JOSEPH E. DAVIES

MISSION
TO
MOSCOW

BY

JOSEPH E. DAVIES

UNITED STATES AMBASSADOR TO THE SOVIET UNION FROM
1936 TO 1938

A record of confidential dispatches to the State Department, official and personal correspondence, current diary and journal entries, including notes and comment up to October, 1941

SIMON AND SCHUSTER, NEW YORK

MANUFACTURED IN THE UNITED STATES OF AMERICA
BY THE H. WOLFF BOOK MFG. CO., NEW YORK, N. Y.

TO TWO GREAT WOMEN

MY MOTHER

and

MY WIFE

We surely can not deny to any nation that right whereon our own government is founded—that every one may govern itself according to its own will, and that it may transact its business through whatever organ it thinks proper, whether king, convention, assembly, committee, president or anything else it may choose.

—THOMAS JEFFERSON

TABLE OF CONTENTS

LIST OF ILLUSTRATIONS

FOREWORD

It was August 25, 1936. I remember the date because it was my mother's birthday. I was up in the Adirondacks. I received a long-distance telephone call from my old friend, Secretary "Steve" Early at the White House, saying that the President wanted to see me. I went to Washington immediately. The President received me in the executive offices of the White House. Over a lunch which was served to us on his office desk he told me that he wanted to talk to me about a possible diplomatic appointment abroad.

The background of this situation is found in the old days of President Wilson's administration when we had been young men together, devoted to the progressive cause in the Democratic Party, both before and during the Wilson Administration. A warm friendship had developed in those old days. We golfed together as regularly as our work would permit, had much in common in our political outlook, and saw a great deal of each other. Even in those days he was a marked man. Early in the Wilson Administration we had an organization called the "Common Counsel Club," which brought us all together twice a month. It was similar in character to the "Little Cabinet" of later days. All of us saw in this tall, handsome young Assistant Secretary of the Navy, the future great progressive liberal whom we were all "for" in connection with some future election to the presidency. In all of his political campaigns thereafter, along with these other men, I was actively engaged

*in his interest along with Louis Howe and other political man-
agers. During all these years our friendship has been both
warm and steadfast.*

*One of the strongest bonds of our friendship was our
mothers. As a young man I was rather a favorite of Madam
Roosevelt among her son's friends; that friendship ripened as
the years went on, and that great lady and wonderful woman
never failed to show kindnesses to my children. When they
were at Vassar College, to their great delight she would have
them over frequently for tea at Hyde Park. My mother was a
minister of the gospel. She had the greatest admiration for
the young Assistant Secretary of the Navy. Among all the
young men of that period he was her great favorite. She was
completely convinced that someday he would be President of
the United States. In the early years of his administration he
had frequently suggested to me that he would like to have me
identified with his official family, but then I was busily engaged with my professional practice and could not leave it.*

*During lunch we visited along, discussing old times for
a while. Then he told me that after discussing the matter with
the Secretary of State ("Cordell," as he called him), he had
decided that he wanted me to serve in his administration in a
diplomatic post abroad. He asked where I would like to go. I
replied, "Either to Russia or Germany." They were, in my
opinion, the most dynamic spots in Europe. His reply was
characteristic. He thought that he himself "would mighty well
like" to see Russia under these conditions. Jesse Straus, the
Ambassador to Paris, had just died. I told him very frankly that
neither Mrs. Davies nor I would like to go to Paris for many
reasons. The post in Germany, he said, was not open, but would
be very shortly, as Ambassador Dodd was unhappy in Berlin
and would soon resign. So it was decided, he said, that I was to
go to Russia, but he wanted me to be prepared for a transfer to*

Berlin within the year, as he wanted me ultimately to go there. He was glad to know that I spoke German. Russia was bound to be a vital factor in connection with war or peace in Europe, he said, and he would like to have my assessment of the strength and weaknesses of that situation, based upon personal observation. Moreover, service in Moscow would be of value in connection with later service in Berlin. The situation in Germany would determine, he thought, whether there was to be peace or war in Europe. That, said he, would determine whether there was to be world peace or world war. While he was not overly sanguine that peace could be preserved, nevertheless, he wanted to contribute in every proper way to prevent war in Europe, if that were possible. That was a very vital matter to us in the United States. It was his opinion that it all rested with Germany, or rather with Hitler. It depended upon whether Hitler had a "Will for Peace" or a "Will for Conquest." If the latter, there was probably nothing that could be done about it, and war would be inevitable. But, if the former, then Germany should have the co-operation of all peace-loving nations in an effort to compose any economic or other situations which bred war. Access to raw materials, political security, and disarmament were all necessary, if the world was not going to be deluged with the horror of war, with the inevitable terrible hardships which would be visited upon the peoples of the world and subsequent generations. He thought my training and experience equipped me to be of help to his plan to try to aid in the preservation or composition of peace, if that were possible. Both sides in his opinion were professing a desire to preserve peace and both sides were charging each other with bad faith and a desire to secure special advantages or world domination through extension of power. There was a simple test of the real purposes, whether for peace or for conquest, in their attitude toward disarmament. That issue had been confused by technicalities and degrees of limitations upon specific weapons of war. He developed the idea that if all nations should agree to stop manufacturing any weapon of war which was heavier than that which a man could carry on his shoulder that such disarmament agreement, in conjunction with an agreement upon fair access to raw materials, etc., might preserve peace. Military forces under such a plan would be reduced to the power of police only and no one nation could, through military power, threaten its neighbor or achieve such military domination as would menace the rest of the community of nations. The President said to me that he wanted me to be giving this thought and to explore the European situation from this angle. In any event it would provide a test of sincerity as to the Hitler attitude on the preservation of peace.

In preparing at the State Department for my work, he stated that I should do so with the ultimate plan in mind that I was to go to Berlin as Ambassador within the year. In the interim, however, he wanted me to go to Moscow. In expressing to him my gratification in being able to go to Russia as his Ambassador, I gossiped with him about the old Wilson days and he remembered that the first time I had been tendered the Ambassadorship to Russia was in 1913, when President Wilson had offered me this appointment, which I declined, because I wanted to run for the Senate in Wisconsin.

Pursuant to the suggestion of the President, I immediately saw the Secretary of State, my old friend, Cordell Hull, who told me that he and the President had discussed my appointment and that he was in very hearty agreement and that he was very glad to have me identified with his Department. We discussed the entire European situation, including Germany and the Soviet Union, at length.

That was how I came to go to Moscow.

The reader may also question why this volume should be

*published at all. As a matter of fact, I had not intended writing
a book, but times have changed. Russia is in the thick of this
fight, the issue of which will determine whether the community of the nations of the earth shall be an ordered and peaceful
world society, or whether it shall be run by a group of bandits
and outlaws, with the destruction of all that we value in life.*

*Only a very short time ago, the U.S.S.R. was associated with
Hitler. Each entered into a solemn engagement not to attack
the other, but today hundreds of thousands of Russian men,
women, and Soviet leaders, whose homes were attacked in the
night by a professed friend, are now very gallantly fighting and
dying for a cause which is vital to our security. They are now
our allies.*

*In our country there has been and is much violence of opin-
ion, some prejudice, and much more misinformation about
Russia and the Soviet Union. Without being partisan or argumentative, I hope that the material contained in this book will
give a factual basis and possibly a more accurate concept of the
Soviet government, its leaders and its people.*

*In assessing the material in this book and in making up your
own judgments on the facts and their interpretations, I think
that it is fair that you should know something of my background and that you should also know just what is my creed
and my political philosophy. If I were the reader I would want
these facts in order to assess the weight to be given to the
material.*

*As I stated to Mr. Stalin, President Kalinin, and the others
of the Soviet leaders, I am definitely not a Communist. I am
called a capitalist. I am proud of the designation, but I think
that the better word is "individualist." Capitalism with its attendant property rights is simply the result of an individualistic order in society which permits to each of us an opportunity to acquire property according to our respective abilities*

in a fair competitive society. The real test of individualism is not property. It is individual freedom in thought and in opportunity. Capitalism is only one facet of individualism. As a matter of fact, I am peculiarly the product of such an individualistic system under a government and in a society in this country of ours, which is the best that civilization has yet evolved for the common man.

My boyhood was spent in the Middle West; my education was received at the University of Wisconsin. I was a progressive in politics and a believer in and follower of Woodrow Wilson and the New Deal of Franklin D. Roosevelt.

Under the faith which my mother had bred in me, I find no difficulty in accepting the idea in connection with Communism, that all believers in Christ and Christ's teachings are theoretical communists, to the degree that they are "for" the brotherhood of men. On the other hand, I am equally firmly convinced that Communism, as such, cannot work on this earth, with human nature as it is; and will not work for another aeon or two and until human nature has evolved upward to a point where men will be willing to work "each for the joy of the working," and each in a selfless society. It is also my firm belief that if any idea is projected too rapidly it will not only fail to cure the alleged evils, but will probably induce even greater evils than those which it seeks to cure. I am a firm believer in evolution as against revolution. I think our system is doing the best job for the common man and doing it more slowly but more surely because it seeks advance through evolution rather than through revolution.

Those convictions with which I went to Moscow, I brought back unchanged. I had, however, seen and learned much that I had not known, and I saw forces in being and apparently evolving which would have far-reaching effects on social and political conditions of the future. It renewed my faith in the

Christian religion as indestructible and in the beneficences of our own form of government and our own way of life.*

When I went to Russia, I made up my mind that I was going to go there free from prejudice and with an open mind. The reports which I sent to the State Department, the letters which I sent back home, the entries in my diary are the honest record

---

* *Excerpt from extemporaneous farewell talk to the Embassy Staff at Moscow, delivered by Ambassador Davies on June 9, 1938.*

ENCLOSURE NO. 1 TO DISPATCH NO. 6 OF JULY 21, 1938, FROM EMBASSY, BRUSSELS.

I never go back home from Europe but what I reverently thank my mother's God that my forebears had the courage and self-reliance and the hardihood to brave the wilderness, 100 years ago, and migrate to the United States of America, and through their sacrifices make it possible for my children and my grandchildren to enjoy the beneficences of a democratic form of government and the privilege of living in the United States. I never go back home from Europe but what I feel how blest the American people are. Think of what we enjoy in contrast to many European countries!

We have liberty—personal freedom.

We have the right of free speech.

We have the right of peaceful assembly.

We have the right to think freely.

We have the right to worship God as our conscience may dictate.

Our liberty, our lives, our property, our rights are protected even as against the government itself.

Every man is a king in his own castle.

Our liberties and our lives are protected by laws under which even an all-powerful government is required to prove guilt beyond a reasonable doubt, before a man may be punished by the state.

What would millions of men and women in Europe today give to be assured of and enjoy these blessings!

The dignity of manhood and womanhood, the sanctity of human life and liberty, the self-respect of the human spirit, is the best product which civilization has brought into this world. These are found in the United States of America to a degree that is found no place else in the world.

I don't care how much totalitarian states or dictatorships may provide in material benefits or social benefits to childhood or old age, if liberty and freedom have to be sacrificed therefor, then the price is too high to pay.

*of and reactions to the situations, personalities, and events as
I saw them. There was always present a deliberate effort to be
fair, judicial, and objective-minded. When I left Russia, President Kalinin said to me, in effect, "We are sorry you are leaving. While you are not in accord with our belief and our
political ideology, we believe you to have been honest in your
appraisal and honest in your effort to see what was being done.
The worst that you have had to say you have said to us, and
the best that you have had to say you have said to our enemies."*

*An old French philosopher said, "When you know a man
you cannot hate him." Leaders of the Union of Soviet Socialist
Republics I came to know. They are a group of able, strong
men. I disagree with them in many respects; but I accord to
them, that which I assume unto myself, namely, credit for
honest convictions and integrity of purposes. In my opinion,
these men believe that they are doing right. There can be little
doubt, on the face of the record, but that, consistent with their
own security, they are devoted to the cause of peace for both
ideological and practical reasons. I came to have a deep respect and affection for the Russian people. They have great
qualities of imagination and idealism which they have reflected in their literature, in their music, and in their art. They
have equally great spiritual qualities which they have translated into aspirations to better the conditions of life of common men, and which they have heroically demonstrated in
their capacity to make the supreme sacrifice of life itself, for
the cause in which they believe.*

*When I left Moscow, I prepared a dispatch entitled "A Brief
on the Facts as to the Soviet Union." It was an effort to set forth
objectively and dispassionately the facts connected with this
extraordinary situation, both favorable and unfavorable, upon
the theory that when the facts are fairly presented, conclusions
will naturally flow from these facts and need not be argued.*

This volume is intended to be a continuation of that report and is addressed to my fellow Americans.

This is the background which you should know when reading and assessing the record contained in this book.

Washington, D. C.
October 1, 1941

AUTHOR'S NOTE

THE material in this book is made up of the following: official reports made by me to the Department of State, sent from either the Embassy at Moscow or Brussels or from some place where I was on special mission; personal letters to officials or friends; entries from a single-page calendar diary; excerpts from a journal which, for purposes of my work, I kept to supplement diary entries, and footnotes or special memoranda interpreting or commenting upon certain facts in the text.

The official dispatches speak for themselves and are in all material aspects in "the exact word." I am indebted to the Department of State for its consent, in the public interest, to their use. They are, of course, conclusive, and the "best evidence" of what my opinions and judgments were on the facts and the situations, as of the dates when written. In a few instances there have been omissions to avoid repetition. The original diary entries were terse and cryptic, and were designed to recall to my mind the events and the personalities and to afford as little information as would be possible to anyone else in case the diary might fall into unauthorized hands. Some of the diary entries, as is obvious from the text, have been expanded for purposes of clarity, others have not. Names of persons where necessary for the protection of either the source of information or the person himself have been omitted and indicated by a dash. The footnotes or memoranda are invariably identified by the date on which they were written, to make it perfectly clear to the reader that they were entries made after the occurrence of the fact. Other than these, there are no *ex post facto* statements in this book.

Material in the dispatches which might be of special value as primary sources of information to the student or of some interest to other readers, but which might possibly slow down the flow in the narration of events, will be found in the Appendix.

In connection with the selection from the rather large amount of material available, which might have been included in this volume, I am deeply indebted to my friend, Jay Franklin Carter. The experience which he himself had in connection with the diplomatic service abroad and in public affairs, together with his recognized editorial good judgment, have been of great help to me. I am also indebted to Spencer Williams whose knowledge of and experience in the Soviet Union were very helpful. To Stanley Richardson, my friend and former secretary, whose splendid capacity and loyalty enabled me to preserve much of this diary and journal material, I wish to make particular acknowledgment. Finally, I wish to acknowledge the great help which has been contributed by my wife because of the constant inspiration, enthusiasm and good judgment which she has contributed in this as in all of my other work.

JOSEPH E. DAVIES

PART I

THE MISSION BEGINS

November 16, 1936—March 30, 1937

I

DIARY   *Washington—November 16, 1936*

The President, this day, signed and issued a commission to me as his Ambassador of the United States to the Union of Soviet Socialist Republics.

DIARY   *Washington—November 20, 1936*

Appointment announced to the press.

DIARY   *Washington—November 23, 1936*

Took the oath in the office of Secretary of State, with many old friends present, including Pat Harrison, Steve Early, Jesse Jones, Dan Roper, Millard Tydings, Joe Tumulty, Dick Whaley, Leo Crowley, Merle Thorpe, George Holmes, and others. The children and Marjorie were also present, which gave me particular pleasure.

DIARY   *Washington—December 14, 1936*

Went to a dinner given in our honor by Ambassador and Madame Troyanovsky at the Soviet Embassy. It was a very beautiful dinner and well done. We both enjoyed it.

DIARY   *Washington—December 15, 1936*

Conferred with Sumner Welles today on the Soviet situation. He has had long and varied diplomatic experience. In the course of my work at the Department these days to familiarize myself with the Soviet situation and my duties there, his suggestions have been very helpful.

It appears that outside of routine work, such as promoting American interests and protecting American citizens, the principal specific matters which are uppermost in connection with this mission to Moscow are about as follows:

First, there are the negotiations looking to the renewal of the Soviet trade agreement with this country, which expires next year, and which provides for purchases here by the Soviet government. Then there is the matter of handling the situation arising out of the misunderstanding which has occurred in connection with the interpretation of the so-called debt agreement. This was a part of the negotiations which the President and Litvinov concluded when the U.S.S.R. was recognized by the United States. The Soviet government has declined to fulfill what appeared to be its obligation to make certain settlements of the Russian debt to the United States, and the payment of claims of American citizens. From this there has arisen considerable bitterness of feeling. It is a matter of real importance, if it can be done consistently with our self-respect, that friendly relations and co-operation should be restored particularly in view of the Chinese-Japanese situation and the possibility of world war starting in Europe. Another matter which it has been suggested I could well investigate is the question of what strength or power there is, politically, industrially, and from a military viewpoint, in the Soviet Union and what is its policy in relation to Germany and Hitler and peace in Europe. From what I can see here, this is about what I am expected to take up in Moscow.

It looks like a very interesting time ahead, particularly in connection with my general survey of the situation as between Germany in its relation to France and England, and the peace of Europe.

DIARY   *New York—December 30, 1936*

Marjorie and I went to the farewell dinner at the Mayflower Hotel, organized by a committee of old friends and presided over by the Attorney General, Homer Cummings. It was handsomely done—my old friend Homer and the committee had gone to a great deal of trouble. It was a very distinguished gathering with most of the leaders in all three of the branches of the government regardless of party affiliation. I was quite touched by it.

As a matter of fact, one of the unimportant but very pleasant phases of this appointment by the President has been the generous interest and kindness of old friends. There was the dinner given by my old buddies at the Federal Trade Commission, including all those who had worked with me when I was Commissioner of Corporations under President Wilson —before that bureau had been merged into the Commission.

Then, there was a group in New York, who, headed by Jim Moffett, had conspired together to give a dinner in our honor at the Ritz. It was entirely unexpected and a lovely thing to do. What surprised and really got me was the large contingent that came up from Washington—Jim Byrnes, Jim Farley, Bill McAdoo, Pat Harrison, Alben Barkley, Frank Murphy, Jesse Jones, and dear old Steve Early. Friends of many years, they were on the job because of that friendship. Of course, things which were said in kindness were extravagant and indicative of the generosities of the speakers—but they meant a lot to me just the same. The dinner given, just prior to my departure, by Reeve Schley, President of the American-Russian Chamber of Commerce, was very helpful.

DIARY   *Washington—January 2, 1937*

Marjorie and I had dinner informally with the President and Mrs. Roosevelt at the White House prior to attending the White House reception. All the family were present, except Anna and John Boettiger. The President was in rare form.

After dinner, the President and I retired to his study, the Oval Room, on the second floor for last instructions in connection with my mission. In view of the differences which were pending between the Soviet government and ourselves over the debt agreement, he thought that my position should be one of dignified friendliness, so long as diplomatic relations existed between the two countries; but such attitude should be characterized by a definite reserve, with the clear intimation that the President and the Secretary of State were deeply disappointed in the failure of their government to live up to what appeared to us to be a plain obligation. The position, he said, should be that we would not seek further negotiations; that it was up to the Soviet government to make the next move; and that it was relatively of far greater importance to them than it was to us. Then wait, he said, and see what would happen. In the meantime, he thought it would be advantageous for me to make every effort to get all the firsthand information, from personal observation where possible, bearing upon the strength of the regime, from a military and economic point of view; and also seek to ascertain what the policy of their government would be in the event of European war.

I told him of Judge Moore's suggestion that Dodd should be urged to serve out an additional year before my transfer to Berlin. The President decisively and immediately said, "No," that the plan should go through as originally outlined.

JOURNAL   *Washington—January 3, 1937*

Had a visit with Ambassador Troyanovsky. He was apprehensive, he said, lest my stay in Moscow might be embarrassed at the beginning by some little coolness on the part of the Soviet officials arising out of differences or misunderstandings such as had developed between the United States and the Soviet government. In that connection he wished to assure me that my welcome would be very cordial and that the Soviet government knew about my capitalistic outlook and professional and business experience as well as my governmental work under President Wilson as Chairman of the Federal Trade Commission. They were familiar with my work and had confidence that I would look at their situation and their problems objectively and without prejudice. He was quite right, I told him, so far as my attitude was concerned. I was going with an open mind. He hoped that any controversial matters that had developed could be adjusted through clear understanding of the position of each party. The principal matter in difference between the governments was the question of the debt. I told Troyanovsky that I was going under instructions of the President and Secretary of State. Personally I felt it would be a great mistake of the Soviet government to permit a misunderstanding on the debt question to cloud the confidence which the President of the United States and our government had in the integrity and reliability of the promises of the Soviet government.

I shall want to discuss this with Bill Bullitt.

DIARY   *Washington—January 4, 1937*

Formal dinner given in our honor by Ambassador and Madame Saito at the Japanese Embassy. Saito is an old friend and golfing companion at "Burning Tree." It was a very pleasant gesture on his part to want to entertain for us. I was perplexed, however, for I was going to Moscow, and Japan and Moscow were scarcely on speaking terms. So I decided to be entirely undiplomatic and go to Saito frankly with the problem. He saw the point at once and said, "That's simple. We shall ask my colleague, the Soviet Ambassador, and Madame Troyanovsky," and my problem was solved with a most pleasant evening. Over the coffee international relations were furthered by a suggestion of organizing an international group of "Burning Tree" Golf Clubs similar to International Rotary. There was no question but what Washington's "Burning Tree" would have to be number one. Party almost broke up over whether number two was to be Tokyo or Moscow. It was referred to the League of Nations!!

DIARY   *At Sea—January 5, 1937*

My old friend, Owen D. Young, Chairman of the Board of General Electric Company, was good enough to come up and spend a couple of hours with me discussing Russia. The General Electric has done millions of dollars' worth of business with the Amtorg, the official agency of the Soviet government in this country. He tells me that the Soviet government has an exceptionally high credit rating in banking and business circles in New York and this country; that they have the reputation of being meticulously careful to meet their financial obligations promptly and even before the due date. In the course of business relations which the General Electric has had with the Soviet government, running into millions of dollars, and covering ten or fifteen years, he stated that the Soviets had been scrupulously prompt in their payments and had lived up to their promises in every respect. He gave them a most excellent reputation for living up to their promises, quite in contrast to nonbusiness and politically minded people with whom I have discussed the Soviets here.

Marjorie, Ekay,* and I sailed at midnight on the *Europa* for Bremen. Walter Duranty is aboard.

DIARY   *Berlin—January 14, 1937*

Arrived in Berlin and immediately made my official call on Ambassador Dodd.

DIARY   *Berlin—January 15, 1937*

Suretz, the Soviet Ambassador here, is particularly kind in the attentions which he and his staff are showing to us. Moscow, he tells me, has given express directions that everything possible is to be done in order to make our stay agreeable and pleasant; and added that the Foreign Office (Litvinov) had received express instructions from the Kremlin (Stalin) to treat the new diplomatic representation with every courtesy and not to permit any friction which may have existed in the past to influence their attitude toward the new Ambassador. I was glad to hear it.

DIARY   *Berlin—January 16, 1937*

We stopped off here for a few days' rest. Ambassador and Mrs. Dodd gave us a very pleasant luncheon. Dr. Schacht and his wife, the former German Ambassador to Washington,

---

* Emlen Knight Davies—my daughter and a senior at Vassar.

Von Gaffron-Prittwitz, the Polish Ambassador Lipski and the
Russian Ambassador and Madame Suretz, along with my old
University of Wisconsin classmate and friend, Louis Loch-
ner, made it a very pleasant occasion.

Had an extended conference with the head of the "Russian
desk" at the German Foreign Office. To my surprise he stated
that my views as to the stability of internal Russian political
conditions and the security of the Stalin regime would bear
investigation. My information, he thought, was all wrong—
Stalin was not firmly entrenched. He stated that I probably
would find that there was much revolutionary activity there
which might shortly break out into the open.

Called on Ambassador Dodd to say good-by and report
what I had gathered in his bailiwick.

Pursuant to the arrangement made at luncheon, I called
upon Dr. Schacht at the Reichsbank. He had arranged to cut
himself off from all interruption and we had a good two hours
together. He was rather bitter upon the alleged lack of fairness on the part of Britain and France to Germany's economic
problem.

Schacht expressed the greatest of admiration for the President. He said that he was pre-eminently one of the great men
in the world; that he had the unusual capacity to reduce any
situation to elemental factors and apply simple common sense
to its solution. That, said he, was the characteristic of genius
and real greatness.

DIARY   *Berlin—January 17, 1937*

Tea at the Russian Ambassador's and saw his beautiful
Russian pictures. It was a "sit-down" tea—a regular meal.

The "snow" pictures were particularly beautiful, all by old
Russian masters.

The Embassy building was of the old regime—extraordinarily handsome—great rooms, high ceilings, all in the royal manner.

The Ambassador is an old Revolutionist intellectual—highly intelligent and interesting. They took us down to the train—a blustering cold night. We had to scramble into the train as it stopped only for a short time for passengers, but we managed to get on and were "off."

Left at 11:40 for Warsaw.

JOURNAL *Berlin—January 17, 1937*

This is an interesting statement made by the Nazis which I picked up in the paper yesterday:

We expect a change of epoch, a total breakup of political and social ideologies. Democracies are done for. They are today consciously or unconsciously nothing more than centers of infection, carriers of bacilli and handymen for bolshevism. That is one group; we are the other. Future turns away collectivism from the uncertain reaction of the masses. Democracies—they are like sand, like shifting sand. Our state political ideal is rock-granite peaks.

This strikes me as being a pretty terse, clear, and threatening statement of the German attitude toward the world. It is frightening. I fear that it indicates a spirit of conquest rather than a desire for peaceful settlement over here.

DIARY *On the Train—January 18, 1937*

It is a cold, bleak country—this Poland which we are passing through.

John Cudahy came down to see us going through Warsaw. He seems to be enjoying it here. The train is clean, but rather gray and cold in the diner and not too comfortable in the sleeper.

Frontier U.S.S.R.—Later

The Counselor of the Embassy, Loy Henderson, met us at the border town of Negoreloye. Everyone had told me that he is a mighty fine man and splendid career officer. I find him modest and apparently capable. I like him, I am sure we will get along all right. Henderson, the poor man, had eaten some "bad food" (an experience here quite common) the night before and had been pretty sick, but he carried on in good shape.

TRAIN JOURNEY INTO RUSSIA: MOSCOW—FIRST IMPRESSION

JOURNAL   *Moscow—January 19, 1937*

The city of Moscow itself was a real surprise. Of course it is a beautiful old city but in addition thereto the activity that you see on the streets, the amount of building that is going on, and the comfortable clothing which seems to be quite common surprised me very much. There is no question but what the tempo here is most active and these people seem to be making strides.

SPAZZO HOUSE—THE AMERICAN EMBASSY

DIARY   *Moscow—January 19, 1937*

Arrived this morning. We were all most agreeably surprised by the Embassy residence, the Spazzo House, so-called.

According to Mr. Huddle, Inspector of Posts for the Department of State, it is one of the finest of our embassies and compares favorably with any embassy of the countries of Europe. In front of the house on the right is rather an unusual (for Moscow) situation—a very pleasant little park. Still farther to the right, a beautiful old church, which makes one sick at heart by its dilapidation and tragedy. It is now occupied by many families, and the indications of lack of care and its run-down appearance make one sad. Between the church and the Spazzo House is what used to be a charming old palace, formerly the city home of some Russian noble, but here, too, this tragedy hits one for it also is all run down, occupied by families of workers and soldiers.

Later

PRESENTATION OF CREDENTIALS TO
FOREIGN OFFICE

Litvinov is in Geneva and will not be in Moscow for several days. It was arranged that I should present my credentials promptly to his first assistant, Krestinsky. After calling on Krestinsky we also called on Mr. Stomoniakov, the second assistant, who impressed me much more favorably than did Krestinsky.

Krestinsky is a shortsighted little man with professorial glasses and rather a repulsive face. He impresses me as being of the furtive type. My disposition would be not to trust him.

FIRST IMPRESSIONS

NO. 1   *Moscow, January 19, 1937*

TO THE HONORABLE THE SECRETARY OF STATE

REPORT OF AMBASSADOR DAVIES

Strictly Confidential

Sir:

I have the honor to report that prior to sailing from the United States I had several conferences with Mr. Troyanovsky, the Soviet Ambassador in Washington. On their face, these conferences were of a social character. On this last occasion, Troyanovsky (speaking "personally") suggested that he was apprehensive that my stay in Moscow might be embar-

rassed at the beginning by some little coolness on the part of
the Soviet officials arising out of differences and misunderstandings which he had heard had developed between Mr.
Litvinov, People's Commissar for Foreign Affairs, and Ambassador Bullitt. To this I, of course, rejoined that I was entirely sympathetic with the very great disappointment which
Ambassador Bullitt had experienced in the failure of the
Soviet government to live up to what appeared to me to have
been a plain commitment. I did not permit the subject to
develop controversially, but expressed the hope that my mission might be helpful in improving relations between the
two countries.

On the occasion of a previous meeting, Ambassador Troyanovsky had suggested that he felt and hoped that we might
be able to adjust and smooth over some of the controversial
matters of the past and by clearer understandings adjust some
of these matters to the mutual satisfaction of both parties.
Upon the previous occasion I had frankly touched lightly upon
what appeared to me to be a regrettable fact, to wit: that a
very great man, the President of the United States, had agreed
in principle with the representative of the Soviet government
upon a broad-gauged settlement, the terms of which settlement, in the light of existing conditions, were well known to
all parties and, in my opinion, were unequivocally clear under
the express terms of the written memorandum; that this agreement had not been fulfilled; and that a situation had developed
which indicated to my mind confusion over nonessentials and
an attempted gradual whittling away of the broad principle
of the agreement to which the Soviet Union had been committed. The writer did not amplify upon this except to express
his regret, pointing out at the same time the relative unimportance of the matter to the United States and the supreme

importance to the Russian people of having in the future a body of liberal public opinion in the United States sympathetic to the Russian people, particularly in view of the uncertain international situation.

These incidents seem significant of the attitude of the Soviet government relative to the debt question. Throughout these discussions the writer has for the most part merely listened with the single exception above noted of the talk with Troyanovsky.

In Berlin the writer had several visits at the German Foreign Office. These talks were all informal and unofficial. The subject matter has been heretofore submitted by code message together with a report of my unofficial interview with Dr. Schacht.

We left Berlin at 11:00 o'clock in the evening and arrived at Negoreloye on the Russian border the following evening. Conditions on the first-class German train to the border indicated some deterioration of service as contrasted with service in Germany a few years ago. The *wagon-lit* from Negoreloye (the Soviet border station) to Moscow was definitely superior, immaculately clean, and with excellent service. The roadbed was rough. The combination of railroad station and customhouse at the Russian border was a new building, neat, substantial, and impressive. The officials were courteous, alert, and efficient. Secretary Henderson met us at the border and it is probable that the conditions existed by reason of his prearrangements. The following morning at 11:30 we arrived at the White Russian Station in Moscow. The villages through which we passed in the morning showed evidence of new construction everywhere. The people at the railroad stations seemed warmly clad and not much different, in so far as being dressed warmly is concerned, from country people to be seen

in rural frontier districts of the United States. At the station
in Moscow we were met by Mr. Barkov of the Protocol Division of the People's Commissariat for Foreign Affairs, who
escorted us to the Ambassador's residence (the "Spazzo
House") which, due to the foresight of Mrs. Davies, was in
livable condition. The house had been empty and run down
since Ambassador Bullitt's departure.

Mr. Barkov, the Chief of the Protocol Division of the People's Commissariat for Foreign Affairs, informed me on arrival
(morning of January 19) that in the absence of Mr. Litvinov,
who is in Geneva, Mr. Krestinsky, the Assistant People's Commissar for Foreign Affairs, would be glad to receive me at 3:00
o'clock of the same afternoon.

Accompanied by Mr. Henderson, the First Secretary of the
Embassy, the writer called at the appointed hour upon Mr.
Krestinsky and found with him Mr. Neymann, Chief of the
Third Western Political Division, the Division of the Foreign
Office which handles American affairs. The writer stated that
he brought greetings to the Foreign Office and to Mr. Krestinsky from the Secretary of State. A copy of letters of credence
were left with him as was also a note requesting an appointment with Mr. Kalinin in order to present the letters of recall
of the writer's predecessor and his own letters of credence. He
said that in view of the fact that a Congress of the R.S.F.S.R.
was in session and that there was to be a meeting of the Central Executive Committee of the R.S.F.S.R., Mr. Kalinin's time
was almost completely occupied but that he hoped that it
would be possible for Mr. Kalinin to receive me on either
January 23 or January 25. The writer rejoined that there was
no need for haste and that he would not wish to occasion Mr.
Kalinin inconvenience, particularly in view of the important
public matters that were pressing.

Accompanied by Mr. Henderson and Mr. Neymann, the writer called immediately upon Mr. Stomoniakov, the Second Assistant People's Commissar for Foreign Affairs. Mr. Stomoniakov specializes on Far Eastern, Middle Eastern, and Eastern European affairs. He also received us most courteously.

The Constitutional Convention of the R.S.F.S.R. was holding its final session on January 21 and, upon the request of the writer, Mr. Barkov of the Protocol Division of the Foreign Office arranged for us to attend. The report of my impressions with reference thereto will follow in the next pouch.

I cannot conclude this report without expressing the appreciation of the excellent and efficient help which I have received from the members of the Embassy staff, a fine group of men, efficient and loyal.

I have the honor to be, Sir, respectfully yours,

Joseph E. Davies

DIARY *Moscow—January 20, 1937*

Slept late. Sent cable congratulating the President on the inauguration. Spent all afternoon getting my office arranged, going over, sorting papers, getting organized for work.

Dinner in the evening for newspapermen and their wives at the Embassy. The wives are attractive and fine types. Mrs. Joe Barnes impressed us very much—she is quiet and reserved but has very definite opinions and lives up to them which is an "awful lot" in these days. She is much more radical than is her husband, I am informed.

It was good fun to get them going on Russia. It was quite apparent that clearheaded Demaree Bess and his able, fine little wife are natural conservatives—while the Joe Barnes are natural radicals. Both Barnes and Bess are men of extraordinary ability, both honest mentally, but of diametrically op-

posite innate points of view. The Deuels and the Charles Nut-
ters are neither extremely radical nor conservative but highly
intelligent and keen. I am very sorry Joe Phillips is leaving.
He knows Russia. He gave me his notes covering his studies of
collective farms, made on the ground in an extended trip
through the Ukraine last year. They are of real value as giving
the actual observations of an exceptionally able and trained
observer and journalist at this critical time in the development of this major operation of the Soviet government. The
debate on Russia was hot and heavy. It was a fine plunge right
in medias res and helpful. I like them all. I think we will get
along together all right.

JOURNAL   *Moscow—January 21, 1937*

Made my first formal protocol call upon the British
Ambassador, Chilston. The Embassy is beautifully located on
the river, just across from the Kremlin, and is a handsome old
palace. The Ambassador was most friendly and cordial. He
impressed me as being a very steady, sound type of man. He
has had a distinguished career in the British Diplomatic Service. He came here from Vienna and Budapest.

He thought that this government was securely entrenched;
that the European situation, so far as peace was concerned,
was very precarious and looked none too good. He wanted me
to feel that I was free to call upon him at any time. I thanked
him and told him I felt that the interests of the United States
and Great Britain, without need of formal agreements, could
always be trusted to go along more or less on parallel lines,
because fundamentally the political, legal, ethical, and religious ideals of both peoples were the same, and because
further through our common language and similarity of institutions there was little danger of misunderstanding.

KREMLIN & DIET DON'TS

Moscow, January 21, 1937

THE HONORABLE MARVIN MC INTYRE

Dear Mac:

Moscow itself is a beautiful old city. The Kremlin is imposing and handsome. It is surrounded by a brick wall 30 or 40 feet high with tessellated top and what looked like arrow apertures in the turrets for defense. The façade from one side is distinctly French and feudal in type with Oriental influence. The domes and minarets from three churches are each topped with the star and crescent and the scythe and sickle on these ornamental peaks add a most unusual and Oriental touch to the picture.

Dr. Bunkley, our Embassy doctor, has given us a list of "don'ts" * as to what we should eat and avoid at diplomatic dinners. There is a lot of contagion in foods here, practically everything is taboo. There is no cream, save for ice cream, nor

---

* (These were compiled and impressed upon us by Dr. Rumreich and Commander [Dr.] Bunkley of our Embassy.)

Until you are here long enough to be immunized:
Don't drink unboiled tap water.
Don't drink milk or cream.
Don't eat any milk products (ice cream, butter, custards, etc.) of local origin.
Don't eat raw vegetables.
Don't eat canned vegetables unless you know they are from the U.S.A.
Avoid rare and underdone meats.
Avoid *all* sausages.
Be very careful about fish (for two reasons: fish may not be very fresh and also the fish tapeworm is very prevalent in Europe).
Don't eat gefüllte fish.

———

British Embassy safest.
French next.
All the rest questionable as they depend on local products.
No wonder that the staff here have their own commissary for supplies.

vegetables that are safe, so Bill Bullitt's advice was helpful in every way, and particularly very sound in suggesting that we bring a supply of food.

The weather is wonderful. The air is crisp, clear, with no wind. The snow and even the air is clear and fresh and in the bright sunshine the trees glitter with snow-whiteness that clings to the branches. Give my regards to the "Bunch."

Hastily,

DIARY   *Moscow—January 21, 1937*

At 12:45 by courtesy of Foreign Office we attended the Constitutional Congress—its final session—Marjorie, E.K., J.D.,* Henderson, and myself, under the guidance of Mr. Barkov (Protocol). We had the box of honor. It was unusually interesting. Hall new and impressive. 2000 or more delegates in pews. Presidium with about 40 on a dais. Cossacks (men and women). Speeches by young air and chemical air force. 400 to 500 strong.

Walked around Kremlin.

CONSTITUTIONAL CONVENTION

Moscow, January 25, 1937

THE HONORABLE STEPHEN EARLY

Dear Steve:

We were most fortunate in getting here in time to see the closing sessions of the Constitutional Convention of the largest single autonomous unit of the Soviet Union.

The Convention was held in the Kremlin. The hall in which it was held was most amazing. It was about 400 feet long, 80 or 90 feet wide, with a very high ceiling. On one side of the

---

* My personal secretary, John Davies Stamm.

room were the diplomatic boxes on what would ordinarily be
the second story. The other side wall consisted mainly of very
large handsome windows about 8 feet wide and 30 to 40 feet
high. The lighting fixtures were modernistic (plain but handsome) of frosted glass. The room was decorated in white and
light blue with handsome hangings. At the end of the room
was an elevated platform about 8 feet high on which were
seated approximately 50 dignitaries of the state. Kalinin, the
President, presided. Immediately beneath this "presidium"
was a sort of pulpit or dais to which the various speakers
ascended for their addresses. Below this were the stenographic
force with facilities for three stenographers and in front of
them in the aisles were innumerable cameramen, newspapermen, and klieg lights. There were microphones scattered about
freely. The body of the hall was filled with what looked like
pews and on the back of each was a collapsible desk. In this
long navelike hall were about 2800 delegates with printed
copies of the constitution before them and back of them was a
gallery with probably 1000 spectators. It was an imposing
sight. The people themselves were interesting. I saw several
Mongolian faces among them. In the body of the hall the faces
were for the most part rather younger-looking and while not
intellectual were generally intelligent and eager. About 25%
were women. There were men among the delegates in military
and naval uniforms, country men and country women, all com-
fortably dressed and self-respecting-looking. Some of the
women wore white shawls, others wore brilliant-colored
sweaters, and some had indications of marcelled hair. They
were all intent upon examining their printed copies of the constitution as article by article they were called upon to vote.
The men on the platform were generally distinctive by reason
of rather more intellectuality in appearance. The Commissar
for War, Commissar for Transportation, and head of the

cavalry unit were all in uniforms; others were in civilian costume, including women in black dresses and white collars.

Prior to voting there were three speeches by two men and one woman, all not over 40 and each with a dramatic personality and a great deal of oratorical power, who apparently sensed their opportunities and worked up to their climaxes, punctuated by applause, with oratorical skill.

A woman speaker came in at the head of a delegation from the Caucasus. They marched to the speakers' dais. The Cossacks were in their picturesque uniforms; and a third of the women were in costumes of shiny satin skirts and white bodices with picturesque shawls over their heads. It was quite a show. The third speaker was a young man of 28 or 30 who wore long plus fours. He had a fine athletic face and had a good deal of fire. He was head of the young people's societies and preliminary to this speech a very dramatic spectacle was put on. In the rear of the hall about 10 feet above the floor in front of the gallery there were eight buglers in sky-blue aviation uniforms. To the blare of their silver bugles there marched in to the rear of the hall and up each of the four aisles about 400 young people with standards, banners, variegated uniforms; women and men all with a great manner and military precision and stood at attention in all of the aisles. They represented every branch of the military and naval forces, even to chemical warfare and parachute jumpers. The man with the record for parachute jumping was pointed out.

Amidst the waving of their banners and flags the speaker put on a fiery but self-contained speech, punctuated with applause. Then to the blare of bugles again they marched out to enthusiastic applause. It was well done and impressive.

The voting on the constitution was upon each article separately, with voting by hand, each delegate holding up a red card to vote "yes." When the voting was completed the convention was permanently ended with applause and various delegates calling for cheers for the various dignitaries. Then this happened: a small group in the rear of the hall started singing the Communistic anthem. Gradually it was taken up and it became a uniform tempo without leadership and they sang several verses. The melody was characteristically Russian with a plaintive minor quality. Its cadence was slow and dignified in contrast to the martial characteristics of the *Marseillaise*. The voices automatically seemed to fall into harmonic parts with tenors and contraltos quite distinct. It was really a moving thing and left an impression of power and earnestness. The assembly broke up and filed out.

I am informed that the purposes of these conventions are educational as well as anything else and the delegates are expected to return to teach their people. Marjorie joins in love to the kids and in affectionate greetings to Helen and yourself.

As ever,

DIARY   *Moscow—January 23, 1937*

There is much excitement in the Diplomatic Corps over the fact that some seventeen old Bolsheviks are being tried before the Supreme Court of the U.S.S.R. here on the charge of treason against the country. They call it the "Radek Trial." This man Karl Radek is a very well-known publicist and brilliant person, who has many friends abroad. The trial opened this morning, and I am told is being held in the Hall of the Nobles which, in the old regime, was a fashionable club of the noblesse of Moscow. At 12 o'clock noon, accompanied by Counsellor Henderson, I went to this trial. Special arrangements were made for tickets for the Diplomatic Corps to have seats. The trial lasted until 3 o'clock in the afternoon, when court adjourned to 6 P.M. I attended the evening session from

6 P.M. to 10:30 P.M. It is particularly fascinating and interesting to me. Upon the adjournment of the evening session, the newspapermen came up with me for beer and sandwiches. They all go out of their way to be helpful to me in getting oriented in this situation.

DIARY   *Moscow—January 25, 1937*

According to the Protocol, the entire official staff of the Embassy were required to and did accompany me to the Kremlin on the occasion of the presentation of my credentials. They were all formally presented to the President before we retired into his office for our conversation. After the ceremony the staff returned with me for a very good luncheon which Marjorie had arranged and J.D. * snapped pictures of the group in the large formal dining room. Caviar, caviar everywhere and not an egg to eat, except at the table of the Commissars!! We simply could not get it! At least so we were told—when it was brought up at lunch. (The subject, not the caviar.)

REPORT TO THE PRESIDENT ON DEBT MATTER
AND KALININ
                                          Moscow, January 25, 1937

THE HONORABLE FRANKLIN D. ROOSEVELT
My dear Mr. President:

Fortunately the custom of representing formal speeches on the presentation of credentials has been abolished. I had twenty minutes with Kalinin. His greeting was cordial, and when I mentioned that you had spoken of him personally he wished me to return his greeting to you, "a very great man." This meeting was cordial.

---

* John D. Stamm, my personal secretary.

He stated that he believed that all matters in difference be tween the two countries could be adjusted. My reply was de liberate: that I sincerely hoped so, and believed that it were possible if matters were approached with the same big-mind edness with which the agreements were projected by the President of the United States, and that I would be glad to take up matters upon Litvinov's return if they desired at their convenience. The impression which I sought to leave (and successfully, I believe) was that it was up to them, and a mat ter of not serious importance to us. Kalinin expressed satisfac tion that in his opinion my professional training would assure objectivity and independence of judgment regardless of what I might hear of an adverse character from diplomatic sources in Moscow.

I am awaiting Litvinov's return to see whether he will broach the debt question. There are evidences that they wish to forget it. If so, I will pursue the lines which you have laid down.

With great respect,

Faithfully yours,
Joseph E. Davies

PRESIDENT KALININ ON SOVIET CONDITIONS

NO. 11   *Moscow, January 25, 1937*

TO THE HONORABLE THE SECRETARY OF STATE

REPORT OF AMBASSADOR DAVIES
IN RE: PRESENTATION OF CREDENTIALS TO MR. KALININ

Strictly Confidential

Sir:

I have the honor to report the following with reference to the formal presentation of my credentials to President Kalinin.

It appeared that the custom of interchanging formal addresses on the occasion of the presentation of credentials has been abandoned.

The President, Mr. Kalinin, sat back of his desk and assigned a chair to me facing Mr. Krestinsky with Mr. Neymann, the interpreter, between. Two others were present; namely, Mr. Unschlicht, Secretary of the Union Soviet of the Central Executive Committee, and Mr. Khatskevich, Secretary of the Soviet of Nationalities of the Central Executive Committee.

President Kalinin offered me a cigarette and I thanked him in Russian with the word *Spasibo* which elicited laughter. I stated I wished to express for myself and family and staff appreciation for the courtesies at the border and otherwise in making our coming to Moscow comfortable and pleasant. I then presented the recall of my predecessor and my own letters of credential.

I then stated that my government through the Secretary of State, Mr. Hull, wished to extend greetings to Mr. Kalinin and cordial good wishes; that prior to my departure I had a conference with President Roosevelt, and that he had referred to President Kalinin, personally. Mr. Kalinin expressed pleasure at being mentioned by our "great President," and stated that matters in difference between the countries could be settled to the satisfaction of both. To this I rejoined, very deliberately, that I hoped so—and also believed so. Certainly that could be done if the broad-mindedness could be applied to matters in the manner in which President Roosevelt had projected in the agreement arrived at with Litvinov.

I stated I was not a professional diplomat and was accustomed to work directly. To this Mr. Kalinin replied that their government was a government based on popular support and that their leaders all believed in directness and forthright discussion. I then stated my government was particularly fortunate in that we were isolated and far removed from any possible threats of other nations and that consequently we were accustomed to direct diplomacy, whereas general European diplomacy was perhaps influenced by the necessities of national fears or national ambitions. President Kalinin then stated that so far as Russia was concerned it had no fear from outside aggression, being confident that their army and their people were strong enough to protect themselves.

He then stated that he hoped my impressions were favorable. I replied that Moscow was a beautiful city and that I was impressed at the activities everywhere in evidence which indicated new construction and progress; that I had been much impressed by the general character and appearance of the people on the streets who were generally well and warmly clothed and generally busy.

President Kalinin then stated that they were making very substantial progress, that their industrial output had increased greatly; that the people's needs were being furnished as rapidly as possible; but that the demand was so great that it was like a great consuming flame that devoured the supply as quickly as produced, to meet the great need of the people.

He then stated that they were glad to have an Ambassador who by his training would take an objective view of conditions and would reserve his judgment until all the facts had been fairly seen in perspective.

He then intimated that his government had probably been prejudiced somewhat by the overzealousness of people who were too friendly and had been agreeably surprised at times by those who had been originally cold in their approach. He stated that superficial snap judgments on conditions were unfair.

He illustrated this by saying that a visitor might see some drunkenness on the streets of Moscow and therefore draw the conclusion that all Russians were drunkards, which, of course, was not the fact. He expressed the hope that the writer would see as much as possible of what they were doing and trying to do for the people and assess it judicially and objectively.

To this I replied that while I was the product of an individualistic and capitalistic system, I had sprung from small beginnings, that I had worked hard all my life, and that my sympathies were with the common people as I knew were the sympathies of my government, that I could assure them my purpose was to attempt to see with an open mind and judicially arrive at conclusions, and report them faithfully to my government. That this they could be assured of, for it was not only my purpose but that it would result by reason of my training and my habit of mind from years of past experience.

I have the honor to be, Sir, respectfully yours,

Joseph E. Davies

DIARY   *Moscow—January 25, 1937*

Kalinin lives in the Kremlin. Both the anteroom and his office into which I was ushered were neat and simply furnished. Kalinin looks like a fine type. He has serious eyes and a simple, kind demeanor. He is reputed to be very popular with the Soviet people. He started out as a worker in one of the foundry plants. He is as comfortable as the proverbial "old shoe."

Kalinin impressed me as being a kind, good man and very able in a simple way.

UNPREPAREDNESS OF FRANCE

JOURNAL   *Moscow—January 26, 1937*

The press reports M. Reynaud as giving some interesting facts in Paris as to war strengths in Europe. The factor of speed, he said, had changed everything. Germany had 2000 airplanes and Italy 1900, while France had only 1300. So far little had been done; France had one bomber to Germany's two; and against a few hundred tanks in France, Germany and Russia had thousands. It seems to me that everyone talks of the inevitability of European war, but no one except Germany and Russia seems to take it seriously.*

DIARY   *Moscow—January 27, 1937*

11 A.M.—Called on Shigemitsu, the Japanese Ambassador. He is lame—a very able man. He spoke of the "Shanghai incident" when he lost his leg and of the help which the American Ambassador, Nelson Johnson, had given him.

4 to 5 P.M.—Walked around Kremlin with Marjorie. Today at one of the museums we went to see a special exhibition of Rembrandts. There must have been over thirty canvases, including *The Prodigal Son, The Nativity,* and many others. It was quite extraordinary. We also visited the Tretyakov Gallery. Wonderful pictures by Gerasimov, *Order of Lenin;* Surikov—extraordinary large pictures—*Soldiers in the Alps,* etc. Grabow, Yuan, and Shishkin—snow pictures. Went to Commission Art Store and had a field day seeing canvases by modern Soviet artists. They are fascinatingly interesting.

DIARY   *Moscow—January 28, 1937*

Started in on the round of official calls: Chinese, German, Persian, British. Had lunch with the Turkish Ambassador.

---

* My main source of current news was through the short-wave radio. I listened in daily and made notes in order to keep a perspective of European developments. My single-page diary did not afford sufficient space and I made it a practice to make journal entries for amplification of matters which could not be taken care of in diary entries.

After lunch Marjorie and I went downtown again to see another exhibition of modern Russian paintings at one of the art shops. We had an interesting two hours. Secured several fascinating oils (snow, revolutionary, etc.) for my University of Wisconsin Collection.*

---

* The following is taken from the catalogue issued by the Alumni Association of the University of Wisconsin of the City of New York of the Davies Collection of Russian Paintings and Icons Presented to The University of Wisconsin:

*Excerpts—*Ambassador Davies' letter of March 9, 1937, to Governor La Follette tendering the collection to the University:

Dear Phil:

Ever since I have been in Russia a thought has been bruiting about in my mind and I would like to ask your advice with reference to it.

Russian painting is extraordinary in its imaginative vigor, strength, and color. While generally speaking, it may not be characteristic of the finesse of the artists trained in other schools, they are nevertheless doing some great painting. From my own point of view, I have always been more interested in the story which the painting tells, and the impression which it makes upon the senses, than I have been in the technique.

So I have been collecting some of these pictures. For the most part they are originals. In some instances, they are copies. The artists are working for the state here, as you know, but I have obtained permission from the authorities to arrange in some instances to have duplicate originals made by the same artists. My purpose has been to have a group of paintings which will more or less cover the various fields of the activity and the life of the country; the people, the soldiers, activities of the revolutionary movement, the building of these great plants, and life in the remote sections of Russia.

The thought which has occurred to my mind is that it might be interesting for the University of Wisconsin to have this collection; and I have been considering the gift of it.

The collection of paintings, while containing some exceptionally fine work, might not be from the strictly artistic viewpoint one of the most important; it would be interesting and interpretive.

The icons, however, are all of the highest type of that kind of painting. They are exceptional and very unique. . . . They were selected by the leading technical experts on icons connected with the Soviet government and particularly with the Tretyakov Museum. They are designed to cover the best types of the various periods.

*Excerpts—*From Governor La Follette's formal announcement of the acceptance of the collection on May 20, 1937:

Ambassador Davies' gift of his collection to the University is a gracious and generous act. It is an outstanding artistic contribution to the University and will be especially valued because of the donor.

DIARY   *Moscow—January 29, 1937*

11 A.M.—The ——— Minister, a fine old gentleman, called. He discussed his reaction to the trial. He thinks they are guilty.

12— ——— Ambassador called. We discussed economic development and gold reserves. He discounts some of the confessions, but thinks that they are telling substantially the truth.

1 P.M.—Went to last day of the trial. Heard Radek, Sokolnikov, Sykinsky, Serebryakov, and others make their final pleas. Adjourned at 3 P.M.

4—With Marjorie and E.K.* called on Madame Litvinov for tea.

5:15—Called at Turkish Embassy.

5:30—Called at Persian Embassy.

9—Went to bed—dead tired.

Madame Litvinov was not in Moscow when we arrived. Various rumors were characteristically spread over the community that she had been "liquidated"; that she had vanished; etc., etc. Marjorie, E.K., and I were asked to come to tea at the Spiridonovka House—an old mansion used by the government for entertainment purposes. Madame Litvinov greeted us with all the poise of the charming Englishwoman that she is. She had been in the Urals teaching "basic English," in which she is very much interested. She gave every indication of charm and mentality, but characteristically gave little attention to her appearance. Her hands were red and chapped. She is a sister of my old friend, Sir Sydney Lowe, whom I knew in Washington during the Great War. It was in London that she met Litvinov and married him.

---

* My daughter—Emlen Knight Davies.

BEHIND THE MOSCOW TRIALS

no. 57   *Moscow, February 17, 1937*

to the honorable the secretary of state

the radek treason trial (jan. 23-30)

Strictly Confidential

Sir:

I have the honor to report the following with respect to certain features of, and impressions made upon my mind in connection with, the recent so-called Trotsky-Radek treason trial.

the immediate political background

This trial was the outgrowth of the Kirov murder of December 1, 1934. Kirov was one of the prominent party leaders of the Stalin government located in the Leningrad area, and his murder at that time created a sensation. The dispatches to the Department at that time indicated that it gave rise to great activity and concern on the part of the leaders of the government at Moscow, and that Stalin himself, Voroshilov, the People's Commissar for Defense, and other heads of the government hastened personally to the scene of the crime, apparently apprehensive that there was a widespread conspiracy to overthrow the Stalin government. The Kamenev-Zinoviev trial held in Moscow from August 19 to August 24, 1936, when sixteen defendants were arraigned, found guilty, and subsequently shot, was the outgrowth of that incident. The present trial finds its origin in the same source and by reason of revelations made at the trial and upon alleged evidence subsequently discovered.

The defendants in the present trial were seventeen in number, consisting of five or six prominent political leaders. The others were of different type—engineers, adventurers, and the like, of no particular prominence—the tools alleged to have been employed for espionage, sabotage, terrorism, and the execution of the various criminal acts. The indictment was founded upon specific criminal statutes. It charged treason against the country, espionage, sabotage, and generally the execution of terroristic activities.

THE CRIMINAL CODE

The statutory definitions, prohibitions, and definition of punishment are specific. These statutes have existed since January 1, 1927. An accessory is equally guilty with the executor of the crime. Even participation in any organized criminal political activity, looking to preparation of commission of any of these acts, entails the same punishment as attaches to the specific criminal act. The criminal code is predicated primarily upon the exaltation of the state. Punishments for crimes against the state are much more severe than crimes against civilian property or life. Their maximum penalty for ordinary civilian murder actuated by greed, avarice, and the like is ten years' imprisonment; whereas the maximum penalty for an offense against the property of the state is death. Another feature of the criminal law, the effects of which were apparent in this trial, is the lack of gradations of punishment. Thus, for instance, Radek's testimony indicates that when, in 1935, after drifting for four years into what developed into a conspiracy to destroy the government, and when he had considered making "a clean breast of it" because conditions had so changed that his views were other than those which he held in 1931, he then found himself in a position where the maximum penalty had already been incurred.

BACKGROUND OF THE PRINCIPAL DEFENDANTS

To appraise this situation, it should be borne in mind that practically all of the principal defendants were bred from early youth in an atmosphere of conspiracy against established order. As intellectuals they had conspired against the Tsar in their youth, in their university days, and had daily faced death "on the doorstep" because of their activities up to the time of the success of the Revolution. Conspiracy was bred in the bone.

After the death of Lenin in 1924, a struggle developed among the leaders for the succession. The two outstanding contenders were Trotsky and Stalin. The former was of the brilliant, versatile, dynamic type; the latter, a Georgian, was simple, hard-working, with great capacity for work—a genius for organization and a man of great physical and mental power and an Oriental patience. As Secretary of the Communist Party, he slowly built up his party machine which resulted in the defeat of Trotsky and his final banishment in 1927. Apparently the struggle at that time was not so much a conflict of principles as a conflict of these two personalities; as is indicated by the fact that many of the things which Stalin is now projecting were a part of the Trotsky program. This should be somewhat qualified by the fact that Stalin apparently, even in those days, was disposed to a program of the development of the communistic idea in Russia as *"the first thing to do first,"* leaving the world revolution to take care of itself, whereas Trotsky was then and is now the ardent proponent of the idea that the world revolution was foremost. During this entire period Trotsky had drawn to himself a very large number of enthusiastic adherents among the leaders in the party. These men, upon his downfall, were sent into the interior and deprived of their places in government officialdom. Some few later recanted, were taken back into the party, and were again given official position. Always, however, the cloud of suspicion hung over them. None of them were entrusted with positions of first-class importance and it is generally recognized that they never would be so entrusted by the present authorities. Such men were the six principal defendants.

OTHER CONDITIONS MATERIAL TO THE SITUATION

It should also be borne in mind that it was Stalin who projected the Five-Year Plan in 1929 after Trotsky's banishment. This involved both the industrialization and agricultural collectivization programs. During 1931 and 1932, when it was alleged the conspiracy originated, these plans were imposing terrific hardships upon the population. Conditions then were definitely much worse than in 1935. The results of the plans only began to indicate their possible successful fulfillment in 1934 and 1935. It is admitted that the Stalin regime was very much stronger in 1935 than it was in 1931. This improvement in the situation is referred to many times in the course of the testimony of the principal defendants as justification for their change of heart and final reasons for repentance and confession.

Another factor making up the background of this extraordinary trial is that Communism amounts to a religion with these men. Devotion to it is fanatical.

THE COURTROOM AND ATMOSPHERE

I attended the trial, which lasted six days, assiduously. It was terrific in its human drama. The sessions were held in a long high-ceilinged room, which had formerly been part of a fashionable Moscow club in the old regime. On both sides of the central aisle were rows of seats occupied entirely by different groups of "workers" at each session, with the exception

of a few rows in the center of the hall reserved for correspondents, local and foreign, and for the Diplomatic Corps. The
different groups of "workers," I am advised, were charged with
the duty of taking back reports of the trial to their various
organizations.* Three judges, all in uniform, presided on an
elevated dais at the front of the hall. They were members of
the military collegium, a part of the Supreme Court, charged
with the conduct of trials of offenses against the state. The dais
was a part of a platform about five feet above the level of the
floor in the center of which was a well; the witness box was a
stand (about a foot high) in the well, about eight feet in front
of and facing the presiding judge. In the well there were also
tables for the defense counsel. On the right side of the dais sat
the defendants enclosed by a plain wooden railing about three
or four feet high (a kind of jury box). They sat in four rows of
four chairs each facing the center of the well. At thirty-minute
intervals four soldiers were marched in under the command of
an officer and were stationed on all but the well side of the
prisoners' box. On the opposite side of the well, on the platform, were the prosecutor and his two assistants, one in military uniform. The court convened at noon, 12 o'clock, each
day, remained in session with a thirty-minute recess until 4
o'clock. It again resumed at 6 and adjourned at 10 o'clock at
night.

---

* The following is an excerpt from a letter to the President, dated Feb. 4, 1937:

During the afternoon recesses between 4 and 6 in the afternoon, I made
it a point to go to various establishments, stores, and the like; and in each
place were groups of 20 to 60 assembled, being addressed by some man
describing the trial and the iniquities of the accused. This, I am informed,
occurred all over the country, with the radio working overtime. Their
political and propaganda organization extends down into every community.
The lowest unit, called the "cell," consists of three party members charged
with the organization of their particular subdivision. Jim Farley might get
some pointers if he were to come over here.

THE TRIAL

The proceedings opened with the reading of the indictment by the secretary of the court. It was a lengthy recital of alleged crimes, set forth in great detail—much evidence being pleaded. The allegations of the existence of alleged corroborative proof, in the form of written documents, created somewhat of a sensation among the journalists and diplomatic observers. Whether there was serious variance between the allegations of the indictment and the documentary proof submitted, as the trial developed, it was impossible to say, as the documents themselves were, in some instances, not produced (alleged to have been destroyed as self-incriminating), and in other instances only referred to in the course of the testimony or reserved for presentation to the military court in chambers.

Each of the defendants arose in his place in response to a question from the chief justice and pleaded guilty. The prisoners' box or pen was interspersed with microphones placed conveniently for their speeches. The prosecutor, with notes which were apparently signed confessions before him, asked but comparatively few questions and each defendant then gave a chronological narrative of his criminal activities. The prosecutor conducted the case calmly and generally with admirable moderation.

There was nothing unusual in the appearance of the accused. They all appeared well nourished and normal physically. For the first few days of the trial they manifested considerable curiosity as to the crowd, and, while serious, did not seem to be much concerned. As the trial wore on, however, there became more evidence of despair in their positions— holding their heads in their hands or bowing their heads upon the rail. Generally they all seemed to listen with eagerness to the testimony of the principal co-defendants. It would appear

that to many much of the testimony came as a surprise as to
some of the details.

The principal defendants were Pyatakov, Radek, Sokolnikov, Serebryakov, and Muralov. Pyatakov was the first witness
and stood before the microphone facing the prosecutor across
the well and looked like a college professor delivering a lecture. He was the Assistant People's Commissar for Heavy Industry; was reputedly largely responsible for the success of
the Five-Year Plan; and is alleged to have come of an old
manufacturing family. In detail, calmly and dispassionately,
he set forth the narrative of his criminal activities. As he proceeded (as was the case with the others), his testimony would
be interrupted by the prosecutor who called upon different
defendants to corroborate the certain specific instances which
he described. In some cases they modified or disputed some
fact but in the main would corroborate the fact that the crime
was committed. All this was done by these defendants with
the greatest degree of nonchalance. I noted particularly that
after Serebryakov, who was an old railroad man, was called to
his feet to corroborate the fact of a peculiarly horrible crime
(which he did laconically), he sat down quite unconcerned
and yawned.

Radek, the second defendant to be called, was quite a different type (short and stocky but with an aggressive and brilliant personality), and rather dominated the courtroom. He
was dressed like a peasant and his personality was accentuated by a fringe of whiskers underneath his chin. His attitude
was that, as a matter of course, he was one of the political
leaders in the plot and that, while he had not personally
participated in these specific crimes ancillary thereto, he had
knowledge thereof, and assumed, and did not seek to evade,

responsibility therefor. He continuously insisted, however, that these were "man-made" crimes and constantly justified himself on the ground that they were political in character and for a cause that he had then believed in. He had several sharp colloquies with the prosecutor and did not come off second best. Throughout his testimony he gave indications of spirit; but upon his final plea to the court he asked them to remember that he it was who had disclosed the Trotsky conspiracy, with the implication that, but for him, that which the government desired to establish would not have been forthcoming. Serebryakov was as mild-mannered a pirate as ever slit a throat (with a cherubic face), who casually recited horror after horror which he had projected. He seemed more or less resigned in his demeanor. Sokolnikov, former Ambassador to London, Assistant People's Commissar for Foreign Affairs, was quite a different type, with a round face, swarthy, and high forehead. He again delivered himself of what might appear to be a dispassionate lecture upon his participation in the conspiracy, and expounded logically and clearly the reasons which prompted him and his associates to launch upon a plot with Japan and Germany; the basis of which was that there was no possibility of projecting their plans for the betterment of the Russian people internally because the Stalin government was so strong that mass action within could not overthrow it and that historically they had reason to believe that their best chance was to rise to power through a foreign war and to create a smaller state out of the embers, because of the friendly disposition of the victors (Germans), and the probable attitude of other western powers of Europe in the resultant peace arrangements.

Muralov was a soldierly looking man with a goatee, a shock of gray hair, and fine aquiline features. He was well over six feet tall, and wore a plain dark Russian blouse buttoned up to the neck. He conducted himself with fine dignity, and appeared manly and straightforward. He had at one time been in position of high command in the military forces in Moscow. There were many indicia of truth speaking in the natural manner in which he told of his reasons for supporting Trotsky as one of his oldest and best friends and a great man, who had been a man "when others were mice," and again when he spoke of his reasons for refusal to confess, and ultimate recantation. He denied that there had been any pressure put upon him; and stated that for eight months he had refused to confess, because he resented his arrest and became angry and stubborn; that at first he thought he would prefer to die as a hero and forward the cause in that way, but that, when he gradually understood the whole plot, he had finally concluded that the Stalin government had made much progress and was doing such great things for the Russian people that he had been mistaken, and that his duty lay in making a clean breast of it. The remainder of the defendants all testified at length with reference to their particular crimes, and were of widely different types.

All defendants seemed eager to heap accusation upon accusation upon themselves—*mea culpa maxima*. They required little cross-examination by the prosecutor. In the case of one defendant the prosecutor had even to admonish him to get down to the case and not embroider his testimony with additional crimes. The attitude of the prosecutor generally was entirely free from browbeating. Apparently, it was not necessary.

At the conclusion of the testimony, the prosecutor made a long address to the court, based in part upon evidence but largely upon extraneous historical matter. It was a scholarly, able presentation.

July 20, 1941.

My dear Mr. Davies:

As I stated to you yesterday, the publication of the facts which you found in the Soviet Union and in the European situation, as disclosed in your reports and letters to the Department, is of potentially substantial value to the cause which is at issue in this war, both here and abroad, and is definitely to the public interest.

For the Department, therefore, I am glad to advise that it will afford to you complete access to all of your reports here; and that the Department accords you permission to quote therefrom, in reliance upon your judgment as to the proprieties.

Believe me

Yours very sincerely,

Joseph E. Davies, Esquire,
      Davies, Richberg, Beebe, Busick,
         and Richardson,
            815 Fifteenth Street,
               Washington, D. C.

LETTER FROM SUMNER WELLES AS ACTING SECRETARY OF STATE GRANTING PERMISSION TO QUOTE FOR PUBLICATION FROM OFFICIAL REPORTS TO THE DEPARTMENT.

FINAL PLEAS OF THE ACCUSED

The defendant Pyatakov asked for no mercy in his final speech, nor did Shestov, who had been the chief agent for the perpetration of some of the most heinous crimes. Shestov, in fact, stated that he deserved death and wanted to die. Radek did not ask for mercy except by implication, nor did Muralov. Sokolnikov did, but in a very dignified way. The others, without exception, pleaded for mercy.

Upon the conclusion of these "last pleas," the court took a recess and five hours later brought in its verdict.

JUDGMENT OF THE COURT

The defendants were all adjudged guilty and sentenced according to the degree of crime. Pyatakov and Serebryakov, as members of the anti-Soviet Trotskyite center and as those who had organized treason, espionage, wrecking and terrorist activities, were sentenced to the supreme penalty—to be shot. Eleven others, including Muralov, as organizers and direct executors of the crimes, were sentenced to the supreme penalty—to be shot. Two, Radek and Sokolnikov, as being members of the anti-Soviet Trotskyite "parallel center" and responsible for its criminal activities—but not directly participating in the organization and execution of the specific crimes —were sentenced to ten years' imprisonment. Two others, Arnold and Stroilov, were sentenced to imprisonment for ten years for the specific crimes with which they were charged. The judgment also provided that the personal property of all the condemned should be confiscated and that all prisoners condemned to imprisonment were to be deprived of political rights for a period of five years each. The clemency shown to Radek and to Sokolnikov occasioned general surprise.

GENERAL COMMENTS

The most extraordinary part of this trial, from a Western outlook, is that there should have been such a trial at all. The accused had all entered the plea of guilty. There remained nothing for a court to do but to hear possible pleas for clemency and to adjudge the fact and sentence the accused. But here a so-called trial was had which lasted for six days and in which presumably all proof was produced that the prosecutor could possibly adduce—from our point of view an entirely useless proceeding. There were probably two purposes for this program on the part of the authorities.

Off the record, one is admitted, to wit: that the occasion was dramatized for propaganda purposes. It was designed: first, as a warning to all existing and potential plotters and conspirators within the Soviet Union; second, to discredit Trotsky abroad; and third, to solidify popular national feeling in support of the government against foreign enemies—Germany and Japan. During the trial every means of propaganda was employed to carry to all parts of the country the horrors of these confessions. The newspapers were filled not only with reports of the testimony but also comments of the most violent and vituperative character as to the accused. The radio also was working overtime.

The other probable purpose was to disclose to the public in open court the *bona fides* of the confessions of the accused. Had these confessions been made "in chambers," or produced over the signatures of the accused, their authenticity might have been denied. The fact of the confessions could never be disputed in the face of the oral self-accusations made "in open court."

From reports of the previous trials the present case differed in the opinion of many observers here in that there was practically unanimity of confessions here, also greater corroboration, and a more general opinion on the part of disinterested observers that an actual conspiracy was shown to exist against the Soviet government.

With an interpreter at my side, I followed the testimony carefully. Naturally I must confess that I was predisposed against the credibility of the testimony of these defendants. The unanimity of their confessions, the fact of their long imprisonment (*incommunicado*) with the possibility of duress and coercion extending to themselves or their families, all gave me grave doubts as to the reliability that could attach to their statements. Viewed objectively, however, and based upon my experience in the trial of cases and the application of the tests of credibility which past experience had afforded me, I arrived at the reluctant conclusion that the state had established its case, at least to the extent of proving the existence of a widespread conspiracy and plot among the political leaders against the Soviet government, and which under their statutes established the crimes set forth in the indictment. There still remains in my mind, however, some reservation based upon the facts, that both the system of enforcement of penalties for the violation of law and the psychology of these people are so widely different from our own that perhaps the tests which I would apply would not be accurate if applied here. Assuming, however, that basically human nature is much the same everywhere, I am still impressed with the many indications of credibility which obtained in the course of the testimony. To have assumed that this proceeding was invented and staged as a project of dramatic political fiction would be to presuppose the creative genius of a Shakespeare and the genius of a Belasco in stage production. The historical background and surrounding circumstances also lend credibility to the testimony. The reasoning which Sokolnikov and Radek applied in justification of their various activities and their hoped-for results were consistent with probability and entirely plausible. The circumstantial detail, apparently at times surprising even to the prosecutor as well as to other defendants, which was brought out by the various accused, gave unintended corroboration to the gist of the charges. The manner of testifying of various accused and their bearing on the stand also had weight with me. The dispassionate, logical, detailed statement of Pyatakov and the impression of despairing candor, with which he gave it, carried conviction. So, too, with Sokolnikov. The old general, Muralov, was particularly impressive. He carried himself with a fine dignity and with the forthrightness of an old soldier. In his "last plea" he said:

> I refuse counsel and I refuse to speak in my defense because I am used to defending myself with good weapons and attacking with good weapons. I have no good weapons with which to defend myself. . . . I don't dare blame anyone for this; I, myself, am to blame. This is my difficulty. This is my misfortune. . . .

The lesser accused, who were merely tools, amplified in great circumstantial detail their chronicle of crime, and in many instances gave indications that what they were then stating was being uttered for the first time. These and other facts, which I saw, compelled the belief that there may have been much redundant embroidery in the testimony, but that the consistent vein of truth ran through the fabric, establishing a definite political conspiracy to overthrow the present government.

On the face of the record in this case it would be difficult for me to conceive of any court, in any jurisdiction, doing other than adjudging the defendants guilty of violations of the law as set forth in the indictment and as defined by the statutes.

I have talked to many, if not all, of the members of the Diplomatic Corps here and, with possibly one exception, they are all of the opinion that the proceedings established clearly the existence of a political plot and conspiracy to overthrow the government.

In the Diplomatic Corps there is no unanimity of opinion with respect to the testimony with reference to the alleged Trotsky agreement with Japan and Germany. The rationalization of such plan as calmly discussed and justified by Sokolnikov and also by Radek carried weight with some, who pointed out that it was consistent with Lenin's conduct in acquiring power through the use of the German military in 1917, and the rise of the Social Democrats in Germany out of the embers of war. With others, that part of the testimony was discounted. But all agree that the state established a case of conspiracy against the present government.

The trial was quite as horrible in the impression it made upon my mind as the impression of the Constitutional Convention was inspiring.

Ever since the trial there have been constant recurring rumors of wholesale arrests of intellectuals and politically minded people in different parts of Russia, all alleged to be part of the Trotsky conspiracy. In addition to these there are wild rumors that Lenin's widow, a Marshal of the Revolution and Acting Commissar of Defense, and others in high place are imprisoned. There are also rumors which reach here from the outside that Voroshilov, the Commissar for Defense, is marching on Moscow, that the Commissar for Foreign Affairs, Litvinov, has been arrested, and so forth and so on. These last two are untrue to my knowledge. Others may be exaggerated.

It is interesting to note that, at the inception of this revolution, Lenin and the other intellectual revolutionists agreed (reputedly) among themselves that they would profit by the lesson of the French Revolution and would not permit internecine struggle between themselves to breed counterrevolutions. Practically the only original Bolshevik leaders now

left are Stalin, Kalinin, and Voroshilov. All the others have
been banished or are dead, many "liquidated" or shot. In spite
of the recognition of the danger of destruction of their ideal
through ambition, human nature asserted itself here again
as in the French Revolution, only the tempo here was slower.

It is the prevailing opinion here of the Diplomatic Corps,
as well as that of American journalists, that the Stalin government is thoroughly entrenched in power and, in the absence of
foreign war, will continue to be so for a long time.

In conclusion, I wish to say that this whole trial and surrounding circumstances shock our mentality. It is, however,
a most powerful demonstration of the blessings which real
constitutional protection of personal liberty affords. The right
of the accused to have counsel before trial, the right to refuse
to testify against oneself, and, above all, the presumption of
innocence and the application of the old common-law principle that better a thousand guilty men escape rather than that
one innocent man should be unjustly condemned—all these
take on a very real meaning when faced with a trial such as this.

I have the honor to be, Sir, respectfully yours,

Joseph E. Davies

INTERCESSION FOR VLADIMIR ROMM

No. 47   *Moscow, February 12, 1937*

TO THE HONORABLE THE SECRETARY OF STATE

IN RE: THE ROMM INCIDENT IN THE RADEK TREASON TRIAL

Strictly Confidential

Sir:

I have the honor to report an incident which occurred in
connection with the Radek treason trial which, for purposes
of record, should be on file in the Department.

During the course of the Radek trial, Mr. Walter Duranty of

The New York Times came to me with a cable which he had received from a group of journalists in the United States and which reads as follows:

All members of the Washington newspaper corps have read with anxiety of the arrest of our colleague Vladimir Romm of *Izvestiya*. In our dealings with Romm we have found him a true friend and advocate of the U.S.S.R. Never once did he even faintly indicate lack of sympathy for or disloyalty toward the existing government. He did more than any other Soviet envoy to popularize the Stalin regime in this country. We hope this testimonial can be strongly certified to his judges and that you will ask Ambassador Davies also to transmit these representations.

I followed the testimony of Romm with great care. When he had concluded it was perfectly obvious that there would be impropriety in my taking any official notice of the matter at least at that time. The propriety of this attitude was unanimously acquiesced in by the American journalists here.

Attached hereto is a copy of a personal and confidential letter which I sent to Mr. Arthur Krock of *The New York Times* explaining the situation.

LIST OF ENCLOSURES:

No. 1. Copy of letter dated January 26, 1937, addressed by Ambassador Davies to Mr. Arthur Krock.

PERSONAL AND CONFIDENTIAL   *January 26, 1937*

MR. ARTHUR KROCK

Dear Arthur:

    Walter Duranty showed me the cable he received from members of the Congressional Press Association with a list of signatures including your own with reference to Romm's plight.

    Of course my sympathies were enlisted and I watched his testimony with the deepest interest and concern.

Romm was placed on the witness stand on the day of the receipt of your message. His testimony was most extraordinary. Without prompting by the prosecutor or use of leading questions he told a chronological story very clearly and simply. He disclosed that he was an intimate friend of Radek, had received his position from the latter, and in great detail recited the manner in which, upon several occasions, he acted as "go-between" for Radek and Trotsky and Trotsky's son, Sedov, in carrying letters (sewn into the binding of German books) back and forth. He stated that he had been an original Trotsky adherent and that from and after his conversation with Sedov in 1931 or 1932 had become part of the Trotsky organization. These letters, to which Romm and other defendants had testified, were the basis of the conspiracy charge against these defendants. They were relied upon to establish that Trotsky was plotting with those defendants the overthrow of the present Russian government, through sabotage, terrorism, assassination, and for the organization of defeatism among the population and active participation with Japan and Germany through foreign spies in the fomenting of an early war against Russia directed principally by Germany and out of which it was contemplated that the conspirators would rise to power in a new and smaller Soviet Republic, after the dismemberment of the Soviet Union and the cession of the Ukraine to Germany, and the maritime states and Saghalien oil fields to Japan.

The indictment charges innumerable violations of the existing law of the Soviet Union and a typical counterrevolutionary terrorist conspiracy. Romm also stated that he had used government agencies, i.e., the Tass telegraph agency, to communicate with Trotsky.

The poor devil did not leave himself a leg to stand on. He did state that since 1934 when he went to the United

States he had dropped all further participation in the plans.

While his appearance on the stand was rather downcast, he looked physically well and as far as I could judge, his testimony bore the earmarks of credibility.

Under these circumstances it made it impossible for anyone to be of aid to him in the trial.

I would gladly have done anything I could to have helped the poor chap and particularly in view of the interest of you men back home. But after all he is a Soviet citizen, knew Soviet law, and entered into the situation with his eyes open. And of course this situation here is exclusively Russian business and any interposition by me, particularly if my request were turned down, might prove embarrassing to the administration. In fact, under the circumstances, it would have been quite improper.

Immediately at the conclusion of the session I had our press correspondents, including Duranty, Deuel, Nutter, and Bess, up to the residence for a bite to eat and we canvassed the situation thoroughly. They were of one mind in the analysis of the situation as above stated.

Prevailing impressions among the correspondents here is that regardless of motives which may have prompted these extraordinary mass confessions these defendants are, generally speaking, telling the truth at least in part; and that the prosecution has made a strong case establishing the existence of widespread Trotsky conspiracy to destroy the present government. It is the French Revolution over again.

Personally I have found great interest in following this trial and have attended each of the sessions.

If any demonstration of the wisdom and desirability of the principles of Anglo-Saxon jurisprudence for the protection of the accused by the presumption of innocence, the right of counsel, the right of refusal to testify against one's self, the writ of habeas corpus, and the soundness of Anglo-Saxon law from the Magna Charta to the Bill of Rights, were required, it would be found in this proceeding. Such processes, even as the Devil spoke the truth to Christ when he said, "I know thou art the Son of God," may elicit truth sometimes, but God help individual freedom and personal rights whenever it is projected as an institution.

I am writing this to you personally and off the record.*

Sincerely yours,

* I did not say in my letter to my friend, Arthur Krock, that I was going to take the matter up unofficially with the Soviet government because I was not quite sure of the propriety of such an action.

Henderson as usual was helpful. I discussed the matter with him and he seemed to feel that there was no diplomatic impropriety in my taking a personal matter of that kind up with the proper officials if I made it very clear that it was not in my official capacity. Pursuant to appointment I did see President Kalinin, Premier Molotov, and Foreign Minister Litvinov. "Obviously," I said, "it was the purpose of diplomatic representation in the United States and in Moscow to promote friendly relations and better understanding." I, therefore, took the liberty of suggesting to them personally and quite unofficially the desirability of giving serious consideration to the Romm matter. I elaborated upon the ability, high character, standing, and position of the American journalists and that it could not help but have a beneficial effect upon public opinion in the United States if the Soviet government could give consideration to their opinion as to Romm's fidelity to his government so far as his conduct in Washington was concerned. It was quite proper that evidence of this kind should be considered in connection with question of Romm's guilt. The suggestion was received courteously. Molotov stated that he appreciated my good intent; and welcomed my suggestions. On the other hand, he said that unfortunately the "gentlemen of the press" in Washington did not know all the facts as they knew them. He hoped, therefore, that they would defer their judgment until all the facts were disclosed. His government could make no commitment until the whole situation had been thoroughly examined. If, however, there was room for doubt they would consider with much weight the representations of the American journalists in Washington. I went away feeling that if anything could be done it would be done. Of course, poor Romm didn't leave himself a thing to stand on after he got through with his testimony in open court.

In any event, he was not tried by public trial and I have since been informed that he was sent to do work in the interior. Ambassador Oumansky, when later I talked to him about the case, said that it was this action on the part of the American newspapermen that saved him, as "the record of Romm's activity was very bad."

DIARY   *Moscow—January 30, 1937*

1 P.M.—The——Ambassador called. He is very bitter
against the Soviet regime. As to the Radek trial which is the
sensation of the Diplomatic Corps this week, he thinks it is all a
put-up job and an internal fight among the old Bolsheviks.
He believes that the confessions were induced by all manner
of threats and physical police methods. He told me quite an
extraordinary tale which he had just heard. He said that a
Polish citizen had been arrested in the Ukraine on the charge
of being a spy. The Polish Embassy, so he understood, had
been unsuccessful in securing his release so the Polish government arrested two prominent Soviets in Poland. It resulted in
an interchange of prisoners at the border. The Pole appeared
to be a very sick man and was taken under observation and
for hospitalization by Polish medical experts. They arrived at
the conclusion that he had been doped unconsciously by having atropin or some such drug administered to him in his food
for the purpose of weakening his will.* In his opinion this was

---

* In a subsequent discussion of this "atropin" report, another diplomat from
a neighbor country said that he would discount this story because of prejudice
and hostility. He referred to Bruce Lockhart's description of the treatment
(*British Agent*) which he had received at the hands of the Gay-Pay-Oo when
he was arrested on suspicion of being implicated in the attempted assassination of Lenin, and also cited the statements in denial of coercive third-degree
measures by the defendants in these treason trials. For such value as it may
have, however, here it is.

The Soviet government published English translations of the proceedings
in these two purge trials which I attended. With the consent of the Foreign
Office I was able to purchase fifty or sixty copies of each which I sent to
various friends in the United States. It may interest the reader to know that
two very eminent lawyers, one an Assistant Attorney General under President
Wilson's Administration, the Honorable Charles Warren, author of the recent
standard book on the Supreme Court of the United States, and the other the
Honorable Seth W. Richardson, Assistant Attorney General under the Hoover
Administration, told me that they had found interest in reading the proceedings with care and that each had arrived at the conclusion that no other judgment but guilty, in their opinion, could have been sustained by the evidence.

one of the reasons for these confessions at the trial. He also suggested that the reason for Romm's confession was the fact that Romm's wife and child had been induced to come into Russia and that Romm had to return to face the music because of fear of harm to them. This, he said, was pure surmise on his part. It is the first concrete statement that I have heard in connection with this general rumor as to the use of drugs— and this was hearsay and from a biased source.*

The popular celebration of sentences adjudged by the military court went on in the Red Square. This evening there was a most unusual sight consisting of crowds of enthusiastic marching men and women making demonstrations of satisfaction that "the traitors had been discovered and punished."

TO SENATOR JAMES BYRNES   *Moscow, February 18, 1937*

My dear Jim:

In this Radek Treason Trial, the basic vice in the procedure from our point of view was the subordination of the rights of the individual to the state. In these judicial proceedings as in some other European countries the theory is that the accused owes a duty to the state to testify after a prima-facie case has been made.

The guarantees of the common law to protect the personal liberty of the individual from possible oppressions of government, such as the right of the accused to advice of counsel upon arrest, the right to refuse to testify against oneself, the writ of habeas corpus, the right to require that the state shall

---

* In the Bukharin case, a year later, one of the most extraordinary features of the trial was the final plea—Bukharin's "last words." He discussed the confessions. He had read Feuchtwanger's book, which he had found in the prison library, on the last trial, and *seriatim* he took up the various explanations or theories advanced therein, and stated that these were "all wrong." Among them was the "drug" theory.

prove guilt instead of the accused being required to prove innocence—never impressed me with their beneficence in the public interest as they did in this trial. All of these defendants had been kept incommunicado for weeks and months. One by one they arose and told their story quite dispassionately and in the greatest of circumstantial detail, piling self-accusation upon self-accusation. The prevailing opinion is that, objectively viewed in the face of the proceedings, the government established its case at least to the extent of establishing a conspiracy against the present government.

NEYMANN ON GERMAN AGGRESSION

TO THE HONORABLE THE SECRETARY OF STATE:

MEMORANDUM OF CONVERSATION WHICH TOOK PLACE ON FEBRUARY 1, 1937, BETWEEN AMBASSADOR DAVIES AND MR. NEYMANN OF THE PEOPLE'S COMMISSARIAT FOR FOREIGN AFFAIRS

Confidential

On the afternoon of February 1, 1937, accompanied by Mr. Henderson, the First Secretary, I paid my call upon Mr. Neymann, Chief of the Third Western Political Division of the People's Commissariat for Foreign Affairs. During the course of our conversation, I told him substantially as follows:

I have been much impressed with what I have seen in the Soviet Union. It was extraordinary to see the Soviet Union attempt to accomplish within five or six years in the field of industrialization what it has taken the United States several generations to accomplish.

I am particularly interested in your industrial problems and hope that it will be possible for me in the very near future to make a tour of the industrial regions and see actually what is being done. I would like to learn firsthand precisely what has been accomplished, what you are doing now, and what yet remains to be done. I am particularly anxious to gain an idea of the conditions of your steel industry. A number of years ago I made a study of the American steel industry and incorporated my findings in a two-volume treatise which is still regarded as an authoritative work in that field. I am naturally interested in the promotion of American-Soviet commercial relations—but I am also sincerely sympathetic toward the efforts of your government to industrialize the country and to raise the standards of living of the whole population.

I may add that I am not a diplomat. I am a lawyer with an economic training, and a businessman, and I am speaking more as such than as a diplomat. In fact, the United States is so blessed geographically that it may be said that it has little need for diplomacy in world affairs, as it is commonly understood in Europe. Our main desire is to live in peace with the other countries and to promote world peace.

I propose to visit Leningrad in the near future; also a number of industrial areas in the Ukraine. I have already taken up the matter of obtaining railway accommodations and the People's Commissariat for Communications has been very kind in aiding me.

Mr. Neymann replied that the Soviet government was gratified to learn that I was planning to endeavor to obtain a firsthand idea of the developments which were taking place in the country and assured me that the Soviet authorities would do all possible to facilitate me. He said that he would discuss the matter with the appropriate Commissariats and might be able to suggest the names of certain factories which I might find interesting.

He said that he understood that I had been present at the trial and wondered what my impressions were. I replied that the trial was particularly interesting to me since I had at one time been a trial lawyer in the United States and the trial had given me an opportunity to compare Soviet judicial procedure with that of the United States. I said that, based upon my own experience as a lawyer and objectively viewed, I felt that under their laws and their judicial system the government had clearly established its case. There were, however, certain psychological and other factors connected with the proceedings which I was not particularly in a position to evaluate as these factors were foreign to my experience.

Mr. Neymann pointed out that to him the interesting feature of the trial was that it had so pitilessly disclosed the tactics of Germany. He said that he had recently been informed by sources in which he had confidence that the Nazis had been classifying wars in which Germany might become involved into two categories, namely: all-foreign, and partly foreign. The Nazi leaders and German military authorities were of the opinion, he had learned, that Germany would not be prepared until 1938 to engage in an important all-foreign war, that is, a war in which an onslaught from without was not accompanied by an uprising within, but that it might without great risk engage in a partly foreign war, that is, a war in which an attack from without would be accompanied by a civil war. Spain and Czechoslovakia had already been classified as countries in which a partly foreign war might be waged, and the trial discloses that Germany had hoped through Trotsky so to disrupt Soviet unity as to place the Soviet Union in the same category.

Mr. Neymann stated to me later that certain members of the industrial and economic sections of the Soviet government had spoken of my reports as Commissioner of Corporations and Chairman of the Federal Trade Commission, and

that they were favorably known. I replied it would give me
pleasure to send to him for their use a set of such of those reports as might be relevant to their industries and problems.*

DIARY   *Moscow—February 2, 1937*

12 A.M.—The ——— Minister called. He has been in the
U. S. and in Washington several times. Opinion re trial—guilty.
Discussed the Comintern.

4 P.M.—Jenkins, American engineer, called. He is building
a sheet mill in the Don Basin. Gave an interesting description
of industries of that region and the Cooper Dam, second only
to Boulder Dam. Described aluminum factory, sheet factories,
etc. He has a high opinion of the intelligence of Russian
engineers.

5:15—Foreign Office invited us to a preview of Soviet moving pictures of our arrival and meeting with Kalinin as a
"short" and a main picture—a drama—revolutionary picture.

FRENCH DEFENSE BUDGET

JOURNAL   *Moscow—February 2, 1937*

The French Chamber authorized the expenditure of
14,000,000,000 francs ($700,000,000) on national defense dur-
ing the next three years.

What a commentary in contrast to the Soviet! France au-
thorizes about $250,000,000 a year for '38, '39, '40. Russia is
planning to spend in gold values ten times that in 1938.

----

* Within a few weeks thereafter I furnished them with a full set of my reports
as Commissioner of Corporations and as Chairman of the Federal Trade Commission on steel, lumber, coal, farm machinery, etc.

DIARY   *Moscow—February 3, 1937*

12—The ——— Minister called. In discussing trial advised confidentially that defendants, in his opinion, were guilty.

5:30—The German Ambassador, Count von der Schulenburg, came in. He is very jolly and attractive in a fine German way. Discussed trial and plight of German prisoners arrested, to whom access was not given to German diplomatic authorities. He said that there were 40 or 50 Germans arrested or held constantly—three new arrests only yesterday. It kept him busy! He laughed scoffingly at the references in the trial to the alleged activities of Germany.

LITVINOV WARNS AGAINST HITLER

No. 33   *Moscow, February 6, 1937*

TO THE HONORABLE THE SECRETARY OF STATE

CONFERENCE WITH PEOPLE'S COMMISSAR FOR FOREIGN AFFAIRS
LITVINOV AT 3 P.M., FEBRUARY 4, 1937

Sir:

I have the honor to report that I called on the People's Commissar for Foreign Affairs, Mr. Maxim M. Litvinov, on February 4, 1937.

I opened the conversation by advising Mr. Litvinov that I brought greetings from the President of the United States and from the Secretary of State, Mr. Hull, to him as the head of the Foreign Office and to the government which he represents. To this Mr. Litvinov replied that he had an indelible impression on his memory of President Roosevelt and that he felt he was "a very great man" and was devoted to the same ideals in two respects which the Soviet government were pursuing, namely, the alleviation of the masses of the people through

humanitarian efforts and in his advocacy of peace in the world.
He also added that he had very great admiration for the Secretary of State, Mr. Hull, and spoke particularly of his South
American diplomacy. My rejoinder was that in my opinion he
interpreted the President's attitude upon these two matters
correctly and that it represented the attitude generally of the
American people; with the reservation that many people like
myself, while deeply sympathetic with the governmental purposes for the alleviation and elevation of the masses, might
doubt the wisdom of some of the methods that were being
employed and believing that evolution was better than revolution and were fearful that well-intentioned efforts to project it
speedily might deter instead of advance the cause of human
happiness. I took the occasion to state to Mr. Litvinov that he
could rely without reservation upon my personal sympathies
with the purposes and efforts which his government was making in attempting to bring about a better standard of living
and greater freedom for the Soviet people and that he and his
government could be well assured that in so far as my personal attitude was concerned it would be objectively addressed to a fair and impartial report of facts, conditions,
tendencies, and forces as I found them; that we had no diplomatic problems, in the European sense, because of our fortunate geographical position, and that we had no axes to grind.

Thereupon Mr. Litvinov suggested that we were interested
in foreign trade. To this I replied that while in the government
service I had made an expert study of the American foreign
trade for six years and that in my opinion the fact was that
the greatest foreign market in the world was the United States
and that foreign trade was important to us principally in the
fact that it was a backlog for the leveling out of our own
business conditions and that we were quite independent of
it as a vital factor in our national policy. On the other hand,

we were, of course, desirous of aiding and promoting foreign trade, but that it was not so vital or serious a consideration as it would be to a nation less favorably endowed. Mr. Litvinov then suggested that after all America was not so far isolated from trouble in the world and that world conditions were a constantly growing encroachment upon our isolation; and he suggested that we might have our problem with Japan; that as events were moving in America we could not be at all secure in the belief that we were isolated from world affairs. To this I replied that we were fortunate in the fact that Japan and all of our neighbors knew that we had no desire for anything they possessed and that the Pacific Ocean and the Rocky Mountains and our own strength were such as to cause us to believe that relations would continue to be friendly. That so far as South America was concerned, the democratic idea had been firmly planted in that hemisphere and that there was a very thorough understanding between the President and Secretary Hull with the principal governments of the Western Hemisphere in connection with the preservation of their common interests through peace; that one of the greatest achievements of Secretary Hull lies in the fact that there was perhaps a closer mutual confidence and co-operation than ever before between the nations of the Americas.

I asked Mr. Litvinov for his view upon the European situation and whether the situation was quieting. He replied "unfortunately no," and then went on to express vigorously his failure to understand why England and France were "continually bothering" with Hitler in Germany; that he could not understand why they should project notes and questionnaires and constantly stir up the German situation and thereby accentuate Hitler's importance and "feed his vanity" into his self-conception that he (Hitler) is the dominating figure in Europe; that he thought they ought to let him "stew in his own juice"; that Hitler's policy had not changed from that which he had announced in his book *Mein Kampf;* that he was dominated by a lust for conquest and for the domination of Europe; that he could not understand why Great Britain could not see that once Hitler dominated Europe he would swallow the British Isles also. He seemed to be very much stirred about this and apprehensive lest there should be some composition of differences between France, England, and Germany. I did not offer any suggestion of the possible desirability of a settlement of the German problem to preserve the peace of Europe because I wanted to get his full expression untempered by any expression of mine.

At the conclusion of the interview I thanked Mr. Litvinov for the courtesy which the Foreign Office had extended to us upon our arrival in the Soviet Union and up to the present time. He stated that he was very glad to note that we had received his attentions and regretted that he could not be here to greet us upon arrival as he was at Geneva, and also stated that he had given express directions before he left that every possible attention should be given to us for the reason, he stated, that both he and his associates in the government were very glad by reason of their knowledge of my previous career that a man of my type should be nominated to this post, which fact assured them a measure of objectivity and reservation of judgment in reports as to what they were trying to do and what they were accomplishing. I also thanked him for the courtesy which had been extended to the officers of the mission here prior to my arrival.

Pursuant to the policy which I had determined upon before the interview, I brought up no matters in controversy, nor did he.

I have the honor to be, Sir, respectfully yours,

Joseph E. Davies

DIARY *Moscow—February 5, 1937*

Morning spent in dictation of dispatches.

12—Visit of ——— Minister. He said purposes of trial were three: (1) local consumption, (2) foreign consumption, (3) war scare to fortify government in Soviet Union. He told an amusing story of Hitler and his reviewing troops adjacent to an insane asylum. A lunatic, when accosted by a guard, said, "No that man is not Hitler, I am der Führer." The Minister thought perhaps he was right.

FIRST DISCUSSIONS OF A RUSSIAN DEBT SETTLEMENT

No. 68 *Moscow, February 18, 1937*

TO THE HONORABLE THE SECRETARY OF STATE

AMERICAN-SOVIET RELATIONS; INFORMAL DISCUSSION
RELATING TO DEBTS AND CREDITS

Strictly Confidential

Sir:

The People's Commissar for Foreign Trade, Rosengoltz, invited us to his country house (*dacha*) for lunch on February 5th. To our surprise we found there Marshal Voroshilov, the People's Commissar for Defense; Mikoyan, the People's Commissar for Food Industries; Vyshinsky, the prosecutor who conducted the recent Radek trial; and Rosoff, who is the new head of Amtorg in New York.

After lunch and over the coffee and cigars, the conversation was obviously turned by Rosengoltz from a discussion of trade into a discussion of the debt situation. Rosengoltz stated that he thought the matters in difference could be settled if practically approached; that their government recognized no moral obligation to pay the Kerensky debt but even so that he hoped that the matter could be settled; that the matter of the debts to other nations was embarrassing his government; that with Great Britain and France they had arrived at a *modus vivendi* that left debt settlements independent of credit situations. He stated that the matters in difference between our countries could probably be furthered by a similar approach, and asked whether I had any ideas as to how we should approach the matter. My rejoinder was that I had no express instructions from my government to initiate any debt discussions or to project any plan. He then suggested that he thought the matter might be worked out through negotiations with private parties by Rosoff as head of the Amtorg, rather than to take up the matter through the Foreign Offices. To this I replied that I could not speak for my government but that I would take it up with the Secretary of State and of course would naturally desire to know more of the specific plan which they had in mind in connection with the settlement of the whole matter through such process of private negotiation. He stated that he thought it was advisable that Rosoff should explore the situation and return sometime in July and report what he might have been able to develop. My rejoinder was that, speaking personally, I could see no harm in Rosoff making such explorations as his superiors desired. Rosengoltz pressed the position which France and England had taken in recognizing their domestic difficulties and separating the debt question from the credit situation. To this I replied that I was not a diplomat by training and that I was not certain but what my first obligation was to discuss the debt problem through Mr. Litvinov and the Foreign Office when he saw fit to take the matter up with me, but that inasmuch as they were responsible members of the Soviet of People's Commissars and interested in the problem that I would speak quite frankly to them, particularly inasmuch as the discussions had originated

with them. I then stated that I appreciated that there were
difficulties which confronted statesmen of both countries by
reason of the peculiar conditions which were imposed by
forces independent of what simple common sense might require, to wit: perhaps provisions of the Johnson Act in the
United States which I explained in detail on the one hand,
and the embarrassment which Russia might find by reason of
treaty obligations to treat all their debtors the same as they
treated the United States; but that, speaking personally, it was
my opinion that the debt obligation to us was peculiarly important to them by reason of special circumstances; that there
was a very vital distinction between their relation to England
and France and their relations with the United States in this
situation; that their obligations to treat all creditor nations the
same had confronted them, and their difficulty with reference
thereto was as well known to them prior to the Litvinov agreement as it is now; that the irrevocable fact is that the President
of the United States, in a very large-minded and big way, had
projected a plan which was of great value to the Soviet government at that time, and that an agreement between gentlemen
had been entered into with full knowledge of the facts on
their part and under conditions where there could be no misunderstanding as to what that gentlemen's agreement was in
principle; that I had examined a memorandum of the gentlemen's agreement with care and that it had provided that a
loan should be made by either the national government *or* its
nationals; that the matter of the debt which might run up to
$200,000,000 or more was, in our national economy, relatively
but a flyspeck upon a great wall and something that meant
little to us except as a matter of principle was involved; but
that it was a serious matter to them to retain the confidence of
our government in the performance of their agreement; that
we had no aggressive militaristic neighbors threatening our

peace; that we did have a great body of humanitarian democratic thought which did have great influence upon world
opinion among liberal-minded men everywhere which might
be of inestimable value to Russia at some time in the future;
and that, speaking as a friend of the humanitarian impulses
and purposes of the Russian people, personally I felt compelled to say that in my opinion it would be a great pity if a
cloud were to be permitted by the Soviet government to dim
the confidence which my government might have in the integrity and character of the men who were running affairs
here; that this was particularly true in my opinion because
there was no leadership of any of the great nations of the
earth that viewed with as much sympathy the fundamental
humanitarian purposes of the Russian people to the degree
that President Roosevelt and Secretary of State Hull did; that
it would be too bad if a condition were to be permitted by the
Soviet government to exist which would dampen or destroy
their confidence in the integrity of Russian leadership; that
financial credits and business considerations in importance
faded into nothing in contrast with this matter of the principle involved. To this Voroshilov replied that the financial
amount involved was relatively small and that the matter
should be settled on big broad, general principles and that
a way should be found, that he appreciated the greatness of
the President of the United States, and that there was much
force in what I had said. He then stated that, although he was
a friend of Ambassador Bullitt, it was his belief that a great
many difficulties had been created by him. To this I immediately replied, and in no uncertain terms, that I had the
greatest admiration for Ambassador Bullitt, knew him to be
a strong, forthright man who dealt directly and with the
belief that honorable obligations would be fulfilled in the

spirit in which they were entered into, and that the important fact was the continued existence of the condition and not the causes therefor. Rosengoltz also suggested that they had been informed that there was serious opposition to working out any agreement with Russia in certain quarters of the State Department and asked whether that were true. My reply was that I did not believe it to be true, that I had not found it to be the fact; that it might possibly be true "down below" just as it might possibly be true that "down below" in the Foreign Office of Russia there might be men who were bitterly hostile to the American government as a representative of the hated capitalist order of society, but that I knew of no such attitude; and that I did know that such was not the fact so far as my President, the Secretary of State, Judge Moore, or other responsible men in the Department, or I myself were concerned. In conclusion I made it very clear that I had no instructions to project the debt question. The attitude of my government was that it was up to the Soviet government in view of the commitments made; that the problem was in their lap; that my disposition was friendly; that I was here and available for use by them if they saw fit to take the matter up; that I would advise the Department of Mr. Rosoff's plans and would await their further wishes in the situation.

Voroshilov, Rosengoltz, and Vyshinsky stated that they all appreciated my frankness, were very happy that my past experience and what they were convinced was my objective outlook characterized the American diplomatic representation here; that in any event they hoped that I would enjoy my stay in Russia which I assured them I was doing.

The general net result was that these leaders of the government are acquainted with the facts firsthand; that it was our position that an honorable agreement had been made with full knowledge of all facts prior to entering into it; that it had not been performed by them; that it was a matter of relatively little importance to us and might be of vital consequence to them in the future; that it was their problem and their next move.

I have the honor to be, Sir, respectfully yours,

Joseph E. Davies

LUNCHEON AT ROSENGOLTZ' *DACHA*

February 10, 1937

THE HONORABLE STEPHEN EARLY

Dear Steve:

The tempo with which things move here is very rapid. I have been here now about two weeks and events have crowded in so rapidly that it seems like two months.

The luncheon the Commissar of Foreign Trade gave was unusual and interesting. We drove out over the white countryside for about thirty-five miles on a clear, cold day over the Stalin Road, a broad asphalt highway, probably 150 feet wide. It is a part of the new military highway.

On either side for miles was a forest of white birches on one side and green firs on the other, all cleared of underbrush. It was a region of country estates with fences about ten feet high, usually painted green, all with the appearance of being smartly kept up. The winding approach from the road to the *dacha* was attractive. The house was large and comfortable and commanded a beautiful view of the snow-covered landscape on all sides. It was well and attractively furnished after the rather heavy modern German type.

On the way home we passed Stalin's *dacha*. It again was surrounded by a high palisade of painted fence with a few soldiers about. He is almost inaccessible, but I think I will see him before I leave.

These Commissars certainly treat themselves well. They live either in the Kremlin, which is a walled city within the city with the beautiful old court palaces and churches, or out in their country homes or both.

Voroshilov impressed me immensely, as in fact did they all. Voroshilov is 54 and looks about 36. He is not tall but has great dignity and a military personality that is most effective. Moreover, I think he is a man of intellectual power that grasps the elementals of a situation that sweeps the nonessentials aside.

The Attorney General is a man of about 60 and is much like Homer Cummings; calm, dispassionate, intellectual, and able and wise. He conducted the treason trial in a manner that won my respect and admiration as a lawyer.

Mikoyan, the Food Commissar, is a strong type of southern Russian, a Georgian; swarthy, prominent nose, high cheekbones, strong chin, and quick as a rapier.

Rosengoltz is about 50, dark, non-Hebraic in appearance, with rather fine eyes, quite athletic (he has an indoor tennis court to keep himself fit). He is in entire charge of all foreign trade and controls this gigantic monopoly. He is one of the hardest-working men here. I think he is going to be helpful.

They all have a very great admiration for the President and the extent of their information as to what he has done and the manner in which he has done things is quite extraordinary. They all plied me with questions and manifested the greatest interest in everything about him, expressing the opinion that he is the world's greatest figure in government.

Stalin is a simple man, everyone says, but a man of tremendous singleness of purpose and capacity for work. He holds the situation in his hand. He is decent and clean-living and is apparently devoted to the purpose of the projection of the socialist state and ultimate communism, with sufficient resiliency in his make-up to stamp him as a politician as well as a great leader.

Hastily,

DIARY   *Moscow—February 6, 1937*

Spent a hectic morning getting off dispatches and letters in the diplomatic pouch.

12—Called on the Lithuanian Minister—a fine old man. We discussed the trial. He stated that there was evidently a widespread plot. Stalin was still absolute master and that they had the situation in hand. Discussed the silly rumor of Voroshilov marching on Moscow current in foreign press, etc.—The equally foolish rumor that Lenin's widow was arrested. Discussed conditions—opinion was that things were much better and next few years would show great improvement.

1 P.M.—Called on Finnish Minister.

Long-distance call from London. International News, asking about report that Voroshilov and army were marching on Moscow. Also asked the Lithuanian Minister about the atropin story. The old man didn't credit it. He discussed at length the various theories as to why these defendants confessed. He didn't believe that direct physical cruelties (contradistinguished with nervous cruelties) were employed and went into an extended statement of his reasons therefor. He thinks highly of this regime in many ways.

EXCERPT FROM LETTER TO SENATOR MILLARD TYDINGS

February 5, 1937

The protocol requires that a great deal of time be spent in an interchange of calls with the Ambassadors and Ministers. It might be a bore but as a matter of fact I have found it valuable and most interesting. From these visits I have obtained a very great deal of information of value. Moreover, they are interesting types, all of them, and strike me as an able lot of men. Many of them have had long experience here and their judgment is of value. Of course I need not say to you that I have listened more than I have talked, except in generalities.

I have been spending my evenings with different members of the staff who are expert in different fields and feel that I have gotten quite a grasp of the situation and a perspective on the whole picture that at least will be a base for a sounder judgment upon facts here as I will see them.

JOURNAL   *Moscow—February 9, 1937*

Had a very interesting visit with the Afghanistan Ambassador. He is the dean of the Diplomatic Corps, having been here the longest period. (Lady Chilston, a charming, brilliant, and cultivated woman, of the British Embassy said with a twinkle in her eye that the "Moscow official season was always opened by the Afghanistan Ambassador's dinner.") We attended a dinner given by him in our honor the other evening. "Bijou" * was also included in the invitation. It was a delightful occasion. The Ambassador, who is a graduate of Oxford and a cousin of the King of his country, is a man of much ability and charm. He fraternizes a good deal with the musical and artistic people of the Soviet Union and had several excellent artists in for the evening as guests who were generous in their singing and playing.

In discussing the trial, the Ambassador remarked that—from our point of view—the criminal procedure in Russia based upon the Napoleonic Code did not provide those pro-

* My daughter Ekay.

tections for the accused which the common-law system affords. He then went on to tell me how the provisions of the Mohammedan law in his country made provision for such protections. Nothing, said he, contributed so much to the dignity of the human mind and personality of man as the protections which the law provided for his freedom from persecution by those in power in any country. The extent of the advance of civilization, he thought, was the degree to which the individual was protected even against the state itself in charges of crime. He commented upon the right of the accused to refuse to testify against himself and the right of the accused to a presumption of innocence. These principles, he said, were conserved under the Mohammedan system in his country.

He thought also that the Soviets were doing a great deal of good in many ways. But the wisdom of the centuries, he said, disclosed that there was very little progress without the incentive of personal interest. Human nature had not yet arrived at and probably would not for a long time reach a point where men would simply work for the joy of the working. The incentive for work and progress was personal interest and would be for a long time to come. This wise and fine man impressed me with his sincerity and his philosophy. It may be, he said, that this experiment might work out and evolve successfully by making allowances for and being modified by these fundamental facts in human nature. It might be one of the steps in the evolution of progress. Time would tell, said he.

Diary   *Moscow—February 10, 1937*

12 A.M.—Conference with the ——— Minister—six years here—highly intelligent, well read.

Convinced that plot existed and that defendants were

guilty—discussed the fact that these defendants from their youth up, from their university days on to their exile in Europe, were steeped in the psychology of underground plotting.

FINLAND BETWEEN RUSSIA AND GERMANY

NO. 78 *Moscow, February 19, 1937*

TO THE HONORABLE THE SECRETARY OF STATE

THE VISIT TO MOSCOW OF DR. R. HOLSTI,
THE FOREIGN MINISTER OF FINLAND

SIR: *Strictly Confidential*

I have the honor to report the following with reference to the recent visit to Moscow of Dr. R. Holsti, the Finnish Foreign Minister.

There is much speculation here as to the significance and purpose of the visit.

The Russian and Finnish governments now have a pact of nonaggression. Speculation has arisen as to whether this might mean that there was a possible extension of that agreement to include a pact of mutual defense. I have discussed the situation with a number of diplomats here and the consensus is that it was simply a general interchange of friendly discussions upon trade matters, with perhaps a background that Finland desired to establish to the Scandinavian countries that the rumors which have been current that there is an understanding between Finland and Germany in connection with a possible German attack by way of the Baltic were unfounded.

The main reason for the visit was the decision of Finland definitely to assume a position of neutrality vis-à-vis Germany and the Soviet Union and to become a member of the neutral Scandinavian bloc, at present composed of Norway, Sweden, and Denmark. During the last six months there had been a number of informal conversations between representatives of the Finnish government and those of the Scandinavian countries, the purpose of which had been to explore whether it might not be possible for Finland to be accepted as a member in good standing of the Scandinavian bloc, and the Scandinavian countries had given Finland to understand that before it could become closely associated with them it must first convince the Soviet Union of its neutrality. The Holsti visit was a concrete step in this direction.

Dr. Holsti, whom I entertained at the Embassy, stated to me that the disposition of his government was entirely democratic, devoted to the preservation of peace and to a strict adherence to the League of Nations. He impressed me as being an extraordinarily fine man and devoted to the democratic principle. He participated in the agreement for payment of the debt of Finland to us and also in the arrangements for its payment. At one time he lectured at Leland University, and is a journalist by profession.

I have the honor to be, Sir, respectfully yours,

Joseph E. Davies

DIARY   *Moscow—February 11, 1937*

The Belgian Minister, De Tellier, has been here a long time. I had a most interesting discussion with him today. He is experienced, able, shrewd, and wise; and knows his Europe well. The defendants in the trial were guilty, in his opinion. The weakness of the U.S.S.R. in relations with the outside was the Comintern.* "Howard," he said, "had the right idea in his

---

* The organization of the Communist Party, with headquarters in Moscow, which it is alleged aids and directs Communist activities and propaganda in countries outside Russia.

MAXIM LITVINOV

talk with Stalin." "Howard," said I, "whom do you mean?" "Why," said he, "of course, your great editor and publisher, Roy Howard." "Do you know Roy Howard?" said I. "No," he said, "nor was I here when he saw Stalin; but I have followed everything having to do with these matters, and Roy Howard hit the nail on the head in his interview with Stalin as it was reported in the press."

Hitler, he thought, was violent against the Soviets in order to make political capital for "home consumption"; but it was entirely possible for Hitler to tie up with Stalin, if Stalin would agree not to project propaganda in Germany. Stalin, he thinks, is a practical realist who is a nationalist, not an internationalist like Trotsky. Stalin, in his opinion, would "ditch" the Comintern in a minute if he were assured of peace. He holds on to it as a military defensive agency. Stalin's policy is that he must have peace for the development of the U.S.S.R., and to keep his own government securely in power.

DIARY   *Moscow—February 12, 1937*

4:30—Tea and movies—*San Francisco*—which made a great impression on English, Italian, Turkish, and Chinese Ambassadors and their staffs who came in for the afternoon.*

---

* When Ambassador Bullitt established the Embassy in Spazzo House, he arranged one of the large rooms for the showing of moving pictures. It was most helpful in affording contacts both with the diplomatic corps and with government officials. Will Hays continued to be most co-operative and provided new reels regularly. They would be brought in by the courier. Whenever movies are shown it is always "open house" for the whole American colony as well as for the diplomatic corps. The colony certainly appreciated these showings. In fact everyone did. They are quite an institution. It would not have been possible but for the co-operation and fine helpfulness of the moving-picture industry and the co-operation of Will Hays. It gave many Americans a great deal of pleasure in Soviet Russia, and it aided the mission substantially in its contacts.

After dinner, Marjorie and I took a walk in the snowstorm followed by our G.P.U. boys. Found five lipstick and perfume shops and three flower shops in five blocks on the Arbat or main business street near the Embassy.*

Moscow, February 18, 1937

EXCERPT FROM LETTER TO SENATOR KEY PITTMAN

The city of Moscow looks much like any other European city, with red and green traffic lights, large motor busses run on trolleys over the street, streetcars, automobiles, trucks, and the like. There are crowds everywhere. The country people have been flocking here to work in the automobile factories with the result that the city has grown from 1,800,000 to 4,000,000 population in a very short time. The housing conditions are very scant and apparently tremendously overcrowded; but there are no indications on the streets of privation. They look fairly well to do.

---

* Mrs. Davies and I have often talked about these flower shops and perfume shops. It is one of the significant indications of the drift of this government away from the principles of Marxist Communism. Here were shops owned by the state selling flowers in baskets, at prices ranging from $2 in gold value to $15 in gold value. Fifteen dollars was the equivalent of a two weeks' wage to the average workman. A capitalistic profit was being made out of the sale of an article, which found its demand in the fundamental instincts of human nature. The male youth of the country, under the biological urge, all wanted to prove to his particular lady love that he was bigger and better than his rival. To the degree that he could send her better flowers—to that degree he was competitively demonstrating his greater desirability. He therefore had to make more money. He could do so only through the application of the profit motive, the bane of pure Communism. The very essence of Communism, moreover, is a classless society. Here was a stimulus to create a class society, based upon a situation that stimulated the profit motive, because of a state business in a commodity that was desired because of a very primary human instinct.

OPPRESSION OF CATHOLIC CLERGY IN GERMANY

JOURNAL *Moscow—February 14, 1937*

According to the press, the schism between the Church and the Nazis is severe.

Cardinal Faulhaber, preaching at Munich, gave numerous examples of the violation of the Concordat with Rome which had been entered into on Hitler's own initiative, but said that, in spite of everything, Catholics should conscientiously adhere to it, as it had been solemnly signed as an instrument of honest collaboration.

Hitler seems bound to root out religion as the obstacle to his power and his plans. It is an ominous sign as to his purpose. I fear that Hitler is being swept on by these forces which he has set in motion and that there will be but little hope for composing European peace with this arrogant antichrist Nazi philosophy and this policy of cruelty and persecution.*

---

* During this period, I was watching with keenest interest the development of the situation in Europe and particularly the situation inside Germany in connection with the possibility of European peace being preserved through agreement of the principal parties in interest. It, of course, depended entirely upon what the purpose of Hitler and the Nazi party was, either as a matter of deliberate intent or as a consequence of forces which they had set in motion. One of the most significant weather vanes indicating how the wind was blowing, in so far as Hitler's purpose was concerned, struck me as being his attitude toward religion. There could be no real peace if tens of thousands of Lutherans and Catholic Germans were to be the subjects of persecution. Moreover, such persecutions indicated the extent to which the Nazi party was prepared to go in projection of its idea of racial superiority, a part of which was the concept of a new German religion based upon Wagnerian myths and the Hitler concept which deified strength, force, war, and cried down the altruistic virtues of brotherly love, peace, humanity, and kindness. I kept track of the development, therefore, of these various persecutions in Germany with keen interest.

HUMAN NATURE AND COMMUNISM

Moscow, February 18, 1937

THE HONORABLE PAT HARRISON

Dear Pat:

This situation over here was a great surprise to me. The books which I have read preparatory to coming here, and I have read most of them, have the defect of being too extreme either one way or the other. The truth lies somewhere in the middle.

There is no question but what human nature is working here the same old way. There are many indications of it. The bureaucracy all live very well and many have their country houses, or *dachas* in the country. Many of the workers are making more money by reason of the piecework system which is being installed to speed up industry. There are luxury shops on the streets here in profusion: fresh-flower shops, stores exclusively devoted to perfume, fingernail polish, and so forth for women; the old biological urge stimulating both women and men to acquire capitalistic money more than somebody else in order to indulge themselves in luxuries. In the government itself they are swinging to nationalism, exalting the fatherland, singing their national anthem. The world revolution is secondary. The same old processes that appeared in the French Revolution are beginning to manifest themselves here except the tempo is slower. The bureaucracy and the military in France combined with the *bourgeoisie* and the bankers to keep themselves in power against the workers. Here bureaucracy has an ironclad tie-up with the industrial workers against the farmers. They have a strong army and think they can defend themselves against either Germany or Japan or both. They are producing vast amounts of gold and storing it. Their actual balance of trade and payments in the last two years has been favorable. They are not exporting gold any more. In the army, I am told, they devote as much time to political communist instruction as they do to the military and technical field. They frankly admit that they are attempting to change human nature in a generation. It is some job.

DIARY   *Moscow—February 15, 1937*

Conference with Coulondre, the French Ambassador. We discussed at length the Comintern and that it was the block in the way of real international confidence. He stressed the Soviet military necessity therefor and urged that allowances should be made for the Soviets from that point of view. Suggested that the trial might make it easier for Russia to "cool off" on the Comintern because Trotsky would draw all radicals and hence be identified vs. Stalin.

Last election in France showed 40% of Communist party swinging to right toward Social Democrats instead of cleaving to their party line. He said that the Soviets had played the game fairly with France, since the treaty between the two countries had been signed, and cited the foregoing as evidence of their good faith.

LITVINOV WARNS AGAINST WAR AND "NEUTRALITY"

NO. 79   *Moscow—February 19, 1937*

TO THE HONORABLE THE SECRETARY OF STATE

AMERICAN-SOVIET RELATIONS; CONVERSATION BETWEEN AMBASSADOR DAVIES AND MR. LITVINOV, PEOPLE'S COMMISSAR FOR FOREIGN AFFAIRS

Sir: *Strictly Confidential*

I have the honor to report a conversation which I had with Mr. Litvinov, People's Commissar for Foreign Affairs,

on February 15, on the occasion of a luncheon at this
Embassy, extended to Mr. Litvinov and his staff—a return courtesy to the formal luncheon extended to us upon our
arrival.

In the conversation had between the two of us alone, Litvinov commented upon the Runciman visit to the President
and asked directly whether discussions were had with reference to participation in economic aid to Germany. To this I replied that I was not informed except through the press. He appeared to be very much disturbed about it and again voiced
his almost bitter attitude that France and England should be
engaging in discussions at all with Germany. My rejoinder
was that, without any express knowledge of the facts, my
opinion would be that both the President of the United States
and the Secretary of State would be concerned with any plan
that would look to the establishment and restoration of normal international trade and stabilized conditions that would
preserve peace in Europe, but I felt sure that they would exact
reasonable assurances that any plan proposed would involve
a more or less permanent solution which would consider not
only the economic and trade conditions but a mutual disarmament program as well. I then asked him whether he did
not see an indication in Hitler's speech of a differentiation between the Russian people and the Russian government and an opening that would permit some statement
from an official spokesman of the Russian government to the
effect that it would engage itself not to project propaganda
in Germany provided Germany would not project its propaganda into Russia and ventured the opinion that such a
statement would deprive Hitler of his chief argument against
Russia, which he is constantly hammering home. His re-

ply was negative; that Germany was concerned solely
with conquest and it was a mistake to magnify Hitler's importance by engaging in discussions of the character which
France and England were projecting. In that connection
I wish to report that I have very carefully probed the opinion of some of the diplomats who have been here longest
as to their views as to whether or not an arrangement
between Russia and Germany was within the realm of possibility, despite their apparent bitter attitude at the present time, and the opinion is general that both sides might
compose any difficulty if there were advantages to be
gained.

The other matter which Litvinov brought up and concerning which he seemed much disturbed was the matter of pending neutrality legislation in the United States. He urged that
all neutrality laws were designed as a protest against war;
that at the present time such neutrality legislation from that
point of view was misdirected and that it was not an agency
of peace for, he urged, as in the present Spanish situation
the effect of such neutrality legislation would be to project
still greater dangers of war in Europe. To this I rejoined that
the overwhelming public opinion in the United States, as I
sensed it, was in favor of some form of neutrality legislation;
that it was founded upon two ideas: one, to preserve peace,
and the other to prevent the United States from being drawn
into war; that I had not studied the various proposals in
Congress but that undoubtedly the President and the Secretary of State were giving it very great attention and that I was
confident that the executive branch of the government is
provided with such measure of discretion as was reasonable
and would be effective.

ENCLOSURE TO DISPATCH NO. 79 AND PREPARED BY STAFF MEM-
BERS PRESENT

Strictly Confidential

On February 17, the Ambassador entertained at luncheon
a Soviet official, "Baron" Steiger,* who is known to enjoy the
confidence of the Kremlin. Mr. Henderson and Mr. Kennan
were also present.

With respect to the recent visit of the Finnish Foreign
Minister, Baron Holsti, the Ambassador's guest stated that
the visit should be neither overrated nor underrated. It had
been motivated on the Finnish side by the desire of the Finnish government, in the face of the coming elections, to off-

---

* What impresses me as I look back upon this episode is the remarkable
accuracy of Steiger's information. Steiger was a kind of mystery man in
Moscow. His official position at the head of the Cultural Bureau was not
accepted as significant of his real functions. He was regarded as a kind of
liaison man between the Kremlin and the Diplomatic Corps, affording a contact outside of the regular diplomatic channel of the Foreign Office. He was
called "Baron" Steiger.

After lunch I took him off to one side and asked him confidentially, how,
in the face of the purge and terror, he, himself, was faring. He shrugged
his shoulders expressively and pointed his index finger to the back of his neck
behind the ear. This gesture obviously referred to the currently accepted
story that the execution of condemned criminals took place, not before a firing
squad and a stone wall, but in the basement of the Lubyanka Prison in
Moscow. The condemned man would be unexpectedly summoned to appear
before the Commandant, and then, when walking along, would be shot in
the back of the head by his guard, without warning.

Steiger's premonition was well founded. One evening later in the season
we were invited to be the guests of the government in what was once the
Royal Box for the *première* of a new opera. Steiger was in the party. After the
performance, my daughter, Ekay, and Miss Wells, Stanley and Joan Richardson were invited by Baron Steiger to go for a bite to eat and dance at the
night club at the Hotel Metropole. According to the story, shortly after
midnight, seated at their table, Baron Steiger was tapped on the shoulder by
two men in civilian dress. He left with them, excusing himself and saying
he would be back shortly. He never returned and was never seen thereafter.

set the criticisms to the effect that the government was pro-German. The idea of the visit had been supported by the Swedish government. Questioned as to the nature of the sentiments among the Finnish people which had led to the charges of pro-Germanism levied against the government, the guest replied that these sentiments were pacifistic in nature, rather than pro-Russian. The feeling against Russia in general—whether Tsarist or Bolshevik—was still very strong in Finland.

Turning to the situation in Poland, the guest expressed the opinion that the only definite orientation in Poland was an anti-Russian one. The Polish government was faced with a deadlock of forces which made it impossible for it to adopt an out-and-out pro-French or pro-German policy.

Russian-Polish relations, he added, had suffered somewhat from the book recently published by the Czechoslovakian Minister at Bucharest, to which the Czechoslovakian Foreign Minister had written a preface. This book had increased suspicion of the Soviet-Czechoslovakian Pact in Poland.

The talk then turned to Germany, and the Ambassador's guest expressed the opinion that any aggressive actions by Germany at the present time or in the near future would have catastrophic consequences for Germany herself. That was particularly true of any attempt toward expansion in the east. There were only two ways through which Germany could attack Russia. One was through Lithuania and the Baltic States. The other was by way of Czechoslovakia and Rumania. In either case, the lines of communication would be too long and the gateway of the attack too narrow. Furthermore, the German military machine was still not ready for major action. The planes were too slow and the tanks too light. Chances for German expansion were better at the present time in the di-

rection of Austria, Hungary, and Yugoslavia. The latter country, in particular, had fallen into a peculiar form of dependence on Germany in an economic sense. Germany owed her
so much money on past purchases, which could only be paid
in goods, that the predominance of Germany in Yugoslavian
imports was assured for some time to come. As far as economic
conditions in Germany were concerned, the gentleman felt
that Hitler could probably hang on without difficulty for another year or two, even if nothing were done from abroad to
relieve the situation. The British, he felt, would agree to the
return to Germany of other colonies—but not of their own.

With regard to American-Russian relations, the Ambassador's guest expressed the confidence that if things were approached in a quiet, patient way, everything would be "all
right."

DIARY   *Moscow—February 18, 1937*

The ——— Minister called. Re *trial:* There was no doubt
but that a widespread conspiracy existed and that the defendants were guilty.

Re *European peace:* This was a critical year that was coming. The menace was not the Spanish situation but Germany
and Hitler, who was being driven by desperation and who
had to fight, if at all, before England was prepared.

The U.S.S.R. wanted peace above all things else and to get
it, in his opinion, would pay even the price of an agreement
with Hitler. This is an extraordinary view in the face of the
violent way in which Hitler and Stalin are calling each other
all the vile names under the sun.

DIARY *Moscow—February 19, 1937*

12—Conference with Molotov and Litvinov in the Kremlin, at which time I embraced the opportunity to discuss unofficially the testimony of the Washington journalists as to Romm's loyal support of U.S.S.R. in Washington.

8:30—Dinner at German Embassy. Count von der Schulenburg's Military aide, General von Koestrich, was born in Russia. Father was a large landowner. He gave an interesting statement of his estimate of the strength of the Red Army. Believed that government was going to work out its industrial problems in time.

Interesting story was told as to "Baron" Steiger; that his father, a former German of the Ukraine, and his family were permitted by the Bolsheviks to live in Switzerland but on condition that the son was held here as a kind of hostage.

Over the coffee, I asked General Koestrich point-blank for his opinion of the fighting qualities of the Red Army. In reply to my undiplomatic question, he said, in effect, this: that the Russian army, generally speaking, was a good army; that the human material—man power—was excellent, physically strong, brave, and fine soldiers; that the mechanized forces were good, not as good as the German army, but good; that the air force was numerically strong; their flying and reconnaissance planes were good, but that their bombers were heavy and poor. That as a whole, barring superiority in numbers, it could not compare with the German air force; that the Russian flyers were, however, superb—none better; that their parachute troops were excellent (it was just a few years before that in Russian army maneuvers exhibitions were first given of entire regiments with complete equipment being dropped several miles behind the theoretical enemy line).

REPORT ON DEBT DEVELOPMENT

Moscow—February 25, 1937

Strictly Confidential

My dear Mr. President:

Since my last letter I have met Litvinov twice. According to protocol, I made an appointment to make my official call on Molotov, the President of the Cabinet. To my surprise, I found Litvinov present. After the conventional exchanges, Molotov stated that his government hoped that relations between the two governments could be developed along the lines of greater mutual understanding; that certain arrangements which had been entered into had not yet been completed; that he believed that these matters could be adjusted through practical approaches to the problem. I again stated very deliberately that I hoped so, and emphasized again the fact that the President of the United States, in a very broad-minded, big way had entered into certain agreements which had not been performed; that the President of the United States had contributed immeasurably to the furtherance of better relations in the molding of a very great body of liberal democratic thought in the United States through his action in the recognition of the Soviet Union; that the two countries certainly had one great purpose in common, and that was to preserve the peace of the world; that personally I felt that it would be a very great pity, particularly from the Russian viewpoint, if a situation should develop that would cast a cloud upon the confidence which the President of the United States and our government had in the good faith and integrity of the men who were responsible for the conduct of the government here. Molotov again expressed the belief that matters could be worked out in a practical way. He then stated that he assumed that part of my mission here was to adjust such matters. I stated that I had received no express instructions upon these matters but that it was a part of the day's work; that I held myself in readiness to engage in any discussions with Litvinov if it were desired to work out in principle some mutually satisfactory arrangement that would restore that degree of confidence and mutual respect which characterized the initiation of these matters as between the two governments.

Litvinov practically took no part in the discussion except to ask when I would return from my tour of the industrial regions. He stated then that he would like very much to have me come out to his country place for luncheon and I gathered for the purpose of discussions. Following your thought, I have conveyed the impression to them that the matter was of far greater importance to them than it was to us, and that the next move was theirs.

Faithfully yours,

MOLOTOV SHOWS DISPOSITION TO CLEAR DEBT MISUNDERSTANDING

NO. 95 *Moscow—February 26, 1937*

TO THE HONORABLE THE SECRETARY OF STATE

FORMAL CALL UPON COMMISSAR MOLOTOV, FEB. 19;

AMERICAN-SOVIET RELATIONS

Strictly Confidential

Sir:

I have the honor to report that, pursuant to the custom established by the protocol here, I made a formal call upon Commissar Molotov, President of the Soviet of People's Commissars, at his office in the Kremlin. To my surprise, Commissar Litvinov of the Foreign Office was present, as was also Mr. Neymann, head of the American section of the Foreign Office, who acted as interpreter. The following is a report of discussions there had.

I stated to these gentlemen that I brought greetings from the President of the United States and the Secretary of State. His government, Molotov said, hoped that the relations which existed between the two governments could be developed along the lines of greater mutual understanding; that certain arrangements had been entered into which had not yet been completed; and that he thought that these matters could be completed to mutual satisfaction. He stated that he assumed that my government had sent me here with those matters in mind. Further he stated that it was unfortunate that the matters in difference had not progressed and that it was his belief that through a practical approach to the problem all matters could be adjusted. I stated quite deliberately that I sincerely hoped so; that I always regretted a situation where there had been projected broad-minded agreement in principle, and where, in execution, matters had been confused with resultant dissatisfaction; that it was a matter of importance to civilization and the peace of the world that there should be mutual confidence between the American people and the Russian people and their governments. Molotov stated that he agreed with me and felt confident that matters could be worked out in a practical way; that they had assumed that part of my mission here was to adjust such matters. I stated that I had no express instructions upon these matters but that of course it was a part of the day's work, and while it was not a matter of serious importance to us, it would be most advantageous if arrangements could be worked out that would be mutually satisfactory, and if thereby there could be restored that degree of confidence which had caused these negotiations to be initiated. I stated further that I would be glad to discuss the matter further with Litvinov at his convenience.

Molotov expressed gratification that a man of my type with business-legal experience and characterized by a judicial training should come here as the representative of the United States and expressed interest in and gratification over the fact that I was planning personally to see some of the industrial projects of the country.

Litvinov took no part in the conversation at all. The meeting was pleasant. Litvinov has asked me to come out to his country house for lunch and I expect to have a very frank talk with him when we shall have sufficient time to handle the subject adequately.

I have the honor to be, Sir, respectfully yours,

Joseph E. Davies

VISIT TO THE KREMLIN; RUMORS OF ARRESTS

February 19, 1937

MR. MARVIN MC INTYRE

My dear Mac:

We seem far away from the world out here. All the news we get through the English press is three days late. For current events we have to rely on the short-wave radio reports which we get from London. That is rather sketchy so far as the United States is concerned. The American papers come in the diplomatic pouch, and we receive them at intervals of ten days. Otherwise we are dependent on the Russian press and the *Moscow Daily News* in English which is full of

propaganda and has very limited outside news. It seems like
a long way from home.

Recently Marjorie and I and the whole staff were personally
conducted through the Kremlin. It is a walled city built in the
fifteenth century—the walls rising sheer from the street from
40 to 60 feet or more. It is in the center of the city and appears
like a beautiful prison of luxury. Its average diameter I should
say is half a mile. Within its walls are beautiful old court
buildings of the tsars, spacious courtyards, and really noble
avenues. The three main entrances are closely guarded by
soldiers. It is largely occupied as living quarters by Commissars, offices, and assembly halls. Within it are also three great
churches, cathedral in appearance, except for the mosquelike,
gilded domes. We went all over the place due to the courtesy
of the Foreign Office. One imposing building has been converted into a museum. It is most extraordinary. It contains the
old armorial weapons from the Crusades down. The robes and
court dresses of the tsars, crown jewels, vestments of the priests,
the icons and decorated bibles of the churches, the plate and
porcelain of the court, the royal coaches, saddles, harness,
and so forth of the past 500 years are all there. The crown
jewels are startling. The robes of the royal family and the
priesthood, icons, the altar cloths, bookbindings, sword hilts,
and even the saddles are bestudded with profusions of pearls
and innumerable large emeralds, rubies, sapphires, and dia-
monds. It is quite a sight. In the entrance hall there are
streamer banners bearing different legends such as "To the
Prisoners of Capitalism, To the Victims of Fascism, the Workers of Russia extend welcome to the Workers of the World."
I guess I come in all three classes, I felt welcome. The frescoes
on the outside of the churches are very beautiful, but show
lack of attention and in some cases are almost completely

faded out. It was within the Kremlin that I presented my letters of credence to the President and here also that the Constitutional Convention was held.

Diary   *Moscow—February 20, 1937*

12—Called on the ——— Minister, a most interesting man.

Paid a tribute to Frank Simonds' work, *The Price of Peace.* He had a complete lack of confidence in pacts in connection with any promises by Germany re peace of Europe. Despite Hitler's attacks on the Soviets, he could even foresee a possible alliance between Russia and Germany if it suited Hitler's purpose and Russia's interest.

February 25, 1937

Dear Rahel o'Fon: *

LENINGRAD

We had a wonderful experience in Leningrad. Of course we saw it under the best possible circumstances.

The entire city was covered with a blanket of snow and great flakes were falling during the day. The city itself is very beautiful with very wonderful equestrian statues scattered about in squares, parks, and on bridges. It is almost a city of islands. The main street is very long and about 100 or 150 feet wide. To our surprise the show windows were beautifully and almost brilliantly decked out with displays of merchandise of all kinds which, it is said, have just appeared in the last year.

THE HERMITAGE

We spent several hours in the Hermitage and Winter Palace which are located on a huge circular open space which

---

* My daughter, Mrs. Rahel Walker.

it cuts across like the diameter of a large circle, with a cir-
cumference of buildings and a miniature Arch of Triumph
in the center. On the other side of the Palace is the river
Neva. The Winter Palace is an enormous affair and very handsome in red brick and much ornamented. The Hermitage is a
very beautiful building built by Catherine the Great to store
her art treasures and connected by a bridge to the Winter
Palace and by another bridge to an addition on the other
side, subsequently erected. The Hermitage always was a
treasure house of art. It is probably even more extensive now
as the entire Winter Palace is converted into an art gallery
and museum.

ART TREASURES

The rooms are almost innumerable and are filled with
beautiful things—collections of ancient Greek and Roman
pottery, statues, pictures, cameos, and so forth and so forth.
Many of the rooms themselves are entirely ceiled and walled
with different shades of marble and with enormous pillars
of marble. Here are great collections of Rembrandts, Leonardo da Vincis, Andrea del Sartos, Reynolds, Van Dycks, and
everything from primitives to twentieth-century art arranged
by countries and periods.

Leonardo da Vinci's *Madonna Litta,* a small picture, about
15 inches square, is one of the most beautiful things I have
ever seen. Michelangelo's *Crooked Boy* will stay long in my
memory. The most unique experience we had was being admitted to the three treasure rooms, not open to the public and
kept under lock and key. The director took us through and explained the articles of interest. It contains the famous Scythian
Collection of ancient jewelry, watches, cameos, bestudded harness and saddles, of Peter the Great, Catherine,
and other Russian monarchs. The ancient relics, excavated

in the Crimea on the Black Sea, were characteristic of the life of the Greek traders and consisted of ornaments found in the graves of rulers. We saw there the famous earrings of gold which were remarkably beautiful. They are about two and a half inches long and look like remarkable filigrees. Under the microscope they disclose remarkable carvings of horses and charioteers all done with the greatest beauty and delicacy. We were told that there are not instruments known, fine enough to do this delicate work, in modern craftsmanship.

We spent considerable time in the art galleries and museums. There was a very lovely collection of Repin pictures, a very famous artist of the Tsar's period. His portraits of Tolstoy, Liszt, and Rubinstein are particularly great.

CATHEDRAL OF SAINT ISAAC

We motored about the city and stopped at the Cathedral of St. Isaac, a marvelous structure, finished about 100 years ago. The pictures of the saints and apostles, the altar and adjoining walls and ceilings are beautiful. To our surprise closer examination showed they were done in mosaic and with the most marvelous workmanship. The cathedral gives you the impression of St. Peter's. Its red granite monolith pillars and the exterior and interior are very impressive. The ornamentation of lapis lazuli and malachite in the structure of these buildings is startling in its lavishness and beauty.

The massive equestrian bronze statue of Peter the Great overlooking the Neva in the great square between the cathedral and the river is most impressive. It is in a park with the former Senate and Admiralty buildings painted all in yellow and white on either side. Across the river are the beautiful old buildings of the former University of St. Petersburg.

INDUSTRIAL PLANTS

I will not attempt to give you any idea of the industrial district I went into or the big plants I saw. I was impressed with many new buildings for housing the workers. At the most famous old porcelain factory, through the courtesy of the director, three tea sets are being made, one for each of you children, copies of famous past sets, which I think you will enjoy. Each individual piece is hand-painted and the design is baked into the beautiful porcelain. On the back of each piece there is an inscription stating it is made for me as American Ambassador. It will take three months to finish them. I was glad to have this opportunity as they will be lovely souvenirs for you children.

ARTISTS AND THEIR STUDIOS

Another most interesting experience we had was due to the kindness of the director of the artists' industries. All modern artists are working for the state and are engaged for the most part in painting scenes of the Revolution and of typical Russian life. These pictures are characterized by great vigor and color. The studios are in a large house where they work and live and are very interesting. We watched them engaged in painting huge canvases of historical events.

LENINGRAD BALLET

Sunday evening we went to the opera in the beautiful old Opera House. Tuesday we went to the ballet. The audience looked much like the crowd you would see at Keith's. Not an evening dress but all in Sunday clothes and much indication of attempts at style and color, particularly in the women's headdresses.

For weeks there have been celebrations of the centenary of Pushkin's death all over the country. He is a combination of Byron and Shakespeare for the Russian people. He was a liberal in thought and married to a noblewoman who, it is alleged, was a mistress of the tsar. He was killed in a duel, which, as the story goes, was a frame-up. Both the opera and the ballet were based on Pushkin's works and the music was by the great Tchaikovsky. The opera was *Eugen Onegin,* a romantic story of two young men of position whose friendship was broken up over a misunderstanding and lover's quarrel which resulted in a duel in which the poet was killed. It was significant of Pushkin's own end and oddly enough was written by him. The scenic effects, staging, and acting were extraordinarily beautiful and well done. The singing was fine but not great.

The ballet *Christmas Night,* on the other hand, was great in every respect and the most beautiful thing I have ever seen of its kind.

The story was based on the dream of a little girl over her Christmas tree, wherein the dolls come to life, do their dances, the toy soldiers fight a battle with the toy rats, with the doll Prince Charming saving the little girl, and so forth. The ballerina, Oulanova, the most famous at the present time, and Sergeiev were extraordinary and quite as great as Pavlova and Mordkin.

The beauty of some of the scenes was so great as to be almost poignant. In the second scene 30 or 40 little children who participated in the first scene came down in the orchestra pit (there were 100 musicians) and in their clear soprano voices carried the air of the theme of Tchaikovsky's "Dance of the Fairies" while on the stage 40 or 50 women dancers in white danced in the falling snow with a beautiful white background. It was effective and really moving.

DIARY   *Moscow—February 26, 1937*

Spent day preparing for trip down to the Don Basin, Kharkov, Dnepropetrovsk, and to the big dam. Marjorie motored down to the station with me at 5:20 P.M.

We have a complete dining car and sleepers for the exclusive use of our party including the American Moscow correspondents.

REPORT ON DEBT DEVELOPMENT

Moscow—March 5, 1937

Strictly Personal and Confidential

THE HONORABLE FRANKLIN D. ROOSEVELT

My dear Mr. President:

Since my last report I have spent ten days in travel through the country, covering the industrial districts—Leningrad, Kharkov, the big Cooper Dam area, and the Donbas Region which, together with the Moscow area, covers approximately 70 to 80 per cent of the Soviet heavy industry. I wanted to see their equipment, personnel, living conditions, and the forces at work to report and interpret to you more adequately this extraordinary situation.

A voluminous and detailed report is going forward by next pouch to the Department. I think it will be of substantial value.

My observations confirmed and recalled vividly your conversation with Litvinov as to where they were going. What these people have done in the past seven years in heavy industry is unique. They have "painted on a ten-league canvas with a brush of comet's hair." Both in conception and performance it is extraordinary. Bare plains have been transformed into huge industrial areas within six years. The plants and equipment which I saw are first-class, the result of the synthesis of the best engineering judgment of the capitalist countries. The men running the plants are for the most part about thirty-five years of age. They are the serious, studious type and appear to be well equipped and strong. The workers are generally twenty-five per cent women. Fully eighty per cent are less than thirty years of age. The operators in these plants were recruited about twenty-five per cent from established industrial plants, and the remaining seventy-five per cent from the countryside, the latter having been employed to build the plants and then equipped through manual training at night to become the operators of the plants when completed. All these plants have laboratories, technical libraries, nightly lectures. Their factory cost accounting is translated into graphic charts, showing both operations and trends up to the minute. Each plant has its kindergartens (crèches for nursing mothers), workers' clubs, restaurants, and other social provisions for the workers. The wage average is 250 rubles a month, of a gold value (based on the bootleg exchange) of $12.50.

But the communistic principle here has in actual fact been abandoned. "From everyone according to his abilities and to each according to his needs" is gone. They get what they earn. The profit motive and self-interest are the mainspring. From top to bottom production is stimulated by premiums and extra wage for service above the "norm." This applies to management, engineers, and workers. The plant itself is required to make a profit and does, generally, ranging from five to thirty per cent, which goes to the Central Government. This system, they found, was necessary for success. It is a socialistic enterprise based upon capitalistic principle of profit and self-interest, which they had to come to, to make the machine function.

Of course there are many things out of joint. Their factory operations, while fair, do not compare with the appearance of an efficient factory organization at home. The price of a good pair of shoes is twenty-five to fifty per cent of a month's average wage. It is alleged that there is much discontent among the slothful and less efficient workers because of higher wages paid to the skilled.

The big invisible factor that has made this job relatively easy is the enormous wealth of the country and the autocratic power possessed and employed by the leaders. There is undoubtedly enormous waste and tremendous mistakes have been made, but this is *de minimis* contrasted with the resources which they have at their command, and is lost in the size of the picture.

Generally speaking, my judgment confirms the general impression here in the Diplomatic Corps, to wit: that granted five or ten years of peace, extraordinary results will be developed by this industrial program.

With great respect,

Faithfully yours,

RUSSIAN INDUSTRY—HOW IT WORKS AND WHY

NO. 116   *Moscow—March 12, 1937*

TO THE HONORABLE THE SECRETARY OF STATE

RECENT VISITS MADE BY AMBASSADOR DAVIES TO
CERTAIN INDUSTRIAL REGIONS OF THE SOVIET UNION

Strictly Confidential

Sir:

I have the honor to report the following observations in connection with my recent visits to certain industrial regions of the U.S.S.R.

In order adequately to understand and appreciate the forces which are at work in the Soviet Union, it is necessary that reliance should not be placed exclusively upon published sources of information. While these are voluminous they are nevertheless naturally highly colored with propaganda and also do not contain many of the facts which should be known to assess the situation properly.

With this in mind, I had a survey made of the various industrial regions of the Soviet Union and was fortunate enough to procure a map from the government authorities which indicated the various regions, types of natural resources therein, together with the various kinds of manufacturing and producing industries in such districts. Based thereon, I planned a personal visit of inspection to the Leningrad area which has large textile and porcelain plants and other industries which would be natural to a northern seaport but which have not been extended by the Soviet authorities because of probable military vulnerability; and also to the Don Basin and Dnepropetrovsk area in the Ukraine, the regions where, within 400 kilometers, there are huge deposits of coal and iron, in the center of which is located the Dnieproges Dam, which is claimed to be second only to Boulder Dam in the world. These regions produce approximately 78 per cent of the total coal production of the Soviet Union of which 50 per cent is of coking quality, and approximately 60 per cent of the total pig iron of Soviet production. This district contains about 55 per cent of the total number of blast furnaces of the country.

The Dnieproges Dam built by Colonel Cooper with its auxiliary substations had a capacity in 1935 of 587,000 kilowatts. It is probable that within a year or two that capacity will be doubled. The five huge General Electric turbines installed are being supplemented by four of Soviet manufacture. In this region there are to be constructed three other large water-power sites, for which plans are now being projected, which will still further increase the available electric power.

One of the remarkable achievements of the Five-Year Plan has been the conception, projection, and operation of huge manufacturing operations in this district, which has an area of 81,475 square kilometers in the Donets Coal Region alone. In this district are located the largest steel plants, heavy-machine-building and electrical turbine plants, aluminum plant, tractor and chemical plants, agricultural machinery, and other large industrial operations. These plants have been built, operatives trained, and production secured, some employing as high as 38,000 men and women, all within the past six or seven years. The region also contains some of the best agricultural lands in the country.

When it was announced that I contemplated making a trip through these regions, the American journalists asked whether they could accompany me on this trip for the reason alleged that they would have a more advantageous opportunity to see these plants, with me than otherwise. Inasmuch as the Soviet authorities had no objection, I advised the journalists that I would be glad to have them take the trip.

Accompanied by my daughter, a secretary, and four journalists—Charles Nutter of the Associated Press, Norman Deuel of the United Press, Demaree Bess of the *Christian Science Monitor*, and Joseph Phillips of the *New York Herald Tribune*, and Mr. Gordon and Mr. Shiffer of the Embassy staff, we left for Kharkov on a six-day tour of this region on Friday, February 26, 1937.

We visited five cities and the largest plants in this district, covering a wheel and caterpillar-tractor plant (12,000 employees); a plant manufacturing electrical turbine motors, et cetera (38,000 employees); the Dnieproges Dam; an aluminum plant (3000 employees) alleged to be the largest single unit in the world; the Zaporozhe pig-iron and steel plant (35,-000 employees); a steel rolling mill (13,000 employees); a hospital (18 doctors, 120 nurses); crèches and kindergartens; the largest agricultural-implement plant in the Soviet Union (16,000 employees), making seeders, harrows, plows, and combines which are a combination of reaper and threshing machine; and the first "Young Pioneer" House, an establishment of 280 rooms, adapted to the development of school children (27,000), outside of regular school hours, in scientific, artistic, airplane, transportation, and other lines of manual training (320 teachers). These latter institutions are one of the most interesting developments in the Soviet Union and are being established in all the large centers, predicated upon the Stalin idea that the most precious capital of the state is the brains of the youth. Every encouragement and incentive is given to the natural "bent" of the youth, through these agencies, established for the avowed purpose of discovering latent talent.

The impressions which the trip leaves are very distinct.

PLANNING

The planning impresses the mind as being most extraordinary in the boldness of its conception and the vigor of its execution. Five years ago the district of Zaporozhe which now contains some of these enormous plants and a city of approximately 125,000 persons, with modern brick apartment buildings and wide avenues and parks, was a prairie plain. The buildings were constructed, after consultation with the best foreign engineers available in conjunction with Soviet engineers, by unskilled labor for the most part, as I am informed. During the construction, it is stated that the labor was trained at night in technical schools for the operation of the

plants when completed—the nucleus of the workers of the
plant being about 25 per cent in number drawn from other going similar operations in other parts of the country.

BUILDINGS AND EQUIPMENT

The buildings and equipment were generally of the most
modern type. The construction companies, principally American, but also German, French, and English, were selected in
each case to get the best and latest technical and scientific
developments in engineering manufacture.

EQUIPMENT, OPERATIONS, LABOR

It was noticeable that, wherever manufacturing processes
adapted itself thereto, either in individual departments or in
the plant as a whole, the best type of factory efficiency was
employed in the use of conveyor systems and similar operations. The outstanding impressions of factory operations were
two: the extent to which women were employed in machine
operations (averaging about 25 per cent), and the youth of
the average worker; generally from 60 to 80 per cent were
under 30 and a very small percentage were over 40 years of
age. In walking through the plants, while the tempo did not
seem to be as highly speeded as in efficient plants at home,
nevertheless, they were going along very well—approximately
40 to 50 per cent.

MANAGEMENT PERSONNEL

Quite one of the strongest impressions that was left with us
(and it has been a matter of comment by all of the journalists)
is the character of the men running these enterprises. For the
most part they were men about 35 years of age. One was 40
and one was 45 years old. They were all technical "diploma"
engineers, educated in Russia, but all equipped by travel and

technical study in other countries. They all appeared of the steady, studious, scientific type, quiet in manner, but with indications of much reserve in executive strength. In all of these plants, there were large staffs of technical engineers. All plants had libraries, lecture rooms, and a night school for the operatives. In their libraries they had technical magazines of many other countries, a general library, and translators.

WAGES, EFFICIENCY, AND PROFITS

The average wage generally was 200 to 250 rubles a month (about $10 to $12.50 "bootleg" ruble gold value). The factory restaurant supplied a good satisfying meal for two rubles (10 cents *ibid.*). The rental in factory housing buildings varied according to the number in the family and the floor space thereof; but in no instance did it exceed 15 per cent of the monthly wage (a provision fixed by law). The so-called "shock workers" received more wage than the ordinary worker. The so-called "Stakhanovites" (competitive piece-workers) varied from 800 to 2000 rubles per month. There were 15 to 95 per cent Stakhanovites in each factory. A man becomes a Stakhanovite as soon as his performance equals the maximum capacity of the machine. Engineers receive from 800 to 2000 rubles a month, and directors and factory management from 1500 to 2000 rubles a month ($75 to $100 "bootleg" gold value).

Norms are established all along the line, and premiums in wage awarded, based upon productive capacity. This applies also to management. Production cost, overhead, efficiency, and similar factors are all kept in rather impressive efficiency records illustrated by graphs. The management keeps very close track of trends from year to year and quite generally the record discloses marked improvement each year.

Generally each plant is a self-contained unit. The Director enters into an agreement with the Commissar for Heavy Industry as to volume for the year. The price of the product is fixed for resale generally through the Commissar for Heavy Industry and in some instances direct. The price is fixed so as to get a profit of from 5 to 10 per cent on cost of production (one was as high as 30 per cent). A part of the profit over and above that agreed upon is used for betterment of living conditions, improving kindergartens, libraries, crèches, et cetera, and all is in the discretion of the Director, who distributes this "Director's fund" in premiums, bonuses, et cetera, to engineers and so forth or in such other manner as he may determine.

These generalizations will have to be qualified somewhat because these facts were developed in the different isolated plants which we visited, and may not be typical of the entire industry of the country. In the main, however, my impression is that the principle does obtain. Plant extensions are paid for by the state. Ordinary obsolescence is a part of cost.

THE COMMUNISTIC AND SOCIALISTIC PRINCIPLE

There is no doubt but what the leaders of this government have been compelled to abandon the communistic idea of distribution according to needs and accept the principle of distribution for compensation according to earnings. The incentive of personal profit for additional effort impregnates the whole system. First there was the "shock-worker" system, and now the Stakhanovite movement is being projected by the state by every known propaganda. All along the line men are rewarded with premiums for extra work. Everywhere the profit motive is being employed.

Given freedom from European war (many factories are now converted to war uses according to report, as is indicated by the introduction of caterpillar-tractor production), my opinion conforms generally to the opinion of the Diplomatic Corps in Moscow that great economic strides will be seen within the next five or ten years, this always presupposing that there will be no civil war by reason of counterrevolutions and the "revolution chewing up its own children."

The principal factor which would seem to assure this development lies in the enormous wealth and the undeveloped resources of the country. An outlet for the advancement of ambitious youth will be afforded here for a generation at least. There is also the fact that this country is self-sufficient. It is producing enormous agricultural and mineral wealth annually, and it will not be dependent upon import or export for many years to come. It is producing large supplies of gold. While there is no question but what, in its present phase, its efficiency cannot compare with capitalist states and possibly never will, nevertheless, in the absence of competition or need or necessity for competition with capitalist states, such inefficiencies need not and will not appear. There may be enormous waste through bureaucracy, slothfulness, or incapacity of labor or unadaptability to tool production and the like, but still the net profit will probably be such as to continue to enrich the state and through it the general population. Inefficiencies will be absorbed in the fat. In the city of Dnepropetrovsk last year, sixteen large white stone schoolhouses were built, each of 25 or 30 rooms—all alleged to be paid for out of the profits of local industries, which turned over profits to the local municipality.

In the event of being drawn into a European conflict, there is some doubt as to whether the industry back of the line could now support a long war. My guess would be that it could do so to a far greater degree than is expected, in view of what I have seen in this region.

There are reports of sabotage by labor in many instances as a resentment against the piecework and the speeding-up system of the Stakhanovites.

If the present trend of extending higher compensation for greater or more efficient work were to continue and if the standards of living continue to increase, there will soon be no "classless" society in the Soviet Union. At the present rate at which differentiation and increases in compensation are growing, it will be but a very short time before there will be very marked class distinctions based upon property. Human nature is functioning here even as always.

Upon arrival at each plant we generally had a session at the main office at which the Director gave us, universally quite frankly, answers to all questions submitted, and a general picture of the enterprise as well. This was followed by a trip through the plant at which time additional facts were developed and recorded.*

I have the honor to be, Sir, respectfully yours,

Joseph E. Davies

DIARY   *Dnepropetrovsk—February 28, 1937*

An interesting thing occurred here. At the principal commission shop I saw what was in fact a very lovely oil painting. I decided to get it for my University of Wisconsin Collection. The director of the shop represented it to be by a celebrated Italian artist. The price was rather stiff, but I took it and arranged for the picture to be delivered to the sleeping car. That evening we noticed quite a commotion

---

* Attached to this dispatch were exhibits which were technical reports upon the various plants which we saw and which also contained stenographic records of the interviews which I had with the various managers. They were voluminous and technical. To afford a somewhat more detailed account of what these reports show, but in more condensed form, I prepared a memorandum which serves to condense and interpret the various details and stenographic reports made at the time. (See Appendix.)

around a group coming out to our car and to our surprise found that it was our friends the G.P.U., or secret police, who had the director in their charge. They had compelled him to come down and return the purchase price which I had paid and confess that he had misrepresented the fact and that the picture was not "an original." They were highly indignant about it and over the fact that I had been deceived. I thanked them cordially for their interest. As a matter of fact I had a hard time prevailing upon them not to see that the poor devil was severely punished.

While there is no communication or intercourse between me and these men, the mere fact that we see each other daily and smilingly greet each other "good morning" or "good night" has created a sort of comradeship. There is no doubt but what they are deeply concerned with our protection at all times. In fact I am certain that one of the controlling reasons for the practice of having all of the chiefs of mission under constant observation of the secret police when they are out of their own embassies is to afford protection. It was not so long ago that the German Ambassador was bombed and another high diplomatic official was shot through the arm by conspirators who sought to incite a diplomatic incident and create trouble in that way for the Soviet government.

MORE RELIGIOUS PERSECUTIONS IN GERMANY

JOURNAL   *Dnepropetrovsk—February 28, 1937*

News of the day is that Dr. Niemöller announced to his congregation at Dahlem that Herr Weissler, his associate, had died in a concentration camp on February 19, adding that, according to the Secret Police, he had hanged himself. The world will never accept that as a statement of fact. It looks bad for any hope of European peace through German co-operation under Hitler and the Nazis.

DIARY   *Moscow—March 4, 1937*

Dinner at the Italian Embassy. Discussion over the coffee of report of dissension in the "party councils" over new provisions in the new constitution. Stalin, it was reported, insisted upon liberalism of the constitution even though it hazarded his power and party control.

In discussing the war scare the Belgian Ambassador said that England held the balance of power as to European peace and that Germany was wooing England. If Germany sought outlet through war the first attack would be through Czechoslovakia; it would then be up to France either to go to the aid of Czechoslovakia under her treaty commitment or not, and this would depend upon what England would do. England was committed to go to the aid of France only in case of attack on France. England was not committed to aid France, if France herself were the aggressor, said the Ambassador. Germany's solution was through understanding with Russia, so he thought.

He is very positive in his opinions. He may be right.

LITVINOV, SPAIN, AND COLLECTIVE SECURITY

NO. 156   *Moscow, March 26, 1937*

TO THE HONORABLE THE SECRETARY OF STATE

SPANISH SITUATION; EUROPEAN PEACE;
SOVIET PARTICIPATION IN ARMAMENTS
AGREEMENT

Sir: *Strictly Confidential*

Pursuant to an appointment made, I called upon Commissar for Foreign Affairs Litvinov to present my respects before departure for the United States. Explaining that I was leaving for a short visit home, I stated that I would return here in June.

I then asked him how the Spanish situation was coming on. He stated that from the point of view of the Republican forces, very well; that from the point of view of European peace, almost too well. He expressed the fear that the reverses of the Italian forces would stimulate Mussolini to project additional forces into Spain, to rehabilitate his prestige. In that connection, he stated that the International Committee in London was having great difficulty; that the situation looked very bad; that pursuant to German suggestion it had taken up for consideration the evacuation of all volunteers in Spain; that thereupon Grandi had interposed the condition that before such consideration the matter of the embargo upon the gold of the Spanish government should first be considered; that after the other governments had acceded thereto, Grandi announced that the Italian government would not discuss further the matter of the evacuation of volunteers in Spain.

As to his suggestion of the desperate character of the situation, I suggested that it might be natural for Mussolini to wish to re-establish his prestige before engaging in further discussions, but that conditions in Spain seemed to change very rapidly, for it was only two weeks ago that the Spanish Ambassador had stated to me that his government was seriously contemplating the possibility of declaring war on Italy, and seemed very downcast over the reverses that the Republican forces had sustained; and that now, within two weeks, there was a complete reversal in position and that therefore it was possible the situation might change for the better equally quickly. Litvinov stated that was possible, but reiterated as his firm opinion that if the Italians were to send additional forces into Spain the situation would be most serious for European peace. He emphasized strongly that if the democratic governments would now serve firm notice upon Italy that such action would not be tolerated, Mussolini would not take such action, for he said Italy did not want European war; that internal conditions, economic and political, in Italy were not good and that Italy could not stand a European war. When I suggested that perhaps the democratic countries, including England, did not wish to hazard a firm position until they were prepared adequately, he stated that neither Germany nor Italy was prepared adequately. To my expressions of surprise that Germany was not prepared from a military point of view, he stated again that their information was positive that Germany was not ready, even in a military sense, leaving out of consideration the economic background. I then stated that I had heard rumors that the Soviet Union was apprehensive lest France and England might possibly make a peace in Western Europe with Germany and Italy, leaving Russia to face Germany alone. He stated very positively that in his opinion that was not the fact.*

I then stated that the European situation in its elementals looked simple; and that it was difficult to understand why the statesmanship of Europe could not provide that England, France, Germany, Italy, and Russia should agree to preserve the territorial integrity of Europe and through trade agreements provide Germany with raw materials and thereby the assurance that she could live, which would relieve the peoples of Europe and the world of these terrific burdens of armament

---

* There was much rumor, at about this time, that England, France, Germany and Italy might get together on the basis of a new "Western Locarno," whereby peace to Western Europe would be guaranteed by these governments but to the exclusion of the Soviets. The suspicion was that Hitler was to be given a free hand in Eastern Europe as a consideration for preserving peace in the West. (Not a part of dispatch.)

and the fear of catastrophic war. The prompt rejoinder was: "Do you think Hitler would ever agree to anything like that?" I said that I did not know, but that it was my opinion that there was a very substantial body of influential and responsible thought in Germany that such an idea would appeal to. Litvinov rejoined that he thought that might be so; that Schacht was of that type; he did not think they could prevail against Hitler and the political and military forces dominant in Germany. He then stated that the only hope for the preservation of European peace was a prompt, firm declaration of the democracies of Europe that they were standing together for peace; he named France, Russia, and Czechoslovakia. He then said that if the United States were to join in such a declaration it would mean not only European but world peace as well, as it would also settle the Japanese question. I rejoined that we did not feel any serious apprehension with reference to Japan, and that generally speaking our people were seriously opposed to becoming embroiled or entangled in European troubles. On the other hand, I personally felt confident that both the President of the United States and the Secretary of State were devoted to the cause of peace and would be glad to contribute in any way that was possible consistent with our traditional policies, if and when the time was ripe. I impressed upon him, however, that, in so speaking, I was expressing only my personal views.

Litvinov then said there was some information which might be of value to the United States which he would be glad to take this occasion to give to me, which was as follows:

After the last naval-disarmament agreement, the Soviet Union had taken up with Great Britain the question of building cruisers, with certain caliber of guns, et cetera; that it asked that it be included, within the agreement, that it should build cruisers, et cetera, up to the minimum of the limit set as to any of the participating governments; that England took it up with Germany and other governments and that they agreed that the U.S.S.R. should build seven cruisers, whereas the present German limitation was three; that the U.S.S.R. was not to be required to disclose its program to Japan; that thereafter Germany raised the point that it should be permitted to raise its quota to five, and that the U.S.S.R. might then extend her complement to ten; that the U.S.S.R. had made the suggestion that "the initiative" should be made mutual, namely, that the U.S.S.R. should also have the right to extend to ten upon condition that Germany then might increase her complement to five; that the matter was in abeyance with the probability that it would be favorably agreed upon.

Litvinov stated that in his opinion I had acquired more information and knowledge of Russia in the three months I was here than any other Ambassador had obtained in two years. To this I rejoined that it had been my habit to acquaint myself with the facts in a situation before I arrived at any opinion upon which I would express to my principals. He asked my impressions. I told him briefly that I was very much impressed with what they were doing, with the strength of their leadership, the difficulties they were overcoming; that I felt that they were presently sincerely devoted to peace; that the future would determine the result of their governmental experiment; that I was still of the opinion that our system was the best for the alleviation of the masses of men and that our processes of evolution through democracy were better than the revolutionary experiment here.

The conference ended with his expressions of good will to the President of the United States and to the Secretary of State and personal wishes for a good voyage.

I have the honor to be, Sir, respectfully yours,

Joseph E. Davies

EXCERPT FROM A LETTER TO STEPHEN EARLY

March 9, 1937

There is scarcely a day but what our American chauffeur "Charlie" Giliberti is approached on the streets by some American who has taken out Soviet citizenship and who pleads that he intercede with the American authorities to help him to get back home. A thousand Communists came here in 1934-35 from Austria, so I am told by the Austrian Minister, took up citizenship in the promised land, cannot get out, and are all bending every effort to get back home.

DIARY *Moscow—March 9, 1937*

Harrison, one of the undersecretaries in Warsaw, is here for a few days. He is a very well-informed man. His views are interesting. Poland, in case of war, was confronted with a desperate choice, he said; but he thought that the government would be pro-German as against the U.S.S.R. The large landowning class combined with the municipal *bourgeoisie* were really in command of the government. The Baltic bloc, Estonia, Latvia, and Lithuania, were in a desperate situation. They were artificial states created out of old Russia by the League of Nations and in case of European war would probably be destroyed, at least temporarily. Lithuania, he said, was pro-Russian. Estonia had a large Germanic population leading back to the old Hanseatic days. Both Estonia and Latvia were trying to get along between two dangerous, powerful enemies: Germany and the U.S.S.R. He agreed with me that the Little Entente was in the process of breaking up. The existence of Hungarian minorities in Rumania, in Czechoslovakia, and in Yugoslavia and the very selfish problems of these smaller states gave Hitler a good deal to work on to split them up, playing upon the chauvinistic self-interest of each as against the other.

Finland, he thought, was the very bright spot in the Russian Foreign Office, as Finland was very obviously desperately asserting its independence in relation to Germany as well as to Russia.

DIARY   *Moscow—March 11, 1937*

The new Estonian Minister, Colonel Koznic, is an interesting type. We had a long conversation today. We get along very well together in German. He is a Russian; was educated in Leningrad and was an officer in one of the crack tsar regiments. He was one of the group of old tsarist military men who fought the Bolsheviks in Estonia and succeeded in establishing that state. He is still a young man with a very attractive personality and with a good deal "on the ball," and he was particularly well informed on Russia.

His impression is that this is rather a crucial year in Russia; that there is undoubtedly a great deal of political discontent arising, chiefly out of rivalries among the old Bolsheviks. The men running the government are rather the hard-boiled, tough-fibered type of revolutionists of the Bolshevik early days rather than the intellectuals, of which latter class Trotsky was the leader. Stalin is a very strong, able man who is practical, with a lot of common sense and wisdom. Molotov is an exceptional man with great mental capacity and wisdom. Stalin's control of the army through Voroshilov, who is unquestionably loyal, and his control of the secret police has undoubtedly firmly entrenched him in power. They seemed to be conscious of the danger to their government and could undoubtedly be trusted to take strong measures to protect their regime.

From all this, I have the distinct impression that all of the border states are scrupulously careful to offend neither of the two big boys on either side of them.

Another diplomat, Minister ———, made a most illuminating statement to me yesterday. In discussing the trial he said that the defendants were undoubtedly guilty; that all of us who attended the trial had practically agreed on that; that the outside world, from the press reports, however, seemed to think that the trial was a put-up job (façade, as he called it); that while we knew it was not, it was probably just as well that the outside world should think so.

LADIES' LUNCHEON AT THE MOLOTOV *DACHA*

DIARY   *Moscow—March 14, 1937*

Marjorie went to Madame Molotov's luncheon. It was quite extraordinary—a group of wives of the commissars all of whom are actively engaged as engineers, doctors, or factory managers.

Madame Molotov, wife of the Premier, is a Member of Cabinet and has been Commissar for Fisheries and is now Commissar for Cosmetics. She is a very extraordinary woman. The manner in which she has established these very chic perfume shops and cosmetic beauty parlors indicates a great deal of executive direction. She and the rest of these serious-minded women who are engineers, physicians, etc., found great interest in Marjorie particularly in the fact that a woman of her type should be so much interested in serious business matters and should herself be "a workingwoman." This idea of having a "hen luncheon" is something most novel in Soviet experience, as I am advised. So I've asked Marjorie to dictate her account of it while it is fresh in her mind. Here it is:

"The day we went through the factory (one of four she runs) making fine perfumes, creams, etc., Mme Molotov asked us to lunch with her. We accepted with pleasure, but had no idea what a rare and interesting experience we were in for. The day arrived and off we went—an hour in the country out Rublova Woods way— past several large villas, and finally the green fence and guards came into view. Gate was open, and enroute to house we saw many more guards.

"House modern, large (but by no means a palace either in or out), rather plain. Good taste—ample, but not furnished in a cozy or "lived-in" manner, though in every way adequate. Entrance hall, big stairs, dressing rooms, etc. Living room spacious. No photos or bric-a-brac. Dining room large with huge casement windows. Table decorated in cyclamen—at least 3″ each. Standing on floor around room were eight or ten potted lilacs—white and lavender— fine big heads and full of flowers.

"I was on Mme Molotov's right—Mrs. Kennan wife of an Embassy Secretary—Miss Wells—Mme Kubar—Mme Krestinsky—Mme Stomoniakov. The table was filled with hors d'oeuvres. Luncheon was elaborate and many courses—three kinds of meat—six kinds of fish—one very special, a snub-nosed little thing about eight inches long—very good, and comes from the Volga River. I had to eat regardless of the Embassy doctor's warning—so I did, *at length*. (They all have an enmity to the animals, but we Americans are used to inspected and sterilized food!) The whole atmosphere was very cordial—very anxious to have us have a good time—and we did, but OH! if only one could speak the language. Through an interpreter it is difficult, to say the least.

"An interesting reaction to the luncheon came upon my return. I found Joe in the library with one of the newsmen who was greatly astounded upon learning where we had been and asked dozens of questions. Then, at dinner that evening at the Belgian Legation, I was sitting next to the British Ambassador, Lord Chilston, who nearly burst with excitement over my story of our luncheon—inquiring two or three times, 'Where did you say this luncheon was?' Then, after he had satisfied himself that it was Mme Molotov and it was at her *dacha*, he said, 'You Americans are remarkable! I have been here seven years and haven't been able to get so much as a toe in their house—and you come and after only a few weeks you have a luncheon given there in your honor. I don't understand it!'"

JOURNAL   *Moscow—March 14, 1937*

Marjorie told me of a most interesting talk she had with
Mme Krestinsky the other day. Mme Krestinsky is a physician
and the wife of the Undersecretary of State. She is in charge of
the hospitalization of women and children in Moscow. She is
of the comfortable type of middle-aged woman, with a very
handsome head and face. There is no doubt of her sincerity
and fineness. In response to Marjorie's enquiry, she said,
"This government is not against religion, as such. Our people simply had to take steps to prevent the abuses of religion
from destroying our people." She then went on to tell how
under the tsarist regime, the Greek Orthodox Church was
taken over as a part of the government, with the tsar as the
religious head of the Church, as well as the ruler of the state.
All priests were paid by the government. The burden of a
profligate government, she said, was placed upon the backs of
the people. It became, as she described it, a terrible abuse.
Finally, it became so bad that in the "Duma," the legislative
body created by one of the Alexanders, almost a third of its
members were priests and ecclesiastics. This group debased
their religion, she said, and fattened themselves, with all manner of excesses, and with all kinds of oppressions of the poor.
"Religion," she said, "was used as an opiate to lull unthinking
people into an acceptance of these unspeakable conditions."
They therefore had to separate religion from the state, and
did so. The new Soviet constitution expressly provides for
freedom with reference to religion, but provided it should
not be part of the state government, and that there should be
freedom of speech against religion, as well as for it. This,
she said, constituted real freedom, and that she knew that the
leaders of the government had no feelings against religion, as

such, but were determined not to permit these old conditions to return. It is significant that Stalin's wife was buried in holy ground, which was her dying request, as the story goes.

SOVIET GOLD PRODUCTION

Moscow—March 15, 1937

HONORABLE HENRY MORGENTHAU, JR.

Dear Henry:

Since my arrival I have been making every effort to try to get a line on the gold reserve here. It is practically impossible to get anything definite. It is more or less a military secret which is guarded with care and it is available, of course, as a matter of propaganda to project the idea of their power vis-à-vis Germany and Japan.

From the best information I can get, the situation is about as follows: that the production of the Union of South Africa in fine kilograms is between 325,000 and 350,000; the production of the Soviet Union is approximately 175,000; whereas that of the United States and Canada each is about 100,000. These data come from a study which has been made by the Legation at Riga. The general information here is that the 1936 production of the Soviet Union is considerably in excess of the amount hereinbefore stated and runs between 200,000,-000 and 250,000,000 dollars. The gold reserve of the State Bank is stated to be 350,000,000 dollars.

The other day I was privileged to see the collection of treasure and jewels at the State Bank. What surprised me was the size of the gold nuggets. They had two nuggets of solid gold ranging between 40 and 50 pounds each. From their appearance I should judge that they were practically pure gold. There is undoubtedly great wealth in the mountains here. Mrs. Litvinov, who is engaged in teaching in one of the schools of higher education in that region, told Mrs. Davies and me that holidays of school children and, in fact, picnic parties of the populace were generally spent in searching for gold nuggets in the hills, with remarkable success. Litvinov told me yesterday that recently while in the mountains, he had, in the course of a casual walk, picked up a stone which was remarkably high in gold content.

Sincerely yours,

RELIGIOUS FREEDOM IN RUSSIA

NO. 131   *Moscow, March 17, 1937*

TO THE HONORABLE THE SECRETARY OF STATE

ANTIRELIGIOUS MOVEMENT IN THE SOVIET UNION

Strictly Confidential

Sir:

I have the honor to report herewith the following with reference to the antireligious movement in the Soviet Union.

In connection with the adoption of the sections, in the new constitution, having to do with religion, there has recently been much discussion and attention paid by the Soviet authorities to the status of the antireligious movement.

I have learned from one of the members of the Diplomatic Corps, who is very well informed, that, when the religious sections of the constitution were debated, the existing provisions were attacked vigorously by some as being too dangerous; and that it was only Stalin's interposition which saved them; he taking the position that, if there was danger to the Communist Party, it was a challenge to the Communist Party to overcome it.

Now, for some weeks past, there has been much agitation in party circles over what might appear to be very substantial gains by the church within the past year. According to the

Administrator of the Affairs of the Central Soviet, the membership of the Society of Militant Atheists has declined from four million to two million members in the last four years.

I have the honor to be, Sir, respectfully yours,

Joseph E. Davies

EXCERPT FROM MEMORANDUM ON ANTIRELIGIOUS MOVEMENT IN THE SOVIET UNION

Nevertheless, the right to vote in the elections to the Soviets, granted to ministers of religion by the new constitution (Article 135), raises certain fears in the minds of atheist propagandists. "What danger does this right to vote present when the ministers of religion number about 100,000 in the Soviet Union?" asks Yaroslavsky, Chairman of the Society of Militant Atheists of the Soviet Union, in an article in the July-August, 1936, issue of *Antireligionznik*. After pointing out that it is not likely that the masses would vote for a priest, Yaroslavsky makes the following statement:

"If a certain priest took it into his head to place himself as a candidate to a local Soviet or even the Supreme Soviet we would have the right to carry on a struggle against such a candidate in depicting him as an example of the evil of religion and religious superstition."

ADDENDUM (Not enclosed with original dispatch)

On November 16, 1933, normal diplomatic relations were established between the Soviet Union and the government of the United States by an interchange of communications between President Roosevelt and Maxim Litvinov, Foreign Secretary of the Soviet Union, who was then in this country. The correspondence discloses the guarantees which were then given to the government of the United States by the Soviet Union.

Specifically, among other provisions, the following rights appertaining to religion were guaranteed to the American citizens in Russia:

1. The right to free exercise of liberty of conscience and religious worship, and from all disability or persecution on account of their religious faith or worship.

2. The right to conduct without annoyance or molestation of any kind religious services and rites of a ceremonial nature, including baptismal, confirmation, communion, marriage, and burial rites, in the English language.

3. The right, without restriction, to impart religious instruction to their children, either singly or in groups, or to have such instruction imparted by persons whom they may employ for such purpose.

4. That nationals of the United States should be granted rights with reference to free exercise of religion no less favorable than those enjoyed by nationals of the nation most favored in this respect, which assured citizens of the United States that they shall be entitled to hold religious services in churches, houses, or other buildings, rented, according to the laws of the country, in their national language or in any other language which is customary in their religion. They shall be entitled to bury their dead in accordance with their religious practice in burial grounds established and maintained by them with the approval of the competent authorities, so long as they comply with the police regulations of the other party in respect of buildings and public health.

CONSTITUTION OF UNION OF SOVIET SOCIALIST REPUBLICS

Article 124

In order to ensure to citizens freedom of conscience, the church in the U.S.S.R. is separated from the state, and the school from the church. Freedom of religious worship and freedom of antireligious propaganda is recognized for all citizens.

Article 135

Elections of deputies are universal: all citizens of the U.S.S.R. who have reached the age of eighteen, irrespective of race or nationality, religion, educational and residential qualifications, social origin, property status, or past activities, have the right to vote in the election and to be elected, with the exception of insane persons and persons who have been convicted by a court of law and whose sentences include deprivation of electoral rights.*

STALIN INSISTS UPON THE SECRET BALLOT AND UNIVERSAL SUFFRAGE

NO. 138   *Moscow, March 18, 1937*

TO THE HONORABLE THE SECRETARY OF STATE

THE COMMUNIST PARTY; THE PLENUM OF THE CENTRAL COMMITTEE, HELD IN FEBRUARY, 1937

Strictly Confidential

Sir:

I have the honor to report the following with reference to the recent meeting—the so-called Plenum—which discussed and determined certain political policies of the Communist

---

* It was shortly after diplomatic relations had been resumed and the Soviet Union had been "recognized" by the United States that the revision of the Soviet constitution was taken up by that government. I was told in Moscow, and I believe the source to have been reliable, that one of the most important influences in securing the adoption of these sections having to do with freedom of religious worship and extending the right of suffrage and office holding to all citizens without regard to religion was the emphasis and explicit requests which President Roosevelt had made in connection with the Litvinov negotiations in Washington in connection with "recognition."

Party; and the resultant current drive in party cleansing and reorganization.

At this meeting, held a few weeks ago, it is understood that the chief matter of discussion was the projection of the new constitution in connection with the new universal suffrage and secret ballot. Since that time, there has been manifest a great deal of party activity. This situation has been a subject of much discussion in the Diplomatic Corps. The Russian newspapers are full of propaganda with reference thereto. It is quite apparent that a great effort is being made to regalvanize the party organization. The leaders, great and small, are constantly urging through the press that the party must cleanse itself, rid itself of slothfulness and inaction, and assume its function of leadership in projecting the principles of the constitution in aiding the determination of the will of the people at the pending elections.

The Spanish Ambassador advised me that at the Party Council (Plenum), an extended discussion, almost in the nature of a debate, was had as to whether the provisions of the new constitution, according secret and universal suffrage, should be now projected or not; that it was urged that to do so, because of the backwardness of the electorate, might involve serious danger. It is stated that Stalin, himself, decided the issue in favor of projecting actual secret and universal suffrage which the new constitution calls for.

It now would appear to be the situation that the party leaders, recognizing that, with a secret ballot and universal suffrage, the situation might get out of hand, have decided to put on a big political drive to make sure that it will direct and control the electorate in the coming elections.

I have the honor to be, Sir, respectfully yours,

Joseph E. Davies

COMMUNISM COMPROMISES WITH HUMAN NATURE

NO. 132   *Moscow, March 17, 1937*

TO THE HONORABLE THE SECRETARY OF STATE

> POSSIBLE INDICATIONS OF DEPARTURE FROM OR
> MODIFICATION OF CERTAIN BASIC COMMUNISTIC
> PRINCIPLES OF THE RUSSIAN REVOLUTION
>
> *Strictly Confidential*

Sir:

I have the honor to report that in discussions with the Embassy staff, we have canvassed orally the situation here with a view to assembling the various facts and trends which indicate a departure from, or modification by the present regime of, the basic communistic principles upon which the Revolution was founded.

It appears quite clear that the governing powers have, through necessity and for self-preservation, been compelled to abandon, at least temporarily, many of their communistic principles. The idea of a "classless" society has been and is being destroyed in practice. The government itself is a bureaucracy with all the indicia of class, to wit: special privileges, higher standards of living, and the like. An illustration is found in the fact that the only caviar which can be obtained here is served by the high government officials or possibly obtained as a matter of favor through the Kremlin restaurant, which is provided for the high governmental officials living therein. From the top down, there are to be found indications of class.

Writers, artists, even leaders of jazz bands, receive high compensation and have the class privileges which money provides in luxuries and the like.

Membership in the party constitutes a distinctly privileged class.

In industry, classes have been established and are being rapidly intensified and developed through the system of offering greater pay for greater work. This in turn has induced higher standards of living among certain of the workers, and class consciousness is evidenced in differences in housing and living conditions and indications of style consciousness on the part of women and wives of the workers. This condition is admitted by the officialdom here in confidence; but they seek to justify it on the Marxian theory that there is no class distinction except that which exists between the workers and a capitalistic property-owning class which exploits them, and, inasmuch as this is a socialistic enterprise for the benefit of the state and, therefore, has no capitalistic property-owning class, that therefore, in the proper sense of the word, there are no "classes" because of these differentiations. Of course, the fallacy of this is obvious. "Class," after all, is only a word to define an idea; the basis of which is that there are different groups of men which are differentiated, as among themselves. Obviously the principal visible distinctions are found in the various standards of living and special privileges that are enjoyed. There can be no doubt that this is essentially a "class" society, and contains the seed of self-interest which the condition breeds.

The significant thing to my mind about this situation is the fact that these theoretical Communists, when clothed with responsibility and faced with the necessity of maintaining themselves in power, were compelled to resort to the elementals of human nature, to wit: self-interest and profit for labor, in order to make their plan function and justify their bureaucracy. A "selfless" industry system, they found, would stagnate. To succeed they were obliged to resort to the fundamental incentive of profit and individualistic self-interest. It is alleged by the leaders here that this is simply a stage in their effort to attain ultimate communism. There is every indication here, however, that again it will be a case of "the monster that makes the meat upon which it grows great"; and that it will be a long time before this capitalistic-socialistic state, with its rulers enjoying the "fleshpots" of luxury and power, will develop into a communistic state and "selfless" society.

Again, in the army, the old idea of comrade officers and simplicity has been displaced by titles, gold braid, epaulets, decorations, and smart uniforms, distinguishing the one class from the other.

Another striking indication of departure from the communistic idea is to be found in the attitude of the government toward the home, divorce, parenthood, the fatherland, and nationalistic patriotism. The idea of the world proletariat and revolution has been set aside and replaced with the idea of a nationalistic Russia. Great propaganda is being directed to create that national concept.*

I have the honor to be, Sir, respectfully yours,

Joseph E. Davies

"LITTLE RED RIDING HOOD" SPEECH OF SOVIET AMBASSADOR IN LONDON

NO. 139   *Moscow, March 18, 1937*

TO THE HONORABLE THE SECRETARY OF STATE

                                              Strictly Confidential
Sir:

Since the departure of the Spanish Ambassador for London, it may or may not be significant that Maisky, the Soviet

---

* It should be understood as is set forth in the exhibits attached to this dispatch (omitted here for lack of space) that the Soviet officials do not admit the deductions which I draw.

Ambassador in London, made his rather militant speech there, suggesting that Russia was equipped successfully to handle both a Japanese and a German attack, simultaneously if necessary.* The radio also carries the announcement that the legal government of Spain has made overtures in London to both France and England in connection with possible concessions to them in Spanish Morocco.

A long address was also recently published in the official press here, complaining bitterly against Italy. This was signed by many of the prominent publicists, scientists, and well-known men of university circles here. It is regarded in some quarters as a precursor of some more militant action by the Soviet government in the Spanish situation.

Coincident therewith, there are renewals of rumors that the government is contemplating sending supplies to Spain with a naval convoy of Russian vessels.

An official of the Foreign Office also stated to me the other evening at the Belgian Embassy that they regarded the situation with great seriousness and that something ought really to be done.

The impression which I get here is that the European situation is mercurial to the last degree. Changes are sudden, even violent, indicative of the shifting national realistic interests. There is no firm ground upon which a foundation can be laid with any security. All seem to be playing their own games, and nationalistic interests are running riot.

Aside from the Spanish situation, the universal opinion is that England is "stalling" for time in order to rearm; and that she will not again hazard having her fingers burned, as in Ethiopia. It is generally considered that this will require a year and a half or two years. It is also generally considered

---

* Note: Journal, Moscow—March 13, 1937.

that the danger lies in the fact that Germany, through either despair or a paranoiac leadership, might decide to cast all on the die before England can rearm.

The smaller countries of Europe seem to regard the situation with great apprehension. These impressions arise from conversations which I have had with the diplomatic representatives, of these countries, here.

I have the honor to be, Sir, respectfully yours,

Joseph E. Davies

SPEECH BY M. MAISKY, SOVIET AMBASSADOR, IN LONDON

JOURNAL   *Moscow—March 13, 1937*

According to the press, the Soviet Ambassador in London made a strong speech. Maisky said that the danger of war in general and against Russia in particular had increased during the past fifteen months—the German-Japanese *rapprochement* amounted virtually to a military alliance against the U.S.S.R.—but Russia had the satisfaction of knowing that her preparedness and power of resistance had also increased.

Their two frontiers had been "made well-nigh impregnable by the great fortifications, by the large armies well equipped with all the modern appliances of war, and by the huge air force. At the same time our economic preparedness is also beyond question."

It was no part of their policy, he said, to strive after economic autarchy; they strove for independence, not for economic exclusiveness, and they had already achieved the position where, in the case of war, the U.S.S.R. could, for an indefinite period, carry on on the basis of a self-supporting economy.

"I can say today," he went on, "with full responsibility for every word that at the present time we are strong enough to repel any attack on our territories on the part of any foreign power, or any combination of powers, and we can do this singlehanded."

Their main preoccupation, he maintained, was to prevent war from breaking out, and they could not prevent it single-handed. That made it imperative to seek the reinvigoration of the League of Nations and the reinforcement of the principle of collective security.

They believed that Europe had now arrived at a turning point where it had to make a final choice; either to make collective security a real thing or to aim at the so-called "localization of war," the way of constant retreat before the aggressor, in the "ridiculous hope that perhaps, after all, this ravenous wolf will not devour little Red Riding Hood."

DIARY   *Moscow—March 18, 1937*

Duranty, Spencer Williams of the American-Russian Chamber of Commerce, and John Hazard came to lunch.

Duranty placed Soviet gold production at about $450,000,-000 annually.

Williams had interesting information as to American firms' disposition not to find any interest in possible Russian business because of local market demand. One firm offered $3000 per ton premium to cancel existing first quarter's business when approached to supply more material. This to the great surprise of Amtorg (the Soviet agency in New York).

One of the most interesting young American men here in Moscow is John Hazard. He is one of Charles R. Crane's young men who has a scholarship at the Moscow University. He is able, speaks Russian, and is an excellent student. He had lunch with me today and his account of the difficulties experienced

in teaching law at the Moscow University was most interesting and amusing. I have asked him to furnish me with a
memorandum to send on to the Department. It seems there
has been a great deal of confusion at the law school during
these purge trials. Classes have been postponed and there is
much confusion as to the texts which are required to be
studied. Hazard tells me that the head of the law school is in
trouble with the authorities and is in danger of being deposed.
It seems that he made the grave error of not only accepting
the original communist doctrine of brotherly comradeship but
predicting according to classic Marxian dogma that the state
as such would ultimately vanish and disappear because there
would be no need for it; but he made the additional mistake
of setting a time limit within which this particular development, when the state would fade out, would make its appearance. This he did in some publications and legal writings many
years ago. Unfortunately, the time he set was 1937 and he
was in the unfortunate predicament of having taught a principle which was refuted by the facts which everybody could
see.

PITTMAN NEUTRALITY BILL

JOURNAL   *Moscow—March 18, 1937*

   The "short wave" announces that the House of Representatives adopted an amendment to the cash-and-carry
clause of the Pittman Neutrality Bill, limiting the provision to
two years and giving the President discretion in deciding temporarily what goods and materials should be placed under
embargo.

   I wonder whether Litvinov may not be right and whether
we will not find that we are starving those very nations which
constitute bastions for the ultimate defense of democracy and
liberty as against totalitarianism and regimentation.

DIARY   *Moscow—March 20, 1937*

Had an interesting chat with Father Braun who came to lunch. He is a very gallant soldier of the Lord. He came over with Bill Bullitt.* He ministers to all Christians with great fidelity and humility. I have the greatest respect for him. Moreover, I like him. He is simple and humble and a very good man. His task here is a very difficult one. Every now and then the campaign against religion flares up with some new man in charge, and life is made difficult for Father Braun. He lives at the French Embassy. The French Ambassador and I jointly are looking after the extension of his permits from time to time so he can stay in the country. It has given us much pleasure and I think he too has found pleasure in the fact that he comes in and uses our piano whenever he wants to.

DIARY   *Moscow—March 21, 1937*

The "party" in some sections is putting on a drive to destroy all except the most artistic icons, priests' robes, chalices, and the like. It seems a pity that these should be destroyed. I have made a request that we be allowed to purchase some of these sacred relics and I think that the permission will be al-

---

* Father Braun came to Moscow coincident with Ambassador Bullitt's mission immediately following "recognition" of the Soviet Union by the United States. In the course of the "recognition" negotiations, the President had placed primary insistence upon the right of American citizens in the Soviet Union to enjoy freedom of religious worship and the incidental right to have the ministers of their faith perform their sacred duties in the Soviet Union. It was one of the substantial items of the agreement between the two governments. Clergymen, however, were, as I understand it, limited to ministrations with the understanding that they could not personally proselytize among Soviet citizens. Father Braun was practically the only Western representative of the Christian religion in the Soviet Union, and he ministered to all faiths alike. Under the strict letter of the agreement he would have the right to minister only to American nationals.

lowed us. If we can do so, we will save for ultimate sacred
purposes some at least of these beautiful things of the religious
life of old Russia.*

MOSCOW'S SHOPS AND THEATERS

Moscow, March 22, 1937

Dear Eleanor: †

We have been very busy preparatory to get-
ting away. Marjorie has made a great hit with the wives of the
Commissars (Cabinet Members) here. They are all working-
women who are in charge of large affairs as physicians, manager of a perfume factory, engineers, and so forth, and they
find much in common with Marjorie's interests and ability in
business matters.

Among the most interesting institutions here are the opera,
ballet, and theater. Last night we saw Tolstoy's tragedy—*The
Tsar Feodor*. It was produced in Moscow Art Theater which
was built some fifty years ago and is the center of Moscow
dramatic art. It was, of course, in Russian, but we had familiar-
ized ourselves with the plot and enjoyed it immensely. The
acting was superb. Every member of the cast down to the
least important character was an artist. The support given to
the principals and the general effect was most thorough and
artistic. There was not a jarring note and every person on the
stage was contributing artistry and detail in the support of
the general picture and impression. It was quite remarkable
inasmuch as there appeared to be as many as forty or fifty on
the stage sometimes. The principal characters were great. The
stage settings were also most beautiful, of course, for they

---

* Request granted.

† My daughter, Mrs. Millard Tydings.

have available enormous supplies from the old castles and ward rooms which the state has taken possession of. The stage pictures showed indications of the greatest care and artistic pains. It was one of the most remarkable things of its kind that I have ever seen.

One of the most interesting of institutions here are the Commission Shops. These resemble our antique shops and are run by the state and sell all manner of things brought in by the owners, from pictures to bedroom sets and from jewels to china. Every now and then you can pick up something unusually good, but in general the supply has been well picked over. Up to a year and a half ago they had so-called "Torgsin" shops which sold things for dollars (gold shops). Now all these things are being turned over to the Commission Shops. Dollars can't be used now; everything must be paid for in rubles. We have all had a lot of fun doing a little shopping in these places.

The other night we had dinner in honor of the Commissar of Foreign Trade.* He conducts this gigantic monopoly of export and import. No one but Russian officials and the staff and their wives were present. Several other high officials including the Chief of Staff, Marshal Yegorov,* and his beautiful wife, who used to be a cinema star, and the Commissar of Education and his tall, statuesque wife (of the former noblesse) and others I shall not describe. It created quite a sensation in the Diplomatic Corps. The officials make it a point to be very nice to us. We have no ax to grind and only wish them well in all the good things they are doing, even though we may doubt their ability to work out their plans.

Devotedly,

---

* Subsequently condemned to be shot as a traitor in conspiracy with foreign enemies.

DIARY   *Moscow—March 23, 1937*

We had an interesting evening with a dinner at the Embassy given in honor of the Red Army. It came about in this way. We had received many courtesies at the hands of Red Army men and I suggested to Colonel Faymonville, the military attaché at the Embassy, that we have a dinner for the Red Army leaders. It was an innovation in Moscow diplomatic circles. There was some doubt whether the Red Army would accept such an invitation. Pursuant to the protocol, the situation was sounded out and the invitation was accepted "with pleasure."

About 60 sat down at the Embassy table. They included the "High Command of the Army and Navy" and various notables, such as "Hero Flyers" of the Soviet Union, famous parachute jumpers, airplane engineers, and the like. One was impressed by the fine appearance of these men—strong, healthy, and with fine faces. Their uniforms were perfectly tailored and were quite resplendent with the various insignia of rank and various decorations, including the "Order of Lenin," etc. Colonel Faymonville, who knew all of these men very well, greeted them first and presented them to Mrs. Davies and me. Some brought their wives. Others had regretted for their wives. The dinner was gay. Most of our guests had never tasted an American "old-fashioned" cocktail before. They seemed to go down satisfactorily. The only other guests were members of the Embassy staff. The dinner was as handsome as the Embassy could produce, with all the capitalistic trimmings.

Marshal Voroshilov sat on Mrs. Davies' right with one of the Embassy ladies on his right, for translating. Vice-Marshal Tukhatchevsky sat on the hostess' left with my daughter next to him. She speaks Russian quite well; is a graduate of Vassar and is attending the University of Moscow. They got along very well in Russian and he started to sound her out on Karl Marx and the teachings of Communism and asked her whether she had ever studied "Marxism." She said, "Yes, in college." He inquired, "Don't you think it is a wonderful system?" She said, "No," that she was not impressed with it. Whereupon he said, "Wouldn't you like to be as free as the Russian women are free?" That was just too much for E.K. She "went to town" and gave a very concise comparison between the freedom of the American women as compared with that of the Russian women. Later, Marjorie said, "He probably didn't believe it— but on the other hand, maybe he did." *

Following the protocol on such occasions, toasts were proposed. As host, I proposed the health of the Red Army as an army of citizens, workers, and peasants that were a "people's army devoted to peace above all else." Marshal Voroshilov responded extemporaneously in Russian in a very able but simple and impressive way. He spoke in Russian and each sentence was translated as he spoke it. He said that he could personally attest to the truth of the fact that the Red Army was an army primarily devoted to peace. He stated that there was not a man in the Red Army, from top to bottom, who would not gladly discard his uniform and the implements of war if he could and would do so but for the necessity of protection of

---

* Within nine weeks of this dinner, eleven of the principal officers of the army and navy were tried by court-martial and shot, among them Marshal Tukhatchevsky and four other generals of High Command who were among our dinner guests. Tukhatchevsky was charged with being the head and front of a plot to seize the government. The gossip had it that he was stupid enough to divulge some of the plans to his lady love, who apparently followed the rule laid down by Lenin to "trust no one, watch your wife, watch your children, report to the government on their activities." The lady reported to the Gay-Pay-Oo and according to the report that settled Tukhatchevsky. I was told by a high Russian official that in fact Tukhatchevsky was betrayed by a very beautiful woman—a German spy. Neither of these alleged facts were alluded to in the subsequent Bukharin Trial, which divulged in detail the Tukhatchevsky plot for a palace revolution and a *coup d'état*.

their homes, for the preservation of peace of their land in an insane world where the liberties of nations are at all times subject to the attack of war-mad aggressors.

After dinner, we had moving pictures.

THE SOVIETS SUPPORT FREE CHINA

JOURNAL   *Moscow—March 26, 1937*

Prior to my departure I had the opportunity to have a talk with the Chinese Ambassador, Mr. Tsiang Ting-Fu. Ambassador Ting-Fu is a graduate of Cornell University, very friendly to the United States. He came to his present post from the position of Secretary to the President of China, Mr. Liu Shen. My impression is that the relations between China and the Soviet Union have improved immeasurably within the past few days; that a definite understanding has been arrived at; that there is an agreement that the Soviet Union will refrain from communistic activity in China which was antagonistic to the present Chinese government; that this specifically involved that the U.S.S.R. would lend no support to any independent communistic Chinese military forces or local governments; that this means a very great deal to China and gives much promise for the strengthening of the situation in China; that on their part the Chinese government will make provision to take care of those people in China who were thereby deprived of a means of support.

DIARY   *Paris—March 29, 1937*

Arrived here enroute home on a beautiful Easter Monday. In the evening we went to the opera, *Marouf, the Cobbler of Cairo*. We did not stay long. Outside of the singing and one male dancer it was quite below par and couldn't compare with the Russian opera of either Moscow or Leningrad.

DIARY *At Sea—March 30, 1937*

Sailed on the *Queen Mary* from Cherbourg for home.

PART II

WASHINGTON AND POINTS EAST

April 5—June 20, 1937

II

New York—April 5, 1937

Arrived in New York. Immediately on arrival went to see my old friend, Colonel House, who is not too well. During all of these years I have always found his counsel wise and far-sighted. He said that he was very glad that the President had asked me to go to Russia; that it was one of the great potential forces affecting world peace, and that it would be invaluable to have a judgment based upon personal knowledge of the actual strength of the Soviet government, their leaders and their army. There is too much "prejudiced thinking" as to the Soviets in Europe, and that was a mistake. It was not good judgment to be guided by prejudice instead of facts. It was very important, too, in connection with the Japanese question. He deplored the fact that Dodd had become so ineffective in Berlin. The best type of diplomatic representation, he thought, was that which always maintained stanchly the policy and ideals of one's country, but which also recognized that one of its chief purposes was to influence the government to which one was accredited along lines that were conducive to the interests of one's own country and particularly world peace. It was a serious mistake to allow oneself to get into a position of such hostility as to be ineffective in the country to which one is accredited. Dodd was an able man and of high principles and it was a matter of regret to him to see Dodd mistake his function, particularly as he himself had recommended Dodd to the President. The Colonel said that he was very glad that the President wanted me to go to Germany immediately after Russia. He thought there was still a chance of possibly working out a basis, as between Germany, England, and France, which would preserve the peace of Europe. That chance, said he, was becoming less and less and the situation was getting worse every day. It was a tragic pity, but war was inevitable unless something could be worked out. We had a good visit and reminisced over the old Wilson days. We had a good laugh over the manner in which he and I had sat in with President Wilson when he decided upon the membership of the Federal Trade Commission. The Colonel said, "Do you remember, Davies, how Wilson said, 'I don't want any lawyers on that Commission; they will spoil any good thing. I am sorry you are a lawyer, Davies, but I want you to be Chairman.'" Then he chuckled.

It also impressed me that although I have known Colonel House intimately for twenty-five years or more, he has never said one unkind word about our great chief, President Wilson, despite their differences in later years.

Left immediately thereafter for Washington to report to the State Department.

DIARY   *Washington—April 6, 1937*

Reported to Secretary of State, Cordell Hull, at length and in detail immediately upon my arrival in Washington. It gratified me that the Secretary commented upon "the hard work which I put in," and the initiative which I had given to my work, particularly in making these long trips into the interior "actually to see for myself" what the conditions were outside of the capital. He was very generous in his comment upon the quality of my work.

Had dinner in the evening with George and Mary Holmes, Steve and Helen Early and Harry Hopkins, Jesse and Mrs. Jones. They were all there informally for dinner and George insisted on my joining them. George Holmes was at his characteristic best. He conducted his usual and well-known "Open Forum" where the "lid was off" and everyone was put on the "pan." We had a grand time. Harry Hopkins and Jesse Jones were particularly interested in Russia. They got me talking about it. They wanted to know particularly what I thought of the industrial developments which I had inspected.

It was quite obvious that it was difficult for them to believe their ears. It would have been difficult for me to have believed it six months earlier; or if I had not seen it with my own eyes.

DIARY   *Washington—April 7, 1937*

Had lunch with the President at his office. I gave him details as to my trip into the industrial regions, the Radek treason trial, and conditions generally. He questioned at length about the trial. His interest was particularly directed to the charges of treasonable activities of the defendants with Germany and Japan. He wanted to know my impressions as to the judges, the prosecutors, and the criminal procedure.

My trip into the Ukraine and down into the Don Basin and my reports on these industries were very valuable, he thought, in assessing the actual and potential strength of the Russian situation.

In connection with the general European war situation, he suggested that while I was here I should get as much as I could out of the reports at the Department as to Germany and its relation to the European peace situation.

He said that at the Gridiron Dinner he had outlined to Luther, the German Ambassador who was returning to Germany, the idea of a disarmament plan, which provided simply that no nation should manufacture armaments heavier than that which a man could carry on his shoulders. This would in itself prevent aggression by land forces and would go a long way to preserve the peace. He had asked Luther to take up the idea with his government when he got back to Berlin. I might follow this up, he said, when I went through Berlin on my return to Moscow.

Germany, he said, was projecting an unprecedented industrial war mechanism. It would be a new factor in war and a very dangerous one in creating a new kind of war. He asked me particularly to direct my attention to that situation in connection with my investigations as to Germany.

He was particularly interested in the amount of the German public and private debt and the proportion which each bore to the total national wealth and the total national income; also what the tax burden was, both upon business and upon the individual; also what proportion of total national income was being devoted to armaments and war preparations. I said that I would get what I could at the Department at once.

He is pessimistic, but still hopes that something may be done to stem the tide, and possibly to find some ground upon which Hitler, Britain, and France could agree, whereby war could be prevented.

From what I hear, Dodd is holding out at his post and does not want to get out. Unless he does, there will not be much chance so far as we are concerned to do anything about trying to get a meeting of the minds. Events are moving terribly rapidly. Forces are being generated which will be difficult to stop. Animosities and personal hostilities are hardening. Schacht's bitterness to the so-called obduracy of England is indicative of that. It does not look very much as though I would have a chance to try to do what the President has in mind, unless something breaks pretty fast. Unless there is the possibility of doing something of that kind, Berlin would not be a very attractive post. If it is war, these Prussian Germans, who can be very supercilious, could make it very disagreeable for people whom they did not like. I was glad to see the President looking exceptionally well. How he does it, with all of his burdens, is beyond me.

DIARY *Washington—April 8, 1937*

Got to work at the State Department in the room which is set aside for ambassadors on "home leave" for such purposes. Flack, who is "on the German desk," is most co-operative. Personally he has an extraordinary amount of information, and he supplied me with published sources of information and also reports from Germany which will be very helpful. Worked all day.

DIARY *New York—April 12, 1937*

My friend, Bob Field, told me that Colonel House was not too well, so I arranged with Bob to go up and have a visit with the Colonel. He was in bed, very feeble and weak. His mind was as bright as a dollar, however. He and Bob and I discussed at length the situation in Europe. The Colonel was very anxious that Dodd should retire from Berlin before it was too late. He thought events were moving with such rapidity in Europe that it would soon be too late for anyone to "stem the tide." The Colonel felt that there was still a chance of composing the points of view of the British, the French, and Hitler on some working basis of accommodation which would avert war, if someone with capacity and tact could bring the parties together. The issue was so vital nothing should be left undone in the effort to avert war in Europe, for it would engulf us all. It was impossible, he said, for Dodd to be of any service in that matter, because of the situation which he had allowed himself to get into. He sympathized with and understood Dodd's personal point of view; but it was unfortunate in that it eliminated him from any possible influence; that from his personal experience in the World War, he felt that the minds of opposing parties could only be brought together through some mental broker who would take matters up with them separately, and try to find a common ground upon which the minds could meet. He even considered and suggested the advisability of having Bob Field go to Germany to see Dodd and carry these views of the Colonel to him. Bob Field is a very able man who was a Rhodes scholar in England, prior to the war; came from Texas, and was a protégé of the Colonel's and who worked with him during and after the World War, and has always enjoyed very properly the confidence of Colonel House, not only as a matter of character, but also as a matter of capacity. I asked the Colonel not to do this. I do not want Dodd to be pressed into any decision through any activity of mine. Besides I very much fear it is too late.

DIARY   *Washington—April 15, 1937*

Lunched with Henry Morgenthau and Oumansky.

Worked in the Department all day.

The Secretary of Commerce, my old friend, Daniel Roper, called me up and asked if I would come over and talk to his "Business Council," which was then in session. Of course, I was glad to comply. They are the leaders in the American business world and many among them are old friends. I told them what I saw in Russia—also what I saw in Europe. I talked "right off the anvil." The gist of it was that no matter what our tax over here might be—"we did not know the half of it," until one could appreciate conditions which confronted the businessmen of Europe, and the people of Europe, not only as to their taxes, but also the fear under which they are all living. No matter what taxes were levied, from what I have seen, I would be mighty glad to pay anything for the privilege of living in the United States with our laws and our system of individualism which is protected against the tyranny of a state, a party, or of a man.

GERMANY'S AGGRESSIVE INFILTRATION PLANS

JOURNAL *Washington—April 22, 1937*

It is amazing how frankly the Nazis tell the world what they are doing. The official news agency announces that 600 young Germans from Southwest Africa, in Berlin on a visit for vocational training, had formed a Southwest African national group, swearing allegiance to Herr Hitler. They were to be "educated into a community," so as to enable them on their return home to maintain the "German community" there. It is either a colossal bluff to aid their diplomatic maneuvers or it is a desperate danger to other countries in the world community of nations.

DIARY *Washington—April 25, 1937*

Harold Wilkie, Regent of the University of Wisconsin, came to arrange for the acceptance of the Russian pictures and icons, which I had brought back with me to give to the University of Wisconsin. The President and Mrs. Roosevelt had expressed an interest in seeing them, so it was arranged to have them displayed in the East Room of the White House.

After the President and his guest, my old friend, Charles R. Crane, had viewed the pictures in the East Room, he in-

sisted upon Marjorie's and my having tea with him in the
family drawing room on the second floor. The President commented particularly upon the vividness and beauty of the
snow scenes.

DIARY   *Washington—April 28, 1937*

Lunched with the President at his desk in the White
House today and gave him the best estimates available on
Germany's economic condition, war, and such. There were
indications, he said, that Germany's economic, industrial, and
financial strength was much greater than wishful thinking in
certain quarters would have us believe. Germany was stronger
than she is generally given credit for. He was depressed about
the situation. To him, war seemed inevitable. Still, while there
was a chance to avert it, we ought to do everything we could.
It would be disastrous to us as well as to Europe and the rest
of the world. He discussed the Balkan situation, the Little
Entente and their potentialities, both as a means of preventing war and as a military factor in case of war. He thought it
would be a good idea for me to visit these different countries
adjacent to the Soviet Union, and in the possible war zone,
during the summer, and report the situations as I found them.
Dodd was going to resign, and he wanted me to plan on going
to Berlin.

ARREST AND PERSECUTION OF CATHOLICS IN GERMANY

JOURNAL   *Washington—April 29, 1937*

The devil's cauldron is still boiling. Four Roman
Catholics, including a priest named Rossaint, were sentenced
by the Berlin People's Court to long terms of imprisonment for
"preparing high treason." The priest's sentence was eleven

years' penal servitude. He was convicted of associating with
Communists—that's a new one!

DIARY   *Washington—April 29, 1937*

Conferred at length with Secretary Hull, along the lines
of my discussions with the President. The simple clarity and
moral power of our pioneer stock and of the people of the
Tennessee mountains, from which he sprung, come right out
in this great Secretary of State. His moral indignation against
wrong and the judicial quality and strength of his convictions,
coupled with his mildness and patience, are about as fine an
indication of our Americanism as there is left.

Spent the rest of the day in discussing reports with William-
son and Wallace Murray. From all I can get from these reports
and discussions with these men, who are experts, it would
appear that the Little Entente (Czechoslovakia, Rumania,
Bulgaria, and Yugoslavia) was on the verge of breaking up.
If that happens, it will be bad, for it is not only a bulwark to
peace, but a military bastion of defense as well. Was much
impressed with Murray's views. He knows the Balkan situation probably better than anyone here. He has been in the
service a long time and has a splendid, balanced judgment.

DIARY   *Washington—April 30, 1937*

Spent the day working at the Department. Late yesterday afternoon I had a long talk with Sumner Welles. I am always impressed by his exceptional ability and the clarity of
his judgment. He knows the European situation thoroughly;
but what is of particular value is that he applies all of these
potentialities to their reactions upon the situation affecting the
Americas, and their ultimate effects upon South America and
upon our own political and economic future. He is rendering

a fine quality of loyal service to the Secretary and to the President as well as to the country.

HITLER CREATES NEW DECORATION FOR FOREIGNERS; CHURCH AND STATE

JOURNAL   *Washington—May 1, 1937*

It was announced that Hitler had instituted a new decoration for foreigners who rendered service to Germany, entitled the Order of Merit of the German Eagle.

Hitler announced also that the state was going to take all the children of the nation and train them to become new German men and women. "When a child is ten years old it has not yet acquired any feeling for high birth or ancestry," he explained, "but is like other children. It is at this age that we are going to take them, to form them into a community, and not let them go till they are eighteen. Then they will go into the Party, the S.A., the S.S., and the other organizations, or they will go at once to work and into the Labor Front and the Labor Corps, and then for two years into the Army. If that won't make a nation out of such people nothing will."

Blind obedience was imperative; the individual had only one choice; he must bend or break, and he went on: "We cannot suffer this authority to be attacked from any other quarter."

It becomes clearer and clearer that Hitler intends that the humanitarian and peaceful purposes of the Christian religion shall not prevent his making the Reich and himself the masters of the German people and possibly of the world.

DIARY   *At Sea—May 5, 1937*

Sailed on S.S. *Bremen*—12:30 A.M.
Walter Duranty came down to see us off.

We are stopping off in London for a few days during the Coronation.

DIARY *London—May 21, 1937*

Had dinner with Ambassador and Mrs. Bingham. It was interesting. Bingham has made a distinct place for himself here. I am impressed with his ability and his modesty. His talk at the Pilgrim's dinner obviously made a strong impression. He looks every inch an American gentleman and is a credit to our country over here.

The staff has also been very considerate despite my express statement that we are here entirely "unofficial"; they and the Ambassador have gone out of their way to show us every consideration. Atherton, quiet, modest, and rather reserved, impressed me with his grasp of the European situation. Our talks were helpful.

DIARY *London—May 24, 1937*

Webb Miller, European director of the U.P. who wrote *I Found No Peace*, came in for an hour or two today. He had just returned from Spain and the "stench of human beings" as he put it. He was going to Moscow and wanted to secure permission to be with the North Pole Fliers from Moscow, and he wanted me to help him with the Soviet government. Of course, I told him I would go the "limit" and will do so.

In the evening we went to the Ritz for dinner with Mrs. Dwight Morrow. Colonel Lindbergh was there and told us of the birth of his little son on the twelfth of May. He also told an amusing incident when he was entertained at dinner by the Görings in Berlin, of Göring's pet lioness, and the accident (?) which happened in Göring's drawing room when the playful pet ruined Göring's resplendent uniform.

DIARY   *London—May 25, 1937*

Had a long and pleasant visit with Mr. Lloyd George, also with Lord Davies, the head of the New Commonwealth Club, an organization devoted to international peace.

This energetic organization is doing a fine job. Lord Davies, a man of great wealth, is spending a fortune on the cause to avert war, and is the real motive power behind the organization. We attended a large luncheon today at the Carlton given by the Club in honor of Winston Churchill.

DIARY   *London—May 26, 1937*

Marjorie and I lunched with Mr. and Mrs. Winston Churchill at their charming little apartment "in town." The walls were covered with delightful and very interesting oils, which Mrs. Churchill told us were painted by her husband. His hobbies are to lay bricks and stones in hedges and rock gardens, and do landscapes in oil. There were a number of diplomats from European countries at the luncheon. Over the coffee, Churchill was interested "in these purge trials." He plied me with questions. I told him the truth as I saw it. It obviously was a great surprise to the diplomatic guests. That sort of talk is not fashionable here, so violent is the prejudice. Churchill has no love for the Communists. He has had some bitter experiences with them. He is, however, fair and judicial-minded and wants to know the facts. He is definitely not a "wishful thinker." I gave the facts as interpreted from the Soviet viewpoint and briefly outlined the argument of the government in these cases. Churchill said that I had given him a completely new concept of the situation. He asked about the strength of the Soviet industry and the army. Too bad this man isn't more effective in the government here. Peace would be safer! He impressed me as a great man.

PERSECUTION OF THE CHURCH IN GERMANY

JOURNAL   *London—May 30, 1937*

And still it goes on!

The Berlin Special Court sentenced forty-two former members of the International Bible Students' Association to terms of imprisonment on the ground that they "pursued dark political purposes in the guise of religious activity."

DIARY   *London—June 1, 1937*

Maisky, the Russian Ambassador, asked Ambassador Bingham and myself to luncheon. Mrs. M. only was present. Both Bingham (at my request) and I stressed to Maisky that the Soviet Union as the second largest gold producer of the world had a very real interest in the world price of gold and that it was to their interest to co-operate with Secretary Morgenthau in his efforts to sustain the world gold market as a means of maintaining the stability of world trade and exchange. The point was that it was alleged that Russia had been forcing very large gold shipments on the New York market this spring. It was in fact enough to depress the New York market. I told Maisky that I had spoken to Litvinov about it and had stressed that it was evidently to Russia's interest not to "break the market price" of one of their most valuable products. I did not tell him nor did I tell Litvinov that Morgenthau was concerned about their shipments. Bingham made a fine statement and a persuasive one. Maisky was, I think, impressed.*

---

* It subsequently developed that the U.S.S.R. sent a special financial secretary to act as liaison between their Embassy in Washington and the Treasury Department.

THE CATHOLIC TRAGEDY IN GERMANY

JOURNAL   *London—June 10, 1937*

A dispatch from Rome states that His Holiness the Pope received a group of German pilgrims from Augsburg, to whom he said that "the hours through which Catholic Germany is passing are not only grave but sorrowful—indeed, they are so grave, so menacing, and so sad that they make us weep."

RED GENERALS SHOT

JOURNAL   *London—June 11, 1937*

The press carries the startling news that, after a secret trial, the Military Collegium sentenced to death Marshal Tukhatchevsky, Generals Putna, Yakir, Uborevich, Feldman, Kork, Primakov, and Eydeman, for "habitual and base betrayal of military secrets to a certain hostile Fascist power, and working as spies to encompass the downfall of the Soviet state and to restore capitalism."

The court consisted of Judge Ulrich and eight senior army officers, two of whom, Marshal Blücher (who came from the Soviet Far East) and the old Bolshevik hero, Marshal Budenny, were reported to have pronounced the sentence of death.

The condemned generals had, until a short time previously, held nearly all the key commands in European Russia, including those of Minsk, Kiev, and Kharkov, while General Putna had been Military Attaché in London. General Feldman was Quartermaster General and Chief of Personnel; and General Eydeman had been President of Osoaviakim (the Society for Chemical and Aviation Defense and Experiment).

According to the official report of the trial, the prisoners had confessed to the charges and had expressly admitted that for a long time they had acted as spies and agents for a neighboring state to which they had betrayed all the military secrets of the Soviet Union.

June 12—The government announced that the eight condemned men had been shot.

JOURNAL *London—June 14, 1937*

The press reports today that M. Rosengoltz, the Commissar for Foreign Trade, was dismissed from his post.

Poor Rosengoltz! I hope he is not involved. It was only a few weeks ago that we were invited to his *dacha* (country place) to spend the day.

JOURNAL *Berlin—June 20, 1937*

On my way back to Moscow, I stopped off in Berlin and saw Schacht at the Reichsbank. We had a long talk. He went into the wrongs which Germany suffered and was still suffering at the hands of the British and French—with much heat and at length. I heard him through; but then I talked to him quite frankly.

"These things," I said, "might impress the American people but for one factor in the situation—and that was the belligerent and threatening attitude taken by the leaders of the German Reich, the almost insolent and brutal manner in which they threatened what they would do 'unless,' and all with a constant 'rattling of the saber.' " Illustrating my point, I cited the fact that in Minnesota if a farmer, through hard luck, crop failure, or the burning of his buildings, faced destitution and ruin, his neighbors would organize a "building bee" and join together to see to it that an unfortunate but decent citizen had a chance to get on his feet and become a prosperous, self-respecting member of the community; but that if these same neighbors obtained the conviction that this unfortunate man was in fact a Jesse James—a bandit—who would use their help and get strong only to turn on them and prey on his neighbors later, they, naturally, would turn a deaf ear to his suggestions of the wrongs which he had suffered. That, I thought, illustrated the position that Germany was fast getting herself into.

His reply was that they had tried it and failed; that force was the only language that France and Britain could understand. I suggested that I did not think that was so. When I outlined the President's suggestion of limitation of armament to defensive weapons only, such as a man could carry on his shoulder, he almost jumped out of his seat with enthusiasm. It was, he said, so simple as to be the expression of genius. He thought it might possibly be done. He asked me, "Would you say these things to Hitler if an opportunity would be found?" I said, "Of course, I would be glad to." He said he thought it could be arranged. [See letter to the President.]

Well, we shall see! It is a test of whether there is a will for peace or whether the die is already cast and Hitler is on his way—irrevocably—to war.

PART III

THE PURGE HITS THE RED ARMY

June 25—July 28, 1937

III

Moscow—June 25, 1937

Marjorie and I went out to the Novodyevichi (Monastery of the New Virgins). Within the monastery walls there is a cemetery in which Stalin's wife is buried in holy ground. The grave is marked by a shaft of rough white marble, in the center of a green grass plot, around which is a black marble border. Out of this rough shaft of white marble, there is hewn a magnificent head of a lovely woman—fine face, hair simply drawn back over the ears, and knotted at the back of the head. The breast and body is lost in the rough stone of the simple shaft. It is a very beautiful piece of sculpture and was done by the celebrated woman sculptress, Mukhina. She did the magnificent figure of the man and woman which appears on the top of the Soviet building in the Paris exposition. Here, too, Gorky's son is buried. The grave is marked by another beautiful full marble figure portrait—half emerging from the block of marble—a youth wearing slacks, no coat—shirt opened at the neck. It was a remarkably lifelike figure. This was also done by the celebrated sculptress, Mukhina.

Moscow, June 26, 1937

THE PRESIDENT

Dear Mr. President:

Following the line of our last discussions, I stopped off in Berlin enroute here. I find that Ambassador Luther did not return direct to Germany, but is returning via the Orient.

However, I did have a most interesting personal visit with Schacht. He talked with great frankness and deep feeling.

He said that the real cause of Europe's trouble was fear; that attempts to solve the problem through stabilization of currency, the removing of economic trade barriers, and the like were useful, of course, but would be futile in averting the catastrophe of European war, because these still did not remove the cause, i.e., fear of conquest or invasion, physically or economically.

I then stated to him that the President in conversation with me had analyzed the European situation and had considered that a solution might be found in an agreement among the European nations to a reduction of armaments to a sheerly defensive military basis; and this through the elimination of aircraft, tanks, and heavy equipment, and the limitation of armament to such weapons only as a man could carry on his back, with an agreement among the nations for adequate policing of the plan by a neutral state. Schacht literally jumped at the idea. He said: "That is absolutely the solution!" He said that in its simplicity it had the earmarks of great genius. His enthusiasm was extraordinary.

I asked him whether he thought the German government would consider any such plan. He stated confidently that it would.

I asked him whether he had seen Ambassador Luther since his return. He stated that he had not. I suggested that he get in touch with the Ambassador's dispatches at the Foreign Office, prior to his (Luther's) departure from Washington. He said that he would do so. He stated that he would explore this idea with his government and wished then to discuss it further with me.

If the parties really desire peace, here is the formula and the agency at hand. It can be explored with relatively little difficulty. If it can be made effective, then your plan will have saved European civilization. If either side balks, a possible interchange of letters between the President of the United States and the willing party would clarify the atmosphere and place the burden of responsibility for war where it belongs.

With assurances of my great admiration and warm regard, I am,

Respectfully,
Joseph E. Davies

N. B. In view of the fact that this was not an official, but purely a personal visit which I had with Schacht, I made no report of it to Ambassador Dodd.

DIARY   *Moscow—June 27, 1937*

We went out to see a soccer football game at the Moscow stadium. The champion Soviet team was playing the champion Spanish team, who had come to Moscow for the contest. The stadium was an immense bowl of cement construction, made after the most modern manner, and would compare favorably with any of our stadiums. The stadium has a capacity of 100,000 people.

JOURNAL   *Moscow—June 28, 1937*

It is very significant that not only here, but throughout Europe, there is no privacy for anyone, as against espionage of the secret police. There is only one place, it is
said, where there is assurance against being overheard and
that is either out in the open spaces or in a room where you
can tap on wood with a lead pencil and break the sound wave.
That is a common practice in Moscow. I am told it is quite
the same generally all over Europe. The secret police are
omnipresent. No government trusts any other government,
and the horrible part of it is that no confidence is placed by
one government in the express promise of another, even
though it is reduced to writing and is under seal. Moreover,
under the philosophy of the Nazi Party, such betrayal constitutes not only no dishonor but is a badge of strength and
capacity. I was surprised upon the occasions of my two very
first diplomatic calls which I made upon Ambassador colleagues to note that each removed the telephone receiver on
the desk, and explained to me that the telephone afforded the
most common hiding place for the dictaphone apparatus of
the secret police.

KILLING OF THE RED GENERALS

June 28, 1937

THE HONORABLE SUMNER WELLES

My dear Sumner:

Conditions here, as usual, are perplexing.
The judgment of those who have been here longest is that
conditions are very, very serious; the best judgment seems
to believe that in all probability there was a definite con-

spiracy in the making looking to a *coup d'état* by the army—not necessarily anti-Stalin, but antipolitical and antiparty, and that Stalin struck with characteristic speed, boldness, and strength. A violent "purge" all over the country has been going on.

The opinion of the steadiest minds of the Diplomatic Corps is that the government is not in imminent danger and is still strong; this, however, is all subject to the reservation that all depends upon whether the army has been seriously infected and weaned from the Stalin bureaucracy or not. The general impression is that it has not been, but nobody knows. It is the imponderable factor in the situation.

Last winter Eden rejected the German overtures with reference to economic aid through colonies or otherwise, unless political security were assured in Eastern as well as Western Europe. The demonstration of Russian airplanes and tanks in Spain has had a chilling effect on the German and Italian war commands. This is generally admitted.

The strength of the Red Army and the avowed and well-recognized adherence of the U.S.S.R. to peace is regarded as a distinct factor in maintaining peace in Europe. It definitely could contribute to the balance of power, and buttress the Democratic "bloc."

Hastily yours,

DIARY *Moscow—June 29, 1937*

In the evening we had a dinner of 36 in honor of the Lithuanian Minister, a poet,* quite famous and a great friend of the U.S.A. The Chinese Ambassador and the French Ambassador were here and ranking guests.

---

* To my surprise I found that Minister Baltrusaitis was a great admirer of Edgar Allan Poe and had translated his works into Russian.

The choice remark of the evening was that of the charming little Chinese Ambassadress. She said: "No, I'm not a diplomat. I am really sincere. I tell the truth."

LIFE IN MOSCOW

Moscow, June 30, 1937

Dear "Ekay": *

We had a very pleasant evening at the Norwegian Legation with the Urbyes. It was a small dinner and a very charming one. I had a most interesting talk with the French Ambassador who was particularly concerned over the crisis in Spain arising out of the withdrawal of Germany and Italy from the nonintervention committee and participation in policing. The garden of the Norwegian Legation was particularly lovely both before and after dinner and we sat out there long in the twilight. It was still light at eleven o'clock.

Later we "went on" to the soiree at the Bulgarian Legation in honor of the birth of an heir to the throne. Everybody was there and it was pleasant meeting all the friends of the Corps.

Mme Litvinov came in with the Foreign Secretary and immediately singled out Marjorie, and the two went into a huddle and had a long visit. Mme Litvinov was interested to hear about you and your interest in Basic English. She wanted to hear of your work in summer school and when you were going to get your degree at Vassar.

On Sunday night we dined at the Italian Embassy. Both the Ambassador and Mrs. Rosso looked very well. The entire staff were particularly keen about the party you gave at the Embassy during our absence. They told us all about it and how well you had done everything. Apparently it was a great success.

* My daughter.

As usual the impressions were exaggerated and overdrawn. So it is in connection with the description in the outside press of the effect of the "purging" of the Red Army on conditions in Moscow. So far as Moscow is concerned, on the face of things, everything is as serene as this June day. It is just as normal in every respect as when you were here. There is, of course, much agitation and excitement and gossip in the Diplomatic Corps, with numerous and mysterious whispers intimating great consequences of the information being imparted over the tea cups; and, perhaps, underneath the surface there may be and probably is much ferment among the Russian people. But it is Russia and apparently things have definitely quieted down. The crux of the question is whether the morale of the army has been destroyed by the shooting of these generals or whether its loyalty has been alienated from Stalin. If Stalin retains the loyalty of the army he will be more strongly entrenched politically than ever before because he has smashed all potential rivalry and leadership.

JOURNAL   *Moscow—July 1, 1937*

The Soviet government announced the floating of a new defense loan of 4000 million rubles, bearing interest at 4 per cent. It was to be redeemed in full in 1957.

This interests me for two reasons: first, it shows how much they are spending for defense—twice as much as England and France together. Second, it shows that frozen labor (capital) commands payment for use—contrary to the basic Communist idea that compensation shall be paid only for human labor, that no man shall be paid for the use of frozen labor (capital) because that is the vice of capitalism. Interest is payment for use of capital, and here it is paid by the state itself, in direct violation of the fundamental principle of Marxist philosophy.

WHEN JAPAN FOUND RUSSIA WASN'T BLUFFING

NO. 414-A   *Moscow, July 1, 1937*

TO THE HONORABLE THE SECRETARY OF STATE

SOVIET-JAPANESE AMUR BORDER INCIDENT

Strictly Confidential

Sir:

In connection with the reported protests which were made by the Japanese Ambassador, Mr. Shigemitsu, to the Soviet Foreign Office on June 29, I was informed, from a credible source, that the character of these conferences between Ambassador Shigemitsu, Litvinov, and Stomoniakov (Litvinov's assistant) were of an unusually serious character; that they were characterized by very obvious concern of the parties, were long drawn out, and lasted late into the night and into the early hours of the morning.

On the morning of June 30 I was again advised that the Japanese Ambassador had, in practical effect, issued an ultimatum to Litvinov, requiring that the Soviet government should withdraw their military forces from the islands; that Litvinov had yielded somewhat and had finally proposed that both parties should withdraw their military forces, in order to permit negotiation and discussion of the juridical question involved without the danger of the clash of armed forces in the vicinity; that Japan had refused to concur in this proposal of such reciprocal or mutual withdrawal. The situation, it would appear, was left where Japan had made a demand for categorical withdrawal of forces when Litvinov had proposed that both sides should withdraw; but where Japan, on the other hand, had stood pat and had refused to accept anything except its original demand requiring evacuation by the Soviet forces.

On the afternoon of that day, June 30, and before conferences were resumed, there occurred a clash between the armed forces of the Soviet patrols and the Japanese-Manchurian cutters and gunboats on the Amur River in the neighborhood of these islands, with the result that one boat was sunk, another driven to shore with attendant loss of life of a number of persons.

Late that day there were again extended discussions between the Japanese Ambassador and the Foreign Office, as I was informed, which conferences again lasted long into the night and ended in no further agreement.

These were the conditions here on the morning of July 1.

Through the Associated Press offices of London, I obtained the information that the situation was regarded as very grave in Tokyo; that Japan's public sentiment was seriously aroused; that the Japanese government was considering calling a cabinet meeting to consider the problem and it was considered likely that the Stock Exchange of Tokyo would be closed.

You will doubtless recall that in Dispatch No. 152, March 26, 1937, I advised you of a conversation which I had in March with the Japanese Ambassador.

During my stay in Washington, you will recall that I had discussed with the President as well as with yourself the significance of this interview which I had had with the Japanese Ambassador, and that the President had suggested the possible advisability of the Department's considering whether it might not be a good thing for Ambassador Grew and me to meet some place midway, between here and Japan, to discuss what might probably be done in the cause of peace and understanding between these two countries.

Because of these facts and because of the rapidity with which these events were marching, and the possibility that it might suit the book of either one of these parties to project a foreign war at this time and in view of the terrific possibilities which such a war would entail, not only to the parties involved, but to Europe and indirectly to the world, I decided that I would call on both the Japanese Ambassador and Litvinov to ascertain what the exact facts of the situation were, in order that I might report them to you accurately and, incidentally, to express the hope, personally and unofficially, that the situation might be held in such status as not to permit it to become so serious an incident as might project the dangers of war. The Japanese Ambassador responded very promptly and invited me to see him within the hour. I received word from Litvinov that he would be glad to see me on July 2.

I desire to emphasize that I made it specifically clear to the Japanese Ambassador that I came to him on my own initiative, primarily to ascertain the facts, and that in expressing my personal hope that this incident should not be permitted to develop into a major situation that might induce the catastrophe of war, I did not in any way speak for my government or under its instructions as I had received none.

Because of the rapidity with which events were moving, I assumed the responsibility of taking the foregoing action, with a view to procuring the facts as accurately as I could from first sources of information to report to you and to the President; and also because of the hope that I might contribute to pacifying a dangerous situation without serious risk of being misunderstood.*

I have the honor to be, Sir, respectfully yours,

Joseph E. Davies

---

* Later in 1938 in Europe a high Japanese official told me that the Japanese government had deliberately projected these tests of Soviet resistance and military strength; and that the Japanese were surprised and impressed with the mechanized strength and effectiveness of the Red Army in the East.

DIARY   *Moscow—July 4, 1937*

Fourth of July celebration in the afternoon, reception from five to seven. The entire Diplomatic Corps turned out. About 20 to 25 Soviet officials from Litvinov down—including Judge and Mrs. Ulrich (he presided over all these purge trials). Had a fine talk with Litvinov. I told him quite frankly the reactions in U.S. and western Europe to the purges; and to the executions of the Red Army generals; that it definitely was bad, and harmful to the outside reputation of the U.S.S.R. In my opinion it had shaken the confidence of France and England in the strength of the U.S.S.R. vis-à-vis Hitler.

Litvinov was very frank. He stated that they had to "make sure" through these purges that there was no treason left which could co-operate with Berlin or Tokyo; that someday the world would understand that what they had done was to protect their government from "menacing treason." In fact, he said they were doing the whole world a service in protecting themselves against the menace of Hitler and Nazi world domination, and thereby preserving the Soviet Union strong as a bulwark against the Nazi threat. That the world someday would appreciate what a very great man Stalin was.

BLATANCY OF GERMAN PROPAGANDA

JOURNAL   *Moscow—July 4, 1937*

Here is another of these extraordinary manifestations of Nazi obtuseness. To think that they could get away with this report, which has just come out of Berlin, to the effect that Canon Buchholz was sentenced at Königsberg to three years' imprisonment, and three Roman Catholic chaplains to shorter terms, for having acted as "ringleaders" in disturbances during a Corpus Christi procession. Six Catholic laymen were also given sentences of six to twelve months' imprisonment.

"Catholic priests disturbing a Corpus Christi procession"—
what a travesty! The shoe was, of course, on the other foot.

EFFECT OF PURGE ON EUROPEAN PEACE

EXCERPT FROM A LETTER TO STEPHEN EARLY

Moscow, July 4, 1937

Political conditions locally are cooling off. There are indications of arrests and purges still going on. No one can tell what the effect has been on the army. It will take time to disclose that. It now looks as though the loyalty of the army to the Stalin government has not been weakened. If that is so, then, the government will be stronger than ever internally, because he has with characteristic speed killed off all potential leadership. The pity of it all is that in so doing he has destroyed the confidence of western Europe in the strength of his army and in the strength of his government; that has also weakened the confidence of both England and France in the strength of the Russian army, and has weakened the democratic bloc in western Europe, and that is serious, for the only real hope for peace is a London-Paris-Moscow axis.

JOURNAL   *Moscow—July 7, 1937*

The Director General of the Tass Agency, M. Doletsky, was denounced in the press as an enemy of the people.

ADDENDUM TO JOURNAL

I am informed by a Moscow correspondent of long experience that the facts in the Doletsky case are as follows:

The circumstances under which the disappearance of such a prominent figure as Doletsky was allowed to become known, provided a striking illustration of the atmosphere and tactics of the "Great Purge." A rumor that he had been seized by the "Gay-pay-oo" in a customary nocturnal visit circulated almost as soon, apparently, as the next day, but nothing appeared in the Soviet press or was issued officially. The American correspondents, who quickly heard the rumor, felt they found sufficient corroboration to justify their dispatching reports of it, though they risked expulsion from the country for evading the censorship in doing so. They discovered that the Tass offices, with which they maintained relatively close contact, were in a state of utter confusion because a number of Doletsky's assistants and confidants had been arrested also or cleaned out following his downfall. But the conclusive proof came to hand only some weeks later when a provincial newspaper published in the Urals denounced Doletsky as a "Polish spy" and "enemy of the people." It still failed to indicate whether reports that Doletsky had committed suicide when arrested were true or whether instead he had subsequently been executed. But "Purge" victims publicly branded as "enemies of the people" were generally believed to be either dead or certain to be executed. Doletsky had been a veteran Polish revolutionist in tsarist times. He visited the United States immediately after Maxim Litvinov negotiated American recognition of the U.S.S.R. with President Roosevelt in Washington.

DIARY   *Moscow—July 8, 1937*

Reports are current that among other persons arrested for treason were Kaminsky, Rudzutak, Mezhlauk (a member of the Politburo), Karakhan, Krestinsky, Rosengoltz, Ossinsky, Unschlicht, and Stern.

It seems impossible to me that Mezhlauk, Krestinsky, and Rosengoltz should be suspected of treason. Krestinsky is the First Assistant to Litvinov of the Foreign Office. His wife is an eminent woman physician who is a devoted party member. She is in effect giving up her life to taking care of women and children in the hospitals of the city of Moscow. They both give indication of being "zealous for a cause." Still, that might be the very reason for their being Trotskyites. No one can tell in this strange situation.

Rosengoltz is the Commissar for Foreign Trade. We had dinner at his country place only a few months ago. It seems unbelievable that he should be involved in this situation.

Mezhlauk is one of the ablest economists in the Soviet Union. He is widely known in the United States. He was Chairman of the State Planning Commission of the U.S.S.R., which got a very voluminous report on the Five-Year Plan, which is quite a classic in its way and reflects great credit on Mezhlauk's ability. He was recently made head of Heavy Industry. Of course, the simple fact is that ordinary psychology does not apply in this situation. The very earnestness and sincerity of their convictions might contribute to guilt, in so far as these political crimes are concerned. After all, in the last treason trial the question was whether Radek was a devoted idealistic martyr to what he believed was his political faith or whether he was a political criminal. This certainly was true as to the principal defendants. So, there is no telling. I confess the situation has me guessing.

DIARY   *Moscow—July 9, 1937*

Reception given for Sandler, the Foreign Minister of Sweden. Litvinov took me aside and said that Sandler was urging that all of the smaller countries in Europe should be relieved from the obligations of Article 16 of the covenant of the League of Nations which compels them to take common action against any nation which the League advises to be the aggressor, etc. He complained bitterly that this was

"German propaganda"; that Sandler was simply falling for German technique again; that it would ultimately end in "collective security" being destroyed in which alone there was strength against the aggressor, and that Hitler would then dominate them one by one. Litvinov was bitterly annoyed because he said Sandler was using as an argument that if Article 16 were eliminated in the League Covenant, it would make it easier for the United States to join the League, likewise other nations who did not wish to participate in and be bound by League decisions on European matters. Litvinov intimated that Sandler stated that the United States was sympathetic with this idea. He asked what I thought and my reply was that I had no instructions and it was out of my bailiwick and that my personal opinion was that so far as the United States was concerned it was the "bunk"; that the United States would not join the League of Nations *now;* that in my opinion it was unfortunate, but it was nevertheless the fact; and that also in my opinion plain "horse sense" of the American people would compel them to be of the opinion that the only means of safety for the smaller nations in Europe was to unite and compose a common front against the aggressor nations. Litvinov was mad and "fumed" over the tragedy of failure to do the obvious.

Of course, he said, since Abyssinia all of these smaller countries are scared to death and want to be relieved of any obligation that might run them up against Hitler and that Hitler was browbeating them into intimidation one by one.

JOURNAL   *Moscow—July 9, 1937*

Cardinal Pacelli made this powerful indictment of the Nazi Nordic New Religion in consecrating a church at Liseaux:

In all the churches of a powerful nation, which wicked leaders wished to imbue with an idolatry of race, an indignant protest of

an octogenarian Pontiff resounded like the voice of Sinai to recall
the imprescriptible rights of the Personal God of the Incarnate
Word and of the Sacred Magistracy which had been confided to
him.

MAJOR OPERATION GOING ON HERE

July 10, 1937

THE HONORABLE SUMNER WELLES

My dear Sumner:

There is no question but what a major
operation is going on here. On the face of things everything
is quiet. There is nothing unusual on the streets or among the
crowds you see, but there are constant rumors, both unverified
and authenticated, of prominent people in all sections of life
being in prison or liquidated.

The prognosis is not so simple. There are too many factors
here that are imponderable. There is the danger of a foreign
war and also the danger of assassination. Either of these
would upset the applecart and confuse any calculation. If,
however, the army remains loyal to Stalin, and there are indications that it will, then this government will be temporarily
more securely entrenched in power internally, at least for a
while, than it was heretofore.

There are many indications that France has lost faith in
the power of her Russian ally. I was impressed in England by
the general feeling there that England would be in a sad state
if she had to rely on France with her internal weakness and
on Russia under the present conditions.

The opinion as to the Russian power is completely the re-
verse of what it was three months ago. This is so both as to the
strength of the regime here politically and governmentally
and the strength of the Red Army. It would not surprise me if
the opinion would be completely reversed back again in three

months, events move so rapidly. They were not so strong as they were credited with being three months ago and they are not so weak now as is supposed.

The man power here is tremendous. The capacity for ideological concept and devotion to "the cause" found in these people is extraordinary and commands admiration. Moreover, this country is tremendously rich and in spite of all the inefficiencies of bureaucracy and political control of industry, there must be and will be a residue of accomplishment which, because of the size of the country, will be very powerful. Moreover, they have done some extraordinarily good things over here and there is much I see to admire and respect. But the price they pay is too high.

Hastily yours,

"NESTS" OF ALLEGED TRAITORS

JOURNAL   *Moscow—July 13, 1937*

The government is certainly persistent in cleaning up any possible nests of "internal aggression" as Litvinov calls them.

Reports reached Moscow of the shooting in the Far East of 61 "leaders and members of a Trotskyist-Japanese-German terroristic spy, diversionist organization working on the Far Eastern railways and systematically supplying espionage information to a certain foreign intelligence service."

"FLAMING YOUTH" OF THE SPORTS PARADE

July 14, 1937

Dear "Bijou" *

Your letter came on the very day of another one of the national celebrations in the Red Square. It was the

* My daughter Ekay.

Youth Sport Day and was characteristically one of those extraordinary shows they put on here. Stalin and all his Commissars were in their box on the top corner of Lenin's Tomb
in front of the Kremlin. We were in the same diplomatic section where you were on May Day. Both J.D. and I spoke of
how we wished you could have seen this show as it was such
a remarkable supplementary contrast to the military display
of May Day. It was quite wonderful and impressive in its
way.

It was a bright, sunny day. Both ends and the opposite
façade were decorated profusely with flags and red bunting
and various large emblems emblazoned with athletic medal
designs, tributes to Stalin, etc.

Massed around three sides of the Square were companies
of approximately three or four hundred each of men and
women, leaving the Square about half filled for the marching
and the various athletic tableaux and performances.

There were almost as many women as men in the parade
and in the exhibitions. It was "flaming youth." And a very
beautiful youth it was—all bareheaded and tanned to a deep
brown, for the most part wearing only white shorts and colored
jerseys. Each company had a different uniform. Some were in
Jansen suits and others were in regular gymnasium attire. The
combinations of blues and whites, reds and whites, oranges
and whites, crimsons and yellows, maroons and tans—all con-
ceivable combinations—with white sneaker shoes, with colors
in the hair of the women or carried in the hands of the
marchers. It made a beautiful display. Added to this were
thousands of tanned soldiers with shaved heads, in blue shorts
and white "sneakers." Again there were two or three thousand
athletes from various sections of the Soviet Union who were
particularly colorful, especially those from the Ukraine, the
Caucasus, and the Oriental section of the country. The latter

brought reed, horn, and drum bands which made weird music
for their sword dances and all manner of native Oriental religious, athletic, swaying dances and marches. The colored
gowns and robes of the performers as well as the beauty of
the dances were unique and strange.

The parade lasted about four hours. It was estimated that
there were forty or fifty thousand young people participating.
There were all kinds of floral displays; extraordinarily well
done; with bluebells and poppies and all manner of flowers in
profusion. You know how beautifully they make pictures out
of the massing of growing flowers over here.

The floats were designed for the most part to display various
types of club activities. There were skiers actually skiing in
companies of at least 1500 young men. They apparently had
ball bearings on their skis to enable them to get over the
asphalt.

On some floats were horizontal bars with the gymnasts
actually performing; and springboards with acrobats doing
double high somersaults on the float. Others were skating or
tobogganing on the floats as the floats moved along in the
parade. One athletic exhibition consisted of forty or fifty
young men and women, all performing on the floats as they
went moving by.

All in all, it was one of the most beautiful and extraordinary
exhibitions I have ever seen. Of course the day was beautiful;
and the wonderfully fine-looking youth and perfect physiques
and healthful appearance all contributed to making the whole
spectacle most unusual.

DIARY   *Moscow—July 16, 1937*

Worked all day getting things cleaned up at the office.
In the evening had a dinner in honor of Charlie Nutter (Asso-

ciated Press), who is leaving for Spain. We will all miss him.
He commands the respect and admiration of all of us. After
dinner, had movies and the staff as usual came in to see them.
Moonlight Sonata with Paderewski.

DOING BUSINESS WITH STALIN

NO. 433   *Moscow, July 16, 1937*

TO THE HONORABLE THE SECRETARY OF STATE

NEGOTIATIONS IN CONNECTION WITH PROPOSED RENEWAL OF
COMMERCIAL AGREEMENT WITH THE SOVIET UNION

Confidential

Sir:

Immediately upon the receipt of the Department's telegram, I personally called upon Commissar Litvinov and had
an extended discussion with him in connection with the above
matter and enclose herewith for the files of the Department a
copy of a memorandum covering that conversation.

I urged strongly that it was incumbent upon the Soviet
government to increase substantially its commitment for purchases in the United States over that of the preceding year;
and that such commitment should not be less than forty million dollars. Mr. Litvinov seemed to be favorably impressed
with the argument, made notes thereon, and stated that while
he had nothing to do with the commercial treaty, he would
take the matter up with those who were handling it, and impress upon them the consideration of the views and facts I had
submitted.

Subsequent thereto discussions were had with Mr. Neymann and Mr. Rosenblum of the Foreign Office, and Mr.
Kaminsky of the People's Commissariat for Foreign Trade,

with a view to resolving the matter into its ultimate issues. While these discussions with Mr. Henderson, Mr. Kennan, and Mr. Durbrow were proceeding, I had a conference with Mr. Litvinov and two discussions with Mr. Neymann personally and enclose herewith memoranda covering the subject matter thereof. Again on July 15 a very satisfactory conference was had at the Foreign Office with Messrs. Neymann, Rosenblum, Kaminsky, and Vinogradov, at which conference Mr. Kennan was present with me and the results of which were embodied in telegram No. 176, July 16, 11 P.M., to the Department.

It is unfortunate that the negotiation of the renewal of this commercial agreement should have come up at just this particular time. Because of the "cleansing and purging" of the party and government which is going on here, manifested by the shooting of the Red Army generals on June 12, and because of the "hate campaign" which has been projected against all foreigners.

We have now reached a stage where we have practically obtained everything we have set out to obtain. In fact we have been agreeably surprised by the manifest desire on the part of these men to be fair to the United States, which is a unique position in their attitude toward foreign states. During these negotiations they have been compelled to concede on every position except one—the exportation clause. Behind their insistence upon that there are probably two motives, (1) the fact of an *amour-propre* on behalf of their government, and (2) the fact that they must be in a position to show something as a result of their negotiations with the foreigner.

In connection with these negotiations I wish to refer to the exceptional contributions of Mr. Henderson, Mr. Kennan, and Mr. Durbrow. They have not spared either their energies or time in an effort to bring them to a head speedily and have all displayed exceptionally fine judgment and ability.*

I have the honor to be, Sir, respectfully yours,

Joseph E. Davies

TRADE AGREEMENT

EXCERPT FROM A LETTER TO STEPHEN EARLY

August 10, 1937

We did a good job for Cordell on the trade agreement—it was not easy. There was great confusion here, due to this "purging" process. It slowed us up but it was quite an achievement to get a 33⅓% increased commitment for purchases of American goods for next year. This is particularly true when you consider that Great Britain, only six months ago, in order to get $50,000,000 of business loaned, on a long term and at a low rate of interest, a similar sum to the Soviet government.

I am satisfied that I have done a job here. They know exactly where we stand. I have scrupulously adhered to the President's instructions. Nevertheless, we have managed to maintain a position where they indicate a most friendly attitude toward us and which has been reciprocated by this mission. Sometime that may be of particular significance, and even value, in connection with possible developments in the Far East or even in Europe—who knows!

DIARY   *Moscow—July 23, 1937*

Today I sent a report on collective farming here to Henry Wallace. It is one of the most interesting experiments

---

* The negotiations were successfully concluded with the substantial increase in the commitment for purchases in the United States referred to. Because of possible interest to some readers, in either the subject matter or the procedure in such cases, the memoranda referred to may be found in the Appendix.

over here. Individual farming has been practically prohibited by the government. Scientific farming by use of machinery has been forced upon the country. The government provides mechanical stations in each section with mechanized agricultural machinery for large-scale farming. The crops are divided among these mechanical units, the farm workers, and the state. In certain sections of Russia I am told there are so-called millionaire farmers, the farmer's share of the crop being so very large. In other sections this collectivism does not work because the topography of the country is not adapted to mechanical farming. Wheat fares very well under this system. With orchards, vineyards, and the like there is more difficulty. It was in the enforcement of collective farming that so many hundreds of thousands of people were alleged to have died from starvation in 1931 and 1933. I still hear accounts from Americans who were here then as to the horrors of that situation. The farmers apparently struck and refused to produce more than their needs for the winter. When the government was taking its quota after harvest, the farmers protested that if the crops were taken they would starve. The government's reply was that was too bad. It broke the strike.

THE RUSSIAN BEAR WADDLES THROUGH

NO. 455   *Moscow, July 28, 1937*

TO THE HONORABLE THE SECRETARY OF STATE

ALLEGED BREAKDOWN OF SOVIET INDUSTRIAL PLAN

Strictly Confidential

Sir:

I have the honor to report that during the last six months the criticisms by the Soviet press of conditions in industry have been so insistent and so drastic that the impression has become general among observers here that a serious breakdown of the economic industrial structure is imminent.

On the face of the record the picture appears to be a desperate one. No indictment of the inefficiency of Soviet industry could be drafted by the most severe critic but what some corroborative proof as to almost any statement made could be obtained from the charges made constantly in the press of the government newspapers here. Daily there are accounts of the manner in which this or that industry is falling behind in production, or failing to function properly or on time. The genius for self-criticism that obtains in the Soviet mentality has appeared at its best in these attacks upon industry. The failure of heavy industry to properly function has been frequently alleged to be one of the causes for the criticism and discontent of the Red Army generals who were executed in June. It seems to be accepted with practical unanimity, among observers here, that the government faces a most serious test in these conditions.

If the full facts justify the prevailing view of the seriousness of conditions here, then it is a matter of first-class importance, as it vitally affects any estimate of the present or future power, or influence, of this government.

I am submitting herewith the results of an investigation into these alleged conditions, together with an analysis thereof, and the conclusions which seem reasonably to follow therefrom.

That there has been and is now a marked "slow-up" in all industry is undoubtedly true. It would be most extraordinary if industry here, or anywhere else, could undergo the conditions which have obtained here during the past eight months, without being seriously impaired in its efficiency.

In the first place, all of these industrial organizations are controlled, managed, run, and operated by the government.

They are, therefore, peculiarly susceptible to political conditions; and political conditions for the past year have been particularly bad.

DISORGANIZATION DUE TO ALLEGED SABOTAGE

For the past year and a half, the "party" leaders have been "beating the bushes" in a man hunt for Trotskyites, spies, and saboteurs, who are alleged to have conspired with foreign enemies to wreck and sabotage industry. Innumerable prosecutions have occurred of factory managers and directors who were charged, rightly or wrongly, with these crimes. There is scarcely an industry that has not been shaken to the foundation of its organization by charges of this kind and been subjected to the internal intrigues and disruption that such a situation would breed.

PARTY DRIVE TO MAKE "PARTY" CONSIDERATIONS PARAMOUNT IN INDUSTRY

Coincident therewith, following Stalin's speech of last March before the Plenum of the Central Committee of the Party, economic efficiency has been "cried down" by all leaders of public thought. The charge was constantly made that the "true faith" had been forgotten and overlooked by "these economists and managers," who were engrossed in industrial and economic activities; that they had forgotten their first obligation to the "party" and that this must be at once rectified. Business and industrial administration became secondary to party activities and considerations. This could result only in severe interruption and disturbance of production. Factory managers and directors became acutely conscious of political necessities. In many cases they failed to discharge incompetent workers and in many other situations were themselves the subjects of attack by active political subordinates for alleged delinquencies. These and innumerable other results, as reported in the press, were the natural consequence of the drive to re-establish party considerations over the ordinary considerations of efficiency and good judgment which the administration of a business properly and usually would employ.

WAGE AND LABORER PROBLEM

The Stakhanovite movement (the piecework system) has been found to have so increased the cost of production that the wage system has had to be revised. Further, each one of these industries and their managers are concerned with making profit, for it is out of profit that the management and workers receive their "premiums" for production in excess of the planned allotment. Labor costs, therefore, are vital to the system.

In an effort to reduce costs, and to improve the profit position of these industries, an attempt was made to put into operation, by April 20, 1937, a revised standard for Stakhanovites; which revised standards raised the "norms" and reduced the rates of payment. The purpose was to stimulate the workers to produce more to get the same wage. The plan contemplated and promised that the factory management would provide greater efficiency of equipment and plant organization, to enable the workers to produce more, with the same effort and still keep their wages up in spite of the raised standards. The system apparently did not work. A general discontent among the workers was induced. New regulations brought new inequities. Frequently the more skilled earned less than the less skilled, with resultant discontent. Innumerable complaints of inequities were currently reported. Generally, wages went down, and with it both labor productivity per unit and volume of production declined. The Soviet newspapers, trade, and technical journals are full of charges of mismanagement of industry and "wrong organization of wage and labor systems." The natural consequence was to increase discontent among the workers, induce confusion in management, and a very substantial increase of the labor turnover.

INCREASE IN LABOR TURNOVER

The labor turnover has always been a serious problem in Soviet industry. Labor migration normally is very large. It can ill afford to have any substantial increase in this factor. The average per cent for the entire industry of the country, of the number of dismissals of laborers, as compared to the average annual number of workers on the pay roll for the year 1936, was 87.5%. In the coal industry for last year it was 112%; in the oil industry 95%, and in ferrous metallurgy it was 70%. With a labor turnover in the coal industry which in one year changed its entire labor personnel and then 12% more of the new "help," because of discharges or "quitting," it seems extraordinary that the industry made as good a showing as it did.

The resultant falling off in production for the first six months, according to the press, and the resolutions of the Central Committee of the Party, were caused by: (*a*) the after-effects of the wrecking activities of Trotskyists; (*b*) confusion and lack of capacity of managers and engineers; and (*c*) inadequate organization of the wage system and labor.

In addition to these conditions, it should be borne in mind that the entire country is in the throes of an impending political election. The new constitution throws the weight of the electorate out of balance. The party heretofore has been dominated by the industrial working class, constituting about 20% of the entire electorate. Under the new constitution, the agricultural workers are placed on an equality with industrial workers for the first time, and they constitute 80% of the electorate. It is vital to the government that they should make a strong showing of popular support. The result has been an enormous party activity from the top down, extending into every branch of activity over the entire country. The whole party organization is being shaken up. Sixty per cent of all of the officers in the local party organizations (of which there are some 60,000 scattered over the country) have been completely changed. Political pressure and party pressure are being brought to bear upon every industrial situation, along with all other branches of national activity. Politics permeates yard, factory, warehouse, office, and distribution facilities from bottom to top, with consequent disorganization and inefficiency.

Under such conditions it is not surprising that there should be a failure on the part of industry to live up to the planned production for the year 1937. That is the chief and ever-recurrent burden of complaint in the Soviet press.

Under the Soviet method, the State Plan Commission proscribes a plan in advance for each year, under which industry is required to increase its volume by a certain percentage over the previous year. The increase in the requirements imposed each year has been extraordinary. Thus the total revenue (profits) from industry in 1934 was approximately thirty billion rubles; in 1935 this had increased to approximately fifty-one billion rubles, and in 1936 to sixty-two billion rubles. The requirement of the plan for 1937 is 28% over 1936.

The criticisms of the party and the press are constantly directed to failure of industry to bring current performance up to the requirements of the plan for 1937.

In view of the conditions existing, as heretofore described, the question that occurred to my mind was not what was the lag or failure below the planned production for 1937, but what was the performance in contrast with the same period for the preceding year. The year 1936 showed an increase of 25% over 1935, and the year 1935 showed an increase of 66% over 1934. If then, under the conditions existing this year, industry could hold its own in contrast with last year, it would tend to show that the effects of these conditions as portrayed in the press were not as serious or significant as is generally accepted.

INTERVIEW WITH THE COMMISSAR FOR HEAVY INDUSTRY

In that connection, I recently had occasion to have quite an extended discussion with Mezhlauk, the new Commissar for Heavy Industry.* I asked him what the facts in the situation actually were in connection with this alleged "falling down" of industry this year. He stated that there had been much difficulty in the integration of some industries; that in some of the speciality lines there had been a substantial falling off, due to the fact that the suppliers had not been able to deliver parts to the main plant on time; that this had been true, particularly, in the automobile industry and in certain other industries where conveyor systems had been installed. He stated that thus far this year they were not living up to the requirements of the plan for the year 1937, which plan called for a 28% increase over last year; but that they were running along on about a basis of 12% increase over last year. I asked him particularly what the results for this year would show in his opinion. He stated that it would be substantially ahead of 1936. He pointed out that while,

---

* I was much relieved to see Mezhlauk, as it disproved rumor of his arrest reported July 8. As representative of the Soviet government he had signed a contract in Schenectady with the General Electric Company. Later he went to Detroit and it was largely due to the impression he made personally upon Henry Ford that the Ford Motor Company signed a contract to assist Soviet automobile production.

for instance, in the automobile industry, the production was about 33% below the requirement of the plan, it was approximately 70% over last year's production, and that the total output for the year would be better than 200,000 cars. He stated also that there was an unusual condition in coal and pig iron but that he expected that it would be remedied before the year was out.

Following this conversation, I had the economic section of the Embassy run down the figures from available sources of published information (these are generally correct), and I find that production in coal and pig iron for the first six months this year is in fact only 2% less than last year, whereas in steel and in rolled-metal products there has been an increase for the first six months this year, over last year, of 11% and 20%, respectively.

CONCLUSION

It would appear, therefore, that the conclusion which apparently seems to have been arrived at, that this situation spelled so serious a condition as might indicate a breakdown of the system, is not justified by the facts.

OVEREMPHASIS OF INDUSTRY IN SOVIET ECONOMY

It is perhaps true that an overemphasis has generally been placed upon the importance of industrial development here, in contrast with the whole picture of the economy of the Soviet government. Enormous sums in industry in the past eight years in the Soviet Union have been expended in capital investment. It is also true that most extraordinary plant and equipment facilities have been developed, with remarkable results. It is also true that the leaders of the Communist Party and particularly the founders of this Russian plan have repeatedly emphasized the importance of the industrial field as the ideal field for the projection of a communist state. The whole resources and economy of this enormous country were directed to the building up of an industrial economy.

A study and analysis of the budget of the Soviet Union, however, disclose that in so far as the functioning and life of the entire state are concerned, the part which industry contributes is relatively unimportant.

According to the budget of 1935, the total revenues of the U.S.S.R. were approximately sixty-five billion rubles (approximately three billion dollars gold). Loans and contributions from social insurance funds accounted for 3% of this total; 46% was obtained directly from agriculture and was substantially the amount of the tithe or share which the government exacted from the crops of the farmers. An additional 26% of all revenues came from the food industry which is, of course, primarily also agriculture. Commercial trade contributed an additional 12%. Heavy industry contributed but 9% and light industry contributed but 4%. If the entire revenues (profits) of heavy and light industry were dropped completely out of state revenues for 1935, it would still make no appreciable diminution of the 1934 revenue, for there would still remain a sum that would be in excess of the revenues of the preceding year by three billion rubles.

This is again simply an illustration of the fact that it is the enormous wealth of the Soviet Union and, particularly, the agricultural wealth of the country which enables this communistic and socialistic experiment to project and sustain itself with the apparent success which it has.

Not only can it withstand inefficiency and waste in industry, but it could afford to blot out the entire contribution of industry and scarcely feel the impact in the economic or financial administration of the state. With control of the army, it could afford even to disregard the social effects thereof.

The conclusion seems to be established that the plight of the economic industrial organization of the Soviet Union was not as serious as is currently believed; and further it seems probable that even though the most dire predictions of complete industrial and economic disintegration were in fact justified, the complete disruption of industry would not have so serious an effect upon the whole Soviet organism, as might be generally accepted, because of its relative insignificance in contrast to the enormous resources and strength which go to make up the life of the state.

There is, however, one phase of heavy industry that is of vital importance—possibly even to the existence of government itself, i.e., its necessity as a part of war preparedness. Military observers generally maintain that the present Soviet army is first-class in point of man power and officer personnel. It is generally believed that this army would render an excellent account of itself in case of war; but under conditions of modern war—a front line is no stronger than the second line of defense, i.e., the suppliers for equipment, tanks, munitions, and the like. The responsible leaders of the government, to my personal knowledge, are acutely "war conscious." They appreciate keenly the menace of Germany on the one side and Japan on the other. There is no doubt, however, but what President Kalinin voiced the opinion of his associates, when he stated to me that they had every confidence in their army and felt secure against attack, even though it were simultaneous on both sides. Their industries have been so located in the country as to indicate that the industrial plan was organized and projected, in part, as a war measure.

The enormous resources and wealth of the Soviet Union enable it to absorb waste and inefficiencies to an extraordinary degree, without vital impairment of its power. While not nearly so efficient as the industry of capitalistic countries, it is quite probable that Soviet industry would give a very fair account of itself in case of emergency.

It is said that England always manages to muddle through. The Russian bear is so big and rich in fat that the prediction is reasonably safe that he will waddle through most exigencies in the long run.

I have the honor to be, Sir, respectfully yours,

Joseph E. Davies

WHY THEY SHOT TUKHATCHEVSKY

NO. 457 *Moscow, July 28, 1937*

TO THE HONORABLE THE SECRETARY OF STATE

SHOOTING OF THE RED ARMY GENERALS ON JUNE 12, 1937, AND GENERAL CRISIS WHICH FOLLOWED *

Strictly Confidential

Sir:

Several weeks have now passed since the trial and shootings of the high officers of the Red Army. It has occurred to me that it might be of some interest to you, and to the Department, to have my analysis of what happened, from the vantage

---

* In connection with this dispatch, the sequence of events should be borne in mind. The record of the Radek trial which was held in January, 1937, contained practically no reference to Marshal Tukhatchevsky or to Red Army generals. In fact when Tukhatchevsky's name was mentioned, the prosecutor went out of his way to absolve him of any possible guilt.

Immediately following this trial there were evidences of great activity on the part of the Kremlin authorities. These culminated in the shooting of the Red Army generals in June.

The Bukharin trial was not held until the following March, 1938. It was in this trial that detailed and specific charges were made for the first time against the Red Army, implicating some of its leaders in "fifth column" activities.

This dispatch was written before the Bukharin trial and while we were all in the dark. It indicates that many of us missed the real significance of these events, in relation to possible treason and collusion with Germany, which subsequent developments disclosed.

of this perspective; as well as my estimate of the significance
and results of these events upon the present regime.

The trial, condemnation, and execution of these officers,
the flower of the Red Army, occurred June 12. Events had
moved with such lightninglike rapidity and terrific tragic force
that for some time it seemed difficult to obtain a well-balanced
judgment on the situation. There was not only much confusion, but much violence and prejudice of opinion among
the diplomatic and other observers in Moscow.

Both here and in Europe there were all sorts of rumors.
Some of these were that there existed an overt plot in the Red
Army to overthrow the Stalin government; that a Bonapartist
coup, with Marshal Tukhatchevsky as the Corsican, had
failed; that there had been established a definite agreement
between these Red Army generals and the German Reichswehr to co-operate with Germany as part of an impending
German *Putsch* into the Ukraine; that this was part of a larger
Trotsky plot for the purpose of destroying the Stalin regime
through a foreign war so that a new buffer state between the
Orient and Europe might arise therefrom to save "real" communism through the aid of the Red Army; that Stalin was
the "sick man of the Kremlin," who was suffering from a
hysteria complex with mental aberrations of personal danger,
which resulted in these shootings of all who threatened his
prominence, as he saw in them a menace to his safety; that
he had severe heart trouble and was being treated by a famous
Austrian physician (probably true); that his fears were being
preyed upon by a group of new, ambitious members of the
secret police (N.K.V.D.), who were "bending the pregnant
hinges of the knee" and demonstrating their loyalty and effectiveness, ever increasingly, by constantly unearthing new
alleged plots (which did not exist); that the army was engaged in a death struggle with the secret police, arising out

of resentment by the army of espionage by the secret police over army officers, in connection with these political trials and the alleged Trotsky conspiracies; that the entire army was impregnated with anti-Stalin feelings, and was a hotbed of counterrevolution; that Voroshilov—Commissar for Defense—was also a suspect, and in danger of imminent execution; that the entire economic structure was demoralized by these "party purges" and was in danger of collapse; that there were mass shootings going on all over the Soviet Union on a wholesale scale; that economic breakdown with physical revolution and the overthrow of the government was imminent.

A hostile foreign press made the most of these rumors. Stories were carried to the effect that the Red Army was "marching" on Moscow; that the Red Army would probably make a demonstration in the west (Poland), in order to divert attention from its internal troubles, et cetera.

These rumors and theories are an indication of the feverish attitude which would naturally be incident to a situation of so tragic a kind, and which was so completely enshrouded by lack of information. Some of the reports were probably true.

MOSCOW VIEWS OF THESE RUMORS

The "sick man of the Kremlin" theory is quite universally discounted. Stalin has had some heart trouble, as most of these men in the government here have had; but he has been seen on numerous occasions, and only recently by the writer, at very close range, and he looks strong, solid, healthy, and normal.

Moreover, generally speaking, in diplomatic circles here responsibility for these executions, in a strictly personal sense, is not attributed to Stalin. He commands a great deal of respect, outside of these terrible happenings. He is generally considered to be a clean-living, modest, retiring, single-purposed man, with a one-track mind, devoted to communism and the elevation of the proletariat. The responsibility is generally attributed to the "action of the party" through its party leaders. Of course, in that connection, it is generally considered that Stalin is by far the strongest character, and he is what we might term the type of "easy boss," who permits it to appear that his associates make their own decisions.

As to the alleged guilt of these army generals of overt acts —actual conspiracy with the German government—the general opinion is here that the charge is not justified, although it should be said that two very well-informed ambassadors, with whom I have discussed the matter, have stated it to be their belief that there was probably some truth in the allegations.

Several weeks have now elapsed and judgments håve cooled. During this period I have been making an effort to probe the facts and procure the temperate judgments and opinions of people here, who are as well informed as any foreigners could be, in an effort to get a consensus as to what occurred; what is the present strength of the government and what its prospects are.

SURFACE APPEARANCES IN MOSCOW IMMEDIATELY
AFTER THE EXECUTIONS

Upon my arrival in Moscow, I found that on the face of things everything appeared as usual. There was nothing on the streets, in the traffic, or in the crowds to indicate trouble of any kind. There were no indications (as per newspaper stories) of Cossacks either camped near the Kremlin or moving about in Red Square. Very shortly after my arrival I had occasion to meet different commissars and officials of the Foreign Office and I could detect no change in their demeanor or attitude. On the occasion of a conference with Litvinov, Commissar for Foreign Affairs, in connection with the discussion of the Spanish situation and European affairs, I asked him directly whether he appreciated the extent to which these events had weakened the Soviet Union as both a military and political power, in the opinion of western Europe. He stated that the Soviet government, far from being weak, was much stronger than it had been, and that a government must be very strong indeed that could withstand the loss of so many of its leaders through punishment for treason and still go along "on an even keel," without indication of storm or stress, and continue on its way "with business as usual each day."

ACTUAL CONDITIONS—VIOLENT ACTIVITIES OF "PURGE"

Underneath the surface, however, there were manifestations of the fact that a major operation of magnitude was and is going on here. Both in the local and, particularly, in the provincial press there were constant admissions of criminal trials directed against hundreds of defendants, and extensive "purgings and cleansings" of the party. These obtain in industry, agriculture, science, artistic circles, the theater, and in fact in all phases of activity. Constant violent criticisms of different situations and specific individuals appear daily in the news columns of the controlled government press. Even more convincing are the accounts carried by word of mouth of the disappearance or arrest of this or that person, sometimes prominent, and many times unobtrusively unimportant. Oftentimes these rumors were corroborated by first-hand knowledge. There are probably many exaggerations. In my opinion, however, there is no doubt whatever but what the authorities have conducted, and are conducting, a "cleansing and purging" activity with great vigor and relentless purpose and with increasing velocity, within the past few months.

The execution of these Red Army officers is a part of this general situation. The particular tragedy cannot be adequately understood or interpreted, except as a part of the whole picture.

In the course of the Radek trial, the names of General Putna and Marshal Tukhatchevsky were mentioned. Great care at the time was taken by Vyshinsky, the prosecutor, to absolve Tukhatchevsky from possible criminal complicity. Nevertheless, immediately following this trial, Tukhatchevsky disappeared. Rumors were rife that he was imprisoned, et cetera. During this period also, there was a great deal of talk that a bitter internecine struggle was going on between the army and the secret police.

IMMEDIATE CHRONOLOGY OF THE TRAGEDY

In the latter part of March, Tukhatchevsky returned to Moscow. Along with Voroshilov, General Egorov, and others of these defendants, Tukhatchevsky came to the Embassy in April for a dinner which I gave for officers of the Red Army. There were no particular indications of stress as between these men at that time. Tukhatchevsky had the reputation of being a very able man. He did not impress me very much. He had a rather fresh and boyish appearance, was rather overweight for his size, and looked like a man who enjoyed good living. The French Ambassador, M. Coulondre, said that he understood that Tukhatchevsky's downfall could be traced partly to his indiscretions with a lady friend (alleged to be a German spy).

In April it was announced that Tukhatchevsky would be one of the official representatives to the coronation of King George.

On the eleventh of May, it was officially announced that he was deposed from his command as Assistant Commissar for Defense and assigned to a minor command in the Volga district.

On the seventeenth of May, the Central Executive Committee of the Communist Party decreed Soviet control over the army. Each military district thereafter was to be commanded by one military officer and two other members. This meant absolute "party control" of the army, and political dominance over military discipline and action.

On the eleventh of June, Tukhatchevsky and the other defendants were arrested, charged with treason and with plotting with a "foreign state" (Germany). It was announced that they had admitted their guilt. On the following day they were alleged to have been tried, adjudged guilty.

COINCIDENT—PARTY ACTIVITIES—ELECTIONS PENDING

Coincident with these events were developments of a political and economic character that were interrelated with the immediate tragedy of these shootings. In January of this year, the final draft of the new Soviet constitution was ratified and approved by the constitutional conventions of the various constituent republics. It was designed to be a model constitution, providing for the protection of the freedom and safeguards for the liberty of the individual. This constitution contained other provisions that had far-reaching effects. Heretofore, for instance, industrial workers had a great advantage in their representation in government over the agricultural population. Under the old system each 125,000 peasants were entitled to one representative, whereas each 25,000 industrial workers were entitled to one representative. The new constitution changed this. All voters were placed on an equal basis and, in addition thereto, free elections were guaranteed with secrecy and the individual ballot. It was contemplated that these elections would be held in May. They were postponed.

During the months of February and March, I was told by two different members of the Soviet of People's Commissars, or cabinet, that they were working night and day, to the neglect of their strictly official duties, in connection with party preparation for the coming elections. The Spanish Ambassador stated to me at the time that he was informed that in February and March, 1937, at the Plenum of the Central Committee of the Party, it was debated as to whether it was advisable to clothe the agricultural electorate with this enormous power so suddenly; that it was urged that the reason in Spain for the failure of the popular movement was the fact that leadership there attempted to give freedom and electoral equality, without first implementing their democracy through proper organization and preparation in the country districts. He stated that Stalin himself resolved this debate in favor of going ahead, on the ground that it provided a test for the capacity of the Communist Party, and that it should be met immediately and with great vigor and strength.

On March 5, at the Plenum of the Central Committee of the Party, Stalin's epochal speech was addressed to this situation. He berated the party for having given too much attention to economic development and too little to the welfare of the party machinery. He required that each party member become a vigilant soldier, for the protection of their ideals from capitalistic states, foreign spies, et cetera. He made a definite bid for the support of the agricultural workers and for the workers as against the factory managers and party leaders. All during the months of March and April, and even up to the present time, every vehicle of propaganda—press, radio, and popular exhortation—has been addressed to the reorganization, cleansing, and revivifying of the party organization.

By the seventeenth of May, as announced by the Moscow *Pravda,* 55% of the officials of 54,000 primary organizations scattered over the Soviet Union were elected for the first time. By the twenty-second of May, it was alleged that from 56% to 62% of the total party organization, covering tens of thousands of party organizations, had been changed and that "the party is being reconstructed"; that "the party is closer to the masses." All this to the end that "elections do not run themselves."

During this period also party leadership was making definite overtures to the peasants. The government press constantly was criticizing local party leaders who were alleged to be oppressing the peasants of the collective farms. Prosecutions were instituted against local officials for alleged maladministration of agricultural affairs. Taxes, in kind, were being remitted to the agricultural collectives, and thereby to the individual peasants. It all had the earmarks of a political drive for the farmer vote.

COINCIDENT INDUSTRIAL CRISIS

Simultaneous with these political developments, there were economic conditions disconcerting to the government. The bureaucracy was responsible for the expenditure of billions of capital, in the development of these great industrial enterprises. They had made many promises of betterments and advantages to the masses, in consideration for the sacrifices which they had asked the proletariat to make. It cannot be gainsaid but what enormous results had been achieved; but by 1937 it was apparent that the machine was creaking in spots and lumbering along with difficulty in many places. Industry did not seem to function on the basis of a selfless society as well as it should, and the various devices to stimulate production, which were ingeniously projected, were only sporadically successful, and there were many indications of discontent.

The industrial production for 1936 lived up to the plan and was substantially an increase over 1935; but it began to appear that the top had been, more or less, reached and that there was danger of a recession in 1937. There was according to the press much dissatisfaction as against Stakhanovites in the lower classes of labor. That system apparently was not working as had been expected. The wage and labor problems were serious. Political activity in industry, motivated by Stalin's March speech, aggravated this situation and made conditions still worse. The press has been full of accusations, incriminations, and attacks of all kinds upon individuals, factory managers, directors, et cetera, in all classes of industry.

Still another fact aggravated this recession in the economic planned development. The threat of war had required an increase in the budget appropriations for 1935 and 1936, 15 or 20 times, respectively, of that of the budget for 1931. This was a heavy and direct load in the industrial program. Many industries were diverted to war uses. Agricultural-machinery plants, factory plants, steel plants, and the like were turned over to the construction of tanks, airplanes, munitions of war, and the like. This again slowed down the fulfillment of the benefits promised to the proletariat by the "powers that be."

All of these forces were converging into the tragedy of the Red Army. The party in power, that is, the government, was confronted with several grave threats: (1) the possibility of counterrevolutionary conspiracies, plots, and assassinations within; (2) the possibility of counterrevolutionary conspiracies with Japan, Germany, and enemies without; (3) the possibility that the Trotskyists had impregnated the entire community with seeds of revolution; (4) the immediate possibility of being unable to control the electorate in the impending elections; (5) the possibility of the serious lessening of industrial output of both heavy and light industry, and, more or less, industrial disorganization.

In view of these conditions, it appears both natural and probable that the established powers, who are a strong group of men, should direct all of their energies to strengthening and solidifying their position. Self-preservation would require that they do that. Nothing solidifies a political party in power to a greater degree than the fear of foreign war and possible invasion.

THE ARMY AND THE PARTY

It is, of course, the fact also that the source of greatest weakness, as well as the source of greatest strength to this government, is the Red Army. It is the only factor in the equation which could immediately overthrow and destroy the government. Military observers here are practically unanimous in the belief that in point of man power and officer personnel it is a splendid organization. The most intensive tests—physical, nervous, and mental—are applied in the training and selection of its officers. It is fair to assume that under these conditions, an officer class, conscious of its own superiority, has developed in the army. It has manifested itself within the past two years in titles, insignia, rank, orders, decorations of uniforms, and the like. While the discipline of the army and its technical equipment are first-class, no one knows better than these officers that this means that the Red Army is only all "dressed up with no place to go" unless industrial conditions back of the line will support it. It has been reported that there has been much discontent, and a large amount of criticism voiced by the army against the alleged inefficiency of political heads of industry and their failure to live up to commitments in deliveries.

If, therefore, in the face of these other critical situations, the men in the government here were confronted with the possibility of a lack of allegiance in the army itself, it is small wonder that such speed and ruthlessness were employed in establishing once and for all that the army was the creature of the political bureaucracy and not its master. To charge that army generals were a party to the possibility of invasion by Germany was to mobilize the nation to the support of the government.

DEARTH OF FACTS AS TO THE RED ARMY PLOT

Facts are not now available, and it is doubtful whether they will be for a long time to come, which would justify a statement as to exactly what happened and just what constituted the "offense" of these officers of the Red Army. Opinion must be based largely on deductions from known facts and these are few. The press reports here are practically bare of anything, except allegations. The same applies to Voroshilov's manifesto to the army. About all that has been stated is the position of the government, i.e., that these men were guilty of treason in the Red Army, had conspired with Germany to overthrow the government, had admitted their guilt, had been tried by the cream of the Red Army—their own peers—and that the evidence of their guilt was submitted, prior to the trials, to representative officers of all military districts of the Soviet Union. That such a conference was in fact held and that a very large number of officers were present here in Moscow at that time seem to be confirmed by foreign military observers who saw many of these Red Army officers whom they had met in different parts of the Soviet Union.

KLEMENTI VOROSHILOV
*"To Mr. and Mrs. Davies
Marshal of the Soviet Union
Voroshilov"*

DEDUCTIONS FROM KNOWN FACTS

In view of the character of the accused, their long terms of service, their recognized distinction in their profession, their long-continued loyalty to the Communist cause, it is scarcely credible that their brother officers—Voroshilov, Egorov, Budenny, Blücher, and the many other district military commanders—should have acquiesced in their execution, unless they were convinced that these men had been guilty of some offense.* It is generally accepted by members of the Diplomatic Corps that the accused must have been guilty of an offense which in the Soviet Union would merit the death penalty.

From the facts which we have, certain deductions can be reached as to what the situation probably was. It would have been quite natural for strong-minded men, such as these men were, to have criticized political bureaucratic control of industry when it handicapped the army. It is also reasonable to assume that a group of men, such as these, would resent vigorously the imposition of an espionage system over them, through the instrumentality of a secret police system, under the control of politicians. It would also be quite natural for men of this character, and particularly this training, to have resented bitterly the possible destruction of the fine military organization which they had built up, by the imposition of political control over the military command in each military district. It is quite fair to assume that these men would not permit the party, of which they were members, to adopt this course of conduct as a matter of "party principle," without vigorous opposition. It is possible that they continued to voice such opposition.

---

* The Bukharin trial six months later developed evidence which, if true, more than justified this action. Undoubtedly those facts were all fully known to the military court at this time.

However, if after the seventeenth of May, when political control over the army was established as a result of a party decision, the opposition on the part of these officers continued, even though it were simply through discussions among themselves, their action would be treasonable and a felony under Bolshevik rules of behavior. It is a fundamental of party government that once a party action is established by a vote of the majority, any further opposition thereto constitutes treason.

Under all of the conditions it can also be quite reasonably considered that the party leaders responsible for the conviction of these defendants had convinced themselves that these Red Army generals had outgrown their creators and were a serious threat to the party organization and dominance. It is possible also that these party leaders found but little difficulty in spelling out of the conduct of the defendants an overt conspiracy to impose the will of the army over the party, and failing therein to engage in a conspiracy with a foreign enemy to overthrow the state.

In the face of these conditions, and under this stress, Stalin and the party leaders acted with great speed and ruthless severity. They hit first. Communism is their religion and in executing speedy justice for the violation of party principle, they were in the strong position of "serving the Lord." It also served their interests well, for by such action they were entrenching themselves in power. By adding the charge of treason to the state, they became the bulwark of defense for that Russian nationalism that is being constantly stimulated by every form of propaganda available.

PRESENT STATUS OF STALIN REGIME

The Stalin regime, politically and internally, is probably stronger then heretofore. All potential opposition has been killed off. The crux of the situation, however, depends upon the attitude of the army. It is the army that ultimately holds the key. It is not generally believed that the morale of the army has been basically affected by those events. It is still, in the main, a communistic and party "citizen soldiery." "The party" has been insistently drilled into the youth of the army as a religion. It is probably too deeply rooted in the rank and file to have been easily destroyed. So far as the officers are concerned, they doubtless recognize realistic conditions. It has been very clearly and ruthlessly established that the party is "boss." The secret police is the personal agency of Stalin and the party. It is in the saddle and riding hard! The new head of this organization, Ezhov, is comparatively a young man. He is constantly seen with Stalin and is regarded as one of the strongest men in the government.' His effectiveness and ability are greatly respected. Voroshilov, the chief of the army, is an old Bolshevik. He is generally regarded as a strong and vigorous type of man, whose loyalty and convictions would not be swayed by personal ambition. He seems thoroughly loyal to Stalin. All indications are that, for the present at least, the army is and will be loyal to the party. If so, in internal politics, the Stalin regime will be, temporarily, at least, more firmly entrenched in power than heretofore.

EFFECT ABROAD

The effect of these shootings have probably been more serious in their adverse effects on conditions in Europe, outside of Russia, than on conditions within the Soviet Union. There is no doubt that the confidence of France and England in the stability of a potential eastern European ally must have been severely shaken by these events.

CONCLUSION

Barring assassination, or a foreign war, the position of this government and the present regime looks impregnable for the present, and probably for some time to come. The danger of the Corsican for the present has been wiped out.

I have the honor to be, Sir, respectfully yours,

Joseph E. Davies

PART IV

RUSSIA THROUGH HER NEIGHBORS' EYES

July 28—December 24, 1937

IV

ESTONIA "WALKS THE TIGHT ROPE"

NO. 456   *Moscow, July 28, 1937*

TO THE HONORABLE THE SECRETARY OF STATE

POLITICAL CONDITIONS IN ESTONIA IN RELATION
TO THE U.S.S.R.

Strictly Confidential

Sir:

Taking advantage of a week-end holiday, I made an unofficial visit to Estonia, by way of the national capital, Tallinn.

The present government is practically a dictatorship. With the development of Fascist states about them, they found that their system was weak. It could not make speedy and authoritative decisions that were necessary for the protection of the country. Too much time was spent in debate. In order to prevent the country from falling into the error of complete Fascism as happened in Germany, the President—a very high-minded man—with the aid of other strong men usurped power peaceably and established a benevolent dictatorship, which assured a continuity of policies and unified quick action when necessary in the national interest. This action was taken with the understanding that a constitution was to be drafted and submitted to a plebiscite, looking to the creation of a strong form of democratic government.

The dominant internal political note is: Estonia for Estonians. The nationalistic complex is very strong. The Estonian of German descent, even though he date back several hundred years in Estonian residence, is still not pure Estonian, from the political point of view. Great emphasis is placed upon maintaining an Estonian cultural independence.

Their attitude to Russia is friendly and formal. They want to get along with their big neighbor, but they still remember the unsuccessful Communist *Putsch* of 1924.

Together with Latvia and Lithuania, Estonia is a part of the "Baltic Bloc." The whole bloc is concerned with the preservation of their respective nationalistic entities as between Germany and Russia.* They are all vitally concerned with the maintenance of peace.

Like the rest of these eastern European countries, Estonia is chiefly concerned with "walking the tight rope" and preserving its balance, as between Germany and Russia. It is a member of the League of Nations and generally "goes along" in European affairs. As was said to me by one of these gentlemen: "We are a member of the Nonintervention Committee in London. We are, however, fortunate in having representation there that is modest and one that recognizes the limitations of our size and unimportance. We do not take sides. Quite frankly, we do not want to be placed in the position of risk, which taking sides would involve. We tell both sides frankly that we will go with the majority." This is the key of their foreign policy. In the last analysis, however, England now dominates Estonia. Lord Plymouth has only recently visited

----

* See Appendix for similar dispatches on Finland, Latvia, Lithuania, and Danzig.

the country on a commercial, quasi-political good-will tour.

There is a substantial German minority "bloc" in Estonia, as well as in Latvia. This is a disturbing element. There is always the threat that should Germany regain control over Estonia, this group would assume their former dominant position.

From a military point of view, in the event of a German attack on Russia, they seem to think that they are outside of the danger zone. When I called attention to the fact that the Baltic-Leningrad naval and military attack was one of the two major plans that, according to expert opinion, might be projected by Germany, in the event of an attack on Russia, the reply was that they did not agree with that theory; that Estonia was too far north; that the objective of attack would be Moscow and not Leningrad, and that the overland route to Moscow farther south would leave them out of it. They insisted upon this, in spite of the suggestion that Tallinn was the old Russian seaport of Reval and directly connected by rail with Leningrad.

I spent two days in Tallinn, the capital, and one day in the country at Narva—the old seat of the Russian textile industry, which has largely disintegrated.

Both in the cities and in the countryside, there were evidences of thrift, well-being, comfort, cleanliness, and self-respect.

I have the honor to be, Sir, respectfully yours,

Joseph E. Davies

JOURNAL   *Stockholm—August 8, 1937*

I was interested to find corroboration of Litvinov's statement to me on the occasion of Sandler's visit to Moscow, which was previously reported to the Department. I was told in practically so many words that it was their view that Article 16 of the Covenant should be modified so as to relieve the small nations of the obligation of either economic or military sanction in order that they might the better maintain their neutrality.

The existence of the Scandinavian bloc, including Finland, was stated also to be a recognized and accomplished factor in European diplomacy. It was also confirmed that the Swedish government had been desirous that Finland should establish the fact that it was not on unfriendly terms with Russia, prior to Finland's participation, as they were concerned primarily in preserving the integrity and neutrality of the Scandinavian nations in the event of trouble between Russia and Germany or other European outbreaks.

With reference to the prospect of European peace, I was told that the situation had recently looked very much better, particularly in view of the impending *rapprochement* of England and Italy, and the subsiding of the Spanish danger. However, it was definitely a very precarious situation, for any accident might precipitate armed conflict.

DIARY   *Moscow—August 10, 1937*

My old friend, Sam Untermeyer, well over eighty I understand, but hale and hearty, is in Moscow. He has been here before. He is enthusiastic over the extraordinary achievement of the government in the building of the Moscow subway, which, he said, was one of the finest subway systems, physically, in the world. And, said he, "You know that I have made a specialty of subways," referring to his fight for the city of New York in connection with the five-cent fare and the subway problem. Russia to him had a great fascination. He said that I was to be particularly congratulated on having been assigned to this post. To him, it was one of the most interesting diplomatic posts in the world. He had told his nephew, Laurence Steinhardt, that of all posts, the Russian post was the one that was the most desirable. It was dynamic, vital, and would be tremendously potential not only in the European situation, but in the world situation as well.

He went on at great length along these lines. We have been friends for many years. His incisive intelligence, his breadth and soundness of judgment make him a great man.

INTERCESSION FOR FATHER BRAUN

Leningrad—August 10, 1937

HIS EXCELLENCY M. M. LITVINOV

My dear Mr. People's Commissar:

May I intrude upon your attention, in connection with a matter that has given me a great deal of concern. It has to do with an American citizen —Father Braun—who happens to be a Catholic priest, who is now living at the French Embassy, and ministering to the Catholic members of the Diplomatic Corps.

Personally, I know Father Braun very well and have a very high respect for his character and his fine devotion to his convictions. He is in every way, I am sure, a man of honor.

Some differences have arisen between him and the proper Soviet authorities, in connection with the possible turning over of certain birth and marriage records which are in his custody. I understand that he has offered the authorities the opportunity to inspect these records, but he is very anxious not to have them leave his possession for reasons of conscience.

In view of the spirit of the discussions which you had
with the President of the United States, resulting in the agreements of November, 1933,* I am in the hope that your honorable government will see fit not to permit this matter to develop into either an incident or an issue that would, in my
opinion, have an untoward effect upon the sensibilities of a
large section of our American people.

Please regard this note not as an official representation, but
as a personal message and request to your honorable government, as I do not wish to enter into the discussion of the legali-
ties of the situation at this time.

Assuring you that I would appreciate very much any personal attention that you could give to this matter, and with
assurances of my great respect and esteem, I am,

Very truly yours,

INTERCESSION FOR INTERNATIONAL BUSINESS MACHINES COMPANY

Leningrad—August 10, 1937

HIS EXCELLENCY MAXIM LITVINOV

My dear Mr. People's Commissar:

May I call your attention to
a matter which is now pending before the appropriate visa
authorities of the Soviet government, in connection with the
extension of the visa of Mr. Shervdt, who is an American citizen and a representative of the International Business Machines Company of the United States, now in Moscow.

The International Business Machines Company is engaged

---

* See Diary—March 20, 1937.

In this situation, as in many other visa matters affecting Father Braun, the
Foreign Office invariably acceded to my requests.

in the business of making and leasing various types of machines to be used by large enterprises, in connection with bookkeeping and accounting facilities. It has had a long-continued business relationship with different branches of the Soviet government, which relations, I understand, have always been pleasant.

As a matter of fact, many Soviet institutions are now using these machines, which represent a very substantial capital investment, and Mr. Shervdt's presence here in Moscow is partially due to the desire on the part of the company to have a man on the ground to assure that they are kept in proper repair and used to the best operating advantage.

In view of this situation, it would appear to me to be advisable that Mr. Shervdt should be permitted to stay in the Soviet Union.

In addition to this fact, I am interested because of the fact that the head of the International Business Machines Company is Mr. Thomas Watson.

Mr. Watson is the type of citizen who gives a great amount of his energy and time to the furtherance of matters of public rather than private interest. He is widely and favorably known in all of the liberal sections of American business, and is a close friend of our great President. He is distinctly the type of man who would be sympathetic, in connection with the humanitarian impulses and enterprises upon which the Soviet Union is engaged, and I should be very unhappy to have him feel that he had been dealt with in an unfriendly and unfair manner. You may perhaps know Mr. Watson because he has been very active in international affairs, and is now the President of the International Chamber of Commerce.

Please pardon this intrusion of a small matter upon your

attention when you are engaged upon these very important affairs of state.*

With assurances of my great respect and esteem, I am,

Very truly yours,

SITUATION AS TO GOLD

En route to Riga—August 12, 1937

THE HONORABLE HENRY MORGENTHAU

Dear Henry:

When in London in June, Bingham and I had lunch with the Russian Ambassador, Maisky, who is a very able, shrewd man, and we deliberately set out to emphasize under the appearance of casualness the great interest which the Soviet Union had in the protection of the price of gold and I think that we got over to him quite clearly (without direct approach) the wisdom of the Soviet government cooperating with the United States, particularly with the Treasury of the United States. I am sure that he reported it to his government.

When in London I also had quite an extended conference with Litvinov and discussed with him at length the gold situation of the world and he seemed impressed with the desirability of establishing closer contacts with you and stated that he had authorized the appointment of an additional secretary to be attached to the Washington Soviet Embassy for contact purposes with the Treasury. I asked him the di-

---

* In spite of the severity of the campaign which the government is now conducting against all foreigners, and in marked contrast thereto, the Foreign Office acceded to this request. This incident shows the kind of work which the Embassy had to handle; and also indicates the friendly attitude which the Soviet government invariably showed to the United States during my tenure of office there.

rect question as to what the actual production of gold was and what their present gold reserves were. He hedged on the reply. He did say, however, that he could state confidentially to me that the current estimates were rather exaggerated. Of course, under this regime over here, Litvinov has to be very careful to stick within the confines of his own field and he is naturally hesitant about encroaching upon the military powers of the government, who are jealously guarding the facts with reference to the gold supply of the country as a military and strategic secret and who, I have no doubt, are constantly exaggerating its size for propaganda purposes and its possible effect on their enemies.

Sincerely yours,

ARRESTS OF GERMANS IN RUSSIA

JOURNAL   *Riga—August 13, 1937*

I understand the German Ambassador made representations to the Soviet Foreign Office, protesting the arrests of German nationals, which were reported to have been made in Moscow, Leningrad, Kiev, Kharkov, Tiflis, and other places. According to the official reports *most of the arrested persons were under suspicion of espionage.*

CONFIDENTIAL SUMMARY TO THE SECRETARY OF STATE

TO THE HONORABLE THE SECRETARY OF STATE

Prague—September 1, 1937

Dear Cordell:

Following my talks with the President and yourself I planned these trips into the various countries adjacent to the Soviet Union for the purpose, as was suggested, of get-

ting a firsthand perspective on the personalities and forces
which are at work. It has been invaluable to me and I think
that the "Brief on the Facts" which I have been sending in
to the Department should be helpful to you there. It has
been hard work, but very valuable to me.

Thus far I have visited (unostentatiously) all of the coun-
tries of the Baltic and Scandinavian blocs—Estonia, Latvia,
Lithuania, Finland, Sweden, Denmark, and also Memel and
Danzig.* I shall visit Czechoslovakia and Poland en route to
Moscow.

Vis-à-vis Germany is the Soviet Union. It suits Germany's
book to hold the Soviet Union up as the menace to civilization. Russia is in fact, at least for the present, in my opinion,
a sincere advocate of peace. Of course, economically it suits
her book to have peace while she develops her enormous resources and industries and solidifies her government. Geographically, the Soviet Union is fortunate. Her vastness
defeated Napoleon.

THE BALTIC STATES—FOREIGN POLICIES

Estonia, Latvia, and Lituania, created by the League of
Nations, have one basic foreign policy—a desire to protect
their sovereignty and their independence. Between two
neighbors, both of whom they fear, Estonia and Latvia are
less friendly to the Soviet Union than Lithuania. Lithuania
has her quarrel with Poland, arising out of the seizure by
Poland of her ancient capital, Vilna. That situation is tense.
The border between the two countries, partially at least, is
barricaded. All communication is shut off. Again Lithuania
is fearful lest her only real seaport, Memel, now a semiautono-

---

* See Appendix for complete text of dispatches from Latvia, Finland,
Lithuania, and Danzig.

mous League of Nations' state, with a preponderant German population, might be taken by Germany. As a matter of fact, in my opinion, barring military necessities created by an attack by Germany on Russia, Germany would have but little to gain, except the appeasement of national pride, by acquiring either Memel or Lithuania. The standard of living in Lithuania is low and its resources are so meager that the acquisition of Lithuania by Germany could easily dilute Germany's standard of living and any such acquisition of Lithuania become a liability instead of an asset. Because of these facts and her geographical situation Lithuania relies more on Russia than do the other states.

THE SCANDINAVIAN BLOC

Here, too, the foreign policies and the attitudes of these states, respectively, toward the League of Nations are based upon their geographical situation on the North and Baltic Seas and in the possible military zone of conflict between Germany and other European nations and Russia. Their vital purpose is to preserve their integrity and neutrality. Finland's position as almost a certain military German base in the event of a northern attack upon Leningrad places her in peculiar danger. The Scandinavian bloc is a loose organization aimed to protect the neutrality and independence of these northern countries. They rely on the League of Nations, but are disposed (Sweden quite openly) to advocate the modification of Article 16 of the Covenant in order that they might be relieved of sanctions, economic or military, to the end that their neutrality would be made secure.

Similar to the Baltic states, here too the British influence is dominant. Britain is the best customer and their currencies are tied to the pound.

ATTITUDE TOWARD GERMANY

In all of these states the great concern of their foreign policy is to maintain a balance as between Russia and Germany. It is significant that Finland was not accepted in the Scandinavian bloc until Sweden was assured that the relations between Russia and Finland were pacific and friendly. It is their constant effort to maintain strictly correct and formal relations with both countries.

ATTITUDE TOWARD RUSSIA

These countries do not seem to be fearful of being infected with communistic doctrines through Russian radio propaganda or otherwise. They are, however, practically all disposed to discount Russia's development and economic progress or the present strength of her government. They are practically unanimous in the opinion that Russia has a "will for peace." Confidence has been severely shaken by the shooting of the Red generals and the "purge" that is going on.

THE WESTERN LOCARNO AND EASTERN EUROPEAN PEACE

One of the most valuable pieces of information which these visits developed was an indication of the plan that England and France had in mind looking to the preservation of peace in eastern Europe if an agreement as to western European peace were consummated between England, France, and Italy, and if Russia were left out, as the developments of the last three months would indicate. The idea was briefly the following and was stated by Neville Chamberlain within the past few weeks to my informant, the Foreign Minister of Latvia. Inasmuch as it was recognized that Hitler would not sign any treaty with Stalin, it was contemplated that as a part of the Western Locarno arrangement, and simultaneously therewith, Germany would enter into non-aggression pacts with the countries bordering on Russia, similar to the pacts now already in existence between Russia and these states, the result of which would be that conflict between Germany and Russia would be minimized because of this "neutralized" territory between them; and that thereby a "roof" would be provided for these two antagonists which would preserve peace in eastern Europe.

This information I believe is of first-rate consequence as it is the first suggestion of what England apparently has in mind in connection with handling the Soviet-French situation in preserving peace in the East; and explains her apparent recent advances to Germany, which appear to be at the expense of the Soviet Union.

RUSSIA, JAPAN, AND CHINA

Up to two weeks ago I commuted in and out of Leningrad and was in personal touch with the situation in Moscow. Since then I have talked every other day with Mr. Henderson, the Chargé, by long-distance telephone. The Kremlin is definitely "playing down" any possibility of active Soviet participation against Japan. They are making every effort to appear to be "lying doggo." On the face of the situation that is the condition. However, I have my own reservations with reference to *bona fides* of that attitude. There is no doubt in my mind but what Russia is innately desirous of helping China. What deters her is fear of possible German attack in the event of her participation and possibly also fear as to the solidarity of her eastern military forces until the internal situation has cooled off and solidified, after the shootings and "purgings" that have been going on. In the event that Japan through China should seriously threaten the railroad line of

communications and Lake Baikal, the Soviet Union would
undoubtedly get into the fight.

INSPECTION COLLECTIVE FARMS AND OIL FIELDS

Upon my return, it is my present plan to make an inspection trip covering some of the principal collective-farm activities and also some of the social-welfare projects in the Black
Sea area. There still remains one very important economic
activity in Russia which I wish to cover, to wit, the oil situation at Baku and in the Caucasus. The contacts and possible
conflicts of Persian, English, Turkish, and Russian interests
there are important; and I should like to report to you on
these conditions from firsthand information. With reports
completed on these activities I feel that from firsthand contact I shall have covered fairly comprehensively the economic,
as well as political, activities of the Soviet Union. By October
15 these will be completed.

I have tried to summarize the situations as I have found
them.

I have the honor to be, Sir, respectfully yours,

Joseph E. Davies

DIARY   *Paris—September 4, 1937*

Arrived here for the day. Had a "home folks" dinner
in the evening on the roof of the German Building at the Ex-
position. Madame Roosevelt, Senator Barkley and daughter,
Senator and Mrs. Bob La Follette, Senator and Mrs. Alva
Thomas, Senator McKellar, Senator Henry Hollis, Mrs. Mul-
downey, and a Miss Young (who were with the La Follettes),
Mr. and Mrs. Bess from Moscow, Charlie Nutter (A.P.),
Moscow en route for Madrid. It was a very pleasant party.

Bob La Follette has developed into an exceptionally strong
man, well-balanced character. He might make a good Presi-

dent some day. Alben Barkley looks well and is a really great man—much greater than he seems because of his modesty and simplicity. I have enjoyed my visit with my old friends McKellar and Thomas. It is comforting to know that men of their caliber are serving our country.

There is something about meeting one's old friends in a foreign land that has a "punch" to it.

PIRACY IN THE MEDITERRANEAN

JOURNAL   *Paris—September 6, 1937*

It is reported that the Soviet government sent a strongly worded note to the Italian Foreign Office accusing Italy of responsibility for the sinking of two Russian vessels in the eastern Mediterranean, claiming indemnities and demanding punishment of the guilty persons.

The Italian government replied repudiating responsibility for the attacks on Soviet shipping, and rejecting en bloc the demands for indemnification and punishment of the guilty persons.

Invitations to a conference to be held on September 10, at Nyon, on the prevention of piracy in the Mediterranean were conveyed by the French and British representatives in each capital to the governments of Italy, Greece, Yugoslavia, Turkey, Egypt, and Albania—as Mediterranean powers which signed the Submarine Convention of 1936; to those of the U.S.S.R., Rumania, and Bulgaria, as Black Sea powers, having an outlet into the Mediterranean; and to Germany—as being directly concerned in the control scheme and also a victim of attacks.

This is only another of the many instances of the high-handed boldness of the aggressors in this "pirate" submarine situation. Diplomats are snickering up their sleeves, either in

disgust or amusement over the brazen manner these dictators
get away with their pretenses. No one doubts but what these
attacks were actually made by Italian submarines on Russian
ships carrying supplies to Spain.

Acceptances of the Franco-British invitation to the Mediterranean Conference were received from the U.S.S.R.,
Greece, Egypt, Rumania, and Bulgaria.

The Soviet government's reply in "recognition of the intolerable nature of the attacks by Italian warships against
commercial ships" inquired why an invitation was sent to
Germany, which was not a Mediterranean power; and demanded that Spain be also invited.

DIARY   *Vichy—September 7, 1937*

Stopped off for a few days at Vichy, where Marjorie
is taking "the cure," while I am fast qualifying for it by running around Europe.

We walked and shopped—"antiqued." We found a very
extraordinary tea set made by Sèvres workmen in St. Petersburg done upon the order of Catherine for her lover Count
Orlov. Also a Houdon bronze head of Voltaire, which came
from Catherine's desk in the Palace, and a Disrai portrait of
Voltaire, also from Catherine's library in the Hermitage.

ALLEGED GERMAN AND FINNISH ACTIVITIES
IN RUSSIA

JOURNAL   *Budapest—September 22, 1937*

Word reaches me from Moscow that twenty-one
people were reported to have been executed in Leningrad
Province for organized activities against the provincial Soviet.

The discovery of a serious plot in Karelia was announced,
the object of which was to cut off the port of Murmansk and

the Kola Peninsula by the seizure of the railway line to that area below Petrozavodsk. German and Finnish agents were alleged to be implicated.

ALLEGED BLOWING UP OF CHEMICAL WORKS BY GERMAN SPIES

JOURNAL   *Vienna—September 29, 1937*

Reports from Moscow advise of the execution of many officials at Kharkov, Rostov-on-Don, Sverdlovsk, Tiflis, and other places, and in Leningrad sixteen persons were shot for conspiring to murder members of the government and wreck the chemical works. They were described as spies from the German Secret Police.

DIARY   *Moscow—October 4, 1937*

At 5:30 the journalists came in for a press conference. Walter Duranty, Anna Louise Strong, Rodman, Massock, Deuel, Joe Barnes, and Jim Brown. I gave them a prepared statement and then off the record we discussed at length European peace, Japan, China, and the local situation. Duranty was very pessimistic. From what he knew of recent developments in Czechoslovakia and the Balkans, he was of the definite opinion that Hitler's war was approaching very rapidly.

PRESIDENT ROOSEVELT'S SPEECH AT CHICAGO

JOURNAL   *Moscow—October 5, 1937*

The President, speaking at Chicago, made a great speech. He deplored the unrest prevalent in the world and the fact that a haunting fear of calamity had taken the place of the high hopes felt at the conclusion of the Kellogg Treaty. "The present reign of terror and international lawlessness began a few years ago," he declared, "and has now reached the stage where the very foundations of civilization are seriously threatened. . . . The nations are fomenting and taking sides in civil warfare in nations that have never done them any harm. . . . Nations claiming freedom for themselves deny it to others."

He then uttered a warning lest anyone should imagine that, if matters grew worse in other parts of the world, America would escape, and would continue tranquilly to carry on the ethics and arts of civilization. If those days were not to come to pass, "the peace-loving nations," he declared, "must make a concerted effort to uphold the laws and principles on which alone peace can rest secure. They must make a concerted effort in opposition to those violations of treaties and those ignorings of humane instincts which are today creating the '*international* anarchy' and instability from which there is no escape through mere isolation or neutrality."

There was solidarity and interdependence about the modern world, both technically and morally, which made it impossible for any nation completely to isolate itself from upheavals, especially when such upheavals appeared to be spreading. It was a matter of vital concern and interest to the people of America that the *sanctity of international treaties and the maintenance of international morality* be restored.

He then referred to the very high cost of armaments, and said that the United States spent much less on them than many countries, but, "I am compelled and you are compelled, nevertheless, to look ahead. The peace, freedom, and security of ninety per cent of the population of the world is being jeopardized by the remaining ten per cent. . . . The situation is definitely of universal concern." He went on to remark that in the case of epidemics of physical disease spreading the community always approved, and joined in, a quarantine of the patients. Several members of the diplomatic corps telephoned me about the speech. It created a small sensation, and no wonder—it was the clearest statement of the coming issue, yet made.

ANECDOTE TYPICAL OF CONDITIONS IN RUSSIA

EXCERPT FROM A LETTER TO MAJOR GENERAL WATSON

Here is another one that Demaree Bess of the *Christian Science Monitor* told me the other day. It may give the "Boss" a laugh.

Mrs. Bess had employed a Russian of the Embassy Staff, who had been recommended by me, to do some painting. Shortly after, the poor devil was arrested as a suspect. After "durance vile" of ten days he was released. He came back and told Mrs. Bess of his experience with great pride and stated that he had never enjoyed the privilege of being associated with such people and brilliant intellectual companionship as he had found among his fellow prisoners in jail and was quite set up over his advance in social standing.

DIARY *Moscow—October 7, 1937*

Ambassador Troyanovsky came in and spent an hour with me. He gave rather an interesting account of conditions here that justified the executions. He described the naïveté of his people even in the government in extending their trust and making party membership a guarantee of reliability. He stated that the country was in fact infested with spies of hostile countries, which spies were for years engaged upon this service as members of the Communist Party and even the government itself. He stated that he himself had had suspicions many times; that England and France were similarly infested; that Stalin might later give the world "his side" of this situation.

Troyanovsky is returning to the States. He is an able man, loyal to his chiefs and to his party.

Moscow, U.S.S.R.—October 15, 1937

EXCERPT FROM A LETTER TO SECRETARY HULL

During the last few days I have had several most interesting talks, which were again given to me only under condition that I should exercise the most extraordinary care in their transmission. It is a revelation to me to find what little confidence diplomacy here has generally in the privacy of codes. I was compelled to send a courier to Paris to have the information transmitted to you from there. It was a condition upon which I received the information.

DIARY   *Moscow—October 16, 1937*

Ambassador Rosso, Ambassador Shigetmitsu, and Minister Urbaye of Norway came in for dinner and bridge.

The Italian Ambassador Rosso drew the Japanese Ambassador for a partner and spoke of "aggressor nations" in fun. I kidded them when one of the "aggressors" failed to take a trick with his lone ace, when he had the lead against a game bid, and when that trick would have "set" the bidders. Perhaps the "aggressors" were not so smart after all. We had good fun over it.

EUROPEAN CONDITIONS

Moscow, U.S.S.R.—October 25, 1937

THE HONORABLE BERNARD M. BARUCH

My dear Birney:

After I left you I had a most interesting two hours' conference with President Beneš of Czechoslovakia and a similar conference with Admiral Horthy, the Regent of

Hungary, as well as with the Foreign Minister of Austria. While this traveling during the summer was pretty hard work, nevertheless it was distinctly worth while. I got a feeling of, and perhaps an intimate knowledge of, the real attitude of the various Foreign Offices and leading figures of the government of these countries which I visited, not only toward the Soviet Union but also toward European problems and European peace as well.

Prompted, I suppose, by the knowledge that the United States had no ax to grind in Europe, in all of these situations I found the greatest of frankness in the conversations which I had, which were always of an informal character. As a matter of fact, I did receive some most valuable information which was not generally known and which I was committed to disclose orally only to the President and the Secretary of State.

Since our talk in Paris I have given a great deal of thought to your clear and lucid statement of the problem of European peace. It is characteristic of the vision and clarity of judgment which you apply to problems. I wish it could be projected.

The European situation is favorable one day and dark the next. Things move kaleidoscopically. The Spanish situation doesn't look so good, but it may be that Franco will settle the issue by conclusive military success speedily. It then remains to be seen whether the Balearic Islands will still provide an apple of discord. Hitler is again propagandizing the alleged pressure on the German minorities in Czechoslovakia. Apparently he is keeping that situation alive. France seems to be gaining some strength internally. England, as usual, is playing her farsighted objective and realistic game. It now looks as though Japan will have once again demonstrated that she picks an opportunity to strike when the world is absorbed in other problems. It looks as though she would get away with it.

The "terror" here in this "purge" is something terrific and is
done for the purpose of ensuring that this government shall
remain in power, which, strange as it may seem, probably is
sincerely desirous of elevating the condition of the common
man. The weakness which western Europe finds in Russia is
the product of wishful thinking rather than an objective
appraisal.

Hastily yours,

DIARY   *Moscow—October 28, 1937*

Had long conference with the British Ambassador in
a walk through forest. We were both followed by our respective Gay-Pay-Oos (secret-police guards) who seemed to enjoy
their walk and their visit. They kept at a respectful distance,
but always kept us in sight. I found general agreement with
the belief that the purge and the killings had not impaired
the political strength of the government.

DIARY   *Moscow—October 29, 1937*

Litvinov came to luncheon.

When the suggestion was made of sending the Russian
ballet to the New York World's Fair he replied jokingly that
they were very beautiful and attractive and might fall in love
in New York and not come back to Moscow. Seriously, he said
that it would probably interfere with the schedule of the
opera and ballet to such a degree that would probably be im-
practical. He suggested, why not the Red Army Male Chorus
—I hope we can get this done. They sing magnificently.

RUSSIAN NATIONALISM IN FILMS

EXCERPT FROM A LETTER TO MRS. DAVIES   *October 30, 1937*

The ever-helpful Bender at my request had arranged for
us to see a showing of the new Soviet film *Peter the Great.*

Litvinov and Barkov received us. They also had the Italian Ambassador, Lord and Lady Chilston, the French Ambassador and Madame Coulondre, the Norwegian Minister, and several others. We were ushered into the nice little theater with the large and comfortable chairs.* We had a two-hour showing of this very creditable motion picture. The picture was good not only from a technical point of view, but also by reason of the extraordinary settings and the acting. The actors are really great and I use that word advisedly. We must have it when you come back. It is extraordinary how they are resorting to old historical characters, even royalty, to elevate the conception of Russian nationalism.

JOURNAL   *Moscow—October 31, 1937*

The Protestant Evangelical Churches of Germany celebrated Reformation Day by the reading of a special prayer in which it was declared:

The Church of Christ is today being oppressed. . . . Belief in Christ is being reviled. . . . A new religion is being expounded that there may be no longer a place for Biblical teaching.

Poor Niemöller and the other scores of God's ministers being taken by the Gestapo! One hundred and thirty under arrest, so it is reported in the news today.

----

* This small theater for previews of Soviet films was used frequently by the Soviet Foreign Office to entertain members of the Diplomatic Corps. The furnishings were all of domestic manufacture—modernistic, rather handsome, and exceedingly comfortable. The picture was always shown in the afternoon. Tea and cakes were served with small tables adjacent to each deep comfortable chair.

RUSSIA'S REVOLUTION—TWENTY YEARS YOUNG

NO. 735   *Moscow, November 15, 1937*

TO THE HONORABLE THE SECRETARY OF STATE

CELEBRATION OF THE TWENTIETH ANNIVERSARY
OF THE SOVIET REVOLUTION

Sir:

Three days—November 6, 7, and 8, 1937—were designated by the Soviet government as national holidays for the celebration of the twentieth anniversary of the Soviet Revolution.

GENERAL PROGRAM

The outstanding events provided for by the official program were:

(*a*) A large public meeting (by invitation) held on Saturday evening, November 6, at the Bolshoi Opera House.

(*b*) A celebration in Red Square on Sunday, November 7, with a review of the Red Army units as well as marching civilian clubs by Stalin, the Secretary General of the Communist Party, and a party consisting of President Kalinin, Premier Molotov, Marshal Voroshilov, and other party leaders.

(*c*) A reception extended to the members of the Diplomatic Corps by the Foreign Office which was held at the Spiridonovka which is the formal entertainment house provided by the government for such occasions.

CELEBRATION AT THE BOLSHOI OPERA HOUSE

This meeting was scheduled to begin at 6 o'clock on Saturday afternoon. Tickets of admission for this celebration were not delivered, however, to the members of the Diplomatic Corps until late Saturday afternoon. Long before that hour the square in front of the handsome old Royal Opera House

was crowded with people. Immediately in front of the theater
there were two white, large, and beautiful statues of Stalin
and Lenin surrounded by flags and standards of the various
Constituent Republics of the U.S.S.R. with a background of
red bunting and flowers indirectly lighted. The façade of the
old opera house was similarly decorated and most effective by
reason of indirect-lighting effects with four large portraits of
Marx, Engels, Lenin, and Stalin extending across the entire
front of the theater. The interior was similarly and impres-
sively decorated. The six tiers of boxes on the horseshoe curve *
were separated by long continuous red streamers bearing
Communist slogans, all lettered in gold. The stage, which is at
least eighty feet wide, was hung with huge red plush draperies
as a background for still another white statue of Lenin, with a
large portrait of Stalin immediately back of it—all profusely
banked with flowers. A long table extended across the front of
the stage—at which were seated President Kalinin and a group
of officials of the government. In the second tier, and immediately behind Kalinin, sat Stalin, Voroshilov, and Ezhov (head
of the secret police). At the opening of the meeting there was
much enthusiasm and continuous applause.

Premier Molotov delivered an address from the speaker's
dais. It was a scholarly address. The speech lasted approximately two hours. Delivery was uninspiring but met with
frequent applause, particularly whenever the name "Stalin"
was mentioned. During the long discourse it was noted that
Stalin, Voroshilov, and Ezhov in the rear line were quite ob-,
viously whispering and joking among themselves.

Following the speech there was an intermission of thirty
minutes, and a cold buffet supper was served to the Diplo-

----

* The profuse red-banner decorations of Communist Russia against the background of this exceedingly beautiful opera house of the tsarist regime
startled me.

matic Corps in the foyer immediately back of the diplomatic
boxes.

After the intermission there was shown a Soviet motion
picture depicting Lenin and his activities for the three days
immediately prior to the overthrow of the Kerensky government. The picture was well done. Propaganda was, of course,
omnipresent. Stalin was quite obviously dragged into the picture for several "shots" apparently to establish that affectionate confidence existed between Lenin and Stalin.

The program following the movie consisted of songs, folk
dances, and so forth and lasted well along into the morning.

THE RED SQUARE CELEBRATION

All holders of the tickets were required to be in their places
by 9:30 Sunday morning. Tickets were delivered only the
night before and, in some instances, at 8 o'clock that morning.
Only heads of missions and first secretaries could secure
tickets. Practically the entire Diplomatic Corps was present
in the diplomatic box, which was immediately adjacent to the
reviewing stand on top of Lenin's Tomb, where Stalin, Kalinin, Voroshilov, Ezhov, and others stood. Immediately opposite and facing the reviewing stand in front of the Kremlin,
and at both ends of the Square also, were companies of soldiers and sailors, with standards, standing at attention. These
were probably six or seven thousand in number. The band,
of approximately six or eight hundred pieces, was impressive.
On the walls of the building facing the spectators were the
omnipresent red banners and flags with slogans. Outstanding,
among these, translated in all the languages was the slogan
"Workers of the World Unite." Promptly at 10 o'clock Voroshilov, the head of the Red Army, galloped out of the Kremlin
gate on a very beautiful horse and reviewed each unit of the
standing troops, accompanied by the head of the Moscow

Military District, Marshal Budenny, and their aides. The parade, thereafter, followed, proceeding in front of the reviewing stand, with Stalin, Molotov, Kalinin, Ezhov, Dmitrov (head of the Comintern), and Marshals Voroshilov, Egorov, and Budenny standing at attention. The various military units which passed in review are described in the attached memorandum prepared at my request by the Military Attaché, Colonel Faymonville, who is attached to this mission.

With the conclusion of the military exhibition at about 12:30, the Diplomatic Corps quite generally departed. Stalin and the leaders of the government, however, remained to carry on the review of the civilian marchers who continued to pass through the Red Square all afternoon, until dusk.

RECEPTION AT THE SPIRIDONOVKA

So far as the Diplomatic Corps was concerned, the festivities of the celebration were concluded with the reception for the Diplomatic Corps at the Spiridonovka, the official entertainment building of the government. This is a very large and rather impressive house, admirably adapted for entertaining. Like these other large houses in Moscow, it was built by a merchant prince prior to the Revolution. In the absence of the People's Commissar for Foreign Affairs, Litvinov, and his first assistant, Potemkin, at the Brussels Conference, the guests were received by Vice-Commissar Stomoniakov and his wife, and also Madame Litvinov. The entire Diplomatic Corps seemed to be present. Three quarters of an hour was devoted to a musical program, which was excellent. The outstanding feature of it was the appearance of two youthful prodigies—a girl violinist, aged 14, and a boy cellist, aged 15—both of whom had won first places at the international contest in Brussels this summer. At 12 o'clock a very sumptuous banquet was served. There was a profusion of excellent food, made the more noticeable by the exceptionally beautiful china and gold plate of the old royalist regime.

GENERAL FEATURES

No effort was spared in the attempt by the authorities to create a festive atmosphere throughout the city. For days preceding, scaffoldings were being erected and workers were engaged in placing huge flags and a profusion of red bunting with their various slogans throughout the city.

OIL PAINTINGS FOR POSTERS

Several months ago I had occasion to visit the institutes where artists, all working for the government, were engaged in their work. I found that practically all of the more noteworthy artists were employed in painting large murals for this twentieth anniversary of the Revolution, for the Red Army celebration, and for various government institutions. These paintings were evident in great profusion here. Huge lithographic mural oil paintings depicting historic scenes of the Revolution and portraits of the various government leaders were displayed attached to the sides of the buildings, and some of them were of a size of at least 30 by 20 feet. These were generally illumined at night by indirect lighting. These oil paintings were supplemented by innumerable lithographic posters, not printed but done in crayon either in colors or in black and white.

As heretofore stated, there were also large plaster statues of Lenin and Stalin both in white and in bronze. On the corner façade of one of the prominent buildings in the center of Moscow there was suspended above the street level a huge statue of Lenin attached to the side of the building and measuring at least thirty feet in height.

Shopwindows in all of the principal business streets were

profusely decorated with the ever-present red bunting and many exhibits. There was an obvious motif on one of the principal streets to feature in these exhibits the activities of the Soviet Union in the care and attention devoted to children and to the youth movement.

SPEEDING UP CONSTRUCTION

It was quite noticeable that the preparations for these holidays were characterized by a speeding up generally of the work of repairing and cleaning the streets and roads leading into the city, and a general stimulus being given to building enterprises under the course of construction so as to be finished in time to commemorate the anniversary of the Red Revolution. The large bridge, for instance, leading from Red Square in front of the Kremlin and across the Moscow River and which has been under construction for the past year, had indications of feverish activity about it prior to the Red Day celebration and work was hurried by night and by day so as to have the bridge open for the "Workers' and Peasants' Army" celebration in the Red Square on November 7.

FOOD STANDS

A feature that attracted my attention was the large number of temporary stands erected by the Food Commissariat in the center of the city for the serving of sandwiches, drinks, et cetera. The food looked attractive, clean, and was well exhibited. There was also a large number of small refreshment automobile vans similar to the ice-cream-cone vendor type found in the cities of the United States.

EXCEPTIONAL AND SIGNIFICANT FEATURES

The unusual features which attracted my attention and which were the particular subjects of notice among members

of the Diplomatic Corps who had seen previous celebrations
of the kind, it occurs to me, might be of value to the Department.

ABSENCE OF SLOGANS ATTACKING CAPITALISTIC NATIONS

It was noted particularly that there was a marked difference
in this celebration as contrasted to that of last year in the
absence of slogans, transparencies, and picturizations assail-
ing capitalistic countries and the Fascist enemies. Personally
I noticed only three caricatures aimed at Germany.

EXECUTIVE ABILITY AND ORGANIZATION

What made a distinct impression upon me among other
things was the fact that these events gave indications of a
high degree of executive ability. They were well planned and
were carried through on the minute with the most exact dispatch. The formal occasions also were very well done with
impressive dignity and precision.

RED SQUARE MILITARY DISPLAY

The show which the naval and military forces put on was
distinctly impressive. The equipment, the man power, and
the officers of these various outfits appeared to be first class.
The mechanized units—tanks, mounted machine guns, and
artillery—which shot across Red Square at a high rate of speed
were exceptionally impressive.

The general report of the military attachés, as I understand
from Colonel Faymonville, is to the effect that it was a first-
class exhibition of military strength; that nothing new had
been uncovered in contrast to the review of last May; and that
there seems to be a disposition on the part of the authorities
not to disclose unduly all they may have had. Generally speak-

ing, the military display was practically the same as that which occurred last May.

RED SQUARE CIVILIAN DEMONSTRATION

The most impressive feature of the Red Square celebration to me personally was the demonstration of the marching workers both during and after the military exhibition. Interspersed among the regular military units reviewed by Marshal Voroshilov, there were approximately several thousand civilians who marched in company formation armed with rifles but all in promiscuous civilian and none too good attire. They were called the Proletarian Rifle Division.* From 12:30 on throughout the whole afternoon, however, the entire Red Square was jammed with the civilian marching populace (workingmen's clubs) who entered the Red Square simultaneously from three converging streets. These streets were jammed for miles with the crowds which had been marching all morning and which would be marching all through the afternoon in order to pass before the reviewing stand in front of the Kremlin. Within the Square itself there was a perfect sea of standards, transparencies, banners with slogans, and small allegorical models and statues which were being carried by thousands of apparently enthusiastic marchers. It was a mixed crowd of both sexes and all ages and there were many babies and small chil-

---

* Guerrilla warfare is much featured by the Soviets. Among the many canvases painted for the Red Army by modern Soviet artists depicting the feats of arms of the Russian soldier, there is a marked preponderance having to do with the guerrilla bands, or Partisans as they are called. It indicates the extent to which the Red Army leaders relied upon this type of warfare and how successful it was in the campaigns of the Bolshevik army. They take on some of the characteristics of the minute men and "embattled farmers" of our early history. These husky-looking civilians who paraded here are doubtless typical of what the Germans are contending with and "complaining about" now as back of their lines. It is the barricade and guerrilla fighting of civil war.

dren carried on the shoulders of parents so that they might
catch a glimpse of Stalin. The enthusiasm was being constantly whipped up by martial music by the band hereinbefore referred to. There was also what appeared to be a kind
of "cheer leader" who every now and then and invisibly but
through large loud-speakers kept calling for huzzahs for the
leaders and ideals of the Revolution.

THE SECRET POLICE (NKVD: FORMERLY GPU)

A distinct impression was left of the prominence of the
secret police (People's Commissariat for Internal Affairs)
during the celebration. The Commissar, Ezhov, who is a man
of very short stature, almost a dwarf, but with a very fine
head and face, was constantly close to Stalin but quite unobtrusively.

During the military review there were probably four or five
thousand marching men of the secret police. They are, in
fact, a strictly military organization. They (both officers and
men) were noticeably exceptionally well clothed, smart, and
well drilled. Their marching was noticeably good. It was a
modified goose step. Their cavalry outfits were especially spec-
tacular and well turned out.

During the civilian demonstration in Red Square it was
very noticeable and significant that scattered through the
crowd which was jammed into this Square there were in four
long parallel lines hundreds of the blue- and green-capped
soldiers of these secret police. While ostensibly this was for
the purpose of preserving marching formation, it was obvious
that the protective purpose was also present, for in front of
the reviewing stand and along the entire square there were
lines of the green-capped secret police, the border guards.

During the course of the afternoon it is estimated that between 800,000 and 1,200,000 people marched in review before Stalin and his associates and Lenin's Tomb.

SUSPENSION OF BUSINESS

For three days during the celebration all government offices were closed and generally business was suspended. There were no deliveries of either mail or newspapers during that period.

UNDERLYING SIGNIFICANCE

The underlying significance of this twentieth-anniversary celebration of the Red Revolution should not be discounted. The fact is important that this regime has persisted for a period of twenty years. Its importance is illumined by the expressions of joy which Lenin was reputed to have given when the first ninety days of the Soviet Revolution had elapsed, that their Revolution had at least outlasted the Paris commune.

Despite the admitted great strengths economically, politically, and from a military point of view of this regime, there are many indications that the evolution of this revolution is following the traditional and accepted lines which human nature has a manner of injecting into revolutions. The tempo in the development of the revolution here is slower; but the yeast appears to be working, just the same.

Barring a European war, assassination, or similar accident, it is the consensus here that the army is loyal, that the agencies of propaganda are working efficiently, that the party functionaries are either fanatic or cowed by the secret police, and that this government, by reason thereof, is at least for the time being firmly entrenched and strong.

I have the honor to be, Sir, respectfully yours,

Joseph E. Davies

DIARY   *Moscow—November 8, 1937*

Albert Rhys Williams, author of *Soviet Russia,* came to lunch. He was full of interesting information concerning his two months' trip into the interior and told an interesting story about his lunch with Kalinin, President of the U.S.S.R., and his mother in the provinces. Mother and son ate out of a a common dish because Kalinin didn't want his mother to think he had become "stuck up." When Williams commented on the numerous icons on the wall, Kalinin replied that he didn't think they did him any harm and that they had served a good purpose for his fathers before him and he didn't "mind" them. This indicates that Soviet official antireligious sentiment may be only "skin-deep." I saw several indications of this character. It is pretty hard to kill the faith which came at the mother's knee.

JOURNAL   *Moscow—November 12, 1937*

I had an hour's conference with one of my diplomatic colleagues who is thoroughly familiar with the Far Eastern situation. His viewpoint in brief was that the situation so far as the Brussels Conference was concerned looked hopeless; but he still clung to the hope that Great Britain, France, and the United States might work something out along an acceptable line. If they failed, he felt that the Chinese would stage a long war of the guerrilla type. He stated that short of actual participation in military operations, the Chinese government has received every possible help that they could expect from Soviet Russia.

"LITVINOV WAS EXCEEDINGLY PESSIMISTIC"

NO. 708 *Moscow, November 9, 1937*

TO THE HONORABLE THE SECRETARY OF STATE

CONVERSATION WITH COMMISSAR FOR FOREIGN
AFFAIRS LITVINOV IMMEDIATELY PRIOR TO
HIS DEPARTURE FOR THE BRUSSELS CONFERENCE

· *Strictly Confidential*

Sir:

The Commissar for Foreign Affairs, Litvinov, asked me to come out to his *dacha*, or country place, for luncheon on Saturday, the day preceding his departure for the Brussels Conference. We had an opportunity to have a long confidential talk, covering approximately an hour and a half. Litvinov advised that he did not plan to remain in Brussels for the entire conference.* He is being accompanied by Potemkin, the Vice-Commissar for Foreign Affairs. The latter has been associated with Litvinov at the Geneva conferences for many years and has until recently been Ambassador at Paris.

Litvinov was exceedingly pessimistic as to the outcome of the Brussels Conference. He stated that he was definitely leaving to attend on the following afternoon. ·

With reference to the possible peace which China might be able to accept, he expressed the opinion very positively that China would not consider any peace through mediation that involved the relinquishment of her northern provinces to Japan. In reply to my rejoinder as to what other alternative China might be called upon to face in such a situation, he stated that China could well "carry on" with a guerrilla warfare and that in this character of military activity the question of supplies was not so serious. Despite the blockade and

---

* To discuss the Far Eastern situation with reference to the Nine-Power Treaty of Washington, 1922.

even the possible cutting off of shipments overland via the
Indo-China route, he was of the opinion that sufficient supplies for guerrilla warfare would be available to the Chinese
forces. The impression which he very distinctly conveyed was
that these supplies could go forward from the Soviet Union—
possibly through Mongolia.

With reference to Germany's refusal to attend the Brussels
Conference—word as to which he had just received—he stated
that sometime ago, according to his information, Germany
submitted the question to the Japanese Foreign Office as to
whether Germany should or should not participate and that
Hirota had replied in the negative. He stated further that
Japan had given her friends to understand that she did not
wish that any of them should seem to countenance the implied
violation of the Washington Treaty by attendance at the Conference. Subsequent thereto he stated that the Japanese ambassadors in western Europe urged upon their Foreign Office
that Germany should be advised to attend but that again
Hirota refused.

With reference to Italy, the Japanese Foreign Office took
the position that it was not of such serious consequence and
that it had no objection to Italy's presence; and that this, in
Litvinov's opinion, was because of a desire to have some ally
who could report from the inside as to the developments in
the course of the discussions.

Litvinov also stated that sometime before the Brussels Conference was called, the British Foreign Office had been approached by Japan soliciting their action looking to mediation; and that the British Foreign Office was greatly disappointed when Japan refused to attend and had brought every
possible pressure to bear to cause Japan to co-operate in the
hope that the proposed mediation might be considered and
negotiated there without further delay.

Despite Germany's attitude with reference to participation in the Conference, he stated that there was a great deal of conflict with reference to China in Germany between the financial and commercial circles and the political obligations of the German government.

In connection with Count von Ribbentrop's visit to Rome, I asked whether he had any information with reference to whether or not Italy had been brought into the present Japanese-German Anti-Communist Pact. He stated positively that Italy had joined Germany and Japan in this situation. In reply to my inquiry as to whether in his opinion this amounted to a definite offensive and defensive military alliance between the powers, he stated that there was no necessity for a formal declaration of commitments of a military character as between these parties because of modern conditions under which wars occurred, without formalities of declaration thereof.

In the course of our talk I obtained a very definite impression as to the attitude of the Soviet government with reference to being associated with or a part of the group of western European powers in these various diplomatic activities that are going on. He outlined at considerable length the attitude of the Soviet Union in the Nonintervention Committee and stated that Ambassador Maisky in London had taken the position that the Soviet Union could not assume any responsibility in connection with the British-French plan, but that nevertheless because it did not wish to embarrass the possibility of results in the projection of peace, therefore, it would not vote against the plan but would simply abstain from voting. Italy, he stated, had refused to accept that attitude. Thereafter, he stated that the French and British Ambassadors had conferred with him here and had strongly urged that the Soviet government should change its position on this subject and "go along with them." Both France and England had urgently pressed upon his government that it should co-operate in this situation, as to do otherwise would place the Soviet Union before the world as a nation that was blocking the possibility of peace and that such action would neces-sarily "isolate the Soviet Union." His reply to them, he said, was that it would be better to be isolated and to be right than to be wrong in good company and foolish as well. He then went on to add that the Soviet Union was definitely prepared to be "isolated" and was quite prepared for this contingency. This confirms a statement which was made to me last July, and which I reported to the Department at that time, which was made by a high official of the government, indicating the indifference of the Soviet Union to the attitude of outside gov-ernments and even to the attitude of Great Britain and France, and that the governing powers here had definitely decided to proceed along the lines of policy which they had deter-mined upon and quite independently, if necessary, confident of their ability to withstand enemies either on the west or the east. In reply to my inquiry as to whether the instructions to Maisky would hold and that the policy as heretofore out-lined would persist, he stated positively that the policy would stand. He denied to me that the Soviet government, as re-ported, had in fact withdrawn the support of its financial contribution to the expense of maintaining the Noninterven-tion Committee.

In the course of the conversation I asked him the direct question as to whether the government felt positive that it could rely upon the support and loyalty of the Red Army in the face of the present purge and particularly because of the shooting of the Red Army generals last June. His reply was: "The army is devoted to the principles of 'the cause'; and its loyalty is unquestionably not to the generals but to the government."

In any assessment of this government as a factor in the international situation it would, in my opinion, be a serious mistake to underestimate the strength of the government here. After many conversations with conservative members of the Diplomatic Corps and other well-informed persons here, I am of the opinion that the government has the army well in hand and, barring some accident, is firmly established. The menace of war and the possibility of attack are being propagandized insistently through all the agencies of communication. Recently a large section of the Commissariat for Heavy Industry has been placed under the direct administration of the army. It is generally believed that this has been done upon the insistence of the army, and on the ground that inasmuch as it is charged with responsibility it must be given power to make this army of the government effective. There are indications of somewhat feverish activity here in negotiations for the procurement of war materials, trucks, etc. While undoubtedly confident of its ability to defend itself against military attack from either west or east, or from both, the government is taking no chances, but is preparing vigorously for any such eventuality. From many indications the masses of the people are supremely "war conscious" and apprehensive.

I have the honor to be, Sir, respectfully yours,

Joseph E. Davies

DIARY *Moscow—November 10, 1937*

Conference with Vice-Commissar Stomoniakov of the Foreign Office—re two citizenship cases.

F———, an American citizen who worked for the oil trust, got mixed up with some troublemakers and was desired here as a material witness and was apparently given a run-around typical of bureaucracy in any country when he applied for an exit visa. They didn't place it on that ground but put him off again and again in granting the exit visa. He got roaring drunk, smacked the jaw of a Moscow policeman, and got set for a good attack of delirium tremens. Nevertheless, within 24 hours after my conference he got his visa.

G——, a naturalized American who married a Russian woman, got in trouble. We were advised last spring that they wished to deport him. Recently he was jailed and we were orally refused opportunity for Durbrow * to see him in Minsk.

When I discussed this matter with Stomoniakov he was fine. We got prompt action in this case, too. They were both tough situations so far as the equities were concerned, which I frankly admitted, but with the rights of American citizenship involved, there could be no question but what the American Embassy was entitled to prompt and affirmative action. It was gratifying to get this prompt consideration which is unique in view of the "hate campaign" which is on against all foreigners.

LITVINOV FEARS EUROPEAN WAR

NO. 722   *Moscow, November 11, 1937*

TO THE HONORABLE THE SECRETARY OF STATE

CONFERENCE WITH PEOPLE'S COMMISSAR FOR
FOREIGN AFFAIRS LITVINOV CONCERNING THE
POLICY OF THE SOVIET GOVERNMENT WITH
REFERENCE TO THE BRUSSELS CONFERENCE

Strictly Confidential

Sir:

People's Commissar for Foreign Affairs, Mr. Litvinov, returned from Geneva and after a very few days here was

* Secretary to the Embassy.

about to depart for Brussels. Upon my invitation he came up to the Embassy and had lunch alone with me. The occasion afforded an opportunity for an extended discussion not only with regard to several small matters affecting American citizenships, but also for discussions of matters with broader significances in the international situation. Litvinov stated that the Soviet Union had received an invitation to attend the Brussels Conference and that he planned to leave sometime in the near future for Brussels with Potemkin, Vice-Commissar for Foreign Affairs. He stated that it would be impossible for him to remain at Brussels, but he hoped to attend at least the opening sessions. The vital interests of the Soviet Union were less affected by the situation in the Far East, he stated, than those either of Great Britain or France, and that he had little confidence in the final outcome of the conference, due mainly to what he considered the weakness of the French and British attitude. He was extremely enthusiastic regarding the President's Chicago speech, but expressed doubt as to whether the United States would be able to bring about any practical or realistic justice to China at the conference. He then went on to add that the British and French at Geneva "had hidden behind the United States" inasmuch as they held that at present they could do nothing unless they had the assurance of the active participation of the United States, and that he suspected that in their representations to the United States they were hiding behind an alleged insecurity as to what the attitude of the Soviet Union would be. He said that the Soviet Union was already prepared to take a strong stand if it were in co-operation with France, England, and the United States; and that the Soviet Union was really seriously interested in the cessation of hostilities and in the immediate establishment of collective security and peace. He expressed the hope

to establish close contact with the American delegation upon
his arrival in Brussels.

When referring to the general European situation he was
extremely pessimistic, particularly regarding Germany,
Czechoslovakia, and Austria, which he again attributed to the
alleged weakness in policy of France and Great Britain.

I have the honor to be, Sir, respectfully yours,

Joseph E. Davies

JOURNAL   *Moscow—November 11, 1937*

Had an extended discussion of the entire Far Eastern
situation with a well-informed colleague of mine, who brought
me up to date:

The Soviet government agreed, last August, to extend to
the Chinese government a credit of 100,000,000 Chinese dollars to be used for the purchase of military supplies. Deliveries
from the Soviet Union had already far exceeded that amount.
He stated that over 400 of the best Soviet bombing and pursuit airplanes have already been shipped overland to China.
There are at least 40 Soviet instructors accompanying these
airplanes. A great many lighter supplies, including airplanes,
have been shipped overland, by air, and by caravans. He
stated that at the present time over 200 trucks were in actual
operation in caravan transport. Plans are now being worked
out for the shipment of heavy supplies, tanks, et cetera, by
oversea route, possibly via Indo-China, providing arrangements can be made for co-operation of the French government. A Chinese military mission has been here about six
weeks in connection with the purchase of military supplies
and for military training. He advised that many European
countries are furnishing military supplies to China on a part-
cash basis, and that England, France, Belgium, and Czechoslovakia had been the big suppliers. Up to a short time ago

it is understood that both Germany and Italy had been furnishing war supplies on a similar basis. Italian sales were made purely on Italian initiative and provided for 50% credit * and payment contingent upon safe delivery of the supplies in China. He added that possibly the German and Italian situation may have changed during the last ten days.

The Soviet Ambassador to China, Bogomolov, arrived in Moscow on October 7, after a nine-day flight from China via Siberia. The Soviet Military Attaché, Lapin, is also expected in Moscow in a few days. It is understood that he is also using the same route. Their visit has two purposes: (1) to work out a better route for shipment of military supplies, and (2) to attempt to urge more direct action through actual military participation. My informant has little faith in the outcome of the latter, as the Soviet government desires apparently to maintain formally correct relations with Japan.

He then added that if the Japanese successes required it the Chinese forces could withdraw gradually into the interior and thus withstand a long war, if necessary, and would be able to obtain sufficient supplies through French Indo-China to withstand such a siege.

JOURNAL   *Moscow—November 11, 1937*

I found occasion to have an extended conference again with my Far Eastern "expert."

He stated that the Soviet government here, despite urging by strong Soviet officials in the Far East and many of the army authorities here, had decided not to engage in any definite commitments with reference to a direct military treaty

---

* Apparently Italy not only solicited this business, but accepted 50% cash payment and made payment of the balance contingent upon safe arrival and delivery of the goods.

with the Chinese government at the present time. Bogomolov, he stated, is still in the Soviet Union and in Leningrad,
and it is understood that he will not return to China nor will
he receive final instructions until the conclusion of the Brussels Conference. He stated also that France was using its
position here to deter any project of direct aid by the Soviet
Union because France would prefer that its ally should reserve its powers against a possible German attack and should
not deplete its energies by a war in the Far East.

He stated further that China was having serious difficulty
in connection with shipments of military supplies through
French Indo-China. This, he stated, was because of fear on
the part of the French government of becoming involved.
Such shipments as were made via this route were required
by shipping restrictions to be split up in different cargoes and
mixed with noncontraband shipments. This, he stated, involved much delay, extra handling, and reassembling upon
arrival. He stated that these conditions were made necessary
to keep down the possible risk of loss of entire shipments
through the loss of one cargo and also because of apprehension on the part of the French government that it might become involved through the shipment of military supplies
through French channels. He stated that both France and the
Soviet Union were reluctant to become committed in the
situation without assurances of the support of the Great
Powers.

China, he stated, could make an extremely strong defense
for an almost indefinite period were it provided with adequate
military supplies. The difficulty lies not in the procuring of
supplies, but in their transport.

Germany, he stated, is not unfavorable to China. Despite
formal objections raised by the Japanese government to the
presence of a large number of German military instructors in

China, the German government refused to require their return, on the ground that their employment was a matter of private enterprise.

England's alleged premature statement prior to the Brussels Conference that sanctions would not be invoked aroused deep disappointment in China. On the other hand he thought that China was deeply grateful for the moral support which it found in President Roosevelt's Chicago speech.

NO. 726   *Moscow, November 11, 1937*

TO THE HONORABLE THE SECRETARY OF STATE

DEPARTURE OF JAPANESE AMBASSADOR IN MOSCOW TO BERLIN

Strictly Confidential

Sir:

The Japanese Ambassador left Moscow on Wednesday, October 20, for Berlin, where it is reported he is to undergo medical treatment, but it is conjectured that his purpose is to confer with the German Foreign Office with reference to the Brussels Conference.

I have the honor to be, Sir, respectfully yours,

Joseph E. Davies

Moscow, November 13, 1937

EXCERPT FROM A LETTER TO MRS. WALKER

Last night Colonel Faymonville took us all to the opera for the ballet. The music was by a Russian composer as was the scenario. There was more pantomime than dancing, but the stage setting and picturization were superb. It was called *Flames of the Revolution* and was a story of the worker and peasant triumph over the old regime. It is the ballet, you recall, which has the mob in storming the Tuileries, rushing violently forward to the orchestra pit, with all their weapons, clubs, etc., brandishing with menace. The dramatic impulse is realistic in the extreme and a terrifying object lesson on what mobs can do once the corsage of society—law and order —is destroyed.

In these respects I do not think any place in the world could afford anything equal to the ballet we saw last night.

Moscow, November 16, 1937

EXCERPT FROM REPORT NO. 737 TO THE SECRETARY OF STATE

During the last few weeks, literally hundreds of executions have been reported in the provincial press on charges varying from sabotage to terrorism. At the same time, such prominent Soviet officials as Bubnov, Lyubimov, Rukhimovich, Veitser, Karp, Orlov, et cetera, have been dismissed from their positions and presumably arrested.

Although there are no exact figures on the subject, it is believed by most competent observers that the number of party and government employees executed since the beginning of the present purge runs into the thousands, and arrests into the tens of thousands.* The purge has affected all phases of Soviet life, including former stalwart supporters of the Bolshevik regime. For example, it is known that over 40 members or alternate members of the Central Committee of the Party, 9 former members of the Politburo, 18 former People's Commissars, 50 Assistant People's Commissars, 16 ambassadors or ministers, and the majority of the Presidents of the Soviet of People's Commissars of the Constituent Republics have been arrested.

----

* Relatively few of the trials were reported in the Moscow press. The American newsmen, however, kept track by obtaining local papers and translating them. They kept a "box score" by weeks on the "purge."

NO. 739   *Moscow, November 16, 1937*

TO THE HONORABLE THE SECRETARY OF STATE

VIEWS EXPRESSED BY THE ——— MINISTER IN MOSCOW
CONCERNING THE BRUSSELS CONFERENCE AND
THE GENERAL EUROPEAN SITUATION

Strictly Confidential

Sir:

I have the honor to report that I recently had an extended discussion with the ——— Minister. He expressed his views as follows:

The Soviet Union has definitely determined, at least for the present, not to become involved in active military participation, but it would aid China to the extent that it could and still maintain a correct diplomatic position vis-à-vis Japan.

So far as Austria was concerned, it was a foregone conclusion that Italy's watch on the Brenner Pass passed out of the picture, when she embarked on her Abyssinian and Mediterranean adventures, and that Germany, so far as Italy was concerned, had more or less of a free hand with reference to Austria; that, in his opinion, everything depended upon Schuschnigg's capacity to resist. In the event that Germany should desire Austria, Czechoslovakia would not be vitally affected, except that it would probably bring closer support from the other Great Powers (France and England) as a matter of self-interest.

While Rumania appreciated the danger from German encroachment toward the Black Sea, nevertheless their position was somewhat different from Czechoslovakia and they were less concerned.

Internal conditions in Germany financially were bad as

illustrated by Schacht's resignation but that in his opinion
they could get along for several years, two or three at least.

I have the honor to be, Sir, respectfully yours,

Joseph E. Davies

DIARY   *Moscow—November 17, 1937*

The Czech Minister came to lunch. In the afternoon an
amusing incident occurred when I took a drive in the country. The car got stalled in the snow turning around in a field
adjacent to the woods, so our inseparable Gay-Pay-Oo boys
brought us back in their Ford car.

The heavy snowfall made the forest and thicket mar-
velously beautiful. The branches even to the tips seemed none
less than two inches thick and the boughs of the trees were
weighed almost to the ground by the snow. I can now understand Shishkin's snow scenes. I thought they had been overdrawn.

DIARY   *Moscow—November 20, 1937*

Tea and movies, *Midsummer Night's Dream*, at 4 to
8 for the Diplomatic Corps. British, Afghan, German, Austrian, Belgian, Bulgarian, Italian, Japanese, Polish, and Turkish. Litvinov came and brought his three children, a son and
two daughters (one adopted) all of whom speak English
charmingly.

DIARY   *Moscow—November 21, 1937*

Worked on dispatches and cleaned up my desk in preparation for leaving to report to Washington.

DIARY   *Moscow—November 23, 1937*

Cable came in this morning from the Department, advising that the President had decided that it was advisable to

send a career man to Berlin, in view of changed conditions, and that Gibson, of Brussels, was to be sent to Germany. The President wanted me to go to Brussels as it was the "listening post" of Europe. That is a relief. I will get all the details when I get back to Washington next month. It has been clear now for weeks that Hitler's course is definitely set. It is important that the right kind of career man should go to Berlin. If Gibson should not go because of his severe public criticisms of Germany in the last war, I hope it will not be either an admirer or a "condoner" of the Nazis.

GERMAN SPIES CONVICTED

JOURNAL   *Moscow—November 23, 1937*

A military court at Leningrad sentenced to 25 years' imprisonment two Germans convicted of espionage on behalf of the German Secret Service.

DIARY   *New York—December 7, 1937*

Arrived in New York, and went to Washington immediately.

DIARY   *Washington—December 8, 1937*

Immediately upon my arrival in Washington, I had an appointment with the President and again lunched with him at his office. He said that he was sure that I understood his reason for changing the plan with reference to going to Belgium, instead of Berlin. It was perfectly clear there was no possibility of doing anything to divert the forces in Germany which, under Hitler's concepts of world domination and conquest, were driving inevitably to war. The last talk I had with Schacht in June was convincing that there was no hope of composing the situation. Under these conditions he wished the Berlin appointment to be distinctly formal for conventional representation only. A career appointment would be one that would have no special political significance as a manifestation of the particular interest of this government. The President said that he wanted me to go to Belgium. It was one of the most important missions in Europe, as it was probably the best "listening post" over there. I said that I was very glad to fill any position where he thought I would be of best service to him. As a matter of fact, frankly it was a relief not to be going to Berlin, and we were delighted to go to Belgium. Furthermore, Belgium was neutral; was on the direct route from London to Berlin in Europe, and would afford an interesting post to get an unbiased perceptive and the truth of the situation, without color or bias of local government interest or prejudice.

We discussed the Brussels Conference and other phases of the European situation. He gave me personal messages to King Leopold, whom he knew both as a young boy and also later when he was here with King Albert during the World War. Characteristic of that warmth which draws men to him, and for which he is famous, the President said, "Here is a little note which please give to the King." Then he wrote on a White House card "Dear Joe: Give my regards to the King. Signed— F.D.R."

I told him that upon my return to Russia, prior to going to Belgium, I proposed to make a trip into the other industrial regions, in order to round out my report on Russia. He said "that was fine" and was characteristic thoroughness. Upon leaving Russia, I told him I felt that our relations between the two countries were better than they had been for some time; and that I would leave a final report in the nature of a "Brief on the Facts," assessing the weaknesses and the strength of the Soviet Union, and its significance in world affairs, and particu-

larly its significance with reference to its relations with the
United States from such observations and studies on the
ground as I had been able to make.

EXECUTION OF BARON STEIGER

DIARY   *Washington—December 19, 1937*

News from Moscow is that the trial and execution for
high treason, terrorism, and espionage of eight officials were
officially announced, including Karakhan, Yenukidze, Zuker-
man, and Steiger.

Poor Steiger. He represented the Bureau of Cultural Relations or something of that sort. He was, in fact, a sort of liaison
man, apart from the Foreign Office, between the Kremlin and
the Diplomatic Corps. He invited some of the party to the
opera for a special performance and thereafter took us to the
"night club" at the Metropole Hotel. Shortly after one o'clock
he was tapped on the shoulder, left the table, did not return,
and was never seen thereafter. He was of an original German
prominent Ukrainian family. He was known as "Baron"
Steiger and was a charming fellow.*

CONDEMNATION BY HIS HOLINESS THE POPE
OF NAZI RELIGIOUS PERSECUTION

JOURNAL   *Washington—December 24, 1937*

According to the newspapers, His Holiness the Pope,
in an address to Cardinals and heads of the Church, said he
wished to establish, first, a fact and, secondly, a principle. The

---

* *See* Diary, February 19, 1937; *also see* Report No. 76, February 19, 1937.
Later in the Bukharin trial, Grinko, the former Secretary of the Treasury, a
native of the Ukraine, testified at great length as to the plans which were
made to aid the Germans in an invasion of the Ukraine. Steiger apparently
was implicated.

fact was that "grievous and sore" religious persecution existed in Germany, and "not often before has there been persecution so heavy, so formidable, so grievous, and so sad in its more profound effects." What a travesty on civilization that on the eve of the birthday of the Saviour of men, the head of the Church of Rome should find it necessary to indict a government for religious persecution in Germany!

PART V

THE PURGE HITS BUKHARIN

January 15—March 17, 1938

V

JOURNAL   *Moscow—January 15, 1938*

Apparently the Kremlin was really scared last summer and still remains so.

A joint session of the two Councils adopted unanimously an amendment to the constitution giving the Presidium (the supreme executive authority) power to declare martial law throughout the country wherever and whenever Soviet territory was threatened by any external foe.

JOURNAL   *Moscow—January 19, 1938*

The Soviets are certainly "spy conscious." M. Molotov publicly denounced certain foreign consulates, "engaged in hostile anti-Soviet spying activities on Soviet territory," and warned Japan that the Soviets would "end Japanese hooliganism on the Far Eastern frontier."

SOVIET OFFICIALS CHARGED WITH TREASON

JOURNAL   *Moscow—February 27, 1938*

Twenty-one prominent men are to be tried for treason, including Bukharin, Rykov, Rakovsky, Grinko, Krestinsky, Rosengoltz, Yagoda, Chernov, and Ivanov, according to announcement by State's Attorney.

Organizing espionage, etc., on behalf of foreign states, to provoke war in order to dismember the Union, and deliver up the Ukraine, White Russia, Turkestan, the Caucasus, and the Far Eastern Maritime Province to enemy countries, being in the pay of foreign states, are the principal charges named.

LITVINOV ON CONFESSIONS

Diary   *Moscow—March 4, 1938*

Litvinov and his daughter came in for the movies at 5:30.

He said he was much shocked by Krestinsky's arrest. He could not understand why men would confess to crimes that they must know were punishable by death unless they were really guilty. He said that Rykov and Bukharin last summer, when haled before the Central Committee of the party and when confronted by Sokolnikov and Radek, faced them down and bitterly protested their innocence even when they broke down in tears; but that apparently they were in fact guilty as subsequently they made complete confessions. He said he could not understand their final confessions, knowing them as he did, on any other theory than that they were actually guilty. "A man could die only once," said he, and these men knew that they would surely be condemned to death after such solemn admissions of their guilt. It was regrettable but the government had to be certain and could take no chances. It was, he said, fortunate that the country had a leadership strong enough to take the necessary protective measures.

UNITED STATES RECEIVES "THE HIGHEST CONSIDERATION"

NO. 1007   *Moscow, March 4, 1938*

TO THE HONORABLE THE SECRETARY OF STATE

CONFERENCE WITH THE PEOPLE'S COMMISSAR
FOR FOREIGN AFFAIRS, LITVINOV, ON MARCH 3, 1938

Strictly Confidential

Sir:

I beg leave to report that on March 3, I had an extended conference with People's Commissar for Foreign Affairs Litvinov at the Foreign Office.

At this meeting I first presented congratulations upon the successful achievement of the Papanin scientific expedition to the North Pole and the rescue of these courageous scientific Russian men. I also advised him of the fact that the President and Secretary of State had both desired that I should return from my visit to the United States to the Soviet Union prior to my transfer to Belgium, in order that I might finish my reports and work here and then take proper leave of the authorities here, upon my official departure. Commissar Litvinov expressed thanks for the congratulations upon the achievement of the North Pole scientists. He was also gracious in his expressions of regret that I was being transferred. He asked particularly after President Roosevelt's health, expressed gratification that he was so well, and again expressed great admiration for the work he was doing for the democratic ideals and peace. He also expressed great admiration for the trade-treaty program which Secretary Hull is projecting with such "ability and distinction."

He then stated that he had been much perturbed by reports from Ambassador Troyanovsky to the effect that the Depart-

ment of State had considered that the diplomatic mission
here had not received proper consideration from this government. He stated that he had been so much concerned that he
had himself studied the memorandum which Ambassador
Troyanovsky had received at the Department; that after careful study of the memorandum he had reached the conclusion
that with the exception of the debt question, practically all
the other matters were either trivial or matters that had
already been disposed of to the satisfaction of the United
States. He stated that he felt particularly aggrieved by the
attitude which this situation disclosed, as it seemed a poor
return for the exceptional manner in which the Soviet Union
and his department had gone out of its way to show the highest consideration for the United States. He stated that the fact
was, as he had stated to me (and which he assumed I had
transmitted to the Department), that the Soviet Union had
done and was disposed to do more for the United States than
for any other country. In elaborating upon the point he called
attention to the fact that more adverse publicity and acclaim
had been given to the detention of one American citizen than
had been given to hundreds of Germans and prisoners of other
nationalities who had been detained and who, after months
of imprisonment, still had not been interviewed by the diplomatic representatives of their country.* He stated that he
could not understand why this publicity should have been
projected or why the matter should have been handled in the
way it was so as to have induced this publicity in view of the
fact that within the last six months he had in two cases secured
immediate relief in similar cases upon my taking the matters
up with him in an informal manner. He emphasized that in the

* Arising out of the Rubens case—which occurred during my absence. As
soon as I learned of it, I took the matter up with the Secretary and also with
Ambassador Troyanovsky and succeeded in getting it smoothed out.

LITVINOV'S "DACHA" (COUNTRY ESTATE)

Front Row (seated) left to right: Miss Litvinov, Mrs. Davies, Miss Litvinov. Second Row (standing) left to right: Mrs. Rahel Walker, Foreign Commissar Litvinov, Chief of Protocol Barkov, Ambassador Davies.

H——— case he had immediately complied with my request
that H———, who was under arrest, should be permitted to
be interviewed by the American diplomatic officers. He also
referred to the P——— case and recalled that here too, under
a serious situation, where P——— was not granted a visa because he was needed as a material witness, he was still permitted to depart, upon my representation, despite the fact that
P——— had made a serious physical assault upon a Soviet
official here. In view of these two recent instances, where all
that was necessary to be done was to call the matter informally
to his attention, that they should receive prompt action, he
found it difficult to account for what had happened.

He called attention to the exceptional conditions that confronted his government and that it felt compelled to arrest
hundreds of Germans and other nationals, and to deny them
access to their diplomatic officials, and indicated the exceptional contrast this afforded to the attitude toward the United
States, which had been demonstrated within recent months.
He stated that in view of these facts he regretted matters
should have developed as they had. To this I rejoined along
the lines of the general situation.

Commissar Litvinov then changed the subject by saying:
"Well, let's discuss not trivial matters but larger issues," and
he inquired as to the effect of the President's speech at Chicago and the status of public opinion in the United States
with reference to the policy of isolation. In reply to his question, I stated it to be my opinion that events in England in
the parliamentary Eden-Chamberlain crisis had, at least for
the present, intensified the isolationist feeling in the United
States.

Regarding the general European situation, Litvinov expressed the opinion that Hitler and Mussolini had Chamberlain on the spot; that Chamberlain would be required to make

good before his public by effecting some sort of arrangement; that the dictators would either drive a hard bargain with him so as to make it impossible, or Chamberlain would be required to make a paper peace that would really amount to nothing more than a sham for home consumption.

I have the honor to be, Sir, respectfully yours,

Joseph E. Davies

OPENING SESSION OF BUKHARIN-RYKOV TRIAL

DIARY   *Moscow—March 2, 1938*

The treason trial of the "rightists"—Bukharin-Rykov and group—opened at the former Hall of the Nobles, now the House of Trade Unions. Each mission was confined to one ticket of admission, so I had to go to the trial without an interpreter. Seated immediately in front of the American press section, I was dependent on their translator, and their help in following the testimony. Fortunately Colonel Koznic, the Estonian Minister, who speaks English perfectly, sat next to me and gave me whispered translations. He served in the Tsarist army and was educated in Petrograd as a young man. It was difficult to look upon the prisoners in the box without shrinking. There was Krestinsky, Undersecretary of State, to whom I had presented my credentials a year ago; Rosengoltz, former Commissar of Trade, with whom I had lunched just a year ago this month at his country home; Dr. Pletnov, the heart specialist who had treated me professionally, and whom I knew quite well, and Grinko, the Secretary of the Treasury. There these men sat not more than ten feet from me in the prisoner's box. I hope they saw in my eyes the sorrow which I felt in seeing them again under these conditions. (See Journal entries.)

DIARY   *Moscow—March 3, 1938*

Lunched with Litvinov at his *dacha*. Report on discussions between us sent on to the Department (see dispatch.)

PURGE CONDITIONS IN MOSCOW

NO. 1011   *Moscow, March 6, 1938*

TO THE HONORABLE THE SECRETARY OF STATE

TRANSMITTING MEMORANDUM OF A
CONVERSATION WITH THE ————— AMBASSADOR

Confidential

Sir:

I have the honor to transmit herewith a memorandum reporting a conversation which I had with the Ambassador of ————— today, March 6, 1938.

He said:

That conditions are worse here now than at any time during his five-year tenure in Moscow, viz., the purge and the imprisonment of so many members of the Communist Party;

That the Soviet regime definitely had determined upon a policy of complete isolation so far as other nations are concerned.

Commenting on world conditions, he spoke feelingly of the fact that the United States government is the greatest gift of "nature or God" (as he expressed it) to the world, because of the protection it accords to freedom of religion, safety for individual and property rights, and guaranties of personal liberty.

I have the honor to be, Sir, respectfully yours,

Joseph E. Davies

DIARY   *Moscow—March 8, 1938*

Again went to Bukharin trial, which I have been attending daily since it started a week ago.

Dr. Levin testified relative to coercion by Yagoda, chief of secret police, compelling him and associates to "cure to death" Maxim Gorky and his son and others, as a part of the plot to discredit the Kremlin. It was a gruesome and bizarre tale.

Beneath it runs the tale that Yagoda, one of the defendants, was infatuated with young Gorky's beautiful wife and that Gorky Senior had aroused Yagoda's enmity because of his interposition in that triangle. Yagoda, it was said, feared the elder Gorky because of his great popularity with the Russian people. That was in part the motive, it was alleged, for Yagoda's action in blackmailing these physicians into a conspiracy to "cure to death" Gorky Senior (who was suffering from tuberculosis) by prescribing treatment which would kill instead of cure.*

JOURNAL   *Moscow—March 8, 1938*

Reynaud in Paris commented on the Russian trials. This trial situation, he said, was a disturbing factor when considered in connection with the difficulties of preserving peace in Europe; although, he continued, it could not be doubted that the enormous resources of that country (Soviet Union) in man power and raw materials were a factor for peace, because it was a factor in the balance of power.

This is one of the very serious effects of these trials. From

---

* Yagoda, in a later confession in open court, when he touched upon this phase, requested permission to give his testimony on these personal matters before the court sitting in secret session. So, as a matter of record, there was strictly no confirmation to these rumors but it is generally accepted here as true.

the point of view of European peace, it is too bad as it discounts the real strength of this government as a reliable factor against Hitler.

BUKHARIN TREASON TRIAL

March 8, 1938

Dear "Bijou": *

For the last week, I have been attending daily sessions of the Bukharin treason trial. No doubt you have been following it in the press. It is terrific. I have found it of much intellectual interest, because it brings back into play all the old critical faculties involved in assessing the credibility of witnesses and sifting the wheat from the chaff—the truth from the false—which I was called upon to use for so many years in the trial of cases, myself.

All the fundamental weaknesses and vices of human nature —personal ambitions at their worst—are shown up in the proceedings. They disclose the outlines of a plot which came very near to being successful in bringing about the overthrow of this government.

This testimony now makes clear what we could not understand and what happened last spring and summer. You will recall that the folks at the chancery were telling us of extraordinary activity around the Kremlin, when the gates were closed to the public; that there were indications of much agitation and a changing of the character of the soldiers on guard. The new guards, you will remember we were told, consisted almost entirely of soldiers recruited from Georgia, Stalin's native land.

The extraordinary testimony of Krestinsky, Bukharin, and the rest would appear to indicate that the Kremlin's fears

---

* My daughter Emlen—now Mrs. Robert Grosjean.

were well justified. For it now seems that a plot existed in the beginning of November, 1936, to project a *coup d'état,* with Tukhatchevsky at its head, for May of the following year. Apparently it was touch and go at that time whether it actually would be staged.

But the government acted with great vigor and speed. The Red Army generals were shot and the whole party organization was purged and thoroughly cleansed. Then it came out that quite a few of those at the top were seriously infected with the virus of the conspiracy to overthrow the government, and were actually working with the Secret Service organizations of Germany and Japan.

The situation explains the present official attitude of hostility toward foreigners, the closing of various foreign consulates in this country, and the like. Quite frankly, we can't blame the powers-that-be much for reacting in this way if they believed what is now being divulged at the trial.

Again, it should be remembered that it cannot be conclusively assumed because these facts were adduced through statements of confessed criminals that they were therefore untrue.

I must stop now as the trial reconvenes at 11 A.M. and I'll have to run.

                                                        Hastily,

---

DIARY   *Moscow—March 12, 1938*

Went to the trial. The "last words" of Pletnov, Rosengoltz, and other defendants were harrowing in their interest and tragedy. Rosengoltz particularly so. It was only a year ago that we were at his country home for the day with Grinko, Krestinsky, the prosecutor Vyshinsky, Judge Ulrich, Mikoyan, Rosoff, and Voroshilov at dinner. I then made no impression upon some of them in stressing the dangers of foreign war as an inducement for them to pay their debt to us. The defendants in this trial, including some of these men, according to their statements wanted war! Not so Voroshilov and some of the others. He was then, a year ago, strong for the debt payment to the U. S.

SO-CALLED BUKHARIN MASS TREASON TRIAL

NO. 1039   *Moscow, March 17, 1938*

TO THE HONORABLE THE SECRETARY OF STATE

Confidential

Sir:

I have the honor to report that this confirms cable sent in confidential code with reference to the judgment of the court in the so-called Bukharin mass treason trial.

Paraphrase of the cable is as follows:

On March 13, 1938, at approximately five o'clock in the morning, all of the defendants in the trial were adjudged guilty and the sentences were imposed. Three of the defendants were condemned to imprisonment and the remainder to death through shooting. Eight of the most prominent former members of the Soviet government, including a former premier, six former cabinet officers, one of the most prominent party leaders and member of the Politburo, and also a former president of one of the constituent republics were among those condemned to be shot. Condemned to imprisonment were a former Ambassador to England and France, a former Counselor of the Soviet Embassy in Berlin, and one famous heart specialist.

Notwithstanding a prejudice arising from the confession evidence and a prejudice against a judicial system which affords practically no protection for the accused, after daily observation of the witnesses, their manner of testifying, the unconscious corroborations which developed, and other facts in the course of the trial, together with others of which a judicial notice could be taken, it is my opinion so far as the political defendants are concerned sufficient crimes under Soviet law, among those charged in the indictment, were established by the proof and beyond a reasonable doubt to justify the verdict of guilty of treason and the adjudication of the punishment provided by Soviet criminal statutes. The opinion of those diplomats who attended the trial most regularly was general that the case had established the fact that there was a formidable political opposition and an exceedingly serious plot, which explained to the diplomats many of the hitherto unexplained developments of the last six months in the Soviet Union. The only difference of opinion that seemed to exist was the degree to which the plot had been implemented by different defendants and the degree to which the conspiracy had become centralized.

I have the honor to be, Sir, respectfully yours,

Joseph E. Davies

FIFTH COLUMNISTS IN RUSSIA.
A STUDY IN HINDSIGHT—1941

NOTE: Although this was written after the German invasion of Russia in the summer of 1941 it is inserted here because this seems the logical place to illustrate how the treason trials destroyed Hitler's Fifth Column in Russia.—J. E. D.

Passing through Chicago, on my way home from the June commencement of my old University, I was asked to talk to the University Club and combined Wisconsin societies. It was just three days after Hitler had invaded Russia. Someone in the audience asked: "What about Fifth Columnists in

Russia?" Off the anvil, I said: "There aren't any—they shot them."

On the train that day, that thought lingered in my mind. It was rather extraordinary, when one stopped to think of it, that in this last Nazi invasion, not a word had appeared of "inside work" back of the Russian lines. There was no so-called "internal aggression" in Russia co-operating with the German High Command. Hitler's march into Prague in 1939 was accompanied by the active military support of Henlein's organizations in Czechoslovakia. The same was true of his invasion of Norway. There were no Sudeten Henleins, no Slovakian Tisos, no Belgian De Grelles, no Norwegian Quislings in the Soviet picture.

Thinking over these things, there came a flash in my mind of a possible new significance to some of the things that happened in Russia when I was there. Upon my arrival in Washington, I hastened to reread my old diary entries and, with the permission of the State Department, went through some of my official reports.

None of us in Russia in 1937 and 1938 were thinking in terms of "Fifth Column" activities. The phrase was not current. It is comparatively recent that we have found in our language phrases descriptive of Nazi technique such as "Fifth Column" and "internal aggression."

Generally speaking, the well informed suspected such methods might be employed by Hitler; but it was one of those things which many thought just couldn't really happen. It is only within the last two years, through the Dies Committee and the F.B.I., that there have been uncovered the activities of German organizations in this country and in South America, and that we have seen the actual work of German agents operating with traitors in Norway, Czechoslovakia, and Austria,

who betrayed their country from within in co-operation with
a planned Hitler attack.

These activities and methods, apparently, existed in Russia,
as a part of the German plan against the Soviets, as long ago
as 1935.

It was in 1936 that Hitler made his now famous Nuremberg
speech, in which he clearly indicated his designs upon the
Ukraine.

The Soviet government, it now appears, was even then
acutely aware of the plans of the German high military and
political commands and of the "inside work" being done in
Russia, preparatory to German attack upon Russia.

As I ruminated over this situation, I suddenly saw the picture as I should have seen it at the time. The story had been
told in the so-called treason or purge trials of 1937 and 1938
which I had attended and listened to. In re-examining the record of these cases and also what I had written at the time
from this new angle, I found that practically every device of
German Fifth Columnist activity, as we now know it, was
disclosed and laid bare by the confessions and testimony elicited at these trials of self-confessed "Quislings" in Russia.

It was clear that the Soviet government believed that these
activities existed, was thoroughly alarmed, and had proceeded
to crush them vigorously. By 1941, when the German invasion came, they had wiped out any Fifth Column which had
been organized.

Another fact which was difficult to understand at the time,
but which takes on a new significance in view of developments, was the manner in which the Soviet government was
"bearing down" on consular agencies of Germany and Italy
in 1937 and 1938. It was done in a very highhanded manner.
There was a callous and almost brutal disregard of the sensibilities of the countries involved. The reason assigned by the

Soviet government was that these consulates were engaged upon internal, political, and subversive activities; and that because of these facts they had to be closed up. The announcements of the trials and executions (purges), all over Russia that year, invariably charged the defendants with being guilty of treasonable and subversive activity in aiding "a foreign power" to overthrow the Soviet state.

Every evening after the trial, the American newspapermen would come up to the Embassy for a "snack" and beer after these late night sessions and we would "hash" over the day's proceedings. Among these were Walter Duranty and Harold Denny of *The New York Times*, Joe Barnes and Joe Phillips of the *New York Herald Tribune*, Charlie Nutter or Dick Massock of the Associated Press, Norman Deuel and Henry Shapiro of the United Press, Jim Brown of the International News, Spencer Williams representing the *Manchester Guardian*. They were an exceptionally brilliant group of men. I came to rely upon them. They were of inestimable value to me in the appraisal and estimate of men, situations, and Soviet developments. I had myself prosecuted and defended men charged with crime in many cases in the course of my professional life. Shapiro, too, was a lawyer, a graduate of the Moscow law school. His knowledge of Soviet law was most helpful. The other men were all very familiar with Soviet conditions, personalities, and Russian psychology. We had interesting discussions, which lasted long into the night.

All of us there in Moscow at the time paid comparatively little attention to that side of these cases. Some of us seemed to have "missed the boat." I certainly did. There is no doubt but that, generally speaking, we were centering our attention on the dramatic struggle for power between the "ins" and "outs" —between Stalin and Trotsky—and the clash of personalities and policies within the Soviet government, rather than upon any possible German Fifth Column activities, which we were all disposed to discount at the time.

In my own case, I should have known better, for there were two facts which should have placed me on notice. They had come to my knowledge and were not known to the others. One of these occurred during an interview which I had shortly after my arrival in Moscow with an official of the Soviet Foreign Office; the other occurred before I reached Moscow, in the Berlin Foreign Office in January, 1937, during an interview which I had with a German Undersecretary of State.

The story which was unfolded in these trials disclosed a record of Fifth Columnist and subversive activities in Russia under a conspiracy agreement with the German and Japanese governments that were amazing. The gist of the testimony, which the record of the case discloses, is as follows:

The principal defendants had entered into a conspiracy among themselves, and into an agreement with Germany and Japan to aid these governments in a military attack upon the Soviet Union. They agreed to and actually did co-operate in plans to assassinate Stalin and Molotov, and to project a military uprising against the Kremlin which was to be led by General Tukhatchevsky, the second in command of the Red Army. In preparation for war they agreed to and actually did plan and direct the sabotaging of industries, the blowing up of chemical plants, the destruction of coal mines, the wrecking of transportation facilities, and other subversive activities. They agreed to perform and did perform all those things which the German General Staff required should be done by them pursuant to instructions which they received from such General Staff. They agreed to and in fact did conspire and co-operate with the German and Japanese Military Intelligence Services. They agreed to and in fact did co-operate with German diplomatic consular representatives in connection with espionage and sabotage. They agreed to and actually did transmit to Germany and Japan information vital to the defense of the Soviet Union. They agreed among themselves and with the German and Japanese governments to co-operate with them in war upon the Soviet government and to form an independent smaller Soviet state which would yield up large sections of the Soviet Union, the Ukraine, and White Russia in the west to Germany and the Maritime Provinces in the east to Japan.

They agreed after the German conquest of Russia that German firms were to have concessions and receive favors in connection with the development of iron ore, manganese, oil, coal, timber, and the other great resources of the Soviet Union.

To appreciate fully the character and significance of this testimony, which I personally listened to, it should be borne in mind that the facts as to this conspiracy were testified to by two cabinet members of the first order, the Commissar for the Treasury and the Commissar for Foreign Trade, by a former Premier of the government, by two Soviet Ambassadors who had served in London, Paris, and Japan; by a former Undersecretary of State and by the acting Secretary of State of the government, as well as by two of the foremost publicists and editors of the two leading papers of the Soviet Union.

To appreciate its significance, it was as though the Secretary of the Treasury Morgenthau, Secretary of Commerce Jones, Undersecretary of State Welles, Ambassador Bullitt, Ambassador Kennedy, and Secretary to the President Early, in this country, confessed to conspiracy with Germany to co-operate in an invasion of the United States.

Here are a few excerpts of the testimony in open court:

Krestinsky, Undersecretary of State, said:

We came to an agreement with General Seeckt and Hess to the effect that we would help the Reichswehr create a number of espionage bases in the territory of the U.S.S.R. . . . In return for this, the Reichswehr undertook to pay us 250,000 marks annually as a subsidy.

Grinko, Secretary of the Treasury, said:

I knew and was connected with people both in the Ukrainian organization as well as in the Red Army who were preparing to open the frontier to the enemy. I operated particularly in the Ukraine, that is to say, at the main gates through which Germany is preparing its blow against the U.S.S.R.

Rosengoltz, Secretary of Commerce, stated:

I handed various secret information to the Commander in Chief of the Reichswehr. . . . Subsequently, direct connections were established by the Ambassador in the U.S.S.R. to whom I periodically gave information of an espionage character.

Sokolnikov, former Ambassador to Great Britain, stated:

Japan, in the event of her taking part in the war, would receive territorial concessions in the Far East in the Amur region and the Maritime Provinces; as respects Germany, it was contemplated to satisfy the national interests of the Ukraine.

The testimony of many of the minor defendants went to establish the fact that upon orders of the principal defendants, they had direct connection with the German and Japanese Intelligence Services and co-operated with them in systematic espionage and sabotage; and either committed or aided and abetted in numerous crimes. For instance, Rataichak stated that he had organized and was responsible for two explosions at the Gorlovka nitrogen fertilizer plants which entailed enormous property losses as well as the loss of human life. Pushkin contributed or assumed responsibility for the disaster to the chemical plants of the Voskressensk

Chemical Works and the Nevsky plant. Knyazev told how he had planned and executed the wrecking of troop trains, entailing great loss of life, upon the express directions or instructions from foreign Intelligence Services. He also testified as to how he had received instructions from these foreign Intelligence Services "to organize incendiarism in military stores, canteens, and army shipments," and the necessity of using "bacteriological means in time of war with the object of contaminating troop trains, canteens, and army camps with virulent bacilli."

The testimony in these cases involved and incriminated General Tukhatchevsky and many high leaders in the army and in the navy. Shortly after the Radek trial these men were arrested. Under the leadership of Tukhatchevsky these men were charged with having entered into an agreement to co-operate with the German High Command in an attack upon the Soviet state. Numerous subversive activities conducted in the army were disclosed by the testimony. Many of the highest officers in the army, according to the testimony, had either been corrupted or otherwise induced to enter into this conspiracy. According to the testimony, complete co-operation had been established in each branch of the service, the political revolutionary group, the military group, and the High Commands of Germany and Japan.

Such was the story, as it was brought out in these trials, as to what had actually occurred. There can be no doubt but what the Kremlin authorities were greatly alarmed by these disclosures and the confessions of these defendants. The speed with which the government acted and the thoroughness with which they proceeded indicated that they believed them to be true. They proceeded to clean house and acted with the greatest of energy and precision. Voroshilov, Commander in Chief of the Red Army, said:

It is easier for a burglar to break into the house if he has an accomplice to let him in. We have taken care of the accomplices.

General Tukhatchevsky did not go to the coronation in London as he had planned. He was reported to have been sent down to command the army of the Volga district; but it was understood at the time that he had been removed from the train and arrested before he arrived at his command. Within a few weeks thereafter, on June 11, he, along with eleven other officers of the High Command, were shot pursuant to judgment, after a trial by military court-martial, the proceedings of which were not made public. All of these trials, purges, and liquidations, which seemed so violent at the time and shocked the world, are now quite clearly a part of a vigorous and determined effort of the Stalin government to protect itself from not only revolution from within but from attack from without. They went to work thoroughly to clean up and clean out all treasonable elements within the country. All doubts were resolved in favor of the government.

There were no Fifth Columnists in Russia in 1941—they had shot them. The purge had cleansed the country and rid it of treason.

PART VI

MOSCOW HEARS THE DRUMS OF WAR

March 14—April 1, 1938

VI

INVASION OF AUSTRIA

Diary   *Moscow—March 14, 1938*

Hitler invaded Austria day before yesterday.

Had a long talk with Litvinov and also with Minister Feir-
linger of Czechoslovakia.

On the night of Hitler's invasion of Austria, we had dined
at the Czechoslovakian Legation, and I was awakened later
in the middle of the night by his telephone call, advising that
"it had come." Hitler had marched.

During our visit, he said that he had been advised only
yesterday by his government that it had received definite
assurances from Germany that there was no intent on their
part to disturb Czechoslovakia. He said, of course, there was
nothing his government could do about it anyway; that their
position depended entirely upon what outside support they
would receive from France and England. Czechoslovakia
could do nothing alone. It looks like a Fascist European peace.

These developments are a complete corroboration of the
statements made to me by a prominent head of a Balkan state
last September and which he charged me to deliver from him
personally to the President and to the Secretary of State, and
to them only. He knew what he was talking about, apparently.

LITVINOV DISCUSSES AUSTRIA AND SHOWS CONSIDERATION FOR AMERICAN INTERESTS

TO THE HONORABLE THE SECRETARY OF STATE

MEMORANDUM OF CONFERENCE HAD BY JOSEPH E. DAVIES, AMERICAN AMBASSADOR IN MOSCOW, WITH THE PEOPLE'S COMMISSAR FOR FOREIGN AFFAIRS, M. LITVINOV, AT THE LATTER'S OFFICE ON THE 14TH DAY OF MARCH, 1938

Strictly Confidential

Pursuant to an appointment made at my request, I had an extended conference with People's Commissar for Foreign Affairs, M. Litvinov, at his office on the day and year first above written.

M. Litvinov spoke very frankly in connection with the views of this government with reference to the incorporation of Austria into the German Reich. The following paraphrase of the cable immediately sent to the Department covers the substance of the interview with reference to this subject:

During the course of a conversation which I had with Litvinov today (March 14, 1938), he told me that the situation in Europe was critically dangerous; that the People's Commissariat for Foreign Affairs had been formally advised that Austria had been incorporated in the German Reich. Litvinov further stated that he believed that, as a result of the fact that English acquiescence was indicated by the Halifax and similar conversations, the Chamberlain government was responsible for Austria's predicament; that it was his opinion that Chamberlain would find it difficult, in view of developments, to make a satisfactory arrangement with Mussolini, since Hitler had in all probability agreed to give his support to Mussolini in Spain and the Mediterranean.

Litvinov said that he believed that Czechoslovakia was secure for the present although such security was not permanent; that France because of her treaty would undoubtedly come to the aid of Czechoslovakia in case the latter should be attacked by Germany as "otherwise it would also be the end of France"; and that in such circumstances England "willy-nilly" would be obliged to enter the conflict in order to aid France. He stated, in reply to my question, that the world very likely would witness another example of German aggressiveness before the end of the year and that there was a very definite possibility of war this summer.

I was advised today by the Czechoslovak Minister in Moscow that a few days ago his government had received assurances from Germany that the latter had no hostile intent against Czechoslovakia; that military measures for immediate resistance were not being made by Czechoslovakia; and that actually this was a decision which would have to be made by England and France, not Czechoslovakia.

UNOFFICIAL REPRESENTATIONS

The undersigned then stated to M. Litvinov that he desired to take up with him unofficially three situations in which possibly there was strictly no violation of the legal rights of American citizens, but which nevertheless were possibly prejudicial to the interests of American citizens in the Soviet Union.

M. Litvinov was informed that his personal attention was being called to these situations in a friendly way in the hope that they might be relieved. These situations were the following:

(*a*) THE CASE OF SOVIET WIVES OF AMERICAN HUSBANDS DE-
SIRING TO RETURN TO THE UNITED STATES.

It was pointed out that there were a number of cases where
American citizens—engineers, professional men, and the like
—residing temporarily in the Soviet Union had married Soviet
wives and in some instances had children, and who were now
desirous of or were required to leave the Soviet Union and return to the United States, and where these American citizens
found it impossible to obtain permission from the government
for these wives and their children to leave the Soviet Union.

It was made plain that it was quite clear that under Soviet
law the government was acting strictly within its rights in
asserting its jurisdiction over Soviet citizens and preventing
their departure from the Soviet Union but that nevertheless
such a course did operate as a severe hardship upon normal
human relations and had many cruel aspects. For this reason,
I venture to ask unofficially that the Foreign Office interest
itself in the situation to see whether some relief could not be
accorded.

(*b*) THE CASE OF THE ARRESTS OF SOVIET EMPLOYEES OF THE
AMERICAN CORRESPONDENTS.

The attention of M. Litvinov was called to the fact that
during the course of the recent Bukharin treason trial, a
Soviet citizen who had been employed as a translator by
Mr. Harold Denny, chief of *The New York Times* bureau, for
the last several years and who was taking notes of the trial
proceedings, was arrested in the middle of the trial. This, he
was told, was illustrative of what had previously happened to
the secretary of Mr. Spencer Williams, head of the American-
Russian Chamber of Commerce in Moscow, as well as to the
secretary of Mr. James Brown, the International News Service

correspondent; both secretaries having been arrested. This situation, I stated, causes a great deal of inconvenience to these American interests and also raised the possible implication that these employers had been a party to some violation of Soviet law. M. Litvinov replied that while none of these cases had been specifically called to his attention, and that he did not know positively what the facts were in each case, nevertheless, he was certain that if there had been any suggestion or any implication that any of these foreign employers had been connected with the criminal activity of their secretaries, respectively, he would have known of it and that, therefore, he would give me assurances that there was no implication as against these American citizens in these cases. He stated that the services of these people as employees of these various American interests were only a part of their activities in the community and that what had happened, undoubtedly, was that, apart from their duties to their immediate employers, they were engaged in unlawful activities on the outside. He also pointed out that in such a situation no distinction could be made as between American or Soviet employers of Soviet citizens who happened to have been engaged in unlawful activities, and were, therefore, subject to arrest. He pointed out that the fact of being employed by foreign nationals could not, of course, afford any immunity to Soviet citizens if they were guilty of a violation of Soviet law. He completely exonerated Messrs. Denny, Brown, and Williams and their organizations from any implication of being a part of the alleged unlawful activities of their secretaries.

(c) THE OFFICE QUARTERS FOR THE AMERICAN-RUSSIAN CHAMBER OF COMMERCE.

Last week I was advised by Mr. Stevens, who is here in charge of the office of the American-Russian Chamber of

Commerce in Mr. Spencer Williams' absence, that notice had
been served that the Chamber would be required to vacate
the premises immediately and that he had been unable to
obtain any other quarters or any postponement of eviction
until Mr. Williams got back. I pointed out the extreme inconvenience that this involved to the Chamber of Commerce,
which represents a very responsible and influential section
of the American public opinion. M. Litvinov pointed out that
there was a tremendous shortage of space and that it was
impossible even to accord the Diplomatic Corps the space
necessary to their proper functioning. He stated, however,
that he would look into the matter and asked me to give him
details with reference to the situation.*

DIARY   *Moscow—March 15, 1938*

We all went to the opera to see the beautiful ballet
Snow Maiden. After the performance we went to the Caucasian Restaurant—the leading night club in Russia—and had
shashlik (lamb grilled on long skewers). The orchestra was
from the Caucasus, interesting and unusual, with Oriental
instruments and music.

AUSTRIAN EFFECT ON WAR PSYCHOLOGY

March 17, 1938

EXCERPT FROM A LETTER TO SENATOR MILLARD TYDINGS

Along with the rest of Europe, this country is extremely war
conscious. Enormous shipments are being sent to the Far
East. The shipments include war materials and foodstuffs.
There are many indications of shortage here in food that did
not obtain last winter, in spite of the huge crop last summer.

---

* This was subsequently satisfactorily adjusted.

There are indications that this government is going more isolationist than ever before. War is terribly close.

DIARY *Moscow—March 16, 1938*

The Czechoslovakian Minister called me on the phone to advise that Poland had served an ultimatum on Lithuania. It is an anomaly. The Polish ultimatum states that unless the Lithuanian government will immediately *resume* diplomatic relations that serious consequences will come. The world is certainly cockeyed. An ultimatum is generally accompanied with the *cutting off* of diplomatic relations, instead of a demand for the resumption of diplomatic relations.

DIARY *Moscow—March 17, 1938*

The Diplomatic Corps is excited over the Poland-Lithuania situation. It kept me busy to maintain contacts with the Lithuanian Minister and Litvinov. The aggressive action of Hitler seems to be contagious. Some of my colleagues think that there is a possible German-Polish understanding, whereby Germany will support Poland in its demands upon Lithuania, which will give to Poland the port of Memel, as an outlet to the sea, which Danzig now provides, and in return therefor Germany would have Poland's consent to the return of Danzig to the Reich. All manner and kinds of rumors are afloat.

DIARY *Moscow—March 18, 1938*

Saw the Lithuanian Minister who gave me the details of his conference with Litvinov. The old gentleman was heart-broken. He feared the worst. His confidence in the Soviet government's protection was his only hope.

LITVINOV FEARS A "FASCIST PEACE"

TO THE HONORABLE THE SECRETARY OF STATE

MEMORANDUM OF CONVERSATION BETWEEN PEOPLE'S COMMISSAR
FOR FOREIGN AFFAIRS, M. LITVINOV, AND JOSEPH E. DAVIES,
AMERICAN AMBASSADOR, IN THE EMBASSY, MARCH 23, 1938.

The discussion was opened by my inquiry to the People's Commissar for Foreign Affairs as to his views on the Lithuanian situation.

He asserted that in his opinion, Germany definitely was opposed to the seizure of Lithuania by Poland because she, Germany, was greedy for that territory herself, and that Hitler had designs on all the Baltic states as well. He expressed the view that within a very short time, Germany would take over the Polish Corridor and Danzig and informed me that he had been told here by the German Military Attaché that the German government would "pay" nothing to Poland in return.

He said in response to my request for his views on general European peace that he felt very sure that Czechoslovakia would cause trouble this summer; that the German minorities in Czechoslovakia were exerting pressure on Hitler to move in that direction. He made the rather startling statement that there was danger that Czechoslovakia might voluntarily yield to Germany because she had no confidence in France and because she was completely surrounded. For that matter, Litvinov stated frankly, "France has no confidence in the Soviet Union and the Soviet Union has no confidence in France."

Litvinov said he foresaw a Fascist peace imposed by Germany and Italy and that history would be likely to be repeated in that the present finds Italy making friends with Germany because of fear, with the intention probably of deserting her when the situation seemingly becomes expedient, just as she did during the World War. Italy, he added, is by no means safely anchored to the Hitler axis.

He said the smaller states of Rumania, Yugoslavia, Bulgaria, Hungary, and Czechoslovakia were all frightened and that the only thing that would prevent complete Fascist domination of Europe was a change of government or policy in Great Britain.

In his opinion, Chamberlain will make some arrangement with Italy and Germany which contemplates a resumption of last year's gentleman's agreement to stop Italian anti-British propaganda, "which would be resumed immediately thereafter." He believed Great Britain would have to recognize the Italian conquest of Ethiopia in exchange for such an arrangement, which also would include the withdrawal of troops from Libya and a nonessential understanding vis-à-vis the Mediterranean.

Litvinov voiced doubt that a general election was in prospect in England and in the near future. He thinks the League of Nations is dead, barring a decided change in policy by Great Britain, and he will not attend the League Council meeting in May unless something develops in the meantime.

He thought that within a very short time, a Europe dominated by Fascism would be opposed only by Great Britain in the west and the Soviet Union in the east.

He acknowledged frankly that he does not expect anything to come of his proposals (re Poland and Lithuania) but said that they have served to clarify the situation.

He paid tribute to Secretary Hull's statement of policy last July, asserting that he considered it very strong and able and that it would be helpful if it could be more actively implemented to bring relief to a "force-ridden" world.

He expressed the view that if Fascist Germany does become

dominant over Europe, the long Russian frontier will have nothing to fear from Germany because she, Germany, will have her hands full in the states bordering it.

Regarding the Far Eastern situation, he said that Japan has approximately a million men in China, including 300,000 in Manchukuo, and that the Chinese were putting up a remarkable fight and causing Japan much trouble. He indicated he did not anticipate any aggressive action from Japan against the Soviet Union.

"THERE WILL, THEREFORE, BE NO WAR"

NO. 1074   *Moscow, March 26, 1938*

TO THE HONORABLE THE SECRETARY OF STATE

THE POLISH ULTIMATUM TO LITHUANIA

Confidential

Sir:

The past two weeks here are aptly described by what the British broadcast described recently as the period of "most serious intensity and horror," incident to the absorption of Austria by the German Reich, and on the heels thereof the following of Poland's ultimatum to Lithuania. I submit herewith a report of the situation as it developed from this viewpoint.

The audacity and completeness with which Hitler invaded Austria shocked and generally benumbed diplomatic opinion here. The Soviet government, through Commissar Litvinov, promptly came to the support of France in giving out an announcement through the press that if the Austrian incident were followed by German aggression against Czechoslovakia, the Soviet Union would go to Czechoslovakia's aid and that a "way would be found." The implication generally accepted here was that the U.S.S.R. was serving notice on Poland in particular, and possibly on Rumania as well, that if necessary the Soviets would violate territorial boundaries to go to the aid of Czechoslovakia.

As to the Austrian situation, it was generally accepted from the beginning here that not only would the *fait accompli* succeed, but also that it would not precipitate war. That is fairly illustrative of the then general opinion here. The British Ambassador was very seriously upset; and openly and vigorously condemned German aggression. He did so unreservedly to the Japanese Ambassador and to other members of the Diplomatic Corps, here at the Spazzo House * in conversations during the course of a formal dinner, which happened to fall on the evening of March 19.

The Polish ultimatum to Lithuania on the other hand gave rise to the deepest anxiety lest it should precipitate war. The Czechoslovakian Minister was deeply anxious and came to confer with me several times "to talk the situation over." He feared that it meant another Sarajevo incident which would precipitate general European war.

To be accurately advised as to the developments in the situation from both the Polish and the Lithuanian angle, I immediately called on the Lithuanian Minister and the Polish Ambassador, as well as the Soviet Foreign Office, and kept the Department currently informed by cable. The anxiety here was very serious. The fear was that Poland had some secret agreement with Germany whereunder Germany would support a Polish purpose to absorb Lithuania and find an outlet to the sea, in consideration for which Poland would relinquish the Polish Corridor to Germany under an arrangement whereby Germany would provide some sort of com-

* The American Embassy.

pensation to Poland for her expenditures on the port of
Gdynia and make some peacetime arrangement for free port
facilities for Poland through the ports of Danzig and Gdynia.
If such were the actual facts of the situation, there was a
general conviction here that the Soviet Union would be compelled to come to the aid of Lithuania and that war would
result. While the governments of France and England were
bringing pressure upon Poland to restrain its attitude, the
Soviet Foreign Office here also took a strong position, apparently with both parties.

The People's Commissar for Foreign Affairs, Litvinov,
advised me:

(1) That he had sent for and had three discussions with the
Polish Ambassador; and that he had impressed on the latter the
grave seriousness with which the Soviet Union regarded this
ultimatum;

(2) That the Soviet Union was not concerned with what the
relations between Lithuania and Poland were; but that it *was*
vitally concerned with the fact that Lithuania should actually be
and continue to be independent;

(3) That his government was concerned lest still more serious
demands should be made by Poland if Lithuania should accede to
the present demand, under some similar "innocuous dress" which
would in effect destroy Lithuanian independence.

The phrase "innocuous dress" was used by M. Litvinov to
describe the manner with which Poland had clothed its serious
demands by cloaking its demand in a simple re-establishment
of diplomatic relations, which on its face was so reasonable
that no state could resist it. He pointed out that for Lithuania
to make war based on the refusal to establish diplomatic
relations would alienate the public sympathies of the world.
M. Litvinov stated that while he had pressed hard on Poland,
he had, at the same time, strongly urged Lithuania to accede
to Poland's present request and avoid the possibility of inva-

sion at the present time. He stated that only the future would disclose what the real purpose of Poland was. He also stated that, which gave me considerable surprise, in his opinion, Hitler was opposed to the absorption of Lithuania by Poland, for the reason that "Hitler was greedy for Lithuania and the Baltic states himself." In this connection he stated that Poland would get nothing out of her support of Germany and that "this is not because I say so, but it is the direct statement of the German military aid of the German Embassy in Moscow, which statement he made to me [Litvinov] and at which time he also declared that Germany would very shortly take back the Polish Corridor and that Poland would get nothing therefor."

Fortunately, temporarily at least, the Lithuanian incident is closed. The acceptance of the ultimatum by Lithuania occurred on the afternoon of the evening on which I gave the dinner to the Diplomatic Corps here at the Embassy. The effusiveness with which the Polish Ambassador greeted the Lithuanian Minister and the effort which he made to establish in the Lithuanian Minister's mind that Poland was engaged only in a beneficent policy in its relations to Lithuania was most obvious, and was commented on by several of the other guests in the Diplomatic Corps.

I have the honor to be, Sir, respectfully yours,

Joseph E. Davies

DIARY   *Moscow—March 20, 1938*

Received Mrs. Eisenstein, a former American citizen from California, the wife of a well-known engineering specialist in petroleum machinery and pipe lines, whose husband was employed by the Soviet Oil Trust. It was a most pathetic case. They had been persuaded to leave their beautiful California

home to come to the "New Land" and had burned their
bridges behind them by throwing their American passports
out of the car window, coming on and taking out Soviet
citizenship.* Her husband had been arrested and had disappeared. It was a sad situation, where I was quite helpless,
as they were no longer American citizens and entitled to our
protection.

DIARY   *Moscow—March 26, 1938*

In the evening we had the large party for the entire
Diplomatic Corps. The surprise of the evening was the number of Russians who came, including the Vice-Commissar of
the Navy. Judge Ulrich, the Chief Justice, who presided at
the trials, and a large number of artists, musicians, and writers.
The orchestra was all Soviet and played very good jazz. Due
to Marjorie's management and forethought, the evening was
a huge success and helpful.

Commissar Litvinov and daughter came. He said that Stalin
was arranging to see me before my departure. This surprised
me very much. He sees no one, except it be some visiting head
of government from without the country. It is said that he has
never seen an ambassador formally. It would be interesting to
meet him. I should like to size him up.

GENERAL EUROPEAN SITUATION
AS VIEWED FROM MOSCOW
Moscow, March 26, 1938

THE HONORABLE SUMNER WELLES

Dear Sumner:
Peace in Europe apparently is not going to be
created by ideological considerations of international justice

---

* She was later arrested.

implemented through the League of Nations or other high-minded agencies. The only European peace that seems to be possible is a peace imposed by the stronger of the two groups, or by the most bold and audacious; or otherwise it will be a peace established by the balance of opposing political forces, each yielding to the other by reason of either their fears or the respect which they have for the power and will of the other. In other words, it will either be a Fascist-imposed peace, or a "balance-of-power" peace. Heaven help democracy in the world if it is a Fascist-imposed peace.

I have never held a brief for the balance-of-power type of peace; but it is infinitely better than the dominance of the aggressors and it is a closer approximation to a peace based upon considerations of international morality than a peace that is based upon Fascist projections of power politics.

For some reason, or lack of reason, there seems to be no purpose on the part of the democracies of Europe to fortify their position realistically by availing themselves of such strength as there is here as part of their common front in working out a *modus vivendi* vis-à-vis Mussolini and Hitler. England and France seem to be doing exactly the opposite here and have been playing into the hands of the Nazi and the Fascist aims. The Soviet Union is rapidly being driven into a complete isolation and even hostility to England and indifference to France. This may extend to the point where there might be developed a realistic union of these forces with Germany in the not distant future. That seems farfetched; but it is quite within the range of the possibilities of the future.

Despite the general hostility of attitude here, there is nevertheless a generally begrudging admission that the Soviet regime is more firmly entrenched than it has been for some time and that Stalin and his group have complete control of the army, secret police, and all forms of propaganda. It is also generally recognized that the army is highly mechanized and would give an excellent account of itself, and that the industrial forces back of the line could probably hold for a year or a year-and-a-half siege. There is no doubt of the supreme confidence on the part of this regime in their ability to take care of themselves from an attack from either the east or the west.

From the viewpoint of the struggle for the survival of democracy, which is going on in the world today, and in view of the fact that England and France are being imminently threatened by complete domination of Fascism in Europe, it is rather difficult to understand why the strength that is here available should not be fostered and used, at least to the extent that it is in accord with the maintenance of international morals and justice in world affairs. The man power here is tremendous. The resources here, not only actually, but potentially, are such that inevitably these people here will be of enormous and growing influence on conditions of life both in Europe and throughout the world. In my opinion, they constitute now a lesser actual menace than Fascist states. In any event Hitler is threatened in the East unless his Eastern door is closed. That is a classic accepted by German strategists as a basis for any war against the Western Powers.

I know this is a long letter and I hope it won't burden you. But I know you are giving thought to these things; and while Europe is not our immediate concern *now*, it soon will be, in my opinion.

Hastily yours,

MANCHUKUO BORDER CLASHES—JAPAN AND CHINA

NO. 1065 *Moscow, March 29, 1938*

TO THE HONORABLE THE SECRETARY OF STATE

SOVIET RELATIONS WITH FAR EASTERN COUNTRIES

Confidential

Sir:

There is little change in the border situation, with only one minor incident reported. This may be due in some measure to preoccupation of the Japanese military authorities with the war in China. In this connection, by far the most interesting development regarding the Far Eastern relations during the recent past has been the statement, made to me in the course of a conversation which took place on March 23, last, by M. Litvinov, Soviet Commissar for Foreign Affairs, in which he stated that any aggression against the Soviet Union on the part of Japan is now out of the question, on account of the trouble which China is causing Japan by its (China's) unexpected military success. This, he stated, was shown by the fact that Japan now has a million men under arms in China proper, and another three hundred thousand in Manchuria.

The only developments of interest in connection with the Chinese-Soviet relations have been the reported absence from Moscow of Mr. Sun Fo, Chinese Ambassador on special mission, who is said to have recently visited France and Czechoslovakia; and strong statements made by Marshal Blücher, Commander of the Far Eastern Army, regarding the strength of the Soviet Pacific fleet and Far Eastern Army, which he said will guarantee the integrity of the land and sea frontiers of Russia and "destroy the enemy in his own territory."

I have the honor to be, Sir, respectfully yours,

Joseph E. Davies

NOTHING CAN ULTIMATELY STOP RUSSIA

NO. 1104   *Moscow, April 1, 1938*

TO THE HONORABLE THE SECRETARY OF STATE

GENERAL REVIEW OF CONDITIONS IN THE SOVIET UNION

Strictly Confidential

Sir:

I have the honor to transmit herewith a brief résumé of the situation here.

JAPAN

In the Far East, from what Commissar Litvinov tells me, this government believes that Japan is having a hard time of it in China and that the Chinese are now putting up substantial resistance. This government does not conceal its deep sympathy for China, but is meticulously careful to maintain peace with Japan, at least for the present.

BORDER—NEAR EASTERN AND ASIATIC COUNTRIES

There are serious border and other disputes as between Afghanistan, Persia, and Turkey, respectively, with the Soviet Union. Relations are not good. There are indications of asperities.

BORDER—EUROPEAN AND BALTIC STATES

Since the Soviet diplomat in Rumania * escaped to Rome and the Fascist regime, Rumanian relations here have been somewhat difficult. Relations with Poland are definitely worse than at any time since I have been here, but both governments seem intent upon maintaining relations in spite of those conditions. Finland, Estonia, and Latvia have given some indications of being impressed by the success of German aggres-

---

* One of several Soviet diplomats who quit their posts during the purge, fleeing to other countries.

sion. Up to the Lithuanian incident they were sympathetically
definitely falling away still further from this regime. I state
this only, however, from impressions obtained from discussions with the diplomatic representatives of these countries
here. Since the Lithuanian incident there seems to be a change
of attitude and a recognition of the desirability of the friendship of Russia as a bulwark and support to their independence
as against possible German or Polish aggression.

EUROPEAN AND WORLD CONDITIONS GENERALLY

As I have cabled you, Litvinov's position and the attitude
of this country definitely is that a Fascist peace is being imposed on Europe; that ultimately Europe will be completely
Fascist with the exception of England and the Soviet Union;
that finally Italy will desert Germany, as she did during the
Great War; that Soviet Russia must count on no outside aid
and in fact must be and is completely self-contained and independent; that France cannot be depended upon; that there is
no hope for the maintenance of law and order based on public
morality between nations until the "reactionary elements" in
England in power are overthrown; that they see no immediate
prospect of this; that your great pronouncement before the
National Press Club was a great help, but that without practical implementation it would, "unfortunately, not be effective
against the ruthless forces of Fascism."

INDUSTRIAL PROGRESS

While there are many evidences and admissions of waste
and inefficiencies, and the weaknesses incident to bureaucratic
administration of industry and agriculture are obvious, nevertheless, this great bear is lumbering along and with impressive
results despite these handicaps. There is such an enormous
wealth that these wastes in comparison therewith are rela-

tively small. The wealth of the country is increasing. Last year's crop was the largest in history. The prospect for betterment from a material point of view is improving. Enormous expenditures for war preparations, diverting 25% of total revenues, is holding up distribution of betterments to the masses; but still there are many indications of improvement —notably the appearance of rubbers, boots, and shoes.

PUBLIC WORKS—SCHOOLS

Public improvements—buildings, roads, bridges, canals, and the like are impressive not only in themselves, but in the speed of their projection. The face of certain sections of this city was completely changed during the last year. Stalin, historically, will be recognized probably as the great builder in Russia, following Peter the Great. One hundred and fifty-seven schools are alleged to have been built in Moscow alone during the last year.

THE TERROR

The Terror here is a horrifying fact. There are many evidences here in Moscow that there is a fear that reaches down into and haunts all sections of the community. No household, however humble, apparently but what lives in constant fear of a nocturnal raid by the secret police (usually between one and three in the early morning). Once the person is taken away, nothing of him or her is known for months—and many times never—thereafter. Evidences of these conditions come from many sources. They are: statements made to myself or members of the staff from firsthand witnesses; statements based on actual personal observations of members of the staff (as in one instance, the sight of a struggling unfortunate being arrested and torn from his eleven-year-old child on the street in front of the adjoining apartment house at 3:30 A.M.); or statements made by Russian citizens who for some reason or other come to the Embassy in search of aid. The popular psychology in this situation and the extent of this Terror is again indicated by the fact that, almost daily through the kitchen and servant's quarters, there come reports of whispered and fearful confidences of new arrests, new hardships, new apprehensions, and new fears among their friends. The activities of the secret police have extended and reached down to the arrest of Soviet employees of foreign missions, including our own.

It is commonly alleged that the secret police of this proletarian dictatorship are as ruthless and as cruel as any during the old tsarist regimes. It seems to be an old Russian custom. This particular purge is undoubtedly political. From expressions that I have heard from some of the leaders of the government it is deliberately projected by the party leaders, who themselves regretted the necessity for it, but who nevertheless will not permit themselves to be sentimental or weak in the performance of what they regard as their duty. They believe that great revolutions cannot be projected by spraying perfume; that previous movements in the interests of the proletariat have been destroyed by weakness and false sentimentality. They recognize and regret that there must needs be many innocent who suffer in this situation, but they take the position that they must do this to save their cause, which is supreme, and that the successful elevation of the condition of life of the proletariat will, in historical perspective, justify their present course.

WAR AND WAR PSYCHOLOGY

One fourth of the national revenues were appropriated last year to war purposes. This amounts to approximately twenty-five billion rubles. At the current bootleg gold value of the ruble, this approximates two to two and one half billion dollars. Expenditures this year will probably be still greater. There are indications of an almost feverish preparation for war. Immense stocks of foods and supplies, including military equipment, tanks, submarine chasers, airplanes, trucks, and so forth, are reported by travelers as being sent to the Far East in an unending stream. There is a shortage of fabric here in Moscow, which did not exist last year, and which is alleged to be due to war requirements.

Those industrial organizations which are directly connected with war requirements have been recently placed under direct army control and supervision.

It is variously estimated that the Far Eastern Army consists of from 250,000 to 500,000 men. It is alleged to be completely self-contained with an adequate two-year supply of food and military requirements. Annually 1,200,000 youths are called to the colors for training. There are constant rumors of roads and fortifications being secretly and hurriedly built all along the western frontier. The current strength of the army is reputed to be 1,200,000 men.

TENDENCY TOWARD SOVIET ISOLATION FROM WORLD AFFAIRS

A most significant development and one fraught with portentous significance for the future has occurred within the last year. It is the rapid development of a policy of ruthless hostility directed against all foreigners in the country—individuals or governments.

The present movement undoubtedly began with Stalin's speech of a year ago, in which he pointed out the hostility of all capitalist states and that the U.S.S.R. was surrounded by enemies. It has been stimulated undoubtedly by the disclosures of alleged espionage and spying activity of foreign nations and foreign diplomatic missions in the Soviet Union.

Foreigners all last summer were being expelled from the Soviet Union. Representations even by the French Ambassador in connection with French nationals were unavailing. The secret police were implementing this policy and were thoroughly hard-boiled in their attitude and conduct. They have reached into practically every foreign institution, foreign newspaper bureaus, foreign business offices, and even embassies and legations to apprehend and arrest Soviet employees on charges of one kind or another.

THE CLOSING OF FOREIGN CONSULATES

The consulates of fourteen different nations were closed. The dogmatic and overbearing manner in which these things have been done indicate an almost serene unconcern as to the sensibilities of foreign nations, even—in some instances— to the extent of an apparent indifference as to whether or not it would result in the termination of diplomatic relations. Literally, thousands of foreign nationals, I am told, have been shipped out of the country and returned to Greece, Turkey, Persia, and so forth. Along the entire Afghan border of 2000 kilometers a strip fifty kilometers in width has been provided as a quarantine zone to afford protection against any infiltration.

The purposes of the Fascist governments of isolating the U.S.S.R. among the nations of the world and placing them in quarantine, so to speak, seems to have worked not only successfully from without this country but also seems to have been most effective here. The Soviet Union in retaliation, or for reasons of its own, appears to be perfectly willing to out-Herod Herod in this respect. And they have a faculty for hitting first and hard if they think they are in danger.

SOVIET SELF-CONFIDENCE

Despite the purge, the terror, war propaganda, and the threats of hostile neighbors, there is no doubt but what this government has supreme confidence in its ability to take care of itself. Kalinin, the President; Molotov, the Premier; and Litvinov, the Foreign Minister, have each of them expressed to me (and I think sincerely) that attitude. Only recently Commissar Litvinov expressed regret that the democracies of the world were not willing to go along for collective security and international peace, but was very explicit in saying that in the last analysis the Soviet Union was quite content, if the democracies pursued "their course of present folly and indifference to international peace and justice," to rely only upon itself; and that they had every confidence that the government could maintain itself indefinitely without fear or favor, and quite without fear of the result in the case of outside aggression.

DIPLOMATIC OPINION AS TO THE PERMANENCY OF THE REGIME
AND POSSIBILITY OF A COUP D'ÉTAT

No foreign diplomat with whom I have talked believes that the Stalin regime is weak politically or in any immediate danger. Expressions are quite generally to the contrary. Stalin's natural death in their opinion would not change the regime, particularly if time were afforded the organization to place his successor in power before the news was generally known. If Stalin's death were by assassination and/or accompanied by a palace *coup d'état* directed and executed by a strong group of the army, the present regime would probably be overthrown. In such an event, however, it is the prevailing opinion that still a socialist state would persist. It is generally thought that Stalin has the situation well and strongly in hand, with the various elements of strength balanced off each as against the other and each responsible to him. With the enormous power of the army, the secret police, the press, and all propaganda agencies in good working order there is little possibility of an overt act, barring accident.

SOVIET ATTITUDE TOWARD THE UNITED STATES

Despite some irritations, that must needs arise, in my opinion it can nevertheless be safely asserted that the mission of the government of the United States here has received more consideration and favor from this government during the past year than has any other foreign state. I have it on the word of Commissar for Foreign Affairs, Litvinov himself, that the "Soviet Union would do more for the United States than any other nation." This is probably due to the fact that the officials here, who are a very able and strong group of men, and also the people generally regard the United States with friendly favor. They feel that we are disinterested, friendly, have no direct designs on anything that they have, and have no selfish axes of our own to grind with their immediate enemies at their possible expense. The leaders, too, have great admiration for President Roosevelt and what they consider "his very wonderful achievements." They also have very high admiration for the efforts of the Secretary of State to project international peace through economic appeasement.

This attitude of friendliness does not deter them in matters affecting their vital interests, as indicated by the debt and Comintern situations. They are thoroughly realistic. It is, however, indicative, I believe, of a real "most friendly" attitude and a disposition which is in direct contrast to the prevailing hostility toward foreigners here generally. There are hundreds of foreign nationals—Germans, Poles, and Italians —who were imprisoned, and to whom the diplomatic staffs of

their respective nationalities have been refused access or conference until after trial of the prisoners. In the only two instances that have arisen in connection with our nationals and
where the question has been raised, there has been a direct
compliance with our request in direct contrast to precedent;
and with surprising speed in contrast to the treatment accorded other missions. In both of these cases, representatives
of this Embassy were permitted to see and confer with the
accused before trial.

CONCLUSION

Many fine things are being done under the present regime.
Many noble enterprises have been projected which arouse
sympathy and inspire intense admiration. No degree of altruism, humanitarian effort, or high and noble purpose, and
no amount of material improvement in providing for things
which elevate the standard of living of the proletariat, can
ever compensate for the denial of freedom, of liberty, and
the rights of the individual even as against the king.*

Whether this regime continues in power or falls, in my
opinion, this Russian situation will continue to grow in international importance—both politically and economically.
Enormous and even astounding strides have been made in
industrial and scientific development and achievement within
the past eight years. And the tiger has tasted blood. Nothing
(not even revolution or change of government) can stop the
continued exploitation and development of this country's
enormous resources and wealth. The ambitions of the country

---

* One of two things will happen to this regime, in my opinion. Either it will
destroy itself by reason of its attempt to run contrary to human nature, and
by reason of the methods which it employs; or the government will swing
more to the right and evolve into a more democratic form, and less extreme
type of state socialism. There are indications that such a swing to the right
is now in progress. But nothing can stop Russia.

youth have been fired. Educational facilities have been afforded. Education, scientific and otherwise, is being extensively projected and made universal. Caste or class barriers to individual advancement have been broken down. The inevitable strength of this relatively young nation and a people, fresh from the soil, will inevitably project and continue this development. This country's present position, economically and industrially, appears to me to be now at a point of development where the United States was about sixty years ago.

The next generation, in my opinion, will see these people here exercising a tremendous influence not only upon European but upon world conditions.

Despite many affronts, and despite what would appear to be obvious insults addressed to certain diplomatic missions of certain governments of Europe, these governments nevertheless persist in maintaining their diplomatic representatives and contacts in Moscow. It is, in my opinion, a wise and prudent policy. Great forces exist here and still-greater forces are here in the making. They will inevitably have far-reaching reactions.

I have the honor to be, Sir, respectfully yours,

Joseph E. Davies

PART VII

CLIMAX OF THE MISSION

April 6—July 5, 1938

VII

SOVIET ART & ARTISTS

Moscow, April 6, 1938

MISS EMLEN KNIGHT DAVIES

Dearest Bijou:

We have been finding a great deal of pleasure and exceptional interest in attending the various national exhibitions and performances which are characteristic of the winter in Moscow, the nation's capital. There have been some lovely exhibitions of Soviet art from the different provinces. Each of them was typical of the district from which it came; from the melons and tropical scenes of Bokhara to the frozen wastes of Arctic Siberia. Not the least in interest among these exhibitions was an exhibition of the art of Soviet women. It covered oil, water color, handicraft of all kinds, and also sculpture. Here we found the original model of the beautiful figure of man and woman which crowned the Soviet building in the Paris Exposition last summer. It is quite as extraordinary and beautiful in relief miniature as it was in its magnificent size in Paris.

RUSSIA'S GREATEST SCULPTRESS

Following this exhibition we arranged to call on Madam Mukhina, the sculptress. The invaluable Bender piloted us

313

around to the district where she lives. We found her studio
in an old residence. Despite its desperately run-down condition it still had remnants of great beauty and dignity after the
French style. Madam Mukhina is a fine-looking woman of
about forty years of age, with a splendid head and fine eyes.
Her husband, in a Russian smock, received us with her, as
did also her son of twenty-one, who, to our surprise, spoke
quite good English. We spent a very interesting two hours
at the studio and in her workshop. Like all great people she is
very simple. She certainly sculptured on a monolithic scale.
She showed us some models which she had prepared for the
ornamental approaches to the new bridges which are being
built here in Moscow (eleven in all, all promised to be finished
by the first of May and doubtless will be). The imagination
and beauty which characterizes these plans were really
breath-taking. The figures, of course, were really all symbolic.
The final statues will be about 150 feet high and will be placed
at the abutment approaches of the bridge and also in the center. Some of them provide a sort of stadium in the center of
the bridge, with artificial reflection pools, all designed not
only for beauty but to provide amphitheaters for public
speeches and other performances in the open air. She showed
us several of the smaller models of her statues. Those which
were particularly beautiful were the *North Wind* and the
Fallen Icarus. She and Marjorie became great friends and before we got through she promised to do a bust in marble for
me of Marjorie's head and shoulders. I was very happy about
that. She will do a wonderful thing, I am sure, for to an unusual degree she translates idealism into her work. It was a
most interesting visit.

For the past week the artists of Azerbaidzhan have been
holding their exhibitions here in the national capital, and the
Foreign Office has very kindly arranged for us to see public

performances. The other evening we saw an exhibition of folk dancing in the Hall of Nobles (the old aristocratic officers' club, where also the trials were held). It was the first time that Marjorie had seen the interior. It fairly took her breath away—the majestic and handsome sweeping corridor and broad stairways, the beauty of the wedgwood ornamentation on the blue and white walls, and the noble proportions of the rooms, and particularly the beautiful lighting impressed her very much. The dancing, too, was extraordinary. It was, of course, the best type of native folk dancing that one could find in Russia and the dances were put on by people from various sections of the country. As usual, the tempo was very rapid, the agility and co-ordination were most remarkable, and the charm of the whole thing, with the colorful costumes and the grace and youth of the dancers, made it most enjoyable.

GRAND OPERA FROM THE PROVINCES

Last night we went to see an opera put on by the Azerbaidzhan group. It was staged at the Bolshoi Filial Theater, which we had not seen before. But for the contrast of the Bolshoi Theater this opera house would be remarkable. It is large and quite imposing. There must have been approximately 300 people in the orchestra and in the cast. I counted about 60 in the orchestra and estimated in count about 200 people on the stage at different times. It was a production of a native opera—*Kerogly*—which means "the son of a blind man." It was the characteristic story of the oppression of the people by the ruling Khan, who destroyed the sight of his Master of the Horse because he did not get him a horse that he desired and the vengeance of the son, who became a bandit leader of the people. The performance was very interesting and unique.

That reminds me that on the occasion of the large reception which we gave the other evening, the entire Diplomatic Corps were almost struck dumb with astonishment by reason of the fact that there were 60 or 70 prominent Russians who came to the party. They were all people who are prominent in the drama, in music, literature, art, or official life. They joined in the dancing in the large dining room, which was converted into a ballroom, and seemed to have a good time. A great many of them asked me about you and were so interested in what you were doing. They all knew about your courses in the Moscow University here and they all said very interesting and lovely things about you.

Within the week I expect that arrangements will be made so that we can go to the studio of the greatest living Soviet artist in oils—Gerasimov. He is the man who painted that magnificent, large palace interior, with all of the Soviet generals in conference, which, you will remember, dominated the large room at the Tretyakov Gallery. It was the picture which required repainting by the artist after the treason trials of last summer to eliminate Tukhatchevsky and some of the others before it was exhibited at the Paris Exposition. Gerasimov is the only artist who has received the highest decoration for art, namely, the Order of Lenin. I am told that he speaks excellent English and spent some time as a cowboy in the United States. I am looking forward to meeting him.

Devotedly,

SOVIET ATTITUDE TOWARD JAPANESE PROTESTS

JOURNAL   *Moscow—April 4, 1938*

It is announced by the press that the Foreign Commissar received a protest from the Japanese Ambassador against the military assistance which he asserted the government was giving to China.

M. Litvinov is reported to have replied that their attitude in selling arms, etc., to China was in complete accordance with the principles of international law. He denied that they had sent any military detachments or individual military persons to that country to participate in war action.

Volunteers from many countries were fighting for the Chinese, but as far as was known, the Japanese government had not protested to any of these.

China and Japan enjoyed equal possibilities of obtaining arms from abroad.

COMMUNISM NO WORLD DANGER

Moscow, April 4, 1938

HONORABLE STEPHEN T. EARLY

Dear Steve:

Things sure have been popping here since our arrival. There is nothing unusual. There is never a dull moment in Moscow.

The United States, Canada, and the British colonies would seem to be about the last safe repository for democratic ideals. Russia might be a helpful bulwark for the protection of international peace, if it were utilized. The European democracies, however, seem deliberately to play into the hands of the Fascists in the effort to isolate completely the great power that is here from the rest of the world and particularly from France and England. It is a pity, but it is true.

The Fascists abroad circulate the story that the Stalin regime is breaking up. No diplomat here believes the army is not loyal to the Kremlin, or that their industrial organization is breaking up. As a matter of fact, those who are here on the ground and who are best informed, including even the representatives of hostile states, have all stated to me that barring an accident, or assassination, or a *coup d'état*, this regime is well entrenched in power, has a successful army, has made remarkable strides industrially, and would give a very good account of itself in any world armed conflict.

Personally, I do not think that the world is in any real danger from communism for many years to come. Communism won't work. It hasn't worked here. This government is not communism. It is a socialism. And this socialism has been modified, and is being compelled to accede more and more to the methods of capitalism and individualism in order to make the machine work. And the crowd in power, the government, has got to make the machine work or lose their jobs. So old human nature is working. They are, therefore, constantly forced to modify their methods, with the result that while professing left ideas they are actually projecting rightist methods. The French Ambassador has said to me that the Comintern (the agency for the international revolution idea) is resorted to by Stalin, not because of desire, but purely as a military and strategic necessity. Stalin, he maintains, wishes to prove socialism in Russia first, as a successful object lesson to the world. Trotsky advocates world revolution, without which, he maintains, there can be no successful communism.

Regardless of whether it is Stalin or Trotsky or Tukhatchevsky, or someone else who runs this government, in my opinion, these people here are going to wield an increasing and enormous force both in European and world affairs. That is so because of the enormous man power and the wealth that is here. It is also because this man power has just awakened to its possibilities. Universal education, technical training, the breaking down of caste barriers, and the opening of new avenues of opportunity everywhere have already given the young people of this country a taste of blood. Science and capital have demonstrated what industry can do, and what industrial development means, and have shown the promised land of higher standards of living. The country boys, fresh from the soil, full of "wim, wigor, and witality," are on their way to town and they will not be denied; and it doesn't make any difference *who* is the government, these forces will not be denied. This country is in the position of economic development, in my opinion, that corresponds with the situation that the United States was in sixty years ago and the possibilities here are enormous.

NO. 1149   *Moscow, April 12, 1938*

TO THE HONORABLE THE SECRETARY OF STATE

INSPECTION TRIP INTO THE INTERIOR OF THE
SOVIET UNION—BAKU OIL FIELDS, ET CETERA

Sir:

I am now planning a three weeks' journey personally to inspect the Baku oil fields in Azerbaidzhan, industrial developments in the Donets Basin and in the Caucasus, certain hospitalization projects in the Soviet Union, and collective farms of southern Russia.

The reports thereon will supplement and round out the information obtained and reported in connection with my inspection trips of last year. They should be of value to the Department in assessing both the political and economic aspects of this situation.

This plan necessitates absence from Moscow from May 2 to approximately May 25. During that time, however, I shall be in telephonic contact with the Chancery in Moscow, and will at no time be without the territory of the Soviet Union.

Should an emergency in Europe arise, it would, of course, change the plan. Unless otherwise instructed by the Depart-

ment, however, and in accord with the above exchange of
telegrams, I shall make plans to be absent from Moscow from
May 2 to approximately May 25.

I have the honor to be, Sir, respectfully yours,

Joseph E. Davies

DIARY   *Moscow—April 14, 1938*

Mr. Ralph Blake, Vice-Consul at Kobe, Japan, passing
through en route for home, came in for lunch. He is a keen,
fine-appearing young man—a credit to the service. He is highly
intelligent and well balanced and careful in his expression of
opinions or facts.

He stated that in Japan there were indications of economic
pressure, caused by the war, making their appearance, and
that there was much discussion and fear of possible Russian
air attacks on the "wood and paper" cities of Japan.

JOURNAL   *Moscow—April 14, 1938*

I have just been reading Sir Walter Citrine's book on
Russia. It is admirable. It is neither entirely critical nor entirely enthusiastic. It seems to me that it expresses admirably
the attitude of the British labor movement. It always displays
enthusiasm for any plan which produces a better standard of
living for the worker, a more secure and equitable distribution
of wealth, and greater social security for the underprivileged;
but, on the other hand, there is a very firm insistence that these
benefits shall not be secured at the expense of civil liberties
and those attributes of an individualistic society which have
preserved the freedoms and opportunities of men. In the
world struggle which is now here, between the ideologies of
totalitarianism and Nazism, and our concept of life, one of the

most hopeful things I can see is the sanity, strength, and levelheadedness of the British labor movement, and particularly their steady levelheaded insistence upon making haste slowly—so as to be sure that their hard-won liberties shall not be jeopardized or possibly lost.

Moscow—April 14, 1938

EXCERPT FROM A LETTER TO SENATOR MILLARD TYDINGS

This isolation of Russia is probably more serious to the democracies of Europe than it is to the Soviet Union. The officials purport to be indifferent to this development, except as they regret it on account of collective security and its effect on world peace. They are, without doubt, supremely self-confident in their capacity to defend themselves.

As things are going in this cockeyed world, I am not sure but what the democracies of the world might not be damn glad some day to have the friendship and the power and the devotion to peace which this government could supply in case of another world crisis. And believe me, if these Fascist dictators continue going haywire that crisis is bound to come, and in the opinion of many people whom I know life would not be worth living if it had to be on terms which they would dictate, and it is very close. There is too much wishful thinking—and a refusal to see the simple elemental factors in this Europe.

DIARY   *Moscow—April 23, 1938*

Had a stag dinner. Those present—Denny (*Times*), Deuel (U.P.), Massock (A.P.), Barnes (*Tribune*), Williams (Chamber of Commerce), Shapiro (U.P.), Minor and Anderson of the Staff. Joe Barnes has just returned from a trip into the industrial region east of Moscow, in the Urals, and is full of interesting information as to the extraordinary development which is being projected there. Spencer Williams has just returned from an excursion into Spain, where he saw a good deal of Charlie Nutter. His description of conditions in Madrid were rather harrowing, but also amusing as he told them.

RED BAITING IN MOSCOW

JOURNAL   *Moscow—April 30, 1938*

On March 17 I received a letter from the British Ambassador, acting Dean of the Diplomatic Corps, addressed to all heads of mission, proposing a joint protest to the Soviet Foreign Office over the imposition by Soviet authorities of an examination of all the personal effects which retiring diplomats were taking out of Russia, and the exaction of a tax for such a "service." The letter solicited opinions as to the advisability of the proposed *démarche*.

I saw the British Ambassador, for whom I have great admiration and respect, and told him in my opinion a joint protest would be a mistake; that the grievance was relatively a small matter; that the Soviet Foreign Office was sensitive, especially to joint action by the Diplomatic Corps; that nothing would be gained and that grievous harm might be done where broader issues were concerned. Lord Chilston said that he understood, of course, no action would be taken unless it was the unanimous opinion of the chiefs of mission that it should be done.

I amplified my position by stating that while I recognized that diplomatic privileges have some importance, I regarded as more serious the fact that if this incident assumed a political aspect it might affect larger and more vital objectives of policy of the democratic countries which either existed or would probably exist in the future. If Chamberlain's efforts to secure peace in Europe should unfortunately fail and war should become inevitable, I pointed out, the attitude and position of the Soviet Union with its enormous resources might be of decisive consequence to world peace and to the democratic powers. It was bad judgment needlessly to affront this government on what was relatively a trivial matter. The British Ambassador assured me that he sympathized with this point of view and that nothing would be done about it unless there was complete unanimity on the part of the Diplomatic Corps.

A few days later at a dinner at the British Embassy, two of the guests—the ———— and the ———— Ministers—took me off to one side and asked me to urge the British Ambassador not to project this action because they had word that the Soviet Foreign Office knew all about his letter and was very indignant about it and would certainly rebuff any such action. I asked them why they didn't take it up themselves with the Ambassador. They pleaded that they were representatives of small countries, etc., and wouldn't I please do it. I told them I would, and I did. Lord Chilston saw the point and again assured me that he would not act unless there was unanimous agreement.

Later the British Ambassador advised me regretfully that he felt it would not do to back down, and that they had to see the matter through, and he hoped that he would have my co-operation. I stated frankly that I regretted that under the circumstances I would be obliged to decline to be a party to the *démarche*, and that the Department had left the decision entirely to my discretion.

From the point of view of the conventional diplomat, this situation was a serious one. It was, possibly, a trespass on the

diplomatic rule of immunity which had been set up by the
Congress of Vienna, and, moreover, it was considered important that encroachments upon diplomatic rights should
not go unnoticed or without prompt resistance.

The incident itself was trivial, but it was illustrative of conditions here. It disclosed the rather frayed edges of isolated
nerves; again, it provided a measure of the conventional diplomat's outlook. The real importance of the incident lies in the
fact that it reflected, generally speaking, the attitude of in-
tolerance and covert hostility which existed in certain quarters
in the Diplomatic Corps. It was fashionable for some to "bait
the Soviet" covertly. As a matter of fairness it should be said
that the British Ambassador took no such attitude, and the
reason he was assuming the initiative in this matter was that
he was acting as Dean of the Diplomatic Corps. I am sure he
was sympathetic with my point of view.

I understand the matter was dropped and nothing further
was done about it.*

JOURNAL   *Moscow—May 10, 1938*

Information has come to me, from what is unquestionably a reliable source, of the extent to which this government is "cleaning out" all nonnationals. This is probably due
to zeal as a matter of military defense.

My informant stated that:

1. With reference to the relationship of his government to
the Soviet Union, conditions were very bad indeed; that he
was having very great difficulties; that these arose from two
causes:

---

* See Appendix for dispatches to State Department on the proposed *démarche*.

(*a*) The action of the Soviet government toward nationals in connection with their liquidation, imprisonment, and expulsion from the U.S.S.R., and

(*b*) The inability of the government to facilitate the return of its nationals to their country, due to the inability of their country to absorb and receive them within their own territory.

There were, he said, approximately 80,000 such nationals in the Soviet Union; that at least 20,000 had been arrested; that whole villages in the interior had been denuded of the male population of this nationality by the arrest and deportation into distant parts of the country of the men of the respective communities; that the destitution and desperation of the women and children left behind under these conditions were most serious, and that these unfortunates were flocking in large numbers into Moscow to their legation, importuning help; that if it were a matter of the deportation of 1000 or 1200 of such nationals, their government could probably manage it; that, however, the Soviet government refused to permit deportation in part except and unless it was arranged to take them all; that these conditions made the situation quite impossible and horrible; that in the case of arrest of these nationals, and their imprisonment, their diplomatic representatives were not permitted to confer with or see them. The picture which he painted was a very sad one. I get the same story from several ambassadors. This government is apparently not only closing up the consulates in a peremptory way, but is expelling "foreigners" en masse.

Coincident with this activity, I am told the government is establishing a "no man's land" miles wide along the entire Soviet border to prevent any possible infiltration into the country. The government seems to be war conscious "to the *n*th degree." The evidence of the condition is very obvious; spy trials all over the country, purges, mass deportations, closing of consulates, converting industry into production of tanks, reorganization of the army, etc., etc.

Coulondre, the French Ambassador, tells me the production of airplanes here has been stepped up to 400 a month— 4800 a year. I asked him whether he considered this information reliable and he seemed very certain about it.

DIARY   *Moscow—May 10, 1938*

This morning cables came from that fine old friend Joe Tumulty containing news of my nomination to the Senate as Ambassador to Belgium.

It will be a great change from the atmosphere here. It was a beneficent fate that kept us from being sent to Germany under the present conditions.

DIARY   *Moscow—May 13, 1938*

Called on the new ———— Minister, a very intelligent scholarly man. He stated that, from his observation, many of the Diplomatic Corps here were so hostile to the U.S.S.R. that it appeared to him they had come for the purpose of finding things to criticize. His statement did not surprise me, but that he should have said it did.

DIARY   *Moscow—May 14, 1938*

Worked on my summary, "Brief on the Facts," synoptic survey of the U.S.S.R. It is now practically completed and a thorough piece of work. It may be of some value in the Department files. In any event, I think it gives a fair report of conditions in the U.S.S.R. at this period in the evolution of the Soviet revolution, and at this critical time when European peace is trembling in the balance. When I leave this post, I want to have the record as complete, so far as my observations are concerned, as I can make it.

JOURNAL *Moscow—May 15, 1938*

Coulondre, the French Ambassador, is an exceptionally able man. He is a veteran of the diplomatic service. He also has mental initiative and much vigor in his judgment. We have seen a good deal of each other and he is very frank with me.

The Czech situation and the German propaganda barrage worry him. It indicates in his opinion a definite and aggressive German purpose against Czechoslovakia. To him the German army "maneuvers" on the Czech border are definitely threatening and "might mean anything." His government, he said, had promptly served a vigorous notice on Berlin that in case there was a military attack on Czechoslovakia the French army would march. He was bitter against the Chamberlain Foreign Office in this connection. The British Foreign Office advised Berlin, quite gently, that if France were to go to the aid of the Czechs it would be a very serious situation and that Great Britain would have then to consider whether it would not be obliged to support France, and would give no assurance that it would not do so. That, in his opinion, was not "the kind of language Hitler could understand." It only served to support Ribbentrop in his constant advice to Hitler that "no matter what" Britain would not fight.*

---

* Were it not for the fact that Coulondre's statements of similar character are already published in the diplomatic official Yellow Book of the French government, I would not feel at liberty to quote him.

I SEE FOR MYSELF

NO. 1310   *Moscow, June 1, 1938*

Dictated in Batum, May 19, 1938

TO THE HONORABLE THE SECRETARY OF STATE

INSPECTION TRIP IN MAY, 1938, COVERING THE AGRICUL-
TURAL DISTRICTS OF THE UKRAINE AND CRIMEA. COLLECTIVE
FARMS; COLLECTIVIZATION UNDER SPECIAL CONDITIONS, TEA
PLANTATIONS, CITRUS FRUITS, AND SO FORTH; BAKING PLANT
IN ODESSA; OIL REFINING AND PETROLEUM PRODUCTS IN
BATUM; CEMENT INDUSTRY AT NOVOROSSIISK; THE SANA-
TORIUM PROJECTS OF THE CAUCASUS; AND PORT AND HARBOR
FACILITIES FOR THE EXPORT OF OIL, GRAIN, CEMENT, AND SO
FORTH.[*]

Sir:

During 1937, I made inspection trips into some of the principal industrial regions of the Soviet Union, and reported to
the Department upon various phases of Soviet industry, including plants producing machine tools, electric generators
and transformers, turbines, trucks, pig iron, rolled-steel products, agricultural machinery, aluminum, and electric power,
including the Dnieperstroges Dam. Prior to leaving for my
new post, I wish to supplement and round out the information
then reported with firsthand reports upon various other industries.

In view of the fact that the Soviet Union produces one third
of the world's wheat production, one half of the world's oats,
and 80% of the total world production of rye, and occupies
first place in the production of sugar beets, it occurred to me

---

[*] The following dispatch outlines the entire trip. Some of the subsequent
dispatches appear in the Appendix.

that it might be of value to obtain a perspective upon the facilities which the Soviet Union now has or appears to be projecting in the principal ports of export for these products, which are in the Caucasus and Black Sea region.

PETROLEUM PRODUCTS—PRODUCTION, REFINING, AND PORT FACILITIES FOR EXPORT

This same region produces 75 per cent of the petroleum products of the Soviet Union and has the largest and most important pipe lines. The Batum-Baku district, together with the Caucasus, produces approximately 90 per cent of the entire Soviet output of petroleum products. The petroleum reserves of the Soviet Union are undoubtedly among the largest in the world. Soviet oil production is claimed to be the greatest in Europe. Exports of petroleum and petroleum products have fallen from 6,000,000 metric tons in 1932 to 3,000,000 in 1935, and to 1,929,147 metric tons in the year 1937. In view of the enormous reserves claimed by the Soviet Union it would nevertheless be of interest to obtain some judgment as to the facilities which now exist or are in process of erection for the export of petroleum and petroleum products in the chief Soviet ports of export.

The significant fact in connection with the petroleum industry of the Soviet Union is the enormous increase in Soviet consumption. The efforts made during the last ten years to industrialize the country, mechanize Soviet agriculture, and increase the production and use of automobiles and trucks have resulted in a rise in the consumption of gasoline entirely out of proportion to the increase in the production of gasoline. In 1932 the consumption of gasoline amounted to 647,000 metric tons and was about 25 per cent of production. In 1937 this consumption had increased sixfold to approximately 3,500,000 metric tons, whereas the production of gasoline had

only doubled during the same period, i.e., from 2,459,000
metric tons in 1932 to 4,870,000 metric tons in 1937. The result has been a constantly diminishing export of petroleum
products as stated above. It also partially explains the increase
of Soviet importations of petroleum and petroleum products.
In the last two years imports from the United States alone
have probably increased 600 per cent. These imports consist,
for the greatest part, of high octane airplane gasoline from
California, which is being shipped into the Soviet Far East.
Another reason for imports is undoubtedly to be found in the
fact that the Soviet government is also making great efforts to
preserve and enlarge its war reserves of gasoline.* That is one
of the weakest spots in Soviet war economy. Last summer
there was difficulty in procuring even second- or third-class
gasoline for trucks in Moscow. That situation was then alleged to have been due to the heavy demands put upon available supplies for the harvesting of crops. The scarcity,
however, continued throughout the winter and would seem
to be due to the extraordinary effort which the government is
putting forth in war preparations.

CEMENT BUILDING MATERIALS

One of the important basic industries of the U.S.S.R.
is the cement industry. It is the foundation of the extensive
industrial-construction, housing, and road-building plans
which are being projected. It is particularly important in view
of the alleged enormous construction of military defenses
along the western border. Approximately one third of the
cement in the Soviet Union, up to the present at least, is pro-

---

* Even at that time the government was making great effort to develop additional oil production in the Urals, adjacent to the new military center of
industrial production at Sverdlovsk.

duced in the vicinity of Novorossiisk, which is also in the Caucasus region.

HOSPITALIZATION PROJECTS

It is also in this region that the much propagandized rest-home hospitalization projects both of the government and of the Soviet trade unions are to be found. In the Ukraine, in the Crimea, and also in the Caucasus the great mansions of the moneyed classes of the old regime have been converted into various types of sanatoriums. Various hygienic, radioactive, sulphur, and other types of baths have been developed and exploited. The trade unions, the Red Army, and other organizations have built extensive plants in the subtropical region. It is near Sochi on the Black Sea that Stalin has his summer home. Sochi is the center of hospitalization for heart conditions and is considered as well the show place (of its kind) of the Soviet Union.

COLLECTIVE FARMS

In this region there are also to be found the different types of collective and state farms, covering grain, vineyards, citrus fruits, tea, and other types of tropical agriculture. The advantages of mechanized, large-scale operation of agricultural production of grain on extensive level plains are quite apparent. In connection with fruits and other agricultural produce which would depend more upon individualized attention and care, this value or the effectiveness of collectivized effort is more doubtful. This region, therefore, affords an opportunity to see both types.

With the aforesaid general purposes in mind, I left Moscow on May 15, 1938, accompanied by an expert secretary, Mr. Bartley Gordon, and Mr. Philip Bender, a Soviet employee of the Embassy, who acted as interpreter. All during the follow-

ing day, May 16, we traveled through a very rich agricultural
district between Moscow and the Ukraine. The country looked
much like the rich bottom lands of Nebraska and Kansas,
and the farther south we got, the more prosperous the country
looked. From Kiev, the capital of the Ukraine, to Odessa, there
was an excellent double-tracked roadbed which was oiled for
a large part of the distance.

I have the honor to be, Sir, respectfully yours,

Joseph E. Davies

SOVIET HEALTH RESORT

EXCERPT FROM A LETTER TO MY DAUGHTER, MRS. WALKER

May 30, 1938

Sochi has no harbor. The city reaches from the shore right
up to the hills. It is a city of gleaming white buildings scattered over the hillsides. They peep out from clusters of green
trees, all over the place. It is the show place of the U.S.S.R.
They feature it as one of the great achievements of their
regime. It is here that "Uncle Joe" Stalin spends his vacations
at his winter *dacha,* or country place. It is here, too, that some
of the "faithful," two years ago, took potshots at him from
ambush both on the roadside and when he was motoring
up the coast in a small launch. At least so the story goes. The
place itself is built around the sulphur baths, which are alleged to be peculiarly potent in that they afford sulphur-bath
treatments in rheumatic and other cases which have weak
hearts. But they claim a lot of things—say much besides their
prayers. It (Sochi) never amounted to much until 1925, when
the Soviets started to develop it. Just how coincident with
Stalin's appearance of heart trouble this development was is
not recorded. It now has about 100,000 people, and it is very

impressive. Practically all the habitations in the place (old or new) are either rest homes or sanatoriums.

THE RUSSIAN RIVIERA—BEAUTIFUL CRIMEA

Moscow, June 8, 1938

Dearest Daughter:

We spent three days at Yalta in the Crimea. It is a perfectly beautiful place. The coast is rock-bound and full of beautiful harbors, and the mountains come right down to the sea. They are covered with beautiful trees and vineyards and dotted with lovely, handsome villas of the old regime. It was the playground of the old noblesse.

From Yalta we proceeded to Odessa. It was the one bleak day of the trip. We did nothing in Odessa except wait for the train which departed at 10:40 and spent the time awaiting the train at the local opera. The opera house is physically practically a replica of the opera house in Vienna and was done by the same artist. It was very imposing and very handsome. The opera was *The Queen of Spades* by Pushkin, with music by Tchaikovsky. It was exceptionally well done both dramatically and artistically. The only feature that was not up to the mark was the singing. The director told us that there were 700 people attached to the theater and that they had a performance every day throughout the year of either the opera or ballet; that the artists received all the way from 250 rubles a month to 4000 and even 10,000 rubles, which would be from $20 to $1000 a month at the present rate of exchange. The Moscow government contributes 1,750,000 rubles each year as a subsidy to keep it going at low prices of admission.

That night we took the train and arrived in Kiev, which is the capital of the Ukraine and one of the oldest cities in Russia. Here we stayed for two days. The Ukraine is a tremen-

dously rich, fertile, and beautiful country. Kiev is quite the
most interesting Russian city I have seen. There were many
evidences of prosperity and activity. The shopwindows and
the shops were more attractive than even those in Moscow. I
visited a tile factory and a collective farm. Marjorie spent her
time with the guide enjoying the wonderful old cathedrals
here, which were built at various times from the ninth century on. The Lavra Monastery, which housed at one time
1000 priests and which was in one of the richest of all the
Greek Orthodox dioceses, was particularly interesting, and I
spent an hour there. Here we saw one of the finest collections
of icons and really the most impressive church structure that
we had found in the Soviet Union. Here it is also the cata-
combs are to be found. We also inspected the Institute of the
Masters of Folk Art. It was a school of embroidery and rug
making (being conducted by experts) in the training of young
women. The embroidery work was quite unusual, as was also
the Ukrainian embroidery.

RUSSIA AND JAPAN

JOURNAL   *Moscow—June 4, 1938*

The following is my best judgment as to the situation
here with reference to Japan:

1. Soviet-Japanese relations are very difficult; constant difficulties were being experienced in the Island of Saghalien in
connection with the operation of Japanese concessions; where,
necessarily, reliance was placed in large part upon Soviet employees; these difficulties, it is claimed by some, arise primarily
from the fact that such Soviet employees, fearing charges of
being Trotskyites and Japanese spies and wreckers, refused to
have anything whatever to do with the Japanese; that there
were also other matters of serious difference.

I have the impression that the attitude of Russian diplomacy is definitely hardening toward Japan and more aggressive than last summer.

2. According to reliable information there are approximately 450,000 to 600,000 Soviet armed troops in the eastern area. It is stated, however, that the Japanese believe that for every Japanese soldier in Manchukuo the Soviets maintained, in Manchuria, three Soviet soldiers. The Japanese armed forces in Manchuria are estimated to be from 150,000 to 200,000 in number. This checks with other information current here.

Litvinov recently advised me that the Japanese were extensive buyers of Soviet rubles "outside"; that this accounted for the rise in the price of the "black" ruble, and that in his opinion Japan was procuring rubles for the purposes of bribery in the East.

PLAN TO DIVIDE SPOILS DIVIDES DICTATORS

no. 1339   *Moscow, June 4, 1938*

TO THE HONORABLE THE SECRETARY OF STATE

CONVERSATIONS WITH THE ——— AMBASSADOR IN
MOSCOW WITH REFERENCE TO THE EUROPEAN SITUATION

Strictly Confidential

Sir:

The ——— Ambassador has recently returned. It was reported here that his absence was occasioned not "by leave," but because of a call for consultation.

In reply to my inquiries as to his analysis concerning what had actually happened in the Lithuanian-Polish situation, he stated that this had occurred during his absence, but that upon his return he had checked up on the facts through conversations with Potemkin, the Assistant People's Commissar for Foreign Affairs; the Polish Ambassador, Mr. Grzybowski; and the Lithuanian Minister, Mr. Baltrusaitis. He gave me a detailed account of what he understood had occurred. It coincided precisely with the reports of the situation which I had filed at the time. His conclusions were the following:

1. That Litvinov and the Soviet Foreign Office had handled the matter with great skill as well as with distinct force; that, whereas Litvinov had advised the Lithuanian government to acquiesce in the establishment of diplomatic relations rather than hazard the danger of war by the rejection of the Polish demands on an immaterial issue, nevertheless the Soviet government had made it clear to the Polish government that, while it had no concern with reference to this relatively inconsequential phase of the matter, the Soviet government was none the less vitally concerned with the fact that Lithuanian independence should remain intact; that Litvinov had required a statement from the Polish government to the effect that its ultimate demands were embodied in the pending issue and that it was not merely the precursor of other or similar demands, "clad in equally innocuous dress";

2. That he was very much concerned over the discussions then taking place in Rome between Mussolini and Hitler; that a great deal depended thereon; that his information was that Hitler, after the occupation of the Austrian Foreign Office, had found in their archives indisputable evidence that up to a few days before March 13 * Mussolini had been urging and counseling Schuschnigg to withstand the German demands and that as a result thereof Hitler "was in a fury"; that on the other hand Mussolini had been bitterly upset by Hitler's speedy and ruthless action as to Austria but had

---

* Date of Hitler's occupation of Vienna.

swallowed his pride; that thereafter he was again much disturbed by the fact that air bases for heavy German bombing planes had been established on the Brenner Pass. The Italians could not understand the necessity for this in view of the German professions of peaceful intent; that by reason of these conditions he did not think that Mussolini would go to the extent of engaging in a specific military pact with Hitler, but that there was no assurance that the general staffs did not have an understanding; and that he would have much more confidence in the outcome of this visit if Mussolini were a democratic ruler and not a dictator.

3. That it was the understanding of the French Foreign Office that Hitler's proposals to Mussolini were that Italy should find its "sphere" as a great Mediterranean and African power and confine its European expansion to Spain and to the taking of the French provinces between Italy and Northern Spain along the Mediterranean coast; that Germany should extend its domination east and south through the Balkans.*

4. That the European situation on the whole was somewhat better; that France was going along with England in its attempt to compose the Czechoslovakian situation; that this definite French advantage vis-à-vis England had been procured by Daladier and Bonnet in London, to wit: that, in the event that Czechoslovakia could not comply with the extremes of Henlein's demands, England had agreed to take up the matter with the German government on its own initiative and advise it that if such persistence caused France to go to the rescue of Czechoslovakia, the British government could not give assurances to the German govern-

---

* He stated that the significance of Hitler's proposal was that Mussolini should take the Mediterranean area, including Africa, Spain, and the southern provinces of France and Europe south of a line from Genoa to the Black Sea, and should leave the rest of Europe, including the Balkans, to Hitler.

ment that it would not come into the situation in support
of France; and

5. That while the Spanish situation was troublesome, he
considered that it was a matter of but a very short time
when that situation would be solved, temporarily at least,
by Franco's successes.

I have the honor to be, Sir, respectfully yours,

Joseph E. Davies •

DIARY   *Moscow—June 5, 1938*

Worked all day.

Unexpected conference with Stalin in the afternoon (see
letter).

CONVERSATION WITH STALIN

NO. 1348   *Moscow, June 9, 1938*

TO THE HONORABLE THE SECRETARY OF STATE

THE INTERVIEW AND CONFERENCE HAD WITH MR. STALIN AND
PREMIER MOLOTOV IN THE KREMLIN IN MOSCOW OF JUNE 5,
1938

Strictly Confidential

Sir:

Upon the occasion of making my formal parting call upon
President Kalinin and Premier Molotov on June 5, 1938, a very
interesting situation developed.

When I was in Premier Molotov's apartment in the Kremlin,
and within a very few moments after I had been seated, Mr.
Stalin entered the room alone, came forward, greeted me very
cordially, and he, Molotov, and myself engaged in discussions
for two hours and fifteen minutes. Supplementing my telegram, I have the honor to report with reference thereto as
follows:

After the usual preliminary amenities incident to the occasion of my call on the Premier by reason of my departure and transfer to Belgium, we entered upon a friendly and interesting talk. Stalin was particularly interested in President Roosevelt and asked many questions about him. He also referred in terms of much admiration to your Washington speech.

Stalin brought up the battleship matter which is now pending in the Department, and finally discussed the possibility of a settlement of the Kerensky debt.

A detailed statement of what occurred is set forth in the memorandum hereto attached and made a part hereof. Subsequent developments with reference thereto are also described therein.

Both this dispatch and the memorandum have been dictated under great pressure in the last few hours in Moscow just prior to my departure, and are not at all satisfactory to me as a statement of what occurred, but time presses and I think the memorandum will give you an accurate picture of the situation.

The fact of the conference was announced by the Soviet press and to eliminate the possibility of unwarranted implications I was obliged to issue a short statement to the press, a copy of which I herewith enclose.

The situation created nothing short of a sensation in the Diplomatic Corps here. It was regarded as a unique occurrence in diplomatic history here. I was overwhelmed with requests for appointments. On the occasion of the dinner which Foreign Minister Litvinov gave on the evening of June 7 in honor of our departure (which was again quite unprecedented) and particularly at the reception to the Diplomatic Corps which followed, I was approached repeatedly and delicately questioned with reference to what had occurred. To all inquiries I answered quite frankly that the meeting had been entirely unexpected and had been a complete surprise to me; that I had enjoyed a very interesting visit, in which we had discussed many matters of a general nature. I thought it better to say this much rather than to leave the situation clothed in mystery and possibly thereby cause unwarranted implications to be drawn with reference to the significance of the matter in connection with this international situation.

Enclosed herewith and pursuant to the regulations of the Department you will please find a copy of the talk which Mr. Litvinov made upon the occasion of his dinner, and a memorandum which was prepared by the joint secretarial staff of the Embassy, setting forth the extemporaneous remarks which I made in reply, which I asked them to prepare because of the pressure of matters incident to my departure on the afternoon of this day.*

I have the honor to be, Sir, respectfully yours,

Joseph E. Davies

ENCLOSURE TO FOREGOING DISPATCH

Memorandum of Conference Had This Fifth Day of June, 1938, by Joseph E. Davies with Mr. Stalin, President Kalinin, and Premier Molotov, in the Kremlin at Moscow

Arrangements having been made that the writer should make his formal calls prior to departure on President Kalinin and Premier Molotov on this day, the writer proceeded to the Kremlin at 4:30 P.M.

Considering that it would be advisable to have some member of the staff who also understood Russian accompany me, I suggested that Colonel Faymonville, who speaks Russian

---

* Departmental regulations require that any public utterances shall be reported to the Department.

very well, go with me. Mr. Barkov, Chief of the Protocol Division of the Foreign Office, however, advised that that was not acceptable and when the suggestion was then made that the senior member of the staff should go with me, it was intimated that protocol required that on farewell calls the Ambassador should proceed alone. That made no impression on my mind at the time, but later became significant.

At the former Catherine Palace, inside the Kremlin wall, I was met by Mr. Barkov, the Secretary of Protocol, and was escorted by him to the apartment of President Kalinin, where we were received by the Secretary. Upon entering the President's inner office, Mr. Kalinin came forward cordially to greet me at the door. During our visit President Kalinin sat at his desk. Mr. Barkov, who was also present, Mr. Vinogradov, of the Foreign Office, who acted as interpreter, and I were seated immediately in front of the desk. After the usual social amenities connected with the announcement of my departure were passed, President Kalinin stated that he could quite understand that it might be more agreeable for me at my new post than it would be here. He recognized, he said, that the life of the diplomat in Moscow was not altogether agreeable and had its limitations; for the reason that contacts between officials of the Soviet Union and the Diplomatic Corps did not generally obtain as they did in other countries. He, therefore, could quite understand that I would enjoy the change involved in going to Brussels. I replied that, from an intellectual viewpoint, I had enjoyed this post tremendously. From that angle, I would regret leaving Moscow. Quite frankly, however, the living conditions that obtain in Belgium would be more agreeable. I stated further that I was in entire agreement with his frank statement that the position of members of the Diplomatic Corps here was difficult because of the conditions which he had described. Further, I ventured to say that while this situation contained disadvantages for the Diplomatic Corps, it also had real disadvantages for the Soviet government; that there was much wisdom in the statement of the old French philosopher who had said, "You cannot hate the man you know"; that even though certain Ambassadors and Foreign Ministers might be hostile to this regime, if, through contacts, they come to know the men who were running this government, it might serve to modify the harshness of their judgment; and, certainly, that as to those members of the Corps who were friendly this situation placed them at a disadvantage in not being able to communicate from time to time with the heads of government, as was done in other countries, and thus have the benefit of the point of view of the responsible officials. I stated further that the point of view and outside perspective of friendly foreign diplomats might also be of no small help and real value to government officials here. To this President Kalinin rejoined that the condition which he had referred to was bred by world conditions; that the people of Russia believed that they were surrounded by aggressive and hostile states, particularly Japan and Germany; that in the opinion of his government such feeling was justified and that this basic fact materially prevented free intercourse with the Diplomatic Corps. Another reason for this condition, he said, was that the men in responsible power here, unlike the governing countries of some of the capitalistic classes, were "of the first generation," were confronted with new and great problems, were working overtime and did not have the time for luncheons, dinners, or other social engagements which the Diplomatic Corps were accustomed to employ for such contacts. Time, he thought, would remedy this condition.

President Kalinin spoke of President Roosevelt's speech at Chicago and also of Secretary Hull's speech at Nashville

and expressed the hope that it was an indication of the
United States' possibly becoming more active in the protection of the world peace against the "unruly members of
world society."

In conclusion he stated that he was familiar with the work
which the American Ambassador had done in the Soviet
Union in connection with studying for himself the various
industries and enterprises of the country and of the various
phases of Russian life; that they appreciated the objectivity
of this attitude; and (to my embarrassment) that he and his
associates considered that the American Ambassador, though
he might differ from them, was, nevertheless, an "honest
man," and that they much regretted that he was leaving
this post.

Upon leaving President Kalinin's apartment I asked Mr.
Vinogradov whether he was going with me to Premier Molotov's apartment. He said, "No," that another interpreter would
be available there. Mr. Barkov, however, accompanied me
down the long corridor to another section of the building
where he presented me to a secretary of the Premier. Shortly
thereafter a Mr. Khalotsky (interpreter) came in and I was
ushered into the room of the Premier. Here again on entering
I found the Premier coming forward from his desk to greet
me. Scarcely had we been seated, when I was startled to see
the door, through which I had entered, at the far end of the
room open, and Mr. Stalin come into the room alone. I had
seen him on public occasions heretofore but I had never
had an opportunity to study the man at close range. As he
came in, I noticed that he was shorter than I had conceived and he was quite "slight" in appearance. His demeanor
is kindly, his manner almost deprecatingly simple, his personality and expression of reserve strength and poise very
marked.

As we arose, he came forward and greeted me cordially, with a simple dignity. We then sat down at a large table—a kind of directors' table.

I broke the ice by stating that I had returned to Russia because of a desire, on the occasion of my departure, to express my respects formally to President Kalinin and Premier Molotov, and to express my appreciation of the courtesies that this government and its officials had extended to me. Meeting Mr. Stalin, I then said, was a great surprise, and that I was very much gratified to have this opportunity. I then went on to say that I had personally inspected typical plants of practically all of the heavy industries of the Soviet Union, as well as the great hydraulic developments of the country; that these extraordinary achievements, which had been conceived and projected in the short period of ten years, had commanded my great admiration; that I had heard it said that history would record Stalin as the man who was responsible for this achievement and that he would be recorded as a greater builder than Peter the Great or Catherine; that I was honored by meeting the man who had built for the practical benefit of common men.

To this, Stalin demurred and stated that the credit was not his; that the plan had been conceived and projected by Lenin, who had projected the original Dnieperstroges Dam project; that the ten-year plan was not his work; that it was due to the three thousand able men who had planned this work and those others of his associates; and above all that it was the "Russian people" who were responsible, and that he disclaimed any personal credit therefor. He gave me the impression of being sincerely modest.

After about twenty minutes of conversation discussing my inspection tours of the industrial regions, in the course of which he displayed a knowledge of my work as Commissioner of Corporations and Chairman of the Federal Trade Commission, I started to leave. Stalin asked whether I had to keep another appointment. When I said "No," he suggested that I do not hurry away. I then asked him what were his views on the European situation. He replied that the outlook for European peace was very bad, and the summer might induce serious trouble. He then went on to say that the reactionary elements in England, represented by the Chamberlain government, were determined upon a policy of making Germany strong, and thus place France in a position of continually increasing dependence upon England; also with the purpose of ultimately making Germany strong as against Russia. He stated that in his opinion Chamberlain did not represent the English people and that he would probably fail because the Fascist dictators would drive too hard a bargain. He said that the Soviet Union had every confidence that it could defend itself.

He then asked me whether he might ask me some questions, to which I replied, "Of course."

He then asked whether I was familiar with the pending negotiations which the Soviet government was having with the government of the United States in connection with the proposed contract for the construction of a Soviet battleship by an American firm. He said that the Soviet government had difficulty in understanding why the matter could not go forward; that they were prepared to expend sixty to one hundred million dollars for the building of a battleship, and were prepared to pay cash, both for the battleship to be built in the United States and for the technical aid of American firms to aid them in building a duplicate in the Soviet Union; that this would afford employment to the unemployed, which would be desirable as he was informed that the shipyards were only 60% occupied with present contracts; that the Soviet government could not understand why the matter could not go for-

ward. To this I rejoined that he was misinformed as to the
extent of unemployment as far as shipbuilding was concerned;
that the government of the United States had recently embarked on a huge shipbuilding program which would undoubtedly tax our shipyards to the utmost; that there were
also restrictions imposed by law that would prevent the giving
of plans for battleships, or giving access to manufacturing
plants which were building battleships to foreign countries,
unless the army and navy would declare that this would not
be prejudicial to the military or naval defense of the United
States; that I was familiar only in a general way with the
negotiations which had been projected entirely in Washington and knew of them only through the reports that had been
sent to us as a matter of official routine; that, quite frankly,
it was difficult for me also to understand just what the difficulty
in the situation was from the reading of the reports, but that
I thought the matter had recently given indications of going
forward more rapidly. To this Stalin rejoined that if the President of the United States wanted it done he felt sure that
the army and navy technicians could not stop it, and that it
could be lawfully done. To this I rejoined that in all probability the President of the United States knew nothing about
the matter; that if he did, it was quite probable that among
the many domestic problems which confronted him in connection with the closing session of the Congress, he had not
been able to give foreign affairs his personal attention.

I then asked him which agency of the Soviet government
was negotiating this matter—whether it was the Soviet Embassy in Washington, Amtorg, or the corporation called
"Carp." He asked me whether there was any prejudice against
Carp. To this I said that I did not know. He answered that
Carp was an American corporation; that its president was
an "American patriotic citizen" (a reference, I believe, to

Molotov's brother-in-law), and that it had been considered that it might facilitate the matter, if the contracts were executed by such a corporation. I replied that, in my opinion, there was no prejudice against any agency of the Soviet Union, but that as a practical matter it would clarify the situation for the authorities of the United States to know clearly that the agency presenting this matter spoke authoritatively, and had both his confidence and that of the Soviet government. I then asked the specific question whether the Carp Corporation was the agency to deal with. To this he replied, "Yes."

Stalin then said that there was another matter that he desired to ask me about; and that was a situation that had to do with the possible settlement of the debt of the Kerensky government to the government of the United States.

I stated that I was very glad that he brought this debt matter up; that, with permission, I wanted to trespass upon his patience and ask him to listen to my statement as to this debt matter, which was rather a long story of negotiations, which originated with the President and Mr. Litvinov's agreement in 1933, and which had finally resulted in failure and some misunderstandings and bitterness. I then detailed the facts briefly * as follows: That in 1933 when there were many Japanese attacks on the eastern border of the U.S.S.R. and when it was much to the interest of the Soviet Union to secure recognition by the United States, certain agreements were entered into which also served the interests of the United States; namely, an arrangement whereby the Soviet government would settle the claims of American citizens and those of the government of the United States against the Soviet

---

* Condensed here to avoid duplication of earlier talks with Litvinov, Molotov, and Rosengoltz.

Union; that because Mr. Litvinov was obliged to leave before the arrangement could be fully closed, the matter was left to be worked out as to detail; that for guidance, a memorandum in the nature of a gentlemen's agreement, which set forth the understanding in principle, was written and was initialed by the President and Mr. Litvinov, which expressed the terms under which these debts were to be paid, and that a loan or credit should be made to the U.S.S.R. by the government *or its nationals,* that at the time this memorandum was made and the negotiations were being conducted there was pending in the Congress of the United States a proposal introduced by Senator Johnson, which provided that the government of the United States should in the future make no loan to any foreign government which had not paid its debt to the government of the United States; that this was very well known to everyone and was much discussed, and it was in anticipation that this bill would pass and become a law that the parties entered into an understanding that the loan or credit which was to be made to the U.S.S.R. would be either by the government of the United States *or its nationals:* that there developed misunderstandings in these negotiations; that finally an offer was made by the government of the United States, which in my opinion fulfilled in all respects every honorable obligation that had been undertaken by the President; that this offer had been rejected by Ambassador Troyanovsky upon the direction of his government in 1935 upon the ground that it was not in accordance with the understanding because it offered *not* a *loan* by the government of the United States but by the *nationals* of the United States and upon the further ground that the control of the purchases in the United States was not placed in a Soviet agency but that the purchases were subject to the control of this American agency; that what was offered was a credit and not a loan.

The attitude of the Soviet Union in this respect had been a great disappointment to the President of the United States; that this matter was one of the matters in difference pending between the two governments when I came here and that I would say (with undiplomatic frankness) that my instructions were not to bring up or urge the matter of debt settlement but strongly to take the position that we had done everything that we were honorably committed or required to do and that so far as we were concerned it was a closed book, unless and until the Soviet Union wished to reopen the matter and fulfill its honorable obligations; that I was therefore very glad before my departure to hear from him that the Soviet government was seeking to find a way to settle at least a portion of this debt situation.

To this he rejoined that the Soviet government could not settle with the United States the private claims of American citizens against either the tsarist regime or against the Soviet government without being obliged under treaties to make equally favorable settlement with England and France as to similar claims, and that this would entail too great a burden. What he had in mind was a formula that would eliminate this difficulty. The Soviet government could differentiate a debt of the Russian government to the United States government from a debt claimed to be due to private citizens of the United States. Therefore, the Soviet government could settle the Kerensky debt without such incidental and attendant difficulty with France or England.

I asked whether he knew what the amount of the Kerensky debt was; that I did not have it in mind. He replied that he did not know; that the Kerensky records were not clear; to which I rejoined that I could readily ascertain because I knew our records were clear because it was our money that they had received. This caused a general laugh.

Upon my inquiry Stalin stated that this payment would
have to be in complete liquidation of all claims. To this I
rejoined that if that was the proposition, in my opinion, it
would be useless even to think of submitting it because the
sum was even less than the amount of the previous proposed
agreements. I then asked whether it would be possible for
them to confine the proposal to the Kerensky debt as a governmental debt and leave the other claims for the future. To
this he at first demurred. I then said that my only object in
bringing this point up was frankly to give them my view as
to what, in my opinion, would make it useless to even submit
a proposal, and that the proposal, in my judgment, would not
even be considered unless the arrangement could be made
without prejudice to other claims. I explained that in our
practice in drawing contracts we frequently resorted to that
principle, namely, that a single matter in difference between
parties could be settled, with an express reservation that such
settlement did not prejudice or stop either party from asserting any other claim in the future. He said that was agreeable.

Of course, throughout this discussion it was understood that
the remarks and inquiries I made were designed simply to
explore the exact terms of the offer. It was clearly stated that
I, of course, was not purporting to say what would or would
not be acceptable to my government.

DIARY   *Moscow—June 6, 1938*

Worked all day at the office cleaning up. Discussed the
debt situation with Henderson and Kirk, in an effort to get
down to cases as to just what the proposition was and meant.

Diary *Moscow—June 7, 1938*

Worked on memorandum to define Soviet proposal with reference to matter discussed.

State dinner at the Spiridonovka house given by Litvinov in our honor. Apart from the staff of our Embassy and officials of the foreign office, the only others present were the Belgian Minister and his wife—a rather pleasant and thoughtful gesture.

Litvinov made a very generous and handsome speech to which I replied extemporaneously.

Reception after the dinner, concert and dance thereafter. Came home in the morning, in daylight. It was fine.

Diary *Moscow—June 8, 1938*

Marjorie received a lovely gift of a beautiful pair of vases today, at the Sheremetief House, which is now a porcelain museum. It was presented by Madam Molotov on behalf of the Soviet government and was as a tribute to the first Ambassadress of the United States to the Soviet Union.

NEWSMEN IN MOSCOW

Journal *Moscow—June 8, 1938*

I felt quite a twinge when I told the newspapermen that I was leaving Russia. They have been of inestimable help to me. As a matter of fact, I have come to think of them more or less as "unofficial colleagues." They have performed their job of reporting the news, without regard as to "where the chips might fall"; but they have been scrupulously honorable in keeping faith with me in all "off-the-record" talk. Their judgment upon situations and men, coupled with their far-wider knowledge of Russia, has helped me greatly. They are an unusual group of men, each distinctive in his own personality and each marked by ability peculiar to that personality. I liked the British correspondent Cholerton; he has brittle wit. His phrase, "Habeas corpus has been replaced here by habeas cadaver," is a classic.

Spencer Williams, who writes for the *Manchester Guardian,* and who represents the American-Russian Chamber of Commerce here, has been here since 1930, longer than any American press representative except Walter Duranty. He has a practical mind, with a business twist, is shrewd and able. In my travels into the Ukraine, the Don Basin, and the Caucasus, he was with me daily. His experience here affords a mine of useful information. Demaree Bess is straight as a string and very able. He and Joe Barnes, representing two different approaches to this situation, have been particularly valuable to me. Jim Brown had a matter-of-fact American approach that resolved enigmas to just plain American slang and generally hit the nail on the head. Charlie Nutter is a star. Dick Massock, who took his place, has his feet on the ground all the time. Henry Shapiro speaks Russian and is a graduate of the Law School here, as well as Columbia. His explanation of the Soviet judicial procedure was of value to us all. They are a great credit to American journalism. I shall always feel under a special obligation to Walter Duranty who told the truth as he saw it and has the eyes of genius. Stanley Richardson, my secretary, comes within this group of newsmen. My obligation to him I will never be quite able to express. He had been here before and knew the ground. His clarity and common sense assessed values and situations with great accuracy. His fine loyalty and indefatigable industry made him invaluable. He rendered great service to the Embassy and to us all.

JOURNAL *En route to Berlin—June 11, 1938*

Immediately following my talk with Stalin, I took the matter up with Loy Henderson and Alexander Kirk.* Fortunately, they were both familiar with the whole debt question.

In order to avoid any dispute or misunderstanding, I had decided it would be advisable to have a proposal in writing. The discussion with Henderson and Kirk cleared the situation up very much in my mind and was very helpful.

On June 8, I saw Molotov, upon my request, and stated I wished to clarify in my own mind the debt proposal. We discussed the matter for an hour and a half, and he stated he would let me hear from him later. Upon my suggestion that I would take the matter up with Litvinov of the Foreign Office, he stated that that was not necessary, and that he would "square" the matter with Litvinov so far as diplomatic courtesies were concerned.

On the following day, Premier Molotov's secretary called me up and asked if I could come over to the Kremlin. This I did at 7 o'clock in the evening. Molotov said that he had taken the matter up with his government associates and Mr. Stalin, and that they had agreed upon a written proposal which he gave to me in the Russian language, and which I asked him to have translated into English. Molotov explained that the Russian government did not need a loan, and that this was done purely as a matter of clearing up the misunderstanding with the United States and as a desire to show its high regard for the good opinion of the President and the Secretary of State. Whether or not it failed, he said, it at least would be a manifestation of their good will. He asked that it be kept out of the diplomatic channels and be negotiated direct, and that

---

* The newly arrived Counselor of the Embassy, now Minister to Egypt.

he would provide means for me to communicate direct with
him; that the matter was of such importance that he hoped
that I would return to the United States to discuss it with the
President and the Secretary of State. I told him that I had explained the matter to the Department and that my orders were
to return to the United States before going to Brussels. He
also stated that he thought it would be advisable to give this
matter no publicity, unless it were successfully negotiated.*

Moscow, June 9, 1938

MISS EMLEN KNIGHT DAVIES

My darling Daughter:

Well, I can't tell you how much Mar-
jorie and I have missed you since we returned to Moscow
from our Black Sea trip. It was too everlastingly bad that you
were not here, because you sense and understand all of the
implications that this strange situation involves and would
have enjoyed the experience of the last week in view of that
background, I am sure.

---

* The matters in difference between the Department and the Soviet officials
arising out of this misunderstanding had not been made public as it was one
of those situations in which no useful purpose would be served by making it
public, and in fact the possible solution of the matter might have been
hindered by such publicity. During all the discussions of the matter by my
predecessor or myself, nothing was given to the press.

In all the columns of speculation which appeared in the press of the world
regarding my meeting with Stalin, not even the reputedly best informed of
the political columnists ever even hinted that Stalin had broached a debt-
settlement proposal or that it was under consideration.

Now, in view of the fact that Stalin and his government are resisting Hitler
and his plans of world aggression, it is right that the American public should
be informed of the fact that the Soviet government three years ago reversed
its position in connection with the debt settlement, in order to show its
consideration for the United States and its desire to maintain the confidence
of the President and the Secretary of State in connection with its obligations.

In the Appendix the reader will find the official reports of these conferences
which I had with Premier Molotov.

For surely there have been things doing and the days have been very full of happenings of personal interest that have just followed, one after the other.

The whole Diplomatic Corps has been agog over what has been happening. It is really quite amusing. They almost seem stunned. Well, to give it in chronological order, this is about what happened.

We arrived from Kiev on Saturday, June 4. The entire staff was down to the station to meet us and it was good to see all our old friends again.

On Sunday, June 5, I had an appointment to make my formal calls of departure on the President, Mr. Kalinin, and upon the Premier, Mr. Molotov. This had all been arranged. So at 4:30 in the afternoon I proceeded to the Kremlin and drove up to the entrance of the very beautiful yellow and white Catherine Palace at the extreme end, catercorner from the automobile entrance. You will recall it as just inside the wall opposite the entrance from the Red Square, facing St. Basil's, and inside the Kremlin walls.

When I had presented my respects and my recall to President Kalinin, and also to Premier Molotov, I was very gratified to hear their expressions of regret. The gist of them was that they had been much impressed with the serious manner in which the Ambassador had taken his work and particularly by his studious application to industrial and social conditions in the Soviet Union and the objectivity and honesty with which he had sought the facts, and that while he had always been very frank in his attitude, nonbelief in their political idea, and had always asserted his fundamental confidence in his own country's political philosophy and evolution as against revolution, that nevertheless he had been "honest" and fair. As a matter of fact, I was quite flabbergasted by the extent of their knowledge of what I had done and my travels throughout the country inspecting all of these industries, and also by the intimate knowledge that they had of my work when I was Commissioner of Corporations and Chairman of the Federal Trade Commission under President Wilson. Moreover, I was, of course, very much gratified to hear these things said, because these men are a strong and able group, and I personally give them credit for honesty and sincerity of purpose and an idealism that is based on an effort to serve humanity. Where I disagree with them is not in the end which they seek to project, but in the methods by which they are trying to project their Utopia. They are trying to go too fast and must, therefore, fail. The price which they exact from society and the deprivations of freedom of thought and freedom of speech and in security for life and freedom of the individual is too high to justify what is being done; but as to their motives I give them credit for sincerity and honesty. I am sorry that this great experiment could not have been based on the Christian religion.

Well, after I had left President Kalinin's office and gone to the Premier's apartment—and within a very few minutes after sitting down at the desk—I was perfectly amazed and almost struck dumb with surprise to see the far-end door of the room open and Stalin come in alone. I had not the remotest idea it was going to happen. In the first place, he is not the head of the state, and it is his purpose and theirs, apparently, to keep him apart from the state, and, as you know, no diplomat ever sees him officially or otherwise in a personal way. In fact, he avoids any such meeting. So closely has he been shielded from the public that it has almost become a historical event when he receives any foreigner.

Well, when he came in, of course, I stood up and approached him. He greeted me cordially with a smile and with great simplicity, but also with a real dignity. He gives the impression of a strong mind which is composed and wise. His brown eye is exceedingly kindly and gentle. A child would like to sit in his lap and a dog would sidle up to him. It is difficult to associate his personality and this impression of kindness and gentle simplicity with what has occurred here in connection with these purges and shootings of the Red Army generals, and so forth. His friends say, and Ambassador Troyanovsky assures me, that it had to be done to protect themselves against Germany—and that some day the outside world will know "their side."

We sat down at the table and with an interpreter talked for two hours. Of course, I cannot write here what we talked about, for that is only for the President, the Secretary of State, and our government, but I can say that the discussion ranged over the whole field of economy, industrial conditions in Russia, problems of the United States, personality of President Roosevelt, the European situation, the situation in the Far East—all in a very general way. It was really an intellectual feast, which we all seemed to enjoy. Throughout it we joked and laughed at times. He has a sly humor. He has a very great mentality. It is sharp, shrewd, and, above all things else, wise, at least so it would appear to me. If you can picture a personality that is exactly opposite to what the most rabid anti-Stalinist anywhere could conceive, then you might picture this man. The conditions that I know to exist here and his personality are just as far apart as the poles. The explanation, of course, may be found in the fact that men will do for religion or for a cause things that they would never do otherwise. It is the fanaticism of the world that has brought the greatest cruelties.

There were several amusing sidelights to our conversation. In the course of our talk, I explained that I had always made it clear to the members of the Soviet government that I was a

capitalist—this by way of not having any misunderstanding
as to my point of view. "Yes," he said, laughingly, "we know
you are a capitalist—there can be no doubt about that." I
then explained my point of view frankly—that personally I,
like a great many other capitalists, or rather individualists, in
the United States were sympathetic with what they were trying to do; that we also wanted to have a fairer distribution
of wealth, but we were doing it better in the United States
than they were doing it in Russia; that we were holding fast
to the best and trying to eliminate the worst in the process of
evolution; that we were doing a better job for the common
man than they were; that we were holding on to those freedoms which we cherished and at the same time we were trying to bring about greater distribution of wealth and greater
equality of opportunity, economically and socially, for the
underprivileged.

I asked, as illustrative of the manner in which wealth was
being distributed, "How much of all of Mrs. Davies' property do you think will go to the state and how much to her
children and to her heirs?" He manifested interest. I said,
"More than 80 per cent will go to the Federal and state governments and less than one fifth of her property will go to
her children; that in my own case more than 50 per cent would
go to the state and less than 50 per cent to my children." I
asked him, "How much do you suppose I pay to the government in income taxes alone every year, even including my
salary as a government official—more than 60 per cent;
whereas Mrs. Davies pays more than 72 per cent." This obviously surprised Mr. Stalin, for he looked at Molotov with a
smile and Molotov nodded.

Of course, I am writing this with the confidence that none
of you will disclose it now. But I thought it would be interesting and valuable for you to have in the long years to come;

for it is an honest and objective picture of the man and the conditions under which I met him.

Why he made this exception in the case of the present American Ambassador from both what he said and what he left unsaid, I gather about as follows: first and foremost, this government does have a kindly feeling toward the United States. Beneath that, the Russian people have a kindly and friendly feeling toward the American people. Basically, there is nothing that we have that they could take and nothing that they have that we would want to take and the feeling is that it is just impossible that there would at any time ever be an armed clash between the two countries. Then, from what they say, it would appear that they have been very much impressed with the character of my work and my attitude both. Stalin asked me about my impression of their industrial developments. I told him. He said that I probably knew more about them than any foreigner and probably as much as anyone in the Soviet Union, because I had covered them comprehensively and the most recently. Apparently my interest and work had impressed them all very much. I am enclosing a copy of Foreign Minister Litvinov's speech at the Spiridonovka (Entertainment House) at a dinner which the government gave in our honor the other evening on the occasion of our departure. That is illuminating as to this side of it. It was frank and, while flattering, I am sure he meant what he said.

Then again, I think they have been impressed with the objectivity of my viewpoint and the effort which I made to get the facts and base my conclusions on personal knowledge.

From what they said, they have been impressed by my honesty, as they call it, for, of course, I have been almost brutally frank in my talks with them, privately, in criticism of their system in contrast to our own, both in political thought and methods. I always coupled this position, however, with

a tolerant recognition that everyone has a right to his own
opinion and that no one can be dogmatic or aggressively
positive that in his mind alone there resides a complete in-
fallibility. They have all spoken of that fact. I have even
heard it from London. Lady Williams Taylor told me
that the Russian Ambassador there had said to her: "We like
Davies. He disagrees with us, but we believe him to be an
honest man."

                                                      Devotedly,

                                        Moscow, June 10, 1938

MRS. MILLARD TYDINGS

Eleanor Dearest:

                         My last letter was addressed to Bijou and
I was obliged to discontinue dictating it because I was interrupted. Only now have I been able to resume the account
of our doings since our return to Moscow. And they have been
some doings! ! ! !

Apparently the visit with Stalin created nothing short of a
sensation in the Diplomatic Corps. "It was most remarkable!"
"It was unique in the diplomatic history of the past twenty
years," etc., etc. Such were some of the comments. The
curiosity of the Corps was almost funny.

There were many direct and indirect approaches to the
subject from the various ambassadors and ministers. It
reached even to some of the undersecretaries. The British
Chargé (Vereker—and a delightful fellow he is) asked point-
blank for an appointment, as he apparently had received an
enquiry from his government "and his ambassador was on
leave."

It was quite obvious that all sorts of conjectures and unwarranted implications were afoot. So I gave a short interview to the press, which you undoubtedly read. This I con-

JOSEPH STALIN

"To the Honorable Mr. Joseph E. Davies, Representative of the U. S. in the U. S. S. R. With respect and esteem. J. Stalin"

firmed at great length to my diplomatic confreres with much volubility but no more substance. For after all, it is not their business and my obligation is on occasion *not* to talk (in seven different languages) and if I do, to do so only in reporting to the President or the Secretary of State.

On the evening of June 7, Foreign Minister Litvinov gave a large dinner in our honor, followed later by a reception to the Diplomatic Corps at "Spiridonovka 17" (the official Foreign Office house for entertaining). Those present at the dinner were the Soviet hosts—Foreign Minister Litvinov and Madam Molotov, the wife of the Premier, who is a great friend and admirer of Marjorie's and is now Assistant Commissar of the food industry as well as head of the cosmetic and perfumery trust; the diplomatic staff of our mission and the higher officials of Narkomindel (the Soviet Foreign Office).

The only outsiders present were the Belgian Minister and his wife. (Ekay will remember him as the Councilor of the Belgian Legation when she was here. His name is Heyndrickx, and he was advanced to Minister when De Tellier, the former Minister, was made Belgian Ambassador to Paris.)

It was a beautiful dinner. The food was excellent, the table linen and cutlery and glassware were all of the old regime and the service was quick, alert, and very good. The wines and vodka were also first-class.

Over the dessert and the champagne, Foreign Minister Litvinov gave a simple but thoughtful after-dinner talk preliminary to drinking the health of the President of the United States and his honor guests. It was very well done. He did not rise but spoke naturally and earnestly in perfect English, both in grammatical construction as well as in enunciation.

(Note inserted by M.P.D.: Daddy does not tell you, but it was a really wonderful tribute to your brilliant father and his work here. You would have burst with pride as I did. M.)

One can well understand why he should bear the reputation
of being the ablest Foreign Minister in Europe. I think he is,
and had the pleasure of saying so to Stalin and Molotov the
other day. Thinking you might like to have what he said, I
am enclosing the English copy which was issued the following day by the Foreign Office to the press section. I also am
sending you a copy of my extemporaneous reply which the
staff and Stanley Richardson and the members of the staff
who were present reconstructed for me, as I was simply
swamped in getting dispatches out to take with me to Washington and which had to be done. The boys did a good job
and it faithfully sets forth the subject matter of what I managed to say.

The dinner was better in every way than any we attended
when Ekay was here. Even their menus were very smart, if
modest, with the hammer and sickle embossed in white relief.

Marjorie looked particularly beautiful in a white gown and
with no jewels. She felt it was in better taste to wear none.
She is in every way a great Ambassadress and a credit to our
country. She has been an invaluable asset to this mission.

The reception after dinner was very brilliant for Moscow
or for any capital in the world, for that matter. The entire
Diplomatic Corps was present. The old mansion looked very
much better than when I had last seen it in November of last
year. The furniture was all furbished up and covered with
new tapestry, the doors and windows were all "opened out" to
the garden, which was well groomed as to flowers and foliage
and with sand sprinkled over the winding walks. The summer
houses under the trees were very attractive, with festoons of
strings of many colored incandescent lights and (believe it
or not) there was beautiful tapestried furniture scattered
about in the summer houses and verandas for those who
wished to go out into the moonlight. The verandas were simi-

larly illuminated. A bar was arranged in one of them, where all kinds of hors d'oeuvres—caviar, delicatessen, pastries—and drinks were lavishly served.

As usual, there was an hour of concert music in the white marble ballroom. The artists were the "Honored Artists" of the U.S.S.R., all wearing their "decoration" conspicuously. In other words, they were the best the opera or the Musical Conservatory could produce. The basso was magnificent and the others were first-class. A child of fourteen, who had just won first place in an international contest at Brussels last winter, played the violin remarkably. The power which she displayed in emotional interpretation as well as in technical skill was startling to find in one so young. There is no doubt but what these people have very great emotional and dramatic richness in their physical and nervous make-up.

The artists were all dressed very smartly after the best European fashion. The women were *soignée*—the men wore white ties in very well-fitting evening clothes. Ekay will be interested to know that the dance orchestra of 12 pieces were all in black ties and played the latest jazz and European favorites. The point of this lies in the fact that it indicates a marked change over last year.

It is indicative of the improvement we have seen in the streets—more well-dressed people, more shoes, more color, more handsome automobiles, etc. "Consumers' goods" are at last beginning to make their appearance. They have been long promised and are overdue. As a matter of fact, my own opinion is that it is quite remarkable that this improvement does show so soon considering that the whole manufacturing enterprise—at least 80 per cent of it—sprang practically from the "heel of Jove," beginning only ten years ago.

Well, to get back to the party: after the concert we were again "fed." The tables were laden with good things to eat.

All of the four large rooms were provided with tables, each seating from six to sixteen persons, and all "dolled out" again with the linen, cutlery, and glassware of the old regime. The food, from caviar to the ice, was again bountiful and, like the wine (of which there were six kinds), would be very creditable in any capital anywhere, and was very well served.

After "supper," we danced in the white ballroom until 3.30 A.M. and came home with the dawn breaking over the Kremlin.

Marjorie was the belle of the ball. The Foreign Minister opened the party with her, and he dances very well. So what with the ambassadors, ministers, and young secretaries, the old man "hisself" was sorely put to it to get a dance. But the dear girl, my Marjorie, bless her heart, saw to that.

As you can see, it was a lovely party; and a very memorable evening. It will always be a high spot in the "memories that gild the past." It was a lovely ending to our stay in Moscow.

Devotedly,

Remarks of Maxim M. Litvinov, People's Commissar for Foreign Affairs of the U.S.S.R., at a Dinner He Tendered in Honor of Ambassador and Mrs. Joseph E. Davies at Moscow, June 7, 1938

Ambassador and Mrs. Davies:

The very great pleasure of having here tonight Ambassador Davies and Mrs. Davies is marred by the thought that it is a farewell dinner and that it is perhaps the last occasion of having their pleasant company. It is sad for the simple reason that using plain, undiplomatic language, we all like both Mr. and Mrs. Davies, we continually felt their friendship and good will toward our country and its peoples.

I remember telling you, Mr. Ambassador, during your first visit to me, as I am used to telling every diplomatic newcomer, that Moscow is certainly not a place in which to look for that diversity of amusements and entertainments to which diplomats are accustomed in other capitals, but that a foreign representative who takes an interest in studying and watching the growth and development of a new country, of a new social and political order, of a new life, of the resurrection of the culture of a hundred nationalities, will find here something to occupy his time, his mind, and his faculty for observation.

You, Mr. Ambassador, have proved to be just such a diplomat-student, a diplomat-observer, a diplomat-investigator. You have devoted much of your time and your great energy to the study of this country, losing no opportunity of seeing for yourself anything worthy of study and observation, even undertaking for that purpose fatiguing long-distance journeys. We appreciate it very much. We do not like being just looked at, gullibly talked of, preferring to be studied and, of course, to be properly understood.

You, Mr. Ambassador, have done your best to understand our country, what is going on here, the motives behind our doings, and the aims in front of them. If you will, as I am sure you will, pass on the results of your study and observation and unbiased judgment to your government and to your countrymen, you will certainly contribute much more to the strengthening of friendly relations between our two countries than by any other purely diplomatic activities.

The relationship between the U.S.S.R. and the U.S.A. has not found expression in many diplomatic acts, documents, or external manifestations. But I flatter myself to think that there is a great deal of latent, unexposed, unproclaimed, and unwritten mutual sympathy and respect between the peoples of our two countries. Love and friendship without words are sometimes the truest and the sincerest, for insincerity and hypocrisy not seldom begin with words, with outward expressions. But love and friendship presuppose understanding and comprehension and that is what, I am sure, your country will obtain, thanks to your information in respect of my country.

*Summary of Response of Ambassador Joseph E. Davies to the Remarks of Maxim M. Litvinov, People's Commissar for Foreign Affairs of the U.S.S.R., on the Occasion of a Dinner Tendered by Him to Mr. and Mrs. Davies at Moscow, June 7, 1938 ***

Mr. Commissar, Ladies and Gentlemen:

I am really moved by the very generous character of your remarks and the beautiful hospitality extended to us tonight. From the moment of my arrival, as the Ambassador of the United States, I have received many kindnesses from the government officials and many expressions of friendly feeling from the Russian people, and I wish to express my deep appreciation therefor.

When you, Mr. Foreign Minister, on my arrival presented me to the leaders of your government, I was then, and have been since, much impressed by their evident sincerity and idealistic purposes.

You have commented upon the underlying sympathy and understanding which exist between the peoples of your country and mine. That I believe is pre-eminently true. That feeling found expression in historical events. Catherine the Great refused to loan her troops or her money to the effort to crush the young American republic. Again during the Civil War,

* This abstract of my talk was made by Stanley Richardson, my invaluable secretary and friend, and a member of the Embassy staff.

which threatened the existence of the American republic, Russia refused to participate in any connection which might impair the unity of the United States. Again as an indication of the common point of view of the Russian and American peoples, it is my belief that both peoples are seeking to improve the lot of the common man. Our great President, Lincoln, said, "The Lord must have loved the poor because he created so many more of them than the rich." The political impulse of your people and of the American people is to promote the well-being of the greatest number. That is the end toward which we are striving. Our methods are different. We believe ours to be the best. We concede that you have the right to maintain that yours are the best.

You have commented upon the extent of my study of Soviet institutions and industry and travel in the Soviet Union. I have had the opportunity to see for myself these great industrial enterprises that have sprung up within the past ten years. In my opinion, the extent of that economic development during that short period has been unparalleled.

What has particularly impressed me in that connection is the youth and enthusiasm of the young men and women who have been recruited from the collective farms, given the opportunity to technical and scientific education, and are now administering these great plants. It is a case of where the country boy has come to town, and is on his way. As in the United States, the country boy that is earnest and sincere, who comes to the city, will not be denied.

Whether you succeed or fail, what has taken place here will have a profound effect upon the world. The human forces which have been released and the great resources which you enjoy will inevitably have a powerful effect upon the future.

Mr. Commissar, you have said very beautifully and simply that the Russian people like us. We like the Russian people.

Your literature, your art, your music, your opera and ballet are glorious and reflect the great qualities of your people.

There is one very great noble aim that our two countries share in common, whether it be motivated by God, as we believe, or what you might term great natural forces, or by ideals, or by human nature, and that is that the Soviet Union and the government of the United States are both genuinely desirous of peace in the world, and peace is what the world most needs now. Of this I have been assured by your highest leader.

As you know, I am not a professional diplomat. My experience has been in professional and business affairs. When I was honored by our great President with this appointment, the prospect was of challenging interest. I came here with an objective mind. I am leaving with an objective mind, but possibly less objective and more friendly because of the kindnesses which you and your government have extended to me as the representative of my country.

In conclusion, I wish to thank you again, Mr. Litvinov, on behalf of Mrs. Davies and myself, for your many courtesies, and in particular this delightful evening. I am sure my American staff would be very glad to join with me in raising my glass to you, Mr. Litvinov, your associates, and the traditional friendship of the peoples of our two countries.*

DIARY   *On Train—June 10, 1938*

This has been a hectic day. The Belgian Minister, Mr. Heyndrickx, and his lovely wife had a small luncheon in our honor, prior to going to the train. It seemed strange that our last meal in Russia was at the Belgian Legation, and the first

---

* For Ambassador Davies' farewell talk to the Embassy staff see the Appendix.

official entertainment in our honor when we came to Russia was at the Belgian Legation. The Heyndryckxes are a charming family with lovely little children. All the Diplomatic Corps were present at the station and gave us a great send-off. All of our friends were there from the American colony and the staff. According to statements, it was the largest send-off on record. It was most pleasant.

Spencer Williams' little girl, a perfect dear, brought Marjorie some flowers. In fact she was deluged with flowers, even red roses, the first I have seen in Russia. Barkov came down to bring me an autographed photograph of the Premier—and I had to run to catch the train.

"Our Bender" is with us. He is aboard, going to the Negoreloye frontier to see us through the border. He has been an employee of the American Embassy for years. He is an unusually fine type of Russian—honest, kind, energetic, and most effective. He is thoroughly loyal to his party and I am sure also to us. We are very fond of Bender. He is "an institution" with the American colony.

DIARY *On the train en route to Berlin—June 11, 1938*

When we went through Warsaw at 2 o'clock this afternoon, we were delighted and surprised to see our old friends Tony and Margaret Biddle at the station. They had come down to see us off and, thoughtful as they always are, brought a lovely basket of fresh fruit. We had a visit with these fine people who have made such a distinct and successful career, first in Norway, and then in Poland.

DIARY *On the train en route to Ostend—June 12, 1938*

Marjorie went through Berlin direct to Paris, but I branched off for London via Brussels. Arrived in London at 5:30 P.M.

Mr. Groves, of the American Embassy, came down to the station to see me, and took off some files to be kept at the Embassy. He looks like a very good man—modest, direct, and businesslike.

DIARY   *London—June 14, 1938*

Arrived here, en route for home.

Called at the Embassy to see my old friend, Joe Kennedy. He was out. He came over to the Dorchester later to see me. He is very pessimistic. So am I.

Was lucky enough to get Marjorie's birthday present here at Wartzki's Russian Antique Shop. It is a beautiful dresser set which was presented to the wife of Paul I by the French government on the occasion of her marriage over 150 years ago.

DIARY   *En route to New York—June 17, 1938*

Caught the boat train at 10 A.M. and joined Marjorie on the *Washington* at Southampton. She was delighted with the dresser set. It was sure good to see her.

John Montgomery, Minister to Hungary, an old friend, is also aboard, I understand, going home for summer leave. I am looking forward to a good visit with him.

DIARY   *New York City—June 23, 1938*

Arrived in New York at 6:10 P.M., but fog kept us in the harbor until the following noon. I caught the afternoon train for Washington.

E. K. came with me and Eleanor joined us at Baltimore.

DIARY   *Washington—June 24, 1938*

This morning I had an extended conference with the Secretary of State. Gave him full details of the new developments in the situation in Moscow, arising out of my talk with Stalin. The Soviet government, he tells me, has significance, not only with reference to the Japanese-Chinese situation, but also in connection with possible European peace. He was very gratified by the changed attitude of the Soviet government with reference to agreements made in connection with debt settlements incident to "recognition." In his quiet way he said very generous and kind things as to the success of my mission to Moscow, which these proposals which I brought back had demonstrated. A sound basis of mutual respect and confidence in the promises of each other as between the U.S.S.R. and the United States was a very important thing for the future in these hazardous days of international threat from the "aggressor bandits" in the world.

In Tennessee, he said, and in the West, when outlaws ran amuck, disturbed the peace and the safety of peace-loving citizens, all law-abiding men set their hands against them and put them in jail or made them incapable of disturbing the peace. This kind and patient man is very vigorous when his indignations are aroused. The Secretary is very depressed over developments in the European situation. It looks very bad, he said. All that I told him today confirms this opinion.

DIARY   *Washington—June 25, 1938*

Had a long conference today with the President in his office. Took lunch with him at his desk. He plied me with questions as to the details of the Stalin interview and went over each of the matters discussed in detail. He was very glad that the old misunderstanding which had arisen over the debt agreement in connection with the recognition of the Soviet was being cleaned up and he thought that this was a fine action on the part of the Soviet government. He had always

heard that they had lived up to their agreements and were
particularly scrupulous as to their given word.

The President told me to go ahead and work out the details
of the proposal at the Department with a view to its presentation to the Senate. In that connection, he suggested that I
study the offer which the Hungarian government had made
in connection with their debt settlement, which is now pending before the Foreign Relations Committee of the Senate—
that would be helpful.

Premier Molotov, I said, had delegated Mr. Rosoff, of
Amtorg, the Soviet government agency, to represent him here
for further discussions. Inasmuch as I was not returning to
Moscow, I suggested that it might be advantageous for my
successor to sit in on these discussions with Mr. Rosoff; and
in that connection I suggested that the man appointed be a
liberal, and a man of business training. He asked whether I
had anybody in mind. I told him I thought Sidney Weinberg
would be the type and he would also be very helpful in working out this debt agreement, because of his knowledge of
banking. He told me to speak to Cordell and, if agreeable,
to talk then to Sidney about it, and see how he felt about
going to Moscow. It was a fine idea, he said, to have Sidney
sit in on these negotiations. He wants me to try and clean up
the situation before I leave for Brussels. He said some very
generous things about the success of my representation, which
I shall always value as coming from the greatest man I have
known.

DIARY   *Washington—June 26, 1938*

Sidney Weinberg and Mr. Rosoff came down to spend
the day, and we had an extended conference. We canvassed
the whole debt situation at length, in connection with working
the matter out along the lines proposed in principle.

DIARY *Washington—June 27, 1938*

Conferred today with Sumner Welles. Characteristically, he was thoroughly familiar with the Stalin interview—with all of its implications.

Welles is an indefatigable worker and I was not surprised to find that he had already carefully considered all the material in these dispatches. Moreover, his suggestions in connection with the discussions with Rosoff were very practical and helpful.

He said that it should be pointed out to Rosoff that there was a possibility that the status of the Hungarian proposal in the Senate might make it advisable to defer action on the Soviet proposal for a short time, until it was ascertained what the disposition of the Senate was in connection with the proposal of settlement of the Hungarian government.

DIARY *Washington—June 28, 1938*

Lunched with Oumansky, chargé d'affaires of the Soviet Embassy. Following Premier Molotov's suggestion, I did not mention the debt matter to him at that time.

This afternoon had a long visit with Secretary of State Hull, and reported to him on the debt matter in detail.

DIARY *Washington—July 4, 1938*

Reported to the President with reference to the Rosoff negotiations. He stated that he thought it would be advisable to hold the matter in abeyance until it was known what action the Senate Foreign Relations Committee and the Senate would take in connection with a somewhat similar proposal by the Hungarian government looking to a settlement of its past debt. I told him that I would so advise Mr. Rosoff and would also advise Messrs. Stalin and Molotov, through him, that the matter had been submitted to the President, and that he was much gratified by the gesture of friendship, good faith, and good will which the Soviet government had made, and particularly because it served to clear up misunderstandings which might have affected the confidence of the governments of the two countries, and because it manifested a desire to complete in spirit the Roosevelt-Litvinov agreement appertaining to the recognition of the U.S.S.R.

I told him how gratified and honored Sidney Weinberg felt about his suggestion, and that he would undoubtedly hear direct from Sidney himself.

DIARY   *New York—July 5, 1938*

Conferred with Rosoff, and worked out with him a message which he could send to Premier Molotov, advising that the matter had been discussed at length with both the President and the Secretary of State; both had been gratified by the gesture of friendship, good faith, and good will which these discussions had called for; that the situation had been productive of much good; that it was considered advisable to leave the matter open for the present, and take it up subsequently, if feasible and desirable; that this was for the reason that the disposition of the Hungarian proposal of debt settlement now pending in the Senate of the United States would throw more light upon what would be possible in the matter of a compromise settlement; that when the time comes, if it is desirable, this government would be glad to try to work out some formula which would settle the matter to the satisfaction of both parties; that for the present it was understood that the entire matter will be held in confidence and would be known only to the immediate principals involved.

Made a report to the Department setting forth and bringing up to date the situation as to discussions and negotiations with Mr. Rosoff, preparatory to my departure.

PART VIII

BRIEF ON THE FACTS

June 6, 1938

VIII

"BRIEF ON THE FACTS"—A SURVEY OF THE U.S.S.R.

NO. 1341   *Moscow, June 6, 1938*

TO THE HONORABLE THE SECRETARY OF STATE

FINAL SUMMARY AND REPORT ON THE
SOVIET UNION PRIOR TO DEPARTURE

Strictly Confidential

Sir:

Supplementary to the oral reports on conditions in the U.S.S.R. and the discussions had with the President, the Secretary of State, and with the Department, with reference to the policy of the United States, which under present conditions in contrast to those of several years ago would now seem advisable, I respectfully submit the following general review and summary report of the situation here.

Back of any question of policy, there are questions of fact, which must needs be controlling. These factors, among others, are: the innate strength of the U.S.S.R.; the strengths and the weaknesses of the present regime, politically, economically, and from a military point of view; the attitude of foreign powers with reference to the U.S.S.R.; the future significance of these forces vis-à-vis world conditions and par-

377

ticularly their significance with reference to the United States.

The initial difficulty in assessing this situation lies in the fact that the field is so vast, the forces so great, the prejudices and controversies so violent, that it is difficult to envisage the whole picture and preserve an objectivity of judgment.

There do exist, however, certain definite ascertainable facts which, when marshaled, afford a basis for judgment. Moreover, in the last twenty years during which this regime has existed, certain developments stand out very clearly. They are mileposts in the evolution of the situation, which point to trends and possible future developments.

This report is aimed to present, as far as possible, a "Brief on the Facts." Facts produce their own conclusions and are not susceptible to color or lack of objectivity.

The facts here assembled are based either upon published sources of information without the Soviet Union or upon government sources published here. Where definite facts are not objective, an effort has been made to epitomize the best judgment of the very able staff of this mission, supplemented by the judgment of some of the chiefs of other missions who are stationed here, and as well by the opinions of American journalists, who have made a study of conditions here.

This report is designed to be synoptic and as brief as possible. Necessarily, it does not purport to be exhaustive, complete, or comprehensive in detail. It is aimed at being neither argumentative in spirit nor dogmatic in opinion, but informative, designed to afford a more or less comprehensive picture "in the large."

TERRITORY

The outstanding fact in connection with the U.S.S.R. is its enormous size. It contains one sixth of the earth's surface—

eight million square miles. It has an area two and one half times greater than the entire possessions of the United States. Vladivostok is farther from Moscow than is Portland, Maine. The latitude of the Black Sea is about that of New York City. It encompasses territory greater than the entire North American continent north of the Panama Canal. It covers all zones, from the Arctic to the tropical. It comprises an empire more diverse than that from "Berlin to Bagdad." It includes vast areas of plains, mountains, forests, and waterways.

POPULATION

The latest official estimate (1933) of the population is 165,-700,000—8.29% of the total population of the world—a population 30% in excess of the population of the United States. It consists of 180 different nationalities, with 150 dialects, and 48 different languages.

The density of population is 12.5 to the square mile in contrast to 41 inhabitants per square mile in the United States, 197 in France, 355 in Italy, 363 in Germany, and 668 to the square mile in England. If the entire population of the world were transferred into the U.S.S.R. the territory would not be as crowded as that of Germany. If the population of the entire world were quadrupled and placed in the Soviet Union, its territory would not be as crowded as that of the British Isles.

Birth Rate—According to the most recent Soviet data the birth rate in the Ukraine is about twenty-three to the thousand. The rate for the country as a whole is probably somewhat less, but rapidly increasing. In contrast thereto, the birth rates of the European countries are as follows: Italy

(1935) 23.3; Germany (1935) 18.9; England (1935) 17.8; France (1934) 16.1.

Political Subdivisions—The Soviet Union is made up of eleven political subdivisions (constituent republics), each with a measure of autonomy. These socialist republics are theoretically free to disassociate themselves from the Union. As a matter of fact such liberty is academic. It is obvious that the Federal government and, what is more, the Kremlin (Stalin) would not tolerate disunion. That fact appears very clearly in the recent Bukharin treason trial.

MAN POWER

The nation contains a wide diversity of races, extending from the European Russians and Slavs to the Mongols of the East. Generally speaking, they are a strong, sturdy type. They reflect that physical hardihood, which the survival of the fittest under primitive conditions, close to the soil, would produce. European Russia in the fifteenth century had behind it an economic and historical experience in political development approximately comparable in standards of experience and living to that of Alfred the Great. There are indications of this fact in the vigor, initiative, enterprise, and emotional richness and simplicities of a comparatively young people. Up to a few hundred years ago, Russia had none of the experiences of Europe, incident to the development of civilization.

AGRICULTURAL RESOURCES

Even more significant than the mineral wealth of such a territory are its agricultural resources. Such wealth is inexhaustible. It renews itself each year.

In 1937 the total area under cultivation in the Soviet Union was 367,170,949 acres. This is in contrast to 327,661,000 (1935) acres in the United States and 56,134,000 (1934) acres in Canada. Of the entire population, about 65% are engaged in agriculture. It is interesting to note that in 1913, 57% of the total output of Russian industry was agricultural, whereas industrial output constituted but 43%.* In 1937, however, the industrial output comprised 77% of the total output in contrast to the remaining 23% of agriculture, which quantitatively was slightly in excess of 1913. Generally speaking, the agricultural output in the Soviet Union under the present regime has not been in excess of prerevolutionary production. In 1937, however, there was a bumper crop, which broke all records. The cereal crop for that year is estimated to be about 111,384,000 metric tons (4,451,360,000 bushels). It should be borne in mind, in this connection, that a great effort was made by the planning authorities to diversify agriculture, which eliminated large areas of cereal acreage and diverted them to the development of new crops, such as cotton, sugar beet, et cetera.

The following data indicate the remarkable agricultural wealth of this country.

Wheat—In 1935, the Soviet Union produced approximately *one third* of the total wheat crop of the world. It was two and one half times greater than that produced in the United States; four times as much as Canada; five times as much as Argentina; and more than the United States, Canada, and Argentina put together.†

---

* This comparison is based on value and is somewhat misleading. It still remains significant as generally indicative of the fact of the enormous increase in industrial production.

† In 1934-35 the production of wheat was: total of the world, 3,470,000,000 bushels; Soviet Union, 1,117,000,000; United States, 497,000,000; Canada, 276,000,000; Argentina, 241,000,000.

Oats—During the same year the Soviet Union produced approximately *one half of the world's oat crop.* It was three times that of the United States and four times that of Canada. The production of the Soviet Union equaled the total production of the United States, Canada, and Germany combined.*

Rye—For the same year the U.S.S.R. produced 80% of the total world's rye crop. It was fifty times as much as that of the United States; 40% more than the production of Germany, Poland, and France combined. It was in excess of the combined production of Germany, Poland, France, and the United States.†

Cotton—During the same year the Soviet Union was fourth in the production of cotton. It produced more bales of cotton than did Egypt.

Flaxseed—For the same year the Soviet Union was second only to Argentina in the flaxseed crop. The Russian production was approximately five times that of the United States.‡

Beet Sugar—Germany for many years was first in beet-sugar production. *In 1935* the Soviet Union doubled its production over the preceding year and *took first place.* The production of the Soviet Union for that year was almost double

---

* In 1934-35 the production of oats in bushels was: total of the world, 2,217,000,000; Soviet Union, 1,302,000,000; United States, 526,000,000; Germany, 376,000,000.

† In 1934-35 the production of rye in bushels was: total of the world, 1,400,000,000; Soviet Union, 792,000,000; Germany, 299,000,000; Poland, 254,000,000; France, 33,000,000; United States, 16,000,000.

‡ In 1934-35 the production of flaxseed in bushels was: total of the world, 149,000,000; Argentina, 79,720,000; Soviet Union, 27,558,000; United States, 5,213,000.

that of the United States and almost equal to the production of Germany and Czechoslovakia combined. It was more than 20% in excess of that of Germany. It was more than three times that of Czechoslovakia.*

Cattle—The average number of cattle in the Soviet Union between 1926-30 was 64,900,000, in contrast to 59,191,000 in the United States. It was larger than the combined herds of Argentina and Germany. The Russian herds were three times larger than those of Germany. During the "strike" of the agricultural classes during the collectivization period from 1929-33, the number of cattle had declined to 38,400,000 in 1933. By 1935 it had increased to 49,255,000, which is still twice that of Germany.†

Livestock—*Sheep, Swine, Horses*—During the same period, there was an enormous decline in these herds. They were practically cut in two. By 1935 there had been an increase of approximately 20% over the low period, but still in 1935 the percentage of these herds was from 30 to 40% less than in 1928.

Development of Agriculture—Intensive efforts are now being made to develop extensive regions along the Trans-Siberian Railway in the east. Enormous sums are also being expended for irrigation and the reclamation of lands. In 1929-35 a total of 1,350,000,000 rubles was spent on reclamation and

---

* In 1934-35 the production of beet sugar in terms of raw sugar in short tons was: total of the world, 10,886,632; United States, 1,257,750; U.S.S.R., 2,315,000; Germany, 1,817,430; Czechoslovakia, 615,700.
† In 1926 there were in the United States, 59,191,000; U.S.S.R., 65,900,000; Argentina, 32,212,000; Germany, 17,776,000; in 1933 in the U.S.A., 70,-214,000; U.S.S.R., 38,400,000; Germany, 19,139,000; 1935 in the U.S.S.R., 49,255,000.

irrigation as "capital investment." * It is interesting to note
that in spite of the tremendous effort that has been made to
apply the principles of mechanized, scientific agriculture in
large-scale production, the actual grain crop in metric tons
in 1936 was less than the grain crop of 1913. The bumper crop
of 1937 exceeded the 1913 production by about 20%.

Increase in Use of Tractors and Combines—The extent of
the campaign for the mechanization of agriculture can be appreciated from the following facts. The number of *tractors*
in the Soviet Union in 1928 was 26,000. By 1936 it had increased eighteenfold to 477,000. In 1930 there were 1700
combines in the U.S.S.R., which had been multiplied about
fifty times by 1936, when there were 93,200. The number of
tractors and combines employed in agriculture were:

---

* The official rate of the ruble is now 5.30 to the dollar. It has varied as follows:

            1928—$1.00—1.94½ rubles
            1929—$1.00—1.94½ rubles
            1930—$1.00—1.94½ rubles
            1931—$1.00—1.94½ rubles
            1932—$1.00—1.94½ rubles
            1933—$1.00—1.16-1.12 rubles
            1934—$1.00—1.16-1.12 rubles
            1935—$1.00—1.16-1.12 rubles
            1936—$1.00—5.06 rubles
            1937—$1.00—5.36 rubles

The black bourse, or "bootleg" rate of the ruble, varies in different sections
and fluctuates markedly at different times. It has ranged from five to fourteen
cents, within the past year. It is now approximately ten cents. The actual
value in international exchange is presumably reflected in the bootleg average
rate. That cannot be arbitrarily accepted, however, because of the lack of a
free market and the operation of free forces. Sir Walter Citrine, in his book,
published 1936, gave his estimate at about five cents. Based on food-purchas-
ing power and all factors combined, my opinion is that the gold value is between five and ten cents, although in view of the favorable balance of trade
and large increase in gold production, it is within the realm of possibility that
currency restrictions could be abolished and the value of the ruble could still
be maintained within reasonable limits at the present official rate.

	Number of Tractors (in 1000)	Capacity of Tractors (in 1000 HP)	Number of Combines (in 1000)
1928	26.7	278.1	..
1929	34.9	391.4	..
1930	72.1	1,003.5	1.7
1931	125.3	1,850.0	6.4
1932	148.5	2,225.0	14.1
1933	210.9	3,209.2	25.4
1934	276.4	4,462.8	32.3
1935	379.5	6,534.0	52.1
1936	477.5	7,162.5	93.2
1938	483.5	9,256.2	153.5 *

Number and Role of Machine and Tractor Stations—"During the first three years of the Second Five-Year Plan period, 1004 new machine and tractor stations had been set up. The total number of these stations, which was 2446 at the end of 1932, had risen to 4350 at the end of 1935. During 1935 they served more than 72.8% of the total collective-farm sown area. The machine and tractor stations are not only concentration points for high technique, but also for the application of scientific farming methods, and are the economic and political bases of the state in rural districts." †

*Timber—*The forested area of the Soviet Union is claimed to be the largest of any nation in the world. It constitutes 57% of the total forest area of the world.‡

*Furs and Fisheries—*The wealth in furs is indicated by the fact that it is estimated that approximately one tenth of its purchases abroad are paid for by the value of furs exported.

* Stalin's speech, March, 1939.
† Excerpt from *Fulfillment of the Second Five-Year Plan During 1933-35,* with foreword by Mezhlauk. (Note: Mezhlauk has recently been "liquidated" —whereabouts unknown.)
‡ *New York World Almanac,* 1938.

Fisheries are also extensive, and are being scientifically developed at a rapid rate.

MINERAL WEALTH

The U.S.S.R., through its official publications, claims that it has the richest deposits of the world in iron, manganese, oil, salts, phosphorites and apatites, and the second largest deposits of coal. While these claims may be discounted and taken with some reservation, still, the deposits are undoubtedly exceedingly rich.* Among the state treasures which I have been permitted to see there were solid nuggets of gold of extraordinary size, the largest of which was thirty-nine kilograms, or eighty-six pounds, in weight. These come from the Urals. There were also nuggets of platinum, one of which was fourteen kilograms in weight.

Authorities without the Soviet Union admit that the Soviet Union is second in the world's gold production, and that the prospects are for a still-greater output. While for military reasons no official figures are given out as to the extent of gold reserves, it is variously estimated that the production of gold runs between $175,000,000 and $400,000,000 per year.† The gold coverage for their currency is officially reported at approximately $340,000,000 for 1937. An excellent study of the gold supply is to be found in the report by Mr. Packer of the Riga staff. It is probably the most accurate estimate. In discussions I have had with well-informed men, here on the ground, such as Spencer Williams, Walter Duranty, and certain authorities, including mining engineers from the Far East, and also in London, I find that their estimates approximate $300,000,000 to $450,000,000 per year. My opinion is that it is between $200,000,000 and $350,000,000.

----

* *New York World Almanac*, 1938.
† See *New York World Almanac*, 1938.

In *The Strategy of Raw Materials* (by Brooks Emeny, published by the Bureau of International Research of Harvard University and Radcliffe College), an analysis and study of the military self-sufficiency of the seven leading powers in essential foodstuffs and raw materials are made. The statistical tables disclose the extraordinary extent of the mineral wealth of the Soviet Union. It would appear that, on the basis of percentages of sufficiency, the Soviet Union enjoys 100% in coal, iron, petroleum, manganese, mica, chromite, and potash; 90% in sulphur and pyrites; 85% in phosphates; 80% in mercury; 60% in zinc.

Comparatively, none of the other six great powers—United States, Germany, Great Britain, France, Italy, and Japan—approximate the degree of self-sufficiency of the Soviet Union, with the exception only of Great Britain and the United States.

It is interesting to note that in manganese, chromite, potash, and mercury, in which the percentage of self-sufficiency in the United States is low, the Soviet Union has an abundancy; that in necessary imports such as copper, et cetera, the entire imports come practically from the United States; and that the combined resources of the United States and the Soviet Union constitute complete self-sufficiency in foodstuffs and critical raw materials.

II. What Has the Present Regime Done with These Resources Since It Came into Power?

GENERAL BACKGROUND, HISTORICALLY: 1917-1926; 1927-38

The Bolsheviks seized power in 1917. At that time industry was more than five sixths gone.[*] Transport had worn out most

---

[*] See Pares, *A History of Russia,* 1937.

of its existing reserves. The civil war, immediately following
the accession to power, practically put a stop to production
work. The attempt to apply the principles of communism to
agriculture was bitterly resisted by the bourgeois peasantry.
The agricultural producers "struck" by simply refusing or failing to produce more than their own needs. This, and the utter
lack of distribution facilities, brought famine and even starvation to the towns. Trade, under these conditions and the
disorder existing, dried up. The great drought in the early
days of the Revolution accentuated the distress.

Under such necessity Lenin led an economic retreat and
established the N.E.P. (New Economic Policy), which was
put into operation in March, 1921. This policy attempted to retain communism as a principle of government, but actually
shelved communism in practice. The peasants were in a
measure given the right to property and given the opportunity for some individual profit-making. Private trade was
licensed. There was some improvement in economic conditions. Lenin, who projected this plan against great resistance,
always maintained that it was a necessary step backward only
in order to "take two steps forward." These several years
were marked by the effort of the government to induce capitalistic countries to provide money for the development of
Russia's resources.

The Soviet Union "played off" one country as against another. It was the period of fast-growing friendship between
Russia and Germany, signalized by the Treaty of Rapallo.

Lenin suffered a stroke in 1922 and died in 1924. The N.E.P.
gave rise to a type of economic adventurer, so-called. These
conditions frightened old Bolsheviks. Recourse was had to
purges at different times. These were carried out with great
severity. Strong dissension arose in the party. The result was

that the N.E.P. men were "swept up with their profits" and the policy was abandoned.

Economic decline and chaos during these years threatened the existence of the government. At its base lay the continuing revolt of the peasantry and their refusal to produce more than their needs. The existence of the Central Government and the entire communist principle were in jeopardy. By 1924 the Central Government had managed to balance its budget, but its entire net revenue did not exceed 1,400,000,-000 rubles. The Trotsky wing was advocating world revolution, whereas the Stalin followers were advocating the projection of the communistic principle in the Soviet Union first. Another right-wing group, headed by Bukharin, Rykov, Tomsky, and so forth, differed with Stalin's ideas regarding the policy to be adopted toward the peasantry. In particular, they opposed the forced and rapid collectivization measures advocated by Stalin. It was clear that economic chaos and possibly social anarchy were imminent unless something radical was done to change these conditions.

With the death of Lenin, a struggle for leadership arose. This finally resolved itself into a duel between Trotsky and Stalin. In 1927 Trotsky was expelled from the Central Committee of the party. In 1928 he was banished to Asiatic Russia. His followers were liquidated by banishment or imprisonment. It was a complete Stalin victory.

These were the conditions under which Stalin in 1927 projected the Five-Year Plans of industrial development, which admittedly have produced very remarkable results. The execution of these plans required great courage and utter ruthlessness and a general tightening up of belts in all classes of the community, all based on expectation of future benefits. In the early years of the First Five-Year Plan, however, the government was again threatened by the passive revolt of the agricultural districts. This revolt was ruthlessly crushed. The government employed the simple but cruel expedient of taking its requirement of grain from the peasantry, even though it left nothing to them for food or for seed. The result was starvation in many sections. It was variously estimated that during this campaign from two to three million agricultural peasants died. The program of collectivization and mechanization of agriculture was carried out with similar ruthless force. Thousands of kulaks (large landholders) were "liquidated." The industrial plan and the workers and the government itself were alike dependent on agriculture for not only food, but for revenue for the creation and operation of the industrial plants. The issue was vital. The government won; but at terrific cost of life.

Heavy industry (First Five-Year Plan), however, finally got away to a good start. Enormous new plants were projected. Entire new towns were built and sprung up like mushrooms. Enormous tractor works at Kharkov, automobile factories in Moscow and Gorki, tractor plants in Rostov and Stalingrad, steel furnaces in the Don Basin, fertilizer works in the Urals, enormous dams, were constructed. The great Dnieper Dam (Colonel Cooper's project) was completed in 1935. Over ninety new towns were created during the first five years. Industry in the Ural Mountains was increased fivefold. The attendant dislocation of the populations, the drift to the cities, and lack of adequate housing conditions and other conditions projected an enormous labor turnover that thwarted efficiency. Despite the inefficiencies of inexperience, accentuated by the bureaucratic governmental control and these tremendous difficulties, industrial output quantitatively increased 20% over the previous year in 1929, 38% over the previous year in 1930; with similar large figures later.

This period (the First Five-Year Plan) was characterized

by alternative ruthless purges and oppressions and concilia-
tion policies, for all of which Stalin was extolled. It is interesting to note that the regime became confronted more and
more with the necessity of making a success of these enormous
undertakings. Their continuance in power depended ultimately on making good on the promises made to the proletariat. In order to make good and make the system of industry
work there developed a marked and continuing departure in
practice from the communist principle. The only insistent and
constant stimulus to the workers was found to be the profit
motive. Concessions were also made in the extension of rights
or property to the peasants, as well as to other classes. The
Stakhanovite movement (analogous to the piecework system
—the "speed-up" principle) became a national policy. By 1934
there appeared clearly a very notable advance in heavy industry—both in much larger output and lesser costs.

Meanwhile, despite the withdrawal of millions of hectares
from cereal production in order to project a so-called balanced
scientific agriculture, the collectivization program managed
to produce a normal amount of food. Measurably, the Five-
Year Plan had justified itself. The outstanding fact in the
situation, however, is that it was not *because* of government
operation of industry, but *in spite of it*. The enormous wealth
of the country practically assured, quantitatively, a large
measure of success, despite the enormous inefficiencies,
wastes, and losses which such a system must necessarily entail. What the regime did do, however, was to conceive the
plan and drive it through. It is also significant that in order
to succeed, the regime dropped the principle of communism
in practical application.

In 1924, the total industrial output amounted to 6,000,000,-
000 rubles, whereas in 1937 it is estimated at 85,000,000,000
rubles.

Of the total present industrial output, 75% has been produced by plants that have been built since 1917.

The tonnage in railroad freight had increased from 33,000,000 tons in 1924 to 323,000,000 tons in 1936.

River freight had similarly increased from 9,000,000 tons in 1924 to 69,000,000 tons in 1936.

By 1936 it is claimed that 91% of the total crop area of the country was cultivated by mechanized means through machine tractor stations.

SOVIET PLACE IN WORLD PRODUCTION VOLUME

By 1936 it is claimed that in world production the Soviet Union was *first* in the manufacture of harvester combines and beet sugar; second in total industrial output in machine production, tractors, motor trucks, iron, ore, and gold; third in steel and superphosphates; and fourth in coal.

SOVIET PLACE IN EUROPEAN PRODUCTION VOLUME

In European production it is claimed that the Soviet Union held *first place* in total industrial output, in machine-tool construction, in the manufacture of tractors, harvester combines, motor trucks, and in the production of gold, superphosphates, beet sugar; second place in steel production; and third place in coal output. By 1935, the Soviet Union, in contrast to European production, had also reached first place in oil and peat extraction, copper smelting, production of railroad freight cars and locomotives, and had taken second place in the generation of electric power and the manufacture of aluminum.

I was much impressed by the technical and fixed capital equipment, the methods used, the provisions made for scientific study and experimentation, and by their conveyor and line system of manufacture. The efficiency of the workers, in my opinion, could not be compared with efficiency displayed in plants that I have studied in the course of my work as Commissioner of Corporations and as a member of the Federal Trade Commission in the United States. In my judgment it was not comparable with that which does or would obtain under a capitalistic profit-making organization. It would not equal forty per cent of the effectiveness of our industry. Nevertheless, it was perfectly clear that they were producing an enormous amount of serviceable output. In discussions which I have had with American engineers here, I have also been impressed with the fact that the government secures the best foreign technical skill available in connection with the erection of these plants, their operation and equipment; that the technical schools and universities are producing each year a crop of eager, earnest, young men, fresh from the land, many of whom finished their technical studies by working abroad in the industries of Germany, France, Italy, and the United States; that whereas there is a general disposition on the part of these younger engineers to discount the ability of foreign engineers in contrast to themselves, that nevertheless they are hard-working, ambitious, effective, and exceedingly earnest.

The conclusions which I have drawn from the whole picture are that quantitatively the figures are fairly reliable and reasonably measure the extent of the achievement. Allowing a substantial or even large discount as to their figures, these accomplishments would remain most impressive. This fact is generally conceded in the Diplomatic Corps, even among those who are innately hostile to the regime.

The governing powers, as stated heretofore, are tied irrevocably to the making of a success of this plan. It may even be a condition of their continuance in power. The masses have been constantly fed with the idea that it would result in higher standards and better conditions of living. In order to make this industrial machine effective and even to make an appearance of the performance of these promises, necessity drives. The only permanent and insistent incentive that the government has found is profit. In the evolution, therefore, of this situation I look forward to a still-further constant tendency to the right and an application of capitalistic principles in socialist production.

TRANSPORTATION AND COMMUNICATION

Railroads—The weakest link in the chain of domestic economy is undoubtedly distribution. The government has been making a drive in the past two years, (*a*) to bring up the efficiency of railroads and other means of transportation, and (*b*) to plan agriculture so as to produce local self-sufficiency in foodstuff supply and eliminate the necessity of long hauls.

The mileage of railroads has increased approximately 25%. The double-tracking of the Trans-Siberian Railway has been completed. It is alleged that the government is building a railroad north of Manchukuo into the Maritime Provinces, in order to afford a safer military method of communication with the Pacific provinces. I have been reliably informed that this road has now been finished. The Military Attaché to the Embassy here, Colonel Faymonville, a very careful and able man, advises that there is a marked tendency here to further develop transportation by the extension of highways and the use of trucks, rather than by railroads.

Roads—the mileage of tsarist Russia in kilometers was 24,000, of which 4000 were paved. In 1936 there were two million kilometers of hard-surfaced roads, one fifth of which are main highways.

The military highways, some of which extend out of Moscow, are magnificent, straight, five-lane, asphalt highways.

Airways—In 1936 there were 52,000 kilometers of airlines, in contrast to 15,000 in 1929. The number of airplane kilometers covered have increased from 3,200,000 to 56,000,000 in 1936. The metric tons of freight carried have increased from 1000 in 1929 to 60,000 in 1936.

Waterways—The development of waterways within recent years has been very extensive. The White Sea has been connected with the Baltic Sea (227 kilometers—put into operation in 1934). The Volga River has been diverted into Moscow (1937—128 kilometers), and it is alleged that there now exists complete river transportation from the Caspian Sea to Leningrad. The total navigable river waterways are claimed to be 100,000 kilometers, which is twice the length of navigable waterways in the United States.

Merchant Fleet—The tonnage of the merchant fleet of the Soviet Union in 1928 was 327,000 tons; in 1935 it was 1,350,000 tons, an increase of approximately 400%.

Telephone Lines—In 1928 the total length of telephone lines was 556,110 miles. In 1936 this had increased to 1,343,-750. The number of telephones had increased during that same period from 880,000 to 2,100,000.

Mail—The number of rural postmen in the Soviet Union had increased from 6900 in 1924 to 123,000 in 1936, approximately eighteenfold.

Newspapers, Radios, etc.—The Soviet Union has 10,000 newspapers, with a circulation of 39,000,000. In 1928, there were, it is claimed, twenty-three broadcasting stations in the Soviet Union in contrast to seventy-eight in 1936, with 350,000 receiving sets in operation in 1936. In 1928 there were sixty-five telegraph-telephone service transmitters, whereas in 1936 there were 273.

Books—In 1913 it is alleged that 26,174 books were published with 86,700,000 copies; whereas, in 1936 there were 43,348 books published and 571,000,000 copies issued.

EDUCATION—SCHOOLS—UNIVERSITIES

It is claimed that illiteracy has been completely eliminated; that there is no Soviet citizen who cannot read. Sixty-seven per cent of the population in 1913 were illiterate.

The number of elementary schools in the Soviet Union in 1936 was 164,100, in contrast to 106,000 in 1914, an increase of 64%. The number of colleges and higher technical schools have increased from 91 in 1915 to 592 in 1936, an increase of 500%. The population attending schools in 1936 was 28,-842,000. 1,039,700 children attended kindergarten in 1936. In 1935 there were 1712 schools for manual training, with a total number of students of 246,248. Twenty-six per cent of the entire population, it is claimed, are attending school. It is also alleged that three and one half times the number of children are attending school in the Soviet Union in contrast to the number attending school prior to the war.

Erection of New Schools—In Moscow alone seventy-two big schools were built and fully equipped in 1935. In 1936, 152 additional schools were to be built in Moscow. In 1935 the total number of schools built in cities was 496, while in rural districts 1000 elementary schools and 2000 seven-year schools were erected. The annual current expenditure allowance per pupil has doubled since 1932.

Preschool Training—Preschool training is a constituent part of the educational system of the U.S.S.R. By 1935 the number of children in preschool institutions (kindergartens and playgrounds) had increased by 627,000 as compared with 1932, the number at the present time being approximately 6,000,000.

Higher Education Enrollment—During the three years of 1933 to 1935, 1,300,000 persons were enrolled in colleges, technical colleges, and middle technical schools, while 485,400 specialists with college or middle-school training were graduated. Altogether 509,900 persons studied at colleges and technical colleges in 1935, as against 477,200 in 1932 and 124,000 in 1913.

LIVING AND SOCIAL CONDITIONS

Rise in National Income—The national income has increased from 21,000,000,000 rubles in 1913 to 65,700,000,000 rubles in 1935 (fixed 1926-27 prices). All this income, it is alleged, is being applied directly or indirectly to the betterment of the working classes.

Employment and Wage Increases—It is asserted that there has been no unemployment since 1930; that the number of employed persons has increased in 1935 by 1,800,000 as compared with 1932. It should be noted, however, that the Soviet system admits of no unemployment except of persons who are not fully trusted or who are being punished. Millions of people in the country, however, are not working in the fields in which they desire to be employed and although regularly employed are in a much worse status than those in the United States employed with relief funds. Political prisoners are not unemployed. They are working. The total wage is alleged to have increased from 32,700,000,000 rubles in 1932 to 56,200,000,000 rubles in 1935. The average annual wage per worker had increased from 1427 rubles in 1932 to 2371.5 rubles in 1935.

Remarkable Increase in Expenditures on Armament—Coincident with the rise to power of Hitler, it is interesting to note that from 1934-37 the percentage of the total revenues of the government employed for war purposes grew from 3.3% in 1934 to 22% in 1937. The total expenditures in 1937 reached 22,431,030,000 rubles, which at the official rate of exchange would be approximately $4,200,000,000 and at the current bootleg rate of the ruble it would be $2,200,000,000. At the probable actual gold value it would be probably one half that.

Coincident Increase of Expenditures for Social and Cultural Welfare—No less interesting is the fact that concurrent with this extraordinary increase in military expenditure, the outlay for so-called social and cultural purposes kept pace and exceeded it. In 1928 the total outlay for this purpose was 1,495,500,000 rubles (6.4%), whereas in 1937 it was 26,604,-552,000 rubles (27% of the total). Expenditures for social and cultural welfare cover a broad variety of activities—education, kindergartens, crèches, hospitals, social insurance, housing, drama, cinema, radio, propaganda, books, newspapers, et cetera. The significance of these figures is not in their absolute quality but rather in their classification and point of view. In spite of war necessities, the government has constantly increased its outlay for these activities.

WHAT ARE THE ELEMENTS OF WEAKNESS INHERENT IN THIS SITUATION?

Among the obvious weaknesses, some are the following:

Size—National solidarity finds a constant threat by reason of wide differences in character and other conditions in large sections of the U.S.S.R. Differences in conditions induce different needs, which, in many cases, induce conflicts of interest. It is continuing anticentrifugal force.

Racial Differences—Language, Traditions, Aspirations— There are Slavs, Finno-Ugrians, Turco-Tatars, Japhetic peoples, Jews, Germans, Tadjiks, and Mongols, all with different racial instincts, habits of thought, religion, and concepts of government. These differences, particularly in religion, induce seeds of dissension and disunity.*

*Character of Government Itself—*Based on the idea of a selfless society, the state here is constantly threatened with the fact that it cannot destroy the instincts of human nature toward self-interest. These are imbedded in the glandular, nervous, and physical organisms of men and are the resultant of the atavistic forces of centuries. If these instincts cannot be eradicated in a generation or two, this experiment must fail.

*Bureaucratic Inefficiency—*The very enormousness of the task which this government has undertaken necessitates a tremendous bureaucracy that in itself is a threat. The size and extensive character of the tasks are constantly threatening to break down the administration. The problem of accounting alone as to the thousands of retail stores (necessary to protect honesty and efficiency) is illustrative. It is a staggering project.

*Conflict Inherent Between Agricultural and Industrial Workers—*This conflict is a constant source of possible irritation and is pregnant with far-reaching political consequence.

----

* Colonel Faymonville points out that the Soviet government has frankly recognized the existence of the minor nationalities and has even gone to great lengths to foster national cultures. It is believed that the special needs of each racial group are recognized to a greater extent than formerly. At the same time, transport and other means of communication between regions have been improved and the opportunities for exchange of goods have been improved in order that these special needs and requirements may be met. It therefore seems probable that the conflicts of interest among minor nationalities are less sharp than formerly and less likely than formerly to lead to the disruption of the central power.

Particularly is this true where one class has been so continuously exploited for the benefit of the other.

Russian Character and Habits—The native inertia and fatalistic quality of the Russian type is a constant "drag." *Avos* (perhaps), *osë ravno* (it doesn't matter), and *nichevo* (never mind) are proverbial in Russia.

The Possible Inaptitude of Agrarian Peoples for Mechanical-Industrial Work, Which Threatens Possible Breakdown of Industry Under Pressure—The labor turnover in some industries rises as high as 125% a year.

Difficulties of Arbitrarily Fixing Just Wages—Indications already appear that certain groups of Stakhanovites complain that because of arbitrary classification their rates of wage are not in line with other classes.

Counterrevolution Menace of Military Coup d'État—There is always the possibility of the rise of a Napoleon in the army, who might project a palace revolution and seize power.

The treason trials and recent executions and purges all indicate the weakness inherent here because of the conflicting ambitions inherent in human nature. This revolution is "devouring its own children." In spite of the clear appreciation of this danger and the deliberate determination of the original Bolshevik leaders not to "start" shooting each other, and in spite of the formal declaration of Stalin himself to that effect in 1926, the killing of political offenders began in 1934 and has progressed with horrifying speed.

The Terror—Purge—To a democratic mind, it appears to be inevitable that the tyranny over life and liberty exercised by the secret police, who reach down into all classes of society and whisk men away from family and friends without any protection against possible injustice, must overthrow any regime, in the long run.

Revolt of Youth—As time goes on, with betterment in living conditions, and growing distinctions in class and privileges, youth will probably revolt against these actualities which are contrary to what they had been led to believe communism would induce; and this may ironically result in radical youth espousing in revolt the conservative political doctrine of individualism and capitalistic opportunity.

Dislocation of Agricultural Labor—Through mechanized agriculture, a large number of agricultural workers will be displaced by machines, and will be thrown into the already over-populous industrial centers. What is to be done with them?

Dangers Incident to a General European War—This *would undoubtedly* involve the Soviet Union. A long-drawn-out war would provide fertile soil for revolutionary activities along the conventional line of revolutionary technique. This is a real threat.

The Menace of Possible Hitler Fascist Attack—This menace very obviously is constantly in the forefront of the minds of this government. Hitler's plan, as outlined in *Mein Kampf* and subsequently elaborated upon in his Nuremberg speech, in which the grain fields of the Ukraine were specifically mentioned, the *Drang nach Osten,* all point to this possibility.

The Menace from the East, Japan—The government here is equally conscious of the possibility of Japanese aggression. They are vigilantly active in preparation in anticipation of such an eventuality. Recently there appear indications that as the hostilities in China drag out, the attitude of the government here indicates a "hardening" tendency toward Japan.

Latent Hostility of Adjacent States—Upon economic, religious, and political grounds, in all countries adjacent to the Soviet Union there is great fear of penetration and extension of the Soviet system into their territories. This accounts for the innate hostility that is general and quite obvious.

One-Man Rule—This system of government always contains within itself great danger.

Tyranny—Oppression—In any advancing intellectual experience and education, the innate dignity of manhood must give rise to constant resentments against oppression. No physical betterment of living standards could possibly compensate for the utter destruction of the liberty of thought and speech, and the sanctity of the individual.

Lack of Religion—Every effort is being made to substitute worship of a man or men for the worship of God. It is one of the greatest weaknesses of this situation.

Mistrust Among Leaders Themselves—The philosophy of communism justifies all acts if done in its name. There are no considerations of honor or loyalty which control as against duty to the party. The result is that there can be no confidence or faith between these men, in leadership. No man can trust another. It is a serious and basic weakness and a constant threat to existing government.

WHAT ARE THE POLITICAL STRENGTHS OF THIS GOVERNMENT?

The Communist Party and the Government—The government in fact consists of a very small group of men, who control the Communist Party. The government is no more than the agent of the Communist Party, and takes orders from it. Realistically, the government is in fact one man—Stalin the "strong" man, who survived the contest, completely disposed of all competitors, and is completely dominant. He appears to be the type of "easy boss," quiet, self-effacing, but nevertheless the real power. The government is a dictatorship not "of the proletariat," as professed, but "over the proletariat." It is completely dominated by one man.

Resolute Character of Party Leadership—The Communist Party is governed by a Central Committee of approximately one hundred members. The Politburo, consisting of eleven members, is a kind of board of directors. It runs the party and the government. These organizations do the will of Stalin. There is obviously no "opposition." If it makes its appearance it is promptly "liquidated." The old theorists and mental type of old Bolshevik have practically disappeared. They have either died a natural death or have been imprisoned, exiled, or shot. The survivors, now in control, are of the type of "hard-boiled doers" of the Revolution; such as the Soviet Robin Hood (Stalin), who robbed banks to finance the Revolution; and the top sergeants (Voroshilov, Budenny), who battled their way up from the bottom; or aggressive and able men of the younger generation (Mikoyan, Ezhov). The only notable exceptions are Kalinin, the President; Molotov, the Premier; and Litvinov, the Foreign Minister.

The power resides in Stalin, Voroshilov (army), Ezhov (secret police), Kaganovich (the trouble shooter who built the Moscow subway and reorganized the railroads), and Mikoyan (food). The last treason trial disposed of Bukharin, Rykov, and Grinko, who were of the old "right" opposition. It and the previous trial disposed of Rosengoltz, Krestinsky, Pyatakov, Serebryakov, Sokolnikov, and Radek, of the so-called old "left" opposition. The first treason trial disposed of Zinoviev and Kamenev. Tomsky committed suicide. What of

the old leadership remained after these executions natural
deaths and suicides have practically liquidated.

Technique of Dictatorship—The strength of the government is in fact determined by the strength of this group of
leaders. Constitutional protections to the individual or to
liberty, in the face of any necessity that confronts these men,
are swept aside. These men (the Kremlin) completely dominate and control the bureaucracy. They are, presumably, controlled by a mixture of motives. Generally, however, they are
credited with a sincere and fanatical devotion to the communist ideal, as well as with a natural purpose to protect themselves. They believe that to be weak and not resolute is to
betray "the great project" which they are seeking to promote
for the benefit of mankind. They find justification for their
conduct in the fact that ultimately they will be justified by the
"historical trend." As Stalin is reputed to have said, they will
not hesitate to kill men "as long as it is necessary for the
cause." While idealistically devoted to the elevation of the
proletariat they are realists of a pure type and do not hesitate
to put every man in jail, if need there be, to make men free;
or to shoot, out of hand, even their friends, if they run counter
to their particular brand of communism.

Their private lives are reputedly clean. It is generally admitted that there is no graft in high places. Their habits are
relatively simple. They live well in the Kremlin and have their
dachas (country houses), together with their automobiles and
all comforts. They are careful, however, to avoid ostentation.
The salary of a commissar is reported to be not in excess of
900 rubles per month, but as everything is provided by the
state they do not need money.

They give indication of being indefatigable and very hard
workers. Practically all of them of middle age, including Stalin,

are reputed to be suffering from "tired" hearts. Those that I have met have impressed me, personally, as able, strong men, characterized by personality, energy, and ability as natural leaders. Stalin's entire career indicates an Oriental patience and slowness in action, combined with a capacity for speedy and ruthless striking when necessary. He hits first. Had the General, Tukhatchevsky, been of a Corsican kidney last May, the situation here today might have been entirely different.

Indications of Panic of Last Summer—As late as April, 1937, generally speaking, no question would have been raised by any member of the Diplomatic Corps here as to the immediate strength and political permanency of the Stalin regime. Both at home and abroad the Soviet Union was at the height of its good repute, probably last spring (1937). Then occurred the developments of the treason trials and the executions of political leaders (finding their origin in the Kirov assassination of 1934), the courts-martial and executions of the eleven leading army generals in July, the terrific "purge and terror" that proceeded throughout the summer and resulted in the liquidation of thousands of Soviet citizens, including both the high and the low in the Communist Party, and also those occupying high places throughout the various republics of the Union. The possibility of the existence of either treason in the army or a widespread conspiracy in the country gave rise to doubts as to the strength of the regime. There were and are many indications of a condition bordering on "panic" in government circles. The last treason trial (Bukharin), just finished, with its bizarre confessions, explained (as many of the Diplomatic Corps have stated to me) these perplexing happenings of last summer.

Present Strength of Stalin Government—There is no doubt but what there is much discontent and antagonism toward the government among the intelligentsia of the country and even in the Communist Party, which has been the chief victim of the last purge. All such opposition, however, is undoubtedly thoroughly cowed and under complete control. The horrors of the "terror" everyone here feels. There are indications of it on all sides. It should be borne in mind, however, that the number affected, while actually large, is relatively a very small part of the total population. The Communist Party does not exceed three million in number. The party itself during this purge has been completely reorganized and remanned by fresh blood and young men—all Stalin men. As to the masses generally, it is generally considered that they are more or less indifferent to this characteristic Russian phenomenon and in some instances are even in accord with the liquidation of their tormentors, the "bureaucrats" and the "wreckers" and "traitors" who have threatened the existence of their beloved Soviet Union. It should also be borne in mind that the public is being constantly inoculated by propaganda. The bale of hay—the hope of betterment of living conditions—is constantly being held in front of the youth of the country. And there are some visible indications of progress, which are constantly being pointed out and enlarged upon. Constantly there is being pointed out to them what Stalin the great builder is doing for the Soviet Union. The enormous public works, housing, industrial plants, roads, all of which are being projected on a "ten-league canvas with the brush of comet's hair," are tremendously impressive and give support to the propaganda.

Army Loyalty—The strength of the Stalin regime depends upon the degree to which it may rely on the army and the secret police. As the situation has simmered down during the last several months, prevailing opinion in the Diplomatic Corps grows stronger that the army is loyal to Stalin—at least that he has it well in hand. Voroshilov, Marshal of the army, and Stalin are old "buddies" of the same type, and apparently are very close. In addition thereto, the secret police, an enormous military organization with both soldiery and plainclothes men, that reach down into all classes of society, is actually an arm of Stalin's. It is completely within his control. His personal friend and appointee, Ezhov, has been diligently "cleaning and sweeping up" all anti-Stalin influences in the old Gay-Pay-Oo organization. Army and secret police serve as a check each on the other; and vie with each other in loyalty to the party and to Stalin.

All propaganda agencies are controlled by Stalin. The newspapers, radio, cinema, teaching in the schools, in the party cadres or centers, and in the army itself, are constantly impregnating the public with the religion of communism, with the menace of foreign invasion, with devotion to Russian nationalism, and with the hope of betterment in living conditions. The archprotector of the masses, "Father Stalin," is being constantly extolled. Communism has been drilled into all from childhood as a religion.

Under these conditions, it is not regarded as probable that there is any immediate possibility of the government being overthrown.

Barring the coincidence of two accidents (for such, under present conditions, they would have to be), to wit, the assassination of Stalin and with it a concerted armed revolt and a Kremlin *coup d'état*, this regime would appear to be entrenched in power for some time.

Were a successful revolution to overthrow the present regime, even though the successor were to be a military dictatorship, the prevailing opinion here is that there would still persist a type of socialist government and state capitalism.

WHAT IS THE MILITARY STRENGTH OF THE SOVIET UNION?

Dangers from Without—As to the ability of the Red Army, under present conditions, to prevent invasion of its borders by hostile neighbors, or to withstand a long war, there is some doubt, but it is generally believed here that it would be very difficult and possibly impossible for Japan, or Germany, or both, to "conquer" the U.S.S.R.

Among the leaders of the government, and I have personally talked to some of them, there is absolute confidence that their army is loyal and would be able to protect their borders from either Japan or Germany, or even under conditions of simultaneous attack.

The Regular Army—The strength of the Red Army is approximately 1,300,000 men. In addition thereto the Secret Police (N.K.V.D.) has a military armed force of approximately 200,000 more. In comparison therewith it is interesting to note the numerical strengths of Germany, which is reputed to be 600,000; Italy 528,000; Japan 248,000; Poland 284,000; and Rumania 266,000.

Annual Call to the Colors—Each year approximately 1,500,000 youth are called, of which 500,000 are required for active service.

Accumulated Reserves Available—It is estimated that of the accumulated reserves of the past years there are available approximately five million trained men to fill reserve divisions; and that for subsequent draft there is available an additional reservoir of approximately six million, making a total pool of approximately fifteen million males physically fit for military service.

*Mechanized Units—Tanks—*In tank equipment and mechanized units the Red Army compares favorably with neighboring states. It is estimated that there are available for immediate use approximately 4000 tanks. It should also be borne in mind that the huge agricultural-tractor manufacturing plants are readily adaptable for the manufacture of tanks in large quantities. It is reported that these plants have already been partially converted for such use. As early as a year ago, on the occasion of the inspection trip I then made, we were not permitted to see the foundry sections of many of these plants, and it was then generally thought the reason therefor was that they were being used for war purposes at that time.

*The Air Force—*The air force of the Red Army is considered generally superior in numbers to that of any of the Great Powers. It is estimated that the total number of planes in the Red Army is 4500. The pursuit planes are generally considered to be very good. The heavy bombers are second-rate and very slow. It is generally accepted that foreign planes are known to be superior to the best types available here. I was advised by the French Ambassador that the Soviet Union is presently equipped to produce 4800 planes a year. The Russians are air-minded and considered to be excellent fliers.

*Character of Officer Class—*The officers are considered to be of an excellent quality among the junior commanders and to be fair in capacity so far as higher command is concerned. They are generally younger men. It is generally considered here that the liquidation of the older and experienced generals has weakened the army very materially. Personally, I agree with our Military Attaché, Colonel Faymonville, that while this is measurably true, it is much exaggerated.

Generally speaking, the army is equipped with good hand arms, fair airplanes, and excellent tanks. The artillery is fair

and is being rapidly improved. The defensive position of the
Soviet Union is inherently strong. The army is being constantly indoctrinated with the religion of communism. It is
probable that the Soviet Union could defensively maintain its
entity against any combination of two hostile powers. If confronted by a hostile alliance of more than two such powers,
some territory of the Soviet Union might be occupied, but it
is probable that the present military forces would prevent
decisive defeat and it is unlikely that permanent gains would
accrue to the invading armies. The Russian winter defeated
Napoleon. (See report of Colonel Faymonville attached
hereto.)

The general opinion is that the Red Army is loyal to the
Communist Party and, therefore, to Stalin.

WHAT ARE THE POSSIBLE SIGNIFICANCES OF THE U.S.S.R. IN WORLD RELATIONS?

The future significance of Russian man power and resources
and wealth as a factor in world conditions is obvious from
the foregoing facts. Barring war, the future holds possibilities
of the continued existence of this regime intact for a considerable time. Based upon the industrial and economic progress
of the past eight years and the accretion of wealth during that
period, as is evidenced by the fact that the U.S.S.R. has had an
actual favorable balance of trade for the past two years, an
enormous increase in production of gold, and many other
physical indications, it is probable, and it is generally believed
here, that the wealth and economic power of this situation
will continue to increase. The natural wealth is enormous.
The technical equipment is excellent. Labor and administrative cost are low and in comparison with the capital investments are relatively negligible. There are no capital charges
on investment.

Again in the development of water power, where already the production is second in the world, still-greater capital investments are being planned. The agricultural wealth of the country is reproducing itself each year and is also being increased.

There are great inefficiencies and wastes that are necessarily incident to bureaucratic administration. Nevertheless, the resources are so great that it is probable that the net result will be still-further large additions to national wealth and economic power. Such a condition will inevitably have repercussions and far-reaching effects upon both world economy and upon world politics.

There is still another factor in the situation. The man power here is comparatively that of a fresh, young race. The Russian country youth for the first time in history are afforded opportunities for education, and technical equipment, and they see the opportunity that for the first time gives them "escape" from the restrictions of the peasant caste. In the city of Dnepropetrovsk (population 600,000) there is a university in which it is alleged 25,000 students attend. The country boy has come to town and is "on his way." I was deeply impressed by the earnestness, ability, and balance of the men (all young) who are in charge of these huge industrial plants which I visited. This large class of youthful population are fired by the opportunities which open up new vistas to them through the application of science and industry to the great natural wealth of their country. It is quite reasonable to assume that regardless of who might be at the top of this government this force will not be denied. They have tasted the fruits. With its natural mineral and agricultural wealth, tremendous actual and potential water power, cheap inland water transportation, low labor costs, and the appreciation of the possibilities

of the application of science and machinery to natural resources, this situation appears to me to be analogous to that
imminence of rapid development which confronted the United
States seventy years ago.

It will probably be a number of years before this production will affect world markets. All that can be produced, for
a time, will be required for local consumption, which, as
President Kalinin stated to me, was enormous and like a
"consuming fire." If, however, this regime or a similar successor persists for some time, the world will have to reckon not
only with the potentialities, but the actualities of a very substantial factor in the world economy. Its repercussions on
economic and political developments in Europe and in the
world will be far-reaching.

A possible alternative that the future affords is that this
territory might be subdivided by internal revolution into
several large independent autonomous subdivisions. Similarity of interests would group them naturally into White
Russia (Western Russia), the Ukraine, the Oriental Caucasus,
Mongolia, the Eastern Provinces, and Siberia.

Under these conditions it is interesting to note that the
R.S.F.S.R. comprises that section of Western Russia from Finland to the Caspian and Black Seas, excluding the Ukraine,
and is said to contain 50% of the population and 80% of its
wealth. It has been said that a line drawn from Leningrad
to the Caspian Sea would bound on the east that section of
Russia that contains 80% of the agricultural productivity, 70%
of the population, and a very large part of its water power,
coal, steel, and other basic resources. Were this section to be
cut in two, nevertheless the potentialities, economically and
politically, under the promise of continued development
would be very substantial and would materially affect both
European and world conditions.

A third alternative that the future affords might be the possible but remote contingency of conquest by, or union of, Germany and Russia. It need scarcely be pointed out that if German scientific and industrial methods and German managerial capacity and discipline were applied to the resources of man power and wealth here the effects upon Europe and the world would be very great.

It is probable that it is, in part, because of these considerations that the great western European powers, as well as other nations, maintain diplomatic representation here; and some of them in the face of well-nigh intolerable conditions.

WHAT ARE THE POSSIBLE SIGNIFICANCES OF THE U.S.S.R. TO THE UNITED STATES?

The traditional relationship between the United States and the Russian people has been one of friendship and good will. Catherine the Great refused the importunities of George III to loan or hire her troops for use against the American colonies. Past historical events and other considerations account for the fact that there is undoubtedly great friendliness on the part of the Russian people toward the United States.

As stated in a previous dispatch, the authorities of this government have gone so far as to state expressly to me that their government would do more to accommodate the United States than it would do for any other capitalistic country. They have given recently some proof of this attitude (notably in the Hrinkevich and Rubens cases).

While a dictatorship exists here, it appears to differ from a Fascist dictatorship, at least in one respect. Dictatorship over the proletariat is not the objective or end this system professes to seek, as is the case with Fascist ideology. The fact of dictatorship is apologized for here. It is justified on the

ground that it is a realistic expedient, resorted to only to protect the masses of the people, until they can themselves rule
under a system where ideologically the individual and not
the state shall be supreme. Moreover, there is no doubt of the
present sincerity of this regime in its desire to maintain peace.

Considered objectively, and without regard to ideological
conflicts, there are certain facts which vitally affect the United
States.

The resources of Russia, strategic and necessary in time of
war, complement and supply the lack of those existing in the
United States.

There are no conflicts of physical interests between the
United States and the U.S.S.R. There is nothing that either
has which is desired by or could be taken by the other.

The territory of the U.S.S.R. is contiguous to and lies to
the west and north of Manchukuo and north and east and west
of Japan. As stated heretofore, the U.S.S.R. supports in this
region a complete and self-sufficient army, variously estimated
at from 350,000 to 450,000 men. This armed force is equipped
with modern armament, and it is alleged that it has sufficient
supplies, independent of western Russia, for a two-year aggressive campaign. It is reported to be the fixed policy of this
government constantly to maintain in this region two Soviet
soldiers for every one Japanese soldier in Manchukuo.

The Soviet Union is making great efforts to build up its
navy. It is now claimed that they have 40 submarines in
Pacific waters.

Vladivostok and the Eastern Provinces are the bases for a
large number of Russian bombing planes and pursuit planes
(probably 1500), all within cruising radius of Japanese cities
that are largely built of wood.

Consul Blake, of our service, arriving here from Japan recently, advised that there is much discussion among Japanese businessmen of the danger arising from Russian airplanes.

There is one situation where a very serious issue might develop. That is the possible intrusion of the U.S.S.R. through the Comintern into the local affairs of the United States. Fortunately that has been measurably eliminated by the agreement entered into between President Roosevelt and Commissar Litvinov in 1934. Apparently there is very little activity on the part of the Comintern. The French Ambassador here has stated to me that in his opinion the Stalin government is desirous of lessening contacts with world revolutionary forces and would reduce its interest in the Comintern but for the fact that the government here desires to use the Comintern as an adjunct of military defense in case of war with aggressor states. Recent developments, however, make it clear that the Comintern will not be abandoned. Along with the Red Army and secret police, the "Workers of the World" are held up as the defenders of Russia against Fascist attack.

A common ground between the United States and the U.S.S.R., and one that will obtain for a long period of time, in my opinion, lies in the fact that both are sincere advocates of world peace.

In my opinion, there is no danger from Communism here, so far as the United States is concerned. To maintain its existence, this government has to apply capitalistic principles. Otherwise it will fail and be overthrown. That will not be permitted by the men presently in power, if they can avoid it. I expect to see this government, while professing devotion to Communism, move constantly more to the right, in practice, just as it has for the past eight years. If it maintains itself, it may evolve into a type of Fabian socialism, with large industry in the hands of the state, with, however, the agricultural and smaller businesses and traders working under capitalistic, property, and profit principles.

SUMMARY

I.

The extent of territory, the natural wealth—agricultural, mineral, water power, fisheries, natural ways, and man power of the U.S.S.R.—present a situation pregnant with potentialities of tremendous economic development and power.

II.

The Bolshevik regime floundered on the verge of anarchy and chaos for ten years, but during the last ten years under the Five-Year Plans a most extraordinary record of hydraulic, industrial, communication, social, educational, and army development is quite apparent. It is undoubtedly due to the driving force of Stalin. It has been characterized by a marked departure from the communistic principle in practice. The profit motive had to be resorted to in order to make the system work.

III.

The weaknesses in the system are many and apparent. Communism will fail here. Human nature cannot be changed in two generations. The system is now a type of capitalistic state socialism. Its continued existence and development cannot be forecast, as there are too many imponderables in the problem, such as European war, etc. It is generally considered that if the present government were overthrown from "within" by a military dictatorship or otherwise, a type of state socialism would still obtain, due to the education of each succeeding class of children during the last twenty years, all educated in the religion of their theories.

IV.

The strength of the present regime is found in the resolute, bold, and able leadership of Stalin. He has complete control of the army, the secret police, the newspapers, the radios, and the schools. Stalin is fast becoming, along with Lenin, the "superman" ideal of the masses. For the present this regime is firmly entrenched. There is always, however, the threat that hangs over dictatorships. Barring accident or assassination, coupled with a *coup d'état,* the present regime will persist for some time.

V.

The military strength of the U.S.S.R. is impressive. In both quality and numbers the man power is extraordinary. The standing army of approximately 1,500,000 men is divided into two self-contained units, one in the West and one in the Orient —about 70% in the West and 30% in the East. It is well equipped with side arms and well disciplined and trained to fanatical devotion to Communism. Its mechanized units are very good. The air-force personnel is excellent—their equipment good in pursuit planes, poor in bombing equipment. Numerically the air force is probably the strongest of the great powers. In air equipment, generally speaking, they probably are two or three years behind the Western nations.

The government is supremely confident that it could successfully resist simultaneous attack by Japan and Germany.

It would be exceedingly difficult to conquer or annihilate these forces, with their ally the Russian winter.

The weakness lies, perhaps, in the second line of defense—

the industrial production back of the lines and adequate supplies of high-grade petroleum products.

VI.

The significance of this situation to Europe and the world is very great. Regardless of what regime or what character of government exists, the forces that have been set in motion, as applied to this enormous natural wealth, will inevitably develop an economic factor of substantial character that will make its influence felt in Europe and in world affairs.

VII.

The significance to the United States is quite clear. If Japan should go berserk by any chance, the fact that Russia is at her back door is of consequence to us.

The Soviet Union is more friendly to the United States than to any foreign power. That is quite clear.

If the U.S.S.R. should be excluded from the proposed Four-Power Pact and become isolated (as it now seems to be convinced it will be), there is reason to believe that it may continue to live unto itself and develop indefinitely. It may develop into a very potential threat to world economic and political stability.

Communism holds no serious threat to the United States. Friendly relations in the future may be of great general value.

I have the honor to be, Sir, respectfully yours,

Joseph E. Davies

FINAL REPORT

NO. 1342 · *Moscow, June 6, 1938*

TO THE HONORABLE THE SECRETARY OF STATE

> FINAL REPORT SUPPLEMENTARY TO
> THE GENERAL SUMMARY DISPATCH,
> NO. 1341, JUNE 6, 1938, MADE UPON
> MY DEPARTURE FROM THE SOVIET UNION.
> REPORT ON MATTERS PENDING.
> RECOMMENDATIONS AS TO POLICY.

Strictly Confidential

Sir:

Upon leaving this post to take up my duties in Brussels, I have considered that it was incumbent upon me to render a final report to you, covering my conclusions as to the facts which I have found here, the status of pending matters, together with observations as to the manner in which these matters could be best handled; and finally the policy, which in my judgment, it would be in the best interests of the government of the United States to adopt with reference to the situation here. I therefore have the honor to report as follows:

Reference is here made to Dispatch No. 1341 of June 6, 1938, which is a factual general survey. This report is supplementary thereto and should be read in connection therewith.

SPECIFIC MATTERS STILL PENDING

The major specific matters now pending between the two governments are the following:

1. Payment of the Russian debt and proposed loan by the United States or its nationals; *

---

* The debt and loan discussion is omitted because it is repetitious.

2. The Comintern;
3. The Protection of American Citizens;
4. The Hrinkevich Case;
5. The Rubens Case; and
6. Commercial relationships and the most-favored-nation status.

THE COMINTERN

With references to the Comintern situation, I have at all times made it clear to Soviet officials that the attitude of the United States is that it holds the Soviet Union to strict fulfillment of the promises made to the government of the United States.

There are three factors in this connection, which are important, and which should be borne in mind in this connection:

First: Contacts with the world revolutionary movement in other capitalist countries are now considered by the Soviet officials to be of very vital consequence to the Soviet Union as agencies for military defense. (See dispatch and statement of the French Ambassador with reference thereto.)

Second: There has been some disposition in the past on the part of the Stalin government to minimize its interest in world revolutionary movements in the past. The interest of this government in the Comintern is directly in relation to its apprehensions of danger from military attack of the aggressor nations, and at this moment it is again stressing its interest in the Comintern; and

Third: There appears to be little subversive Comintern activity in the United States at the present time.

The question of the Comintern, therefore, in practical effect, has become largely academic so far as any vital interests of the United States are concerned. Unless, therefore, the idea is implemented in the United States by a greater aggressive and more marked activity than exists at the present time, it would be advisable, in my opinion, strictly to maintain our position with reference thereto as a formal matter, but quietly to ignore the question, unless and until it threatens our well-being. For the present at least under existing conditions, it is not advisable to "use a hatchet to kill a fly."

PROTECTION TO AMERICAN CITIZENS

The traditional policy of the United States which has been reiterated and emphasized by the Secretary of vigilantly protecting the rights of American citizens has been at all times vigorously projected by this mission. Two major situations are pending at the present time. They are the Hrinkevich and the Rubens cases. They are the only two American citizens held in prison at the present time on what appears to be political grounds.*

In connection with these situations the background here, existing at the present time, should be considered. It is a condition bordering on panic. This government is obsessed with the idea that it is being isolated by a hostile world and that the hands of all capitalist nations are against it. The war psychology is strong. A condition of martial law has, practically, been projected. The government is convinced that it is confronted with the actual menace of hostile aggression by Germany and Japan. It is acting with force and vigor to pro-

---

* Hrinkevich was subsequently, upon my representation, promptly released. Mrs. Rubens refused our aid and manifested no desire to return to the United States, where she was confronted with possible prosecution for violation of Federal law connected with alleged passport frauds.

tect itself and is doing so entirely without regard to niceties. Foreign consulates have been ruthlessly closed. Thousands of foreign nationals have been arrested, imprisoned, and held incommunicado. I have been advised recently by the Ambassadors of England, France, Germany, Italy, Turkey, Persia, and Afghanistan that representatives of their governments, respectively, have not been permitted to interview their nationals who were imprisoned here prior to their trial. Thousands of Greeks, Persians, and Afghan nationals, hundreds of Germans and Poles, and substantial numbers of English and Italian nationals have been imprisoned and held under such conditions.

GENERAL POLICY

In view of the shrinkage of the number of American citizens now in the Soviet Union and upon many other grounds a strong argument, from certain points of view, might be made that the continuance of diplomatic relations here is unnecessary under present conditions and inadvisable.

In view of the extraordinary economic and political potentialities which exist here and which will undoubtedly continue to have an increasing effect upon both economic and political conditions of Europe as well as of the world, and particularly in view of the Japanese attitude in the Pacific, it would appear unwise to change the present status or to consider the discontinuance of diplomatic relations except under some severe provocation.

In my opinion the importance of this mission should not be minimized nor should the diplomatic secretariat be reduced.

Equally important with the continuance of diplomatic relations is the matter of policy as to the methods which are to be employed in matters arising between the two governments and the general attitude which this mission should maintain in its relation toward and with the Soviet government and the Soviet officials.

CHANGED CONDITIONS IN CONTRAST TO THOSE OF THREE YEARS AGO

Conditions have radically changed since 1935.

When the Soviet government failed to live up to its obligations under the loan, debt, and Comintern agreements, our government felt properly aggrieved. Under such conditions it was natural that consular representation and staff should be reduced as a gesture of protest. There was then properly directed a policy of the maintenance of strictly formal relations, characterized by a resolute insistence upon the U.S.S.R. living up strictly to each and every obligation in letter as well as in spirit, and characterized also by an attitude of unyielding, unbending, and perhaps of a critical character. Conditions here, particularly in the last year and a half, however, have radically changed. The situation both here as affecting European peace and in the Pacific and the Far East is radically different. An attitude of aloofness which might have created irritations three years ago would have been of little consequence at that time. Larger issues are now concerned. Internal conditions are also very different. Now, this government, apparently, is going through a crisis. The hostility toward foreigners is very intense. Official government organs assert that diplomatic and consular representatives in the Soviet Union are nests for espionage and spying activities of aggressor nations, and that these are actually menacing the Soviet government. Thousands of Afghans, Greeks, and Turks; hundreds of Germans and Poles; scores of Japanese; and even some British nationals have been arrested and confined in prison for alleged carrying on of subversive activities. These foreign-national prisoners have been kept incommunicado. Diplomatic representatives of their governments consistently have been refused an opportunity of interviewing these nationals in prison until after trial.

Despite these conditions and during this period, the Soviet government has gone out of its way to extend particular consideration to the government of the United States. This has been done both by conduct and by oral expressions. It was signally demonstrated in both the Hrinkevich and Rubens cases. High officials of the Soviet Union have stated to me that they would go farther in friendship toward the United States than toward any other nation in the world.

On the assumption that the United States decides to maintain diplomatic relations here, it is, in my opinion, advisable that the conduct of this mission should be projected and maintained in as friendly and harmonious a spirit as is possible, consistent with the strict adherence to the performance of all obligations under the agreements between the two countries. The integrity of our democratic system and our requirement of strict performance of Soviet promises should, of course, always be maintained with vigor; but the methods employed in connection with current matters of relatively smaller importance and, in fact, methods employed in all matters should be based not upon a critical and intolerant attitude that induces irritations, but upon an attitude of tolerant understanding of the difficulties under which the officials here are laboring. It should not be an attitude that would induce suspicion and hostility directed against us. We should not, by reason of our conduct, be classed among "enemy powers."

Such a policy does not involve approving in any manner the ideological concepts of this government. It does, however, recognize the right of self-determination. It is interpretative of the high-minded and Christianlike declarations of the for-

VYACHESLAV MOLOTOV
"To Mr. Joseph Davies, U. S. A. Ambassador
with great respect and all good wishes
Molotov"

eign policy of the United States as expressed by the President of the United States and the Secretary of State in connection with foreign affairs. It is a "Good Neighbor Policy," and one consistent with the best traditions of our diplomatic history.

Subsequent to my conversations with the President of the United States and the Secretary of State on the occasion of my last visit to the United States, and since my return here, and in conformity with instructions as I understood them, I have made an effort to project and pursue this policy. It has, in my opinion, been successful. There is no doubt of the sincerity and the friendliness of the U.S.S.R. toward the government of the United States, in marked contrast and to a greater degree than to any other nation. It has been my experience here that where matters are projected as between the two countries in a spirit of tolerance, understanding, and friendliness, there has been a prompt and generous response on the part of this government to try to accommodate itself to a reasonable agreement.

Upon leaving this post I am able to say that, in my opinion, while at all times we have proclaimed our loyalty to our political ideals and to our system of government, and while we have at all times insistently maintained and asserted with vigor the dignity and rights of the government of the United States, the conduct of the mission here has nevertheless reflected the historical traditions of friendship which have existed between the American and the Russian people.

I have the honor to be, Sir, respectfully yours,

Joseph E. Davies

PART IX

HARVEST OF THE MISSION

September 6, 1938—October 28, 1941

IX

Despite the fact that I am no longer in Moscow, I find much interest in anything that reflects on the Soviet military strength. Here is Hitler's estimate:

"(1) In Russia one has to deal with a nation of 180 millions.

(2) Russia is territorially immune from attack.

(3) Russia can never be overcome by a blockade.

(4) Its industries are safe from aerial attack, as the most important industrial centers are from 4000 to 6000 kilometers from the frontiers.

"These four facts," he said, "should be enough to establish the dangerous power of this country. But added to them comes the strength of the revolutionary idea, and the determined endeavor of those in power to accomplish a world revolution. With this object an army, of the highest perfection technically, has been created. With the same object, with regard to economics, a dangerous dumping policy is being pursued through slave wages in order to undermine the economic systems of other countries.

"The present development of Russia gives cause for reflection," he went on. "In 1917 Russia was down and out. In 1920 she was torn by civil war. In the years 1924 and 1925 the first

signs of convalescence began to appear with the creation of
the Red Army. In 1927 the first Five-Year Plan was begun and
later carried out. In 1932 came the second Five-Year Plan,
which is now in full swing. Russia has a solid trade, the strongest army, the strongest tank corps, and the strongest air force
in the world. These are facts which cannot be ignored."

This I found in a book by the Marquess of Londonderry
just published in London. I don't think much of Londonderry's attitude toward Germany. But I am sure that what he
would say Hitler actually said would be true.

Brussels, Belgium, September 10, 1938

THE HONORABLE V. M. MOLOTOV

Dear Mr. Premier:

You have doubtless heard from Mr. Rosoff
with reference to the matters which we discussed and will
also by this time have received from him the message transmitted by me.

From this you will see that the debt situation might have
been prejudiced if it had been projected at this time.

From my talks with the President and the Secretary of
State, I personally feel sanguine that something can be worked
out within the practical limitations confronting each government, which will be mutually acceptable, after our Congress
has again convened. The President and the Secretary of
State were keenly interested and impressed by the spirit of
your government in connection with this matter. As you said,
even if nothing concrete should develop the situation has,
nevertheless, resulted and should continue to result in better
understanding between two great governments and their
leaders. If at any time I can be of any service in aiding to
bring into agreement this or any other matter of difference I
shall always be glad to be available.

My stay in Russia I shall always remember with keen appreciation of the universal kindness I received at the hands of the fine Russian people, and the many courtesies and kindnesses tendered to me by the representatives of the government of the Soviet Union.

Under separate cover I have forwarded to you an autographed copy of the catalogue of my collection of Russian pictures which, with the aid of your government, I was able to secure to present to my old alma mater, the University of Wisconsin.

We are most pleasantly located in Brussels and I am sure will enjoy our life here; but I miss Moscow and will look forward to going back there from time to time to see the great changes which I am sure you are going to bring about in pursuance of your plans.

Brussels, Belgium, September 10, 1938

THE HONORABLE JOSEPH STALIN

My dear Mr. Stalin:

I found satisfaction in our talk. It is this: it has served to clear up certain possible misunderstandings that existed. It has, I am sure, resulted in better understanding between the governing forces of our two great countries and in better relations between them. As Premier Molotov said to me in parting (and very wisely): Whatever may come of the specific matters we discussed, good will have resulted through this better mutual understanding. I am much gratified that during my tenure as Ambassador to the U.S.S.R., and in no small measure due to the abilities and frankness of your great Foreign Minister, Mr. Litvinov, the relations between the Soviet Union and the United States were never on a better basis of mutual understanding.

Through Mr. Rosoff, who was ever very helpful, I transmitted to you a message concerning the debt question which we discussed. Doubtless you have received it before this and have been advised as to the situation as I found it. It is to be regretted that the exigencies of the moment in my country made it advisable temporarily to defer further discussion just at this time.

I am free to say, however, that the President and Secretary Hull were most favorably impressed with the spirit which you and the government of the Soviet Union manifested in a desire to complete in spirit the Roosevelt-Litvinov agreement. The President hopes quite definitely that some arrangement can be worked out later that will be within the practical possibilities that confront both governments.

I shall keep in touch with the matter and will always be ready to aid in bringing the principals together in a mutually advantageous agreement when it should be considered desirable. In the meantime, the record of these proposals, together with the discussions in my government concerning them, are being kept strictly confidential.

It was a matter of much gratification to me that the battleship matter had been satisfactorily worked out.

If Ambassador Troyanovsky is still in Moscow, please give him and Mrs. Troyanovsky the kindest remembrances of Mrs. Davies and myself.

SOVIET STRENGTH IN CASE OF WAR

EXCERPT FROM A LETTER TO PRESIDENT ROOSEVELT

Brussels, January 18, 1939

It is my judgment that both the Soviet government and its army are a great deal stronger than is generally recognized in certain European quarters. The government is now, at least, devoted to international peace. Moreover, for many years its economic necessities will require peace if that is possible.

The leaders of the Soviet government have stated to me that there is only one government in the world that they trust and that is the United States government under your leadership.

In the event of so dire a calamity as an international conflict between the totalitarian and the democratic states, the Soviet government is, in my opinion, a much more powerful factor than the reactionaries of Europe concede, and might be of the greatest value.

Brussels, January 18, 1939

HONORABLE HARRY HOPKINS

My dear Harry:

When I was at home last, and after our visit at George Holmes' house, I wanted to talk to you more at length. I tried to reach you but you were out and I had to leave without seeing you.

Conditions are hell over here. Chamberlain's peace is a flop. That is the overwhelming opinion in diplomatic circles here. There is no peace. The colonies problem probably was settled by Chamberlain with Hitler at Munich. But appetite grows on what it feeds. The next crisis will be either the Polish Corridor or the Ukraine—and soon. The hell of it is that there is neither collective security nor a balance of power to secure peace and the civilization of Europe.

There appears to be no leadership in England to galvanize the revolt. A lawyer can't win a lawsuit or a battle unless he tells the truth himself and that he believes the defendant is a crook. In other words, unless you get out in front of those you lead, the mass will probably flounder. France is all shot to pieces. The result is that there is no leadership in Europe except on the totalitarian side.

The President picked up the torch which Chamberlain dropped and his press statement on the treatment of the Jews in Germany made him the undisputed leader of world opinion and democratic and moral indignation. But the dictators don't bother about that.

Specifically there is one thing that can be done now in my opinion and that is to give some encouragement to Russia to remain stanch for collective security and peace. The reactionaries of England and France have quarantined her. The bogey that a war would entail communism in a defeated Germany and central Europe is plain bunk. Germany would go socialist or become a sensible military autocracy. Poland and Rumania would still afford a dyke. Moreover, the Soviets have got enough to digest in Russia. That is Stalin's policy—peace to consolidate their position economically is what they need, and they know it. Russia served notice of the renunciation of her treaty of nonaggression with Poland four weeks before the Czech crisis, in order to fulfill her pledge to France, in contrast to the action of England and France in leading Czechoslovakia up to the block under false assurances up to the last minute. The Chamberlain policy of throwing Italy, Poland, and Hungary into the arms of Hitler may be completed by so disgusting the Soviets that it will drive Russia into an economic agreement and an ideological truce with Hitler. That is not beyond the bounds of possibility or even probability—they did it for ten years.

The point of all this is that the President might be able to check this tendency by the appointment of a strong man as Ambassador to Russia immediately. The President agreed with me at home that the type should be a successful businessman with clearly defined ideas of liberalism and an open mind.

Confidentially, he authorized me to proffer it to one man, but unfortunately, he was unable to go.

Apart from the larger consideration, there is the specific fact that it is to the common interest of the Soviets and of our own government—vis-à-vis Japan—to be on friendly terms.

The reactionaries of England and France will shortly be wooing the Soviets' support in their desperation, but it may be too late if the Soviets get utterly disheartened.

Hastily yours,

DIARY   *Brussels—January 30, 1939*

The outline of the Soviet Third Five-Year Plan (1938-42) has just been published. It is most significant that the plan is to be devoted not to the continued production of consumers goods, but primarily to making the country self-sufficient in basic heavy industries, and in the production of armaments and munitions. In other words, they are going back to the First Five-Year Plan which was devoted to heavy industry. Apparently, the feverish defense program which I saw in Moscow two years ago has not subsided or abated.

DIARY   *Brussels—February 2, 1939*

The Russian news agency, Tass, announces today that Foreign Minister Litvinov had served notice on Hungary that the U.S.S.R. was severing diplomatic relations with that country. The reason assigned was that Hungary had joined the Anti-Comintern pact and had "lost its independence and was no longer a free agent." It was yielding to the pressure of "certain states."

DIARY   *Brussels—February 6, 1939*

The British Ambassador, Lord Clive, called me up and told me that Mr. Hudson, head of the Board of Trade, was going to be in Belgium and would like to see me. I immediately asked them over for tea. Hudson, who was going to Moscow on this British mission, was very much interested in talking with me about Russia. I gave him the facts frankly as I saw them. He was surprised—even startled. He said, "This is extraordinary. Why don't we get these same reports from our people in Moscow? Their reports are definitely to the contrary." I replied, "Well, they may be right. I may be wrong. I am simply giving you facts as to what I saw myself, and from which you can draw your own conclusions." If you asked me why our reports differ, my reply would be that it is to be found in the fact that I am not a professional diplomat, but a lawyer and businessman, who was accustomed to making judgments on situations in which it was always important to me personally that I should recognize facts when I see them and not misread them; and that while I would cast no reflections upon the British Embassy in Moscow, with its very able staff (I had great admiration for Lord Chilston's judgment and wisdom), nevertheless, I believed that in any bureaucratic organization there was always a tendency to report to their chiefs what their chiefs wanted to hear. This was pretty strong stuff, but they are British; and the British are good sports and like honest frankness. It will be a first-class disaster to peace, I frankly said, if Britain and France did not tie up definitely with Russia in a common front for the defense of peace against this madman Hitler.

DIARY   *Brussels—March 3, 1939*

At last the ill-fated Spanish Nonintervention Committee is passing out of the picture. The Soviet government recalled its delegate from London. The announcement was couched in typical Litvinov phraseology. The reason assigned was that the committee had long ceased to function and "has even lost the sense of its own existence." All during the period when the German and Italian delegates in the committee were playing fast and loose in connection with the Spanish situation, no one smarted more under what was regarded as "insults to their intelligence" than did Litvinov and the Soviet officials.

JOURNAL   *Brussels—March 11, 1939*

The Moscow radio of yesterday and the press reports of today carry Stalin's speech on the foreign policy of the Soviet Union, made yesterday, before the 18th Party Congress. It is a most significant statement. It bears the earmarks of a definite warning to the British and French governments that the Soviets are getting tired of "nonrealistic" opposition to the aggressors.

Stalin said, in effect: (1) We want peace and friendly relations with all countries and desire also to strengthen our trade ties where possible. (2) We seek neighborly relations, particularly with border countries. (3) We support peoples who have become the victims of aggression in their fight to preserve their own independence. (4) We fear no aggressor and we are ready to deal a "double counterblow" in case of attack from either the east or the west.

He then went on to say that the "nonaggression states," and particularly England and France, were and are "retreating and retreating" and "making one concession after another" to the dictators. They had, he said, completely repudiated the policy of "collective security" and the plan of a united front for protection against "the bandits."

Even more significant, he charged that these two countries in their own interest were inciting Germany to attack the U.S.S.R.; that their purpose in this was selfish, to enable them, after the combatants had exhausted themselves, to intervene "in the interest of peace" and dictate the conditions of peace solely on the basis of their own interests.

Going on, he said that France and Britain had given Austria to Germany; had violated their pledges to Czechoslovakia; and had "shouted lies" in the press about the weakness of the Russian army and disorder in the Soviet Union, in order to push the Germans into a war against the U.S.S.R., on the theory that the Russians would be an easy prey.

That, said Stalin, "looked very much like encouraging the aggressor."

Knowing Russia as I do, I feel that this is very discouraging and really ominous for the negotiations which are going forward now between the British Foreign Office and the Soviet Union in connection with guarantees to Poland and to Rumania, in the event of German attack.

It certainly is the most significant danger signal that I have yet seen. It will be a disaster if the democracies do not use the strengths which exist here against Hitler aggression.

EXCERPT FROM LETTER TO CHIEF JUSTICE RICHARD S. WHALEY

Brussels—March 20, 1939

What a pity Europe hasn't a Franklin Roosevelt! He saw that situation clearly two years ago; but, of course, without intervention in European affairs, he could do nothing effective about it. There is only one clear-ringing challenge to the aggressors on the real issue—of personal liberty and religion—and that is the voice of the Boss. Both in the press and in diplomatic circles, that is common comment over here now. For the sake of civilization, it is too bad that the mental clarity and moral boldness of the President could not have been applied to this situation—before it was too late.

EXCERPT FROM LETTER TO SENATOR KEY PITTMAN, CHAIRMAN
OF THE FOREIGN RELATIONS COMMITTEE

Brussels—March 21, 1939

The next few weeks will disclose which door Hitler will attempt to get closed first: the door on the east or the door on the west. It is axiomatic in German military strategy that Germany must not fight on two fronts at the same time. That he will not be content to remain passive long is a foregone conclusion. The reports which have been published by the German general staff in the technical magazines, describing the power and effectiveness of the Russian army, seem to have dulled Hitler's taste for the *Drang nach Osten*. From information that I get from most responsible sources and that I think is reliable, Hitler is making a desperate effort to alienate Stalin from France and Britain. Unless the British and French wake up, I am afraid he will succeed. If he does, he can turn his attention to western Europe without any concern as to an attack from behind.

EXCERPT FROM DISPATCH TO THE SECRETARY OF STATE

Brussels—March 24, 1939

The diplomatic representatives of the smaller states of Europe here generally point out that although a whole week has gone by since Prime Minister Chamberlain's speech at Birmingham wherein he condemned the invasion of Czechoslovakia by Germany, the government of Great Britain has not been able to create a "united front" even as among Great Britain, France, and the U.S.S.R.—in comparison with the rapid action of the German Führer in the Balkans.

DIARY   *London—April 3, 1939*

Came over here for a week end to see Winston Churchill
at his country place. Had a long visit with Joe Kennedy this
morning. Talked about the European situation at length. Joe
is very pessimistic. So am I.

Took the opportunity of going into the Russian situation
at length with Kennedy and suggested that he could tell
Chamberlain from me that if they are not careful they would
drive Stalin into Hitler's arms. Britain and France had snubbed
Russia, their then ally, by excluding the Soviet from Munich;
that the Soviets did not trust them anyway, and feared that
Britain and France were trying to use Russia as a cat's-paw,
and would leave them to fight Germany alone; that Stalin
wanted peace for Russia above all else; that he might decide
to take Hitler as the best bet for his security, at least for the
time being. I asked him if he had read the copy of my "Brief
on the Facts" report to the Department, copy of which I had
sent him. He said he had. He recognized the value of Russia
in the military situation; but, as a matter of fact, Russia
would have to fight for Poland or Rumania anyway, and regardless of whether there was a formal agreement with France
and Britain or not, because it was vital to Russia's self-interest.
I told him that in my opinion that was a wrong theory. It was
"first things first" in Russia. The Soviets were desperately
trying to keep out of war, unless they could feel assured,
through specific realistic plans and obvious preponderance of
strength, that they in combination with France and England,
could beat Hitler in the event of war or scare him off before
hostilities, by serving notice upon Hitler that he would have
to fight all three. From a number of important and reliable
sources, I was convinced that Hitler was bending every effort
to wean Stalin away from Britain and France, because it was

vital to his military success that he close his eastern door before he made his attack on the western front. Somehow or other it seems impossible to make an impression on this London atmosphere.

About the only man who really appreciates the real imminence of disaster over here is Winston Churchill. It was reassuring to have him tell me yesterday that by the middle of the year this "damnable blackmail menace from the air will exist no longer, because we will be prepared."

EXCERPT FROM DISPATCH NO. 269 TO THE SECRETARY OF STATE OF THAT PORTION WHICH REFERRED TO RUSSIA

Brussels—April 4, 1939

SUBJECT: INFORMAL AND PERSONAL DISCUSSIONS IN LONDON WITH MR. DAVID LLOYD GEORGE, MR. WINSTON CHURCHILL, AND AMBASSADOR KENNEDY

Referring to what Mr. Lloyd George said, the dispatch states:

That it was vitally necessary that England should, wholeheartedly and immediately, aggressively bring Russia into close co-operation with definite and specific mutual military arrangements;

That he had talked with "Neville" (Chamberlain) about Italy and that he (Lloyd George) believed that Mussolini was simply waiting for Hitler to absorb the attention of France, when he would make a military drive in Africa. This would probably result in the Mediterranean being closed to troop ships, and with Franco in Spain, the lines of communication for naval and troop ships, to get troops into the Sudan around South Africa, would be menaced by German submarines from a Spanish base on the Atlantic.

JOURNAL   *Brussels—April 15, 1939*

The President addresses Hitler and Mussolini today: "Are you willing to give assurance that your armed forces will not attack or invade the territory or positions of the following independent countries?" In the twenty-nine enumerated, Russia is also included. The President suggests that if so, he will be glad to notify the various countries and undoubtedly reciprocal nonaggression agreements will come from them.

DIARY   *Brussels—April 17, 1939*

It is announced today in the press that President Kalinin of the U.S.S.R. telegraphed to the President: "Congratulations and profound sympathy with the noble appeal you have addressed to Hitler and Mussolini."

DIARY   *Brussels—April 18, 1939*

Today I sent a personal message to the President and to the Secretary of State that it was my firm conviction that the deciding element in Hitler's determination as to whether it will be peace or war this summer in Europe will be whether Britain and France will make a definite agreement with the Soviet Union which will assure to them the military support of Russia in the event of German attack upon Poland.

DIARY   *Brussels—May 3, 1939*

The German protests in the German papers are "steaming up" in their assaults on Poland. Here it comes! Britain has given public guarantee to assist Poland in the event of attack. More than that, Britain has deprived herself of the capacity to decide her action as events develop. Britain's conduct will be governed solely by the Polish decision. With Danzig and the Polish Corridor in the boiling pot, it is a dangerous situation. Of course, if the British and French tie up definitely in the military pact with the Soviets, this arrangement is all right, for Germany would then be subject to attack on two fronts if it tries to crush Poland. Unless that agreement is assured with Russia, Britain is taking a terrible chance. It probably means that the British, French, and Soviet discussions in Moscow have been successfully concluded.

DIARY   *Brussels—May 4, 1939*

While the British Foreign Office is working on the theory that "unilateral agreements," whereby Britain guarantees the smaller European states against aggression, will afford "collective security," Hitler is taking advantage of the "initiative" and "jumps the gun" by inviting the Baltic and Scandinavian states to enter at once in pacts of nonaggression with him. He will probably "git some of 'em." All these little countries are scared to death. German prestige has risen enormously and the confidence in either the ability or the will of the western democracies to give safety and real help has diminished very rapidly. The reaction to German pressure will be in direct ratio to their proximity to Germany and their fear. In all probability, Denmark, Estonia, and Latvia cannot hold out against this pressure.

NO. 317   *Brussels, May 10, 1939*

TO THE HONORABLE THE SECRETARY OF STATE

SUBJECT: OBSERVATION FROM THIS POST WITH
REFERENCE TO THE SIGNIFICANCE OF THE
LITVINOV RETIREMENT

Sir:

With reference to the above-entitled matter, I beg leave to report as follows:

The announcement of the resignation of Foreign Minister

Litvinov created a sensation in the Diplomatic Corps here.

A theory, which has been stated to me by two diplomatic representatives of countries adjacent to Russia and who, I believe, know the Russian situation very well, is:

(*a*) That Stalin has no confidence in either France or Great Britain and is fearful that the Soviet Union might be involved in European war and left "holding the bag";

(*b*) That Stalin's speech to the Communist Party, delivered to the 18th Congress in March last, definitely indicated a disposition toward withdrawal of Soviet activities so far as Europe was concerned, and a tendency to be extremely cautious "not to allow our country to be drawn into conflicts by warmongers who are accustomed to have others pull their chestnuts out of the fire for them";

(*c*) That the Soviet position is definitely devoted to peace, both because of ideological and economic reasons;

(*d*) That the Soviet government is intolerant and disgusted with the methods of appeasement previously employed, and believes that the aggressors will only understand positive and bold military alliances which are concrete in character, and that these only can preserve peace;

(*e*) That Litvinov in the past two years has been unsuccessful in persuading the western powers to this view;

(*f*) That a new Foreign Ministry is required to project a hard, realistic front in these diplomatic negotiations, which would either secure adequate practical resistance to the aggressors or retirement of the Soviet Union into itself.

Both of these chiefs of mission were definitely of the opinion that Litvinov's retirement augurs difficulty for the British diplomatic negotiations now pending and that the failure to bring Russia in would have a very serious effect on European peace and would ultimately be demonstrated by probable speedy action by Hitler against Poland. I very much fear that this view is correct. I hope England and France can still work it out.

There is a very definite disposition generally in Europe to discount the realities so far as the Russian strength or military power is concerned. The published statements of Hitler, contained in Lord Londonderry's book, in which he expresses great respect for the power of the Russian army, and the published statements of military experts of Germany and other European countries, are discounted.

I have the honor to be, Sir, respectfully yours,

Joseph E. Davies

EXCERPT FROM ENCLOSURE NO. 2 TO DISPATCH NO. 326 FROM EMBASSY, BRUSSELS

MEMORANDUM OF CONVERSATION WITH CAPTAIN VON RINTELEN,* MAY 17, 1939, DICTATED BY JOSEPH E. DAVIES

That Germany is making a desperate effort to succeed in keeping the Soviets neutral and to prevent a new misadventure such as was the case with Turkey. He said that the former Czechoslovak General Syrový, who went over to the Nazis after he had succeeded Hodža as Prime Minister, had been sent twice recently to Moscow to contact army officers and friends in Russia as a Hitler emissary; that every effort was being bent by Hitler to prevent a British-Soviet alliance. He expressed the belief that it was entirely possible that Germany and Russia would get together because of their mutual economic interest, that Nazi Socialism and Russian Communism are brothers ideologically, and that the types of mind of Hitler, Mussolini, and Stalin were the same. It was of vital

---

* Captain von Rintelen, the notorious German agent in the United States during the last war, now claims to be a British citizen. He sought an interview with me. He appeared to be violently anti-Nazi and pro-British. He discussed many topics. Only his observations on Russia are reproduced here.

importance to the western democracies, he added, that Britain close with Russia at once.

DIARY   *Brussels—May 27, 1939*

The press announces that the British and French Ambassadors have handed to Premier Molotov identical memoranda as to the mutual-assistance pact now being negotiated between the three states.

DIARY   *Brussels—May 29, 1939*

The British Ambassador is reported to have been received by Molotov and to have spent a couple of hours with him to reply to questions as to certain points of the Anglo-French proposals which Molotov wanted explained.

MOLOTOV'S ULTIMATUM

JOURNAL   *Brussels—May 31, 1939*

The Moscow radio and the press reported on Molotov's speech on Soviet foreign relations. The gist of the speech as reported was:

The Soviet government would not gloss over the international situation, and the fact that it was very much "worsened."

The Munich settlement was bitterly attacked.

He said: "We stand for peace and against aggression, but we must remember Stalin's admonition that we cannot be used to pull the chestnuts of others out of the fire." He set forth and enumerated the minimum conditions which the Soviet Union would require before entering into a joint pact with France and Britain. They were: (1) There must be an immediate conclusion of a pact for mutual assistance of an exclusive defensive character between the three parties. (2)

There must be a guarantee by all against any attack by an aggressor directed against the nonaggressor states in central or eastern Europe and this guarantee must include, without exception and specifically, all smaller European countries which border on Russia. (3) There must be a definite, concrete, and specific agreement by the three countries as to the exact form, extent, and kind of assistance which is to be given in case of attack, and when.

The British and French did not meet, he said, the requirements of full reciprocity and equality of obligations in their proposals. The British proposals did not include an agreement that Britain and France would give help to the U.S.S.R. if it were attacked; and, in the second place, did not guarantee against aggression the small states bordering on the U.S.S.R. and covering the northwest border frontier of the U.S.S.R., in the event that these smaller states would be unable to defend their neutrality.

Such concessions to the principle of reciprocity as were offered, said Molotov, were so hedged about that they would be a "fictitious step forward."

The new proposals, said he, made no progress at all in connection with giving guarantees to the Baltic states. He concluded with the statement that the Soviet government was asked to assume obligation to assist five central European states whose security was vital to Britain and France. The Soviet Union would refuse to assume such responsibility unless Great Britain or France would assume similar obligations with reference to the three Baltic states whose security and neutrality was vital to the Soviet Union.

In conclusion, there was this rather ominous suggestion, which seemed to be brought in "by the ears," and obviously for a purpose: "We do not refuse to improve our trade relations with Germany. Negotiations may be resumed."

JUSTIFYING THE AGGRESSOR

EXCERPT FROM ENCLOSURE NO. 1 TO DISPATCH NO. 364 OF JUNE 21, 1939, FROM THE EMBASSY AT BRUSSELS

VISIT WITH MR. ———, CHIEF OF MISSION AT BRUSSELS

In reply to a question from me regarding his views on the likelihood of a European war this summer, Mr. ——— stated that he believed such war would be extremely improbable if Russia could be kept out of the agreement with Britain and France, but that perfection of a three-power alliance between Russia, France, and Great Britain would almost certainly precipitate war. His reasoning in this regard, or rather the reasoning that he offered to me, was that Russia would always adhere to a policy of precipitating crises from which she herself would seek to remain aloof. This manner of reasoning, together with other opinions stated by Mr. ———, convinced me that the totalitarian states dread above all the inclusion of Russian power in a solid front against the totalitarian ideology of conquest. Mr. ——— was almost naïve in letting me see his country's keen apprehension about Russia and in disclosing to me the very deeply cherished hope of his government that Moscow's influence would not be exerted to buttress the democratic wall. He also asked my opinion concerning the strength of Russia under the present government, and I replied that Russian military and economic strength either under the present communistic or under any changed form would in any case be immense.

In conclusion, I may say that the main impression I gathered from Mr. ——— is a confirmation of the belief that his country is working in complete sympathy and may possibly even work in formal alliance with the stated policies and the obvious interests of Germany and Italy.

DIARY *New York—July 17, 1939*

When the *Queen Mary* docked today, to my great joy, I found Marjorie on the dock with the girls. All of us had dinner at the Belgian Pavilion at the Fair. Left on the midnight train for Washington, to report immediately to the President and the Secretary. Pursuant to orders of the State Department I had returned to the United States for conferences.

DIARY *Washington—July 18, 1939*

Had luncheon with the President at 12:30 noon. He asked my reasons, specifically, for the confidence with which I predicted that war was immediately imminent through Hitler's aggression and would come either before Hindenburg's birthday in August, or before the Party Rally at Nuremberg in September. I gave him in specific detail the information which I had received direct from Belgians, who had manufacturing plants in Germany and who were in contact with the Nazi party leaders; also the statements which I had received from American businessmen with interests in Germany, whom I had seen just a week before in Belgium, who also had it firsthand from Nazi leaders what was in the making. These men he knew personally. They were men of preeminently sound and steady judgment.

These and many other specific statements I gave to him. Some from high Nazi diplomatic officials. He was particularly impressed with what I told him about the expressions of my diplomatic colleagues in Brussels, who were praying for the amendment of the Neutrality Act, in the belief that it might possibly deter Hitler and at least delay the war.

These statements gave him no surprise. It simply seemed to confirm his deep pessimism. He said that my report simply confirmed his other information.

I asked whether I could be of any help in connection with the neutrality legislation. He said that it might do some good if I saw some of the Senate leaders.

He asked me about the Russian negotiations with Britain and France. I told him frankly that I was very much worried about it. It was a matter of common talk among the Diplomatic Corps in Brussels that Hitler was bending every effort to alienate Stalin from the Western powers. I told him that I was told by a very high and important personage in Europe that Hitler and Ribbentrop were confident they could break Stalin away from England and France. The President told me he had told Ambassador Oumansky, when he was leaving to go to Moscow, to tell Stalin that if his government joined up with Hitler, it was as certain as that the night followed the day that as soon as Hitler had conquered France, he would turn on Russia, and it would be the Soviet's turn next. He told me also to get that word to Stalin and Molotov, if I could.

He discussed the results of a possible Hitler *Blitzkrieg* and its effect on the world, and particularly the United States. He had no illusions as to the tremendous mechanized power of the German army.

Immediately after lunch, I went up to the Capitol and talked with my old friends, Alben Barkley, Jim Byrnes, Key Pittman, Burt Wheeler, Joe Guffey, Claude Pepper, and others in Colonel Halsey's office. Senator Pittman, Chairman of the Foreign Relations Committee of the Senate, asked me to come up to talk to the members of his committee on the following day.

DIARY   *Washington—July 19, 1939*

A conference was held last night between the party leaders on both sides and the President and Secretary Hull, looking to some agreement to pass the amendment to the Neutrality Act. According to the press reports, the President advised them of immediate threat of war this summer, and he urged the passage of the neutrality legislation for the effect it would have in making war less likely. Senator Borah in the conference stated to the President that he had his own sources of information in Europe, and that there was no danger of war breaking out this summer. The President replied that the Senator would have to accept that responsibility. The Republican leaders are very positive that Hitler would not attack, and that there was no necessity for haste in connection with the neutrality legislation. So it was agreed that the legislation should not be pressed until later and that Congress should recess without action thereon.

I nevertheless went up to the office of Key Pittman for lunch with members of the Senate Committee on Foreign Relations. They plied me with questions, both as to the European situation and as to Russia. I gave them the situation as I saw it. Senator George and Senator Gillette were kind enough to say that they were sorry that they did not have the benefit of this information before the meeting occurred yesterday. Senator Pittman stated that had my statement been made to the full committee two weeks earlier, in his opinion, the neutrality legislation may have passed. Of course, the facts are overwhelming.

EXECUTIVE SESSION OF COMMITTEE ON FOREIGN
AFFAIRS OF THE HOUSE OF
REPRESENTATIVES

DIARY   *Washington—July 27, 1939*

Sol Bloom, the very able and effective Chairman of the Foreign Affairs Committee of the House, asked me to appear before his committee at the time when Senator Pittman, Chairman of the Foreign Relations Committee of the Senate, arranged for a meeting with some of the members of his committee. In spite of the fact that the amendment to the neutrality bill had been disposed of, I was nevertheless glad to go up to discuss Russia and the European situation with the committee of the House. Those present were: Chairman Sol Bloom; Republican Luther Johnson, of Texas; John Kee, of West Virginia; James P. Richards, of South Carolina; Ed V. Izac, of California; Robert Allen, of Pennsylvania; Pete Jarman, of Alabama; Laurence F. Arnold, of Illinois; W. O. Burgin, of North Carolina; George Holden Tinkham, of Massachusetts; Bruce Barton, of New York; Robert B. Chiperfield, of Illinois; Robert J. Corbett, of Pennsylvania; John M. Vorys, of Ohio; and Andrew C. Schiffler, of West Virginia.

The members of the committee were considerate in every way. The discussion was held on a high plane without any appearance of partisanship. "We were all beyond the twelve-mile limit"—where partisanship should properly disappear.

The topics which I covered were: Russia's industrial and military strength, which as usual was accepted with some surprise and even incredulity, which I can quite understand, until one has seen it himself; the effort which Hitler was making to alienate Stalin from Britain and France, and the diplomatic battle, then going on in Moscow; the certainty of war in Europe this summer; the desperate military situation in which France and Britain were in, and the menace that confronted us if they fell.

The war maps which I had brought with me, issued by the London papers, were graphically convincing of the military weakness of the democracies. I cited many quotations which I had from books such as Ernst Henri's *Hitler Over Europe* and *Hitler Over Russia*, Fritz Sternberg's *The Military Strength of the Powers,* Auriol Kolnoi's *War on the West,* and Fritz Sternberg's *Germany and a Lightning War,* all of which established clearly not only the military menace of the Nazis, but the horrifying purposes which the Nazis had openly proclaimed, as against the rest of the peoples of the earth. I also outlined the reasons which were undoubtedly driving Hitler into war as his best way out, along the lines of the report to the Department.

The information which I had given to the President and the Secretary of State, and upon which I based the belief that Hitler would make war on Poland either before August 28 (Hindenburg's birthday) or before September 8 (the Nuremberg Party Rally), I submitted very frankly and fully, and stated that this was under the President's express direction, as it was.

THE NAZI-SOVIET BOMBSHELL

New York, August 22, 1939 *

THE HONORABLE SUMNER WELLES,

Acting Secretary of State, Washington, D. C.

My dear Mr. Secretary:

With reference to the above-entitled matter, it occurred to me that in view of the background of my service in Russia, and the information gleaned there, and in Europe, my diagnosis and prognosis of the situation, and of the new status which it has induced, might be of some value to you and to the Department.

As my previous reports, both written and oral, to you and to the Department would indicate, the development of this nonaggression pact between Russia and Germany to me was

---

* The Molotov-Ribbentrop agreement was announced in the press on this day.

not unexpected. My reports from Moscow have pointed out for two years last past that it was perfectly clear that if Europe were to have "peace," it would have to be a "Fascist peace," imposed by the dictators, unless England and France created a countervailing east and west axis, by the inclusion of the Soviets, and established a "balance of power" which would keep peace through an equilibrium of forces.

Moreover, it has always been clear, as I have pointed out in my reports, that there were many advantages to both Germany and Russia in getting together. They had worked together for ten years and could again. That possibility could never be excluded in any objective assessment of the situation.

EVENTS CONTRIBUTING TO PRESENT SOVIET ACTION

During the Litvinov tenure in the Foreign Office, there was to be sure a very strong moral impulse of hostility toward Germany and the aggressor powers beginning with the accession of Hitler to power. During that period the Soviet regime, in my opinion, diligently and vigorously tried to maintain a vigorous common front against the aggressors and were sincere advocates of the "indivisibility of peace."

Litvinov's able battle for peace and democratic ideas at the League of Nations and the vigorous attitude of the Soviet government in being prepared to fight for Czechoslovakia were indications of real sincerity of purpose and a marked degree of high-mindedness.

Beginning with Munich, and even before, however, there has been an accumulation of events which gradually broke down this attitude on the part of the Soviet government.

During my tenure in Moscow I was much impressed with the fact that the Russians were undoubtedly severely irked by what appeared to be a policy of "pinpricking" and an attitude of superiority and "talking down" which diplomatic missions of the Western powers assumed toward the Soviet government. The Soviets are proud and resented this deeply.

Then followed a series of developments which aggravated the relationships between the Soviet government and the Western democracies.

The Soviets were "humiliated" and "deeply hurt" by being excluded from Munich.

Out of "appeasement" there grew still greater distrust, so far as the Soviet government was concerned, in either the capacity, the intention, or even the "pledged word" of the Chamberlain government or the Daladier government.

The Soviet proposals for a "realistic alliance" to stop Hitler were rejected, by the Chamberlain government, out of consideration for the feelings of the Poles and the Baltic states.

During the Soviet-British-French negotiations, including the sessions of the Strang mission and Military Missions to Moscow, this distrust was intensified by the fact that these authorities were not clothed with power to close a final, definite realistic alliance.

The suspicion continued to grow that Britain and France were playing a diplomatic game to place the Soviets in the position where Russia would have to fight Germany alone.

Then there came the Hudson proposals for economic rehabilitation of Germany which again smacked of "appeasement" from the point of view of the Soviets. This was followed by the adjournment of Parliament by the Chamberlain government, without the conclusion of any definite agreement with Russia and the discovery by the Soviet leaders that a British Economic Mission had been sent to Denmark, allegedly with Chamberlain's blessing, to study economic appeasement, along the line of policy which has been initiated by Hudson.

Added to this France and England had persisted in a refusal to enter into an unequivocal agreement to support

Russia in the protection of Russia's vital interest, in preventing the absorption through internal aggression of the Baltic states, whereas Russia had offered unequivocal support to Britain and France to come to their aid if their vital interests were affected by a German attack upon Belgium or Holland, regardless of the character of the aggression.

These events served to feed the suspicion and arouse the dissatisfaction of the realistic Soviet leaders, including Stalin. Apparently they got "fed up" with attempting to stop the aggressors by participation in European affairs, and characteristically boldly reversed their attitude and decided to secure their own position by making a pact of nonaggression with Germany, which would assure peace for Russia, at least for a time, regardless of any possibility of war in Europe.

The foregoing is a theory as to what induced this situation, from such facts and impressions as I have gathered and obtained.

The dominant motive of the Soviets is and always has been "self-interest." For a time they were ardent advocates of active militant hostility against aggressors, in order to preserve peace. This was not only because of love of peace per se but also because it was to their interest.

IMMEDIATE EFFECTS ON EUROPEAN PEACE

The effects of this new development upon European peace in the immediate present are problematical. My own judgment is that with the eastern wall securely closed Hitler will take not only Danzig but the Corridor as well; that he will do this first by diplomatic demand in which there will be neither discussion nor compromise but only ultimatum. Poland will probably wilt, and hope to live to fight another day. If that happens there will probably be no war this year. If, however, Poland refuses to accede and fights, the question then will be whether England and France will come to her defense. It may be that the rapidity of events will make the entry of Britain and France inevitable. If so "the fat is in the fire."

From any point of view, therefore, it is clear that Hitler has won a smashing diplomatic victory. The entire future status of Europe is in the balance. The British Empire, Britain, and France are on the verge of the most disastrous loss of prestige in their history. The peace of Europe, if maintained, is in imminent danger of being a peace imposed by the dictators, under conditions where all of the smaller countries will speedily rush in to get under the shield of the German aegis, and under conditions where, even though there be a concert of power, as I have predicted to you two years ago, with "Hitler leading the band."

LONG-RANGE POSSIBLE EFFECTS

The real menace to the future and to Western civilization probably lies in the possibility that Germany and Russia will find each supplementary to the other in the extension of their ambitions. Economically this union is most efficient. The wealth of resources in Russia supplement the industrial efficiencies and scientific and industrial organization of the Germans.

EFFECT ON AMERICAS

The result of these events should be to accelerate the progress of the solidarity of the North Americas, and possibly the South Americas. The threat of Fascist domination of the world looms larger than ever before.

Respectfully submitted,
Joseph E. Davies

BECK'S GOVERNMENT OVERESTIMATED BY BRITAIN

JOURNAL   *New York—August 26, 1939*

The press announces that the British and Poles have signed a mutual-assistance pact. The horse is already stolen. Up to this date it was a unilateral guarantee which Britain had given to the Poles. Beck, in London last spring, got that "blank check." Litvinov's practical proposal for a conference of all the "nonaggressor states" was rejected, upon the insistence of the Polish and Rumanian governments.

It illustrates the tragic misjudgment of strengths in Europe. Chamberlain placed his confidence in Beck's government and passed up the Soviet strength. The Poles are undoubtedly a brave and gallant people, but from all the information I get, there is too much truth in the essential weakness of Poland, because of racial and other minorities, which the German *Gauleiter* stated to me so clearly in Danzig two years ago. Poland, it is reliably reported, has only eight hundred airplanes. In terms of present-day military strength the mechanized equipment and other strengths of the Polish army are negligible. Among many well-informed men in Brussels, I found little belief in the Polish government because of lack of confidence in Beck. Indicative of this situation, only last spring one of the most prominent officials under Beck, Minister ———, stated to me, positively, that his government would not tolerate proposals that Poland and Germany should get together and compose their difficulties over the Polish Corridor and Danzig. These proposals at that time were generally understood to have been advanced by the Vatican in a desperate last effort to avert war. He expressed himself as being disgusted with what he called the common exaggeration of Germany's military power.

His government, he said, would show them up to the world; within three weeks after the outbreak of war, Polish troops would be in Berlin; the "West Wall" or "Siegfried Line" was nothing but a "cotton line." Poland did not need Russian aid; they could handle the Germans alone and easily.

There appeared to be a complete lack of realism in assessing Germany's strength. It amazed me then and still astounds me. When he saw my surprise he asked me my opinion, and I told him frankly that I thought he was wrong in his estimate of Germany's strength. I feared the time might come when Poland might desperately need any help, including help even from the Soviets, to save itself, and that it was very bad judgment to refuse the water to extinguish the fire which was destroying their house, because of fear that the water would get their feet wet and possibly infect them with a cold.

This mutual-assistance pact should have been made months ago. It now simply serves to aggravate the situation. The die was cast when Hitler closed his eastern gates and when Ribbentrop flew to Moscow a few days ago. The fat is already in the fire. Everyone in Europe knows that Germany is already mobilized for immediate invasion of Poland. The Germans openly boasted, according to Belgian businessmen who have plants in Germany, that they would "clean up" Poland in three weeks. No one to whom I talked had any confidence that they won't.

DIARY   *Brussels—September 16, 1939*

Within two weeks after the declaration of war by Britain and France on Germany, the Russians and Japanese have agreed, according to the press reports, for an armistice on the Far Eastern front. Thus not only has Hitler closed his eastern door in Europe, but he has solidified his position by compos-

ing the differences between Japan and Russia in the Far East.
The Ribbentrop-Molotov agreement was a diplomatic victory for Germany that was far-reaching in its effect.

EXCERPT FROM LETTER TO SECRETARY EARLY

Brussels—September 25, 1939

The Moscow-Berlin pact was a catastrophic calamity. It
was probably one of the greatest diplomatic defeats the British Empire ever sustained. Now, too late, there is coming a
belated appreciation of the power of Russia and its significance as a source of food and supplies to Germany. The possibility of blockade is over. Time is running now to Hitler's
advantage instead of against him.

NO. 497   *Brussels, October 10, 1939*

TO THE HONORABLE THE SECRETARY OF STATE

DISCUSSIONS WITH SOVIET MINISTER,
MR. RUBININ, RELATIVE TO GERMAN-
SOVIET RELATIONSHIPS

Sir:

Some days ago the Soviet Minister to Belgium, Mr.
Rubinin, who, it will be recalled, was an attaché of the Soviet
Embassy in Washington for some years, asked me to have din-
ner quietly with him and his wife and spend the evening.
The gist of the discussions, which consumed the better part
of three hours, was as follows:

He tried to justify the Moscow-Berlin developments on
the following grounds: that for years the Soviets had tried
to contribute to the establishment of a peaceful Europe
through co-operation with the Western democracies, but that
their co-operation and efforts had been spurned and rejected;
that the Soviet Union was now seeking the same end through

co-operation with Germany; and that the ethnical, economic, and political forces in eastern Europe and in the Balkans could be settled by Germany and the U.S.S.R. on a realistic basis which alone would establish permanent peace. More in particular, he cited the following: that the U.S.S.R. had for years advocated "collective security" and the "indivisibility of peace" in efforts to secure a practical combination of the nonaggressor nations in Europe to curb Germany; that Litvinov had carried on these efforts in the League of Nations, in the Spanish situation, and in the Nonintervention Committee in London; that the Soviet government had served notice on Poland that in the event of German aggression against Czechoslovakia, it would cancel its nonaggression pact with Poland, 36 days before Munich, and was prepared to fight for the Czechs; that in April of this year, in response to Chamberlain's query as to whether the Soviets would join in the resistance if Germany attacked either Poland or Rumania, the Soviets had issued a statement in the affirmative and suggested a conference of the nonaggressor states to decide upon a plan of action, which was the only "language Germany could understand"; that Chamberlain had flown to Berchtesgaden himself and had sent a subordinate to Moscow without authority and had then sent a military commission with similar lack of authority, with only "talk"; that the British and French refused to guarantee the Baltic states against internal aggression, in which event the Soviets would have to fight Germany alone; that both the Rumanians and the Poles were obdurate and refused any actual physical help from the Red Army in the event of invasion, etc., etc.—with the result that the Kremlin authorities finally became convinced there was no way out through co-operation with France or Britain.

In response to my query as to whether Russia would per-

mit Germany to establish herself on the Black Sea either at
Constanţa, or at the Dardanelles, he stated it to be his opinion
that this was impossible and contrary to the vital interests of
Russia.

Again in answer to my query, he stated it to be his opinion
that the Soviets would not send their soldiers to the western
front; and that it was not to the interest of the Soviets that
Britain and France should be destroyed, nor was it to the
interest of the Soviets that Germany should be defeated.

He then made an elaborate argument upon the advisability
of accepting the *status quo* and thereby establishing peace in
Europe now by a conference of the belligerents. He asked me
what, in my opinion, the attitude of the United States was.
I told him I could not speak for the government or for the
United States in any official capacity, but if he wanted my
opinion as an individual, I would be glad to give it to him.
It was briefly this: that as far as I could gauge public opinion
personally I believed that, generally speaking, our people
thought that for the conquerors who had resorted to force to
ask now for peace on the basis of the *status quo* was analogous
to a situation where a couple of highwaymen who had robbed
and murdered two inoffensive old ladies now sought to make
friends with the police who were interested in preserving the
peace of the community, by convincing them that they were
not robbers and murderers but law-abiding and honorable
citizens and as such were entitled to be restored as peaceful
and law-abiding citizens of the community without even
offering to restore the loot; that the simple issue involved was
whether the nations in Europe were to live in a society
where law and legal processes, or brute force, was to be the
arbiter for the settlement of differences between nations. To
this he replied that his own point of view was that in the
last analysis the present conflict was simply a conflict be-

tween the British Empire which sought to dominate the world
and the Germans who demanded the right to develop as
equals.

Minister Rubinin is an able and very intelligent man.

As to whether Rubinin was acting under orders in trying
to feel out what the attitude of the United States was, I am
somewhat in doubt. It may possibly have been inspired by
his government as part of the peace offensive which is being
so actively projected. In any event, I was exceedingly careful
to point out that my government was strictly neutral in this
situation and was not mixing up with European affairs; and
that any expressions of mine were purely personal and in no
degree were to be considered as the attitude of my government.

I have the honor to be, Sir, respectfully yours,

Joseph E. Davies

"THE RUSSIAN BEAR HAS TAKEN A HANDSOME REVENGE FOR MUNICH."

Brussels, October 12, 1939

SURVEY OF TRENDS IN THE
EUROPEAN SITUATION
FROM THE POST

My dear Mr. Secretary:

From my knowledge of Russia, it is
my opinion that it may be that Russia will not be able to supply oil in any substantial quantities to Germany for some
time. Russia at the time I was there had over 460,000 tractors
utilized for collective farming and they consumed all the oil
that could possibly be produced. Their pipe-line and transportation facilities are also limited. Oil is very vital, and I
understand that the total Russian supply would only consti-

tute about 20% of Germany's requirements. Ben Smith, of New
York, who knows the oil business thoroughly, tells me, however, that he has just come back from Germany and advises
that one of the best oil men in the world had told him that
he knew that Germany had a supply of oil sufficient to last at
least a year and a quarter. He also said that the oil experts
seem to think that the supply of oil in the Baku district of
Russia could be quickly and speedily developed by high-
pressure methods.

The Diplomatic Corps and official circles here have become
acutely Moscow-conscious. The Russian Bear has taken a
handsome revenge for being thrown out of Munich. Finland
is the only Baltic state that has resisted the importunities of
the Bear so far. The Turkish Foreign Minister is getting the
same treatment from Molotov that Henderson got from Ribbentrop in Berlin, and is being made to cool his heels. The
message of the President to the Soviet government was heralded here with the greatest joy. In diplomatic circles here
the Moscow-Berlin pact is generally conceded to be the greatest tragedy in the development of this war situation. The
shadow of the Soviets, reaching from the Oslo group down
over Poland and into the Balkans, has brought new fear in
addition to the old German menace. The belief is commonly
expressed that a new factor has come into the European
situation which will require a complete revision of alignments
of the different powers. It seems to be generally the impression that Stalin and Hitler had a very specific understanding
of a very concrete and realistic character, based upon the vital
interests of each. Speculation is high as to whether the Russians will come to aid Hitler on the western front. Just as
there was a tendency to belittle Russia a year ago, there is
now a tendency to exaggerate her purposes at the present time.

I find that my own judgment is in accord with neither of

the two extremes. I am disposed to the opinion that the Russian policy may be exactly what she proclaims it to be; namely, a desire to establish peace in Europe if she can, and particularly on her eastern border, and in addition thereto to develop her own resources secure from attack of the capitalistic western nations. To effect this security, naturally, the Soviets would desire to have their western line shoved as far west from Moscow and the Don Basin as possible, as a protection against a possible enemy Germany. It is also vital to her strategic defense and economic and national development that her access to the sea shall be protected by open-water sea bases the year round, and hence her attitude toward the Baltic countries. It may be quite possible that the Soviets are sincere in their statement that they wish to give complete independence and autonomy in self-government to these various countries, but desire to secure by amicable arrangement naval bases that will protect them against possible future German attack. The Soviets believe that with the development of their internal economy in Russia within the next few years, on the basis of the past rate of advancement, the adjoining states with lower standards of living will be clamoring to get into the Soviet Union. Their attitude toward Turkey and the Dardanelles, as well as their attitude toward Constanta and the Black Sea, is equally consistent with a pacific intent and not a war purpose to aid Germany. Stalin's whole plan since 1926 has been to develop an internal economy that would be self-sufficient and create a socialistic communistic community that would be a model for the world; and he said to me himself that they figured that for him and his associates to achieve that was a man-sized job and as much as they could do, without trying to run the whole world.

With great respect, I am,

Sincerely yours,

JOURNAL   *Brussels—November 28, 1939*

Three months have now elapsed since "the state of war" was declared by England.

It has developed many surprises. They were:

The Germans made good on their prediction of demolishing Poland in three weeks. That was surprising to some.

Apparently the Moscow agreement envisaged a complete restoration of the geographical and political spheres of tsarist Russia to the Soviets, and *more*, to wit: the uprooting and abandoning of the Baltic German civilization and life, as well as the restoration of Polish White Russia and Polish Ukraine to the U.S.S.R. as a part of the deal with Germany. The Soviets are willing to risk alienating world opinion and that of many world Communists by attacking Finland to complete the naval outpost fortification of Leningrad against possible future attack by an enemy, who can only be conceived to be their present ally, Germany. Such an anachronism seemed impossible a few months ago.

Nor would the well informed have conceived it possible six months ago that Germany would pay so high a price to Russia in order to close her eastern door when attacking Poland.

The implied threat to England and France contained in Ribbentrop's Moscow statement that "consultations as to the necessary steps" to be taken jointly, unless the western nations stopped their war on Germany, had, apparently no real basis in any agreement with Molotov. The "necessary steps" were not taken, or proved abortive. Instead of embarking on such action, Molotov declared the policy of the U.S.S.R. to be one of neutrality. Thus Hitler closed his eastern door, but he paid a very high price.

THE DEVELOPMENT OF RELATIONS BETWEEN
STALIN AND HITLER

Last September it was stated to me that Stalin was resisting Hitler's effort to secure military and political penetration into Russia—this for the reason that the Russians did not trust Hitler. The full value of the Russian pact depends on the German ability to make it fructify through technical assistance in the organization of staff work and, particularly, industrial production. Conditions now have been changed as between the two by the Finnish developments. Undoubtedly Hitler has made the most of it by playing both the Balkan and the Finnish situations to bring pressure on Stalin to accede to the arrangement that German engineers and technicians shall co-operate with the U.S.S.R. to get greater supplies to Germany. There are indications that the effort is successful and that Germany now has both military and industrial experts in Russia. It is my opinion that, given German technical support, the Russian economy, with Soviet co-operation, will be of great value to Germany. Despite the proximity of the Baku oil fields to Weygand's army air base in Palestine and the threat of air attack on the oil fields, the potentialities of Russian oil production under German administration, and two years' opportunity for development, are enormous.

RUSSIA—FINLAND

Undoubtedly the Finns have set the Russians back in a very heroic way. The probability of negotiated peace between Russia and Finland is, in my opinion, not *now* imminent. The Russian army is a god to the Communists. *Amour-propre* and perhaps even self-preservation itself would require the established authorities to throw all of their might and numbers into the fight to re-establish lost army prestige. Finland can't stand out against such a machine. After that, peace will come on Soviet terms.

OBSERVATIONS AS TO THE WAR SITUATION AS TO RUSSIA AND GERMANY

JOURNAL   *Brussels—November 29, 1939*

Russia, as early as last summer, had become a proponent of Bulgaria's claims to Dobruja, in Rumania, and it is quite within the range of probability that as soon as the Soviets clean up Finland they will turn their attention to Rumania and Bessarabia.

Some of these eastern countries appear to be very confident and, like Poland, conceive their power to be very strong. But Poland was a bitter example and I fear that Finland, also, will be. The result, in all probability, will be that Carol of Rumania will make his peace on the best terms possible and in a very short time be under the vassalage of Hitler and Stalin.

I was told that Russia's demands on Turkey included a military base that would control the Dardanelles similar to those in the Baltic. That is quite possible. Bulgaria now is definitely under Communist influence; Hungary is subject to the immediate threat of Germany, and Yugoslavia is under the threat of both Italy and Germany.

HITLER'S PRESENT POSITION

This all spells out a situation none too advantageous for Hitler. He has given up the Baltic and uprooted and transplanted a Germanic civilization of 400 years; he has cut himself off from the Ukraine; he is confined to an economic power only over Rumania and, as well, to only a limited influence over Bulgaria or Hungary. The Russian Bear will not support the

Germans in the Black Sea. Considering the grandiose concept of *Lebensraum*, which Hitler preached to his people and to the world, he now finds himself confined in a pretty small compass. His only "out" seems to be in the west for the immediate present. These conditions, perhaps, account in a degree for the apparent uncertainty of plans in Berlin; as evidenced in the last-minute change of plan of German attack on Armistice Day and the present continued inaction on the western front. It is another and not the least funny aspect of this so-called "phony" war.

Much depends upon what Hitler's agreement with Stalin really is. If it is an "all in" alliance and he can project into Russia his engineers and scientific men in the same manner that he did in Italy, and if the Soviets will really co-operate, Hitler will still find tremendous advantage in the Russian pact. But there are indications that the Russians will not really co-operate; that the Soviets are pursuing an independent policy based solely on self-interest and that Hitler is not too happy about it.

DIARY   *Washington—January 15, 1940*

Pursuant to order of the Department of State I returned to Washington to take up the post of Special Assistant to the Secretary of State in charge of War Emergency Problems and Policies. I therefore filed my resignation as Ambassador to Belgium and Minister Plenipotentiary to Luxembourg.

DIARY   *Washington—February 16, 1940*

According to report from Rumania, there are two thousand Germans who have arrived in Odessa and who are engaged at that and other Black Sea ports in the laying of mines in Russian waters.

A prominent Belgian businessman who has just arrived from that country and who is familiar with the Balkan situation tells me that his information indicates that Moscow hotels are full of German agents and commercial travelers and engineers; but that they are having a hard time in getting into Soviet industries because of the disposition on the part of the Soviet Union not to co-operate.

JOURNAL   *Washington—March 30, 1940*

In the speech of Premier Molotov, Foreign Minister, before the Supreme Council of the Soviet Union on March 29, this significant statement appeared: "We must maintain our position of neutrality and must refrain from participation in the war between the great powers. This policy not only serves the interests of the Soviet Union, but also exercises a restraining influence on attempts to kindle and spread the war in Europe. If we view the recent past we find that we have achieved no mean success in safeguarding the security of our country. We shall continue consistently with our policy in the future."

This is significant as a reiteration of neutrality. It refutes the implied suggestion of Ribbentrop last fall that unless France and Britain stop their war on Germany, consultations would be had between Germany and the Soviet Union. It cannot be too satisfying to Hitler.

DIARY   *Washington—June 26, 1940*

It is reported that Molotov handed a note to the Rumanian Minister in Moscow demanding the immediate cession of Bessarabia and northern Bukovina within twenty-four hours.

The Russian press is quoted as having declared that this settles a twenty-two-year-old conflict between Russia and

Rumania and is one of the "rectifications" of the Versailles Treaty which is a part of the plan to contribute to European peace.

MOLOTOV REITERATES SOVIET NEUTRALITY POLICY

DIARY   *Washington—August 1, 1940*

Molotov's speech before the Supreme Council in Moscow as reported contains the following with reference to changed conditions due to the defeat of France and the entry of Italy into the war: "All these events have not caused a change in the foreign policy of the Union. True to her policy of peace and neutrality, the Soviet Union is not taking a part in the war." Developments in Europe far from reducing the strength of the Soviet-German nonaggression pact, on the contrary, emphasize the importance of its existence and further development. Contrary to foreign speculations upon possible disagreement between the parties, he stated that these relations were based upon the fundamental interests of the two parties.

MOLOTOV'S "RETURN CALL" ON BERLIN

JOURNAL   *Washington—November 14, 1940*

Molotov and his staff of sixty-five in number left Berlin today after having had extended discussions with Göring and Hess and other industrial experts and after a second long conference with Hitler and Ribbentrop. The official communiqué gives no actual light on what occurred except that "it led to agreement on all important questions of interest to Germany and the Soviet Union." *

---

* This official communiqué does not square with Hitler's Sportpalast speech of October 3, 1941, which described basic differences and alleged demands by Molotov.

In all probability there is more to this than meets the eye. The Soviet Union has been repeatedly emphasizing as the cornerstone of its foreign policy, a position of absolute neutrality and nonparticipation in the European war. It repeatedly describes its arrangement with Germany as a mutual non-aggression pact. The press of Moscow within the past month or so appears also to have been very generous in its comment on effectiveness of the British air force and the fine quality of British soldiery as composed of trade unionists, etc., etc.

DIARY   *Washington—November 30, 1940*

Lunched with the President. Asked that he permit me to resign from the State Department to take effect the beginning of the year. I explained that I had given no attention either to my private business affairs or to my law office during the past five years and that I owed a duty to do so. He was fine and understanding. He said, "Of course," but he wanted me to hold myself available for specific tasks that he might have in mind. He asked me to take on immediately the Chairmanship of his Inaugural Committee, which I was very proud to do.

DIARY   *Washington—January 10, 1941*

It was announced from Berlin today that the so-called "Russo-German Pact of Friendship" was signed. The official spokesman stated that this would put an end to the "foolish gossip" about deterioration of relations between the Soviet Union and Germany and would confirm the fact that the parties were quietly working to improve and consolidate their friendly relations. It provided for settlement of questions, among others, connected with the Soviet annexation of Baltic countries and Polish frontier problems.

DIARY *Washington—February 18, 1941*

The Soviets are taking no chances. The head of the State Planning Commission in Moscow announced that Russia must make every effort to continue and increase production of tanks, aircraft, and warships to keep the country in a state of readiness for any contingency.

RUSSIA OPPOSES GERMANY IN THE BALKANS

JOURNAL *Washington—March 3, 1941*

There is considerable Soviet activity in the Balkans. Last month a report came over the Moscow radio that the Turkish-Bulgarian pact was signed through the intervention of Russia, Greece, and England, and the Soviet speaker said that if Germany intended marching through neutral territories, she must expect to have to fight for it; and that Germany should not forget that there was a pact of friendship existing between Turkey and Great Britain. Later in the month Tass, the Soviet official news agency, stated that the above report which came through a Switzerland paper did not correspond with the facts. Furthermore, a formal statement has now been issued by the Moscow Foreign Office that the Bulgarian government had advised that it consented to the entry of German troops into Bulgaria, in order to "consolidate peace in the Balkans." The Soviet Foreign Office formally notified the Bulgarian Minister that it did not agree with the Bulgarian government as to the correctness of the Bulgarian attitude; that this action on the part of the Bulgarian government led not to peace but to an extension of the sphere of war, and that the Soviet government conforming to its peace policy would not support the Bulgarian government in the execution of their present policy.

This is going pretty far in opposition to Hitler's plans.

RUSSIA'S VITAL INTERESTS BLOCKING HITLER

DIARY   *Washington—March 24, 1941*

The Turkish government at Istanbul issued a formal
statement this day based upon a news item which had appeared in the foreign press. The item that if Turkey were involved in war, the Soviet Union would take advantage of that
situation to attack Turkey. According to the Turkish statement, the Soviet government had formally declared that this
news was untrue, specifically adding that in case Turkey
should be compelled to resist aggression and thus find herself
forced to defend her territory, Turkey could then rely upon
Russia's entire compliance with the nonaggression pact between the two countries, and could count on the neutrality of
the U.S.S.R. This was also confirmed in Moscow. Both Turkey
and the Soviets have a vital interest in preventing the German
military from reaching the Dardanelles.

RUSSIA BUTTS IN ON YUGOSLAVIA

DIARY   *Washington—April 5, 1941* *

A treaty of friendship and nonaggression was signed between the Soviet Union and Yugoslavia. It contained this
extraordinary statement: "That should one of the contracting
parties be attacked by a third state, the other contracting
party pledges itself to preserve its policy of friendship." The
treaty was to stand for five years and to be automatically renewed for another five years unless notice of a year was given
of intention to cancel. Of course the third state referred to
obviously means not only Italy but Russia's ally, Germany.

* The next day, Germany invaded Yugoslavia.

DIARY *Washington—April 29, 1941*

Reports from Moscow from the newspaper *Pravda* state that four German transports arrived in a Finnish port on April 26 with 12,000 troops fully equipped with tanks and artillery.

DIARY *Washington—May 17, 1941*

The Foreign Office in Moscow has prohibited foreign diplomats and consular officials from traveling in any of the frontier zones without express permission from the Foreign Office. There are continuous rumors of the massing of large numbers of German troops on the Soviet frontier in Rumania, Poland, and Finland. I am reliably informed that official reports confirm this situation.

JOURNAL *Washington—June 23, 1941*

Went on visit to Madison for the June commencement of the University of Wisconsin, and stayed with President and Mrs. Dykstra.

After the alumni dinner and my broadcast, when we were driving up to the President's house, a young man came dashing up over the lawn and stopped us as we were going into the house. He was the correspondent for the United Press. He told us the startling news that Hitler had attacked the Soviet Union. It was like a bombshell. He wanted a statement from me. I said that it was all to the good for the Western democracies. In reply to his question, I told him that, in my opinion, the extent of the resistance of the Red Army would amaze and surprise the world; and even though Hitler were to take a substantial part of the Ukraine, his troubles would then just begin, in my opinion. It was just plain common sense for us to give the Soviets all the aid we possibly could, because they were fighting the greatest danger to our security in the world, the menace of Hitler's aggression and lust for world domination. This statement was rather widely carried by the press, as it was directly contrary to practically all of the opinions of the best military experts. It was, however, founded not upon hearsay, so far as I was concerned. It was based upon what I myself had seen in Russia.

ADDENDUM:

Here are some of the facts and impressions which are not set forth in the reports.

NOTE ON THE RED ARMY

During my stay in Russia—1937, 1938—I saw a great deal of the Red Army leaders and the Soviet troops.

The Soviet government paid particular military attention to the young. The utilization of its youth for war purposes was characteristic of the regime. They were constantly under the supervision of local military authorities. When girls and boys reached the age of six years, there existed organizations for them, the Octobristas, which were energetically supported by the state. From this, they graduated into another organization, "Young Pioneers" (from 12 to 16 years), and thence into the "Komsomols" (League of Communist Youth—from 16 to 24 years) (somewhat similar to our Boy Scout organizations).

At Kharkov, I saw a typical "Young Pioneer" club house. It was equipped for the purpose of developing individual aptitudes of young people during their hours of recreation. Here laboratories were provided for boys working under technical instructors. I saw them building model miniature airplanes, tanks, locomotives, railroad systems, etc. The military authorities were intensely interested in these activities.

The "Komsomols" (organization from 16 to 24) were the object of especial attention by the military. They receive intensive physical training, military drill, marksmanship practice, a great deal of parachute jumping, glider practice, all forms of athletic practice, manual training, etc. It was as though we had from the start treated the C.C.C. and the N.Y.A. as preparatory schools for the armed forces of the United States.

Each year approximately 1,500,000 of these prefabricated young soldiers at the age of 20 were called to the colors. At the various military and other reviews in the Red Square, I had an opportunity to see for myself various cross sections of the Red Army forces. These troops, of course, were the best of the army. Nevertheless, it aided me in my assessment of the whole picture.

INFANTRY—MAN POWER

The man power was invariably impressive. Their infantry was striking as they marched by the Kremlin reviewing stand in their thousands; stripped to the waist, heads shaved, bodies brown as nuts, all in the pink of athletic condition—for the most part big, powerful men. It would be difficult to find any group apparently more physically fit or a military group that marched with greater precision than that which they displayed as they marched in close formation with shoulders leaning forward and with bayonets fixed, directed over the shoulders of the line in front. They looked as though they would be a tough bunch to handle across "no man's land."

PROLETARIAN RIFLE DIVISION

Interspersed among the regular military units reviewed by Marshal Voroshilov, there were approximately 6000 civilians who marched in company formation armed with rifles but all in promiscuous civilian and none too good attire. This was a preview of the organized guerrilla bands which the Red

Army is now using to harass German communications in the so-called "defense in depth" by which the Soviet strategists have sought to counter the *Blitzkrieg*. This is also significant as indicating that even in 1937 the Kremlin officials anticipated a German offensive which would succeed in overrunning western Russia and was even then preparing to leave these "Proletarian Rifle Divisions" behind the advancing German lines, as part of the "scorched earth" policy of Soviet Civilian Defense.

MECHANIZED UNITS

The Red Army, I had understood, compared favorably with great armies of Europe in its mechanized equipment. It was then reputed to have about 4000 tanks of various types ready for immediate use, and from what I have seen myself in the plants of heavy industry, and from information gleaned from other informed sources, I was satisfied that they were on the way to producing tanks at a pretty high rate of speed through mass production. Subsequent events have justified that opinion. On Red Army Day in 1938, some 480 tanks, some of enormous size and some of lighter variety, raced across the Red Square at terrifying speeds which were said to be between 35 and 65 miles an hour. The military experts at that time told me that it was a very good performance. It was commented upon that in bringing their tanks into the city and in the marshaling of these mechanized units preparatory to going through the Red Square there had been remarkably few breakdowns or indications of weakness.

AIR-MINDEDNESS OF RUSSIAN YOUTH

There is one thing which made a strong impression upon me in connection with Soviet air power. That was the air-mindedness of the Russian people. In every city of any size in the Soviet Union, there is a so-called "Park of Culture and

Rest," and invariably among the other games and amusement devices these parks have high towers for parachute jumping. On all "rest days" (holidays) these towers were crowded with children and young people eager to try the parachute jumps. In Moscow, it was said that there were several hundred thousand (it was currently claimed at a million) young men and women who had won their official decoration and lapel insignia by reason of having officially completed three parachute jumps from an airplane, from an altitude of 2000 feet or over. Illustrative of this situation, I recall that, on the occasion of a luncheon which Foreign Minister Litvinov was having for some of the Diplomatic Corps, his eighteen-year-old daughter, a lovely young girl, came breezing into the dining room, full of enthusiasm over the fact that she had just completed her third jump to qualify for her much cherished membership in the Parachute Jumpers Corps.

ARMY AND OFFICER TRAINING

In 1939, Voroshilov reported to the Soviet Congress that the Red Army had extended its system of military institutes, which Frunze had started in the early twenties, so that he was able to report that there were sixty-three schools for land troops, in which tens of thousands of young men, equipped with secondary education, were being turned out with training as officers for the army. Graduation qualified them for the grade of lieutenant. Thirty-two flying schools and aeronautical and engineering schools, he said, were turning out aviation experts and aviation personnel. There were also fourteen academies and military universities for men with university education, designed for training of those who were qualified for high command. These universities, he said, also provided evening courses in which some 15,000 commanders and other high officers in the army were enrolled. Soviet books on military strategy, I was informed, commanded general respect in professional army circles in other countries, particularly in Germany.

SEVERITY OF ADMISSION TESTS

In the talks which I had with some of the military experts in Moscow at that time, I was told that in recent years the examinations and tests for admission to these higher military schools were most severe, scientific, and selective. The higher officer class was recruited by processes of competitive elimination from the most fit, the most able, taken from this large reservoir of military man power.

MORALE OF OFFICERS AND TROOPS

By 1937 and 1938, the number of former tsarist officers which had perforce been commanding the Red Army units had become negligible. They had been replaced by younger men, graduates of the large number of military schools which had been built up by Frunze and Voroshilov. The typical Red Army officer in 1937 was a man who had passed through the special school of his arm of the service, and who had in addition been graduated from one of the high military institutes or academies which prepared officers for general command duty and for general staff duty. His military qualifications for the command of smaller units were considered excellent. His qualifications for higher command were yet to be tested. He was generally a man of fine physique, ambitious, full of energy, and accepted as a part of his job hardships and deprivations which ordinarily did not fall to officers in other armies.

The government in power early realized and has never overlooked the fact that its success depends, in the last analysis, on the loyalty and support of the army. There appeared to be nothing too good for the Red Army within the gift of either the people or the government of Soviet Russia. No pains have been spared to impress thoroughly officers and conscripts with loyalty to their government and to their country. The curriculum in the military schools is reported to have been devoted 60 per cent to the military training and 40 per cent to the study of Communism.

The elimination of higher commanders by the purge, I was told, had resulted in the promotion of many of the younger officers who, while lacking the experience of their predecessors, probably made up for it in greater energy and devotion and loyalty to the government. It was also said that these changes had resulted in a feeling of greater security on the part of the average soldier and the belief that his fate was now in the hands of more trustworthy and loyal officers than the "Trotskyite traitors who had met a deserved fate."

In connection with this question of morale, it must always be borne in mind that, so far as the average soldier is concerned, he is generally a man below 30 years of age. That would mean that he was about seven years old in 1917, when the Soviets came into power. During the tender years of Soviet youth, the government sees to it that every possible agency is used to indoctrinate the young idea with the principles of Communism, the greatness of Soviet Russia, and his duty and destiny as a Bolshevik. What is not generally realized is that under these conditions Communism becomes religion, and one of the first principles of the Communist Party is absolute loyalty to the party and unquestioning obedience to its constituted leadership. In the then existing situation, it meant loyalty to Stalin. It should be also noted in this connection that every agency of propaganda—the press, the billboards, theaters, cinemas, schools, books, magazines—are all controlled by the government and utilized for the purpose; that of impregnating the public with devotion to the regime, to

Communism, with fear as to the menace of foreign invasion;
with pride in Russian nationalism; and devotion to "Mother
Russia." Unquestionably, the government at this time was
taking steps to solidify the loyalty of the Red Army. Officers'
pay was raised substantially. The rapidly expanding Soviet
defense program offered increased opportunities for command and responsibility.

During this period military morale was also sustained
by the Red Army's victories over the Japanese Army at
Lake Hanau and on the Amur River. For the Kremlin never
forgot that it faced the Samurai in the East as well as the
Nazis in the West. To meet this situation, two entirely separate armed forces were created, one in Europe and one in
Siberia, each self-contained and designed to fight independently and without any expectation of help from the other. In
the Far East, I was told, the Special Red Banner Army numbered 400,000 men and was equipped with an independent
reserve in the form of a two-year stock of munitions and other
supplies. The greater part of the total Soviet forces was
massed in the districts adjacent to the western Soviet frontier.
It was during this purge crisis that the Japanese strategy
found its first opportunity to "try out" the strength of the
Russian army in the East. The Axis powers derived little comfort from the results of this encounter. I was informed at that
time from a high Japanese official that the strength and effectiveness of the mechanized forces and of the infantry made
a very strong impression and aroused very substantial respect
in the Japanese army circles for the power of the Red Army.

INTERNAL AND EXTERNAL FACTORS AFFECTING
SOVIET MILITARY DEFENSE

There was another very important factor in this situation.
The army and defense activities of the Soviet Union in 1937

and 1938 were by no means static. These years were periods of terrific tension and resultant expansion. There were daily indications that the Soviet government was intensely alarmed and that all leaders were working night and day to defend their regime. On all sides there were indications of great government activity of a defense character.

These were also the months just before Munich, when the Hitler West Wall was being feverishly built by the employment of hundreds of thousands of men. This was the time when the Soviet government had served notice upon Poland that in the event of a German attack upon Czechoslovakia, Russia would fulfill its obligations to fight with France as her ally for Czechoslovakia and formally served notice that it desired to abrogate its pact of mutual nonaggression under the terms of its treaty. War and more war with each recurring crisis was constantly in the air in Moscow during this time. Accompanying these developments, naturally, very radical things were happening in connection with the armed forces and the defense of the Union. After the purge trials, the entire army was vigorously shaken up and reorganized for the purpose of establishing closer centralized control and administration. After the invasion of Austria and with the Czech crisis, new military areas were established. The Japanese situation was critical, seriously so with the Amur incident. The Far Eastern Red Banner Army was divided into two separate administrations. Artillery divisions were increased from 13,000 to 18,000 men. Before and after Munich, the vulnerable parts of the frontiers were feverishly fortified and deep zones of fortified areas were constructed. "Bunkers" were being built. The number of tanks and tank units and other mechanized units were being enlarged.

This enormous and defensive program and expansion in the armed forces are indicated clearly in the budgetary provisions made for war and navy purposes for these years. In 1937 the government expended for war and navy approximately 23 billion rubles. In 1938, the budget appropriated for the following year nearly twice that amount—40 billions rubles for the war and navy and approximately an additional 25 billion rubles for industrial defense, capital and war purposes. In 1939, its defense budget called for a total of 82 billion rubles for the succeeding year; and in 1940, the government's budget called for a total for war and navy and industrial defense of approximately 105 billion rubles. These expenditures were tremendous. The outside world did not know or did not appreciate the huge preparedness campaign that was then being projected for the defense of Russia.

In short, during these three years the average appropriation was approximately 6 billion dollars each year for defense alone, a sum in excess of the total revenue raised by the government of the British Isles, and almost equal to the total annual revenue raised by the government of the United States by Federal taxation.

By the end of 1938, General Voroshilov stated that contrasted with 1934, the number of armored cars had increased seven and one half times; that the number of tanks and tank units had trebled. During the same period armored cars had increased seven and one half times. Antiaircraft guns, antitank guns, and tank artillery were more rapidly increased than any other branch of the service. The chemical-warfare service troops were doubled. It was publicly announced that the ceiling for antiaircraft had been doubled. Voroshilov publicly stated that pursuit planes had been trebled; that their searchlight, motor-transportation, and other services had been completely reorganized both as to quality and quantity; that light, battle, and escort planes had been doubled; that the capacity of bomb loadings for bombing planes had been trebled. He made the astonishing statement in a report to the Congress of the Party that the Red Army had pursuit planes with a capacity for speed exceeding 500 to 1000 kilometers per hour (300-600 miles per hour) and with a ceiling capacity of from 14,000 to 15,000 meters (approximately 44,000 feet—almost nine miles).*

Stalin had then said: "A second universal imperialistic war has become inevitable." Voroshilov had said: "We know more than ever that the only reliable guarantee against military attack upon the Soviet state is to keep the Red Army and Navy in a state of real and constant military preparedness."

The Soviet leaders saw very clearly not only the progress but the ultimate purpose of the technique of aggression as practiced by Hitler and Mussolini. The years of 1937 and 1938 were to Soviet Russia what the years of 1940 and 1941 are to the United States in the matter of military preparedness. Czechoslovakia was then to Russia what Britain is now to the United States. When the bastions of Czechoslovakia fell, and France refused to permit its ally to participate in the Munich Agreement at Hitler's behest, Russia had lost its only hope of defense outside of its own strength. It was because of these facts that enormous new appropriations were made and extensive additional plans were made for the erection or extension of plants and for the manufacture of tanks, airplanes, and war supplies, not only in the Don Basin, but as well deep in the interior of the country.

American aviation and other engineers told me at that time that the efficiencies of plants under the War Commissariat were far greater than under civil control. There were many

---

* At the time, these statements were characteristically brushed aside by many in Moscow. The published reports made by the engineering and technical military experts of the Beaverbrook and Harriman mission seemed to establish that in all probability the conditions were not overstated by Voroshilov.

evidences which I saw in my trips in the inspection of plants in industrial regions that the military were at work.

JOURNAL   *Washington—July 7, 1941*

To my amazement, I find that my friend, Lindbergh, is quoted that he would prefer Nazism to Communism. I cannot believe he has said it, but the reports seem to be authoritative. If he has, I am sorry. It is not in keeping with either the tradition of his people or the career of his father.

It would be a desperate choice to make, but there is a very wide difference between the two. We should be eternally grateful that we do not have to make the choice. Ours is the best form of government yet devised by man, and democracy is not yet dead. It has demonstrated reserves of power and strength when crises develop as they did at Dunkirk and in London in September, and here in the reactions of our own people to Hitler's aggression. It is a defeatist attitude and not good Americanism, in my opinion, to talk about the necessity of choice as between the two. We should not admit that any such choice is necessary or possible. Our democracy is the best form of government.

Both Germany and Soviet Russia are totalitarian states. Both are realistic. Both are strong and ruthless in their methods. There is one distinction, however, and that is as clear as black and white. It can be simply illustrated. If Marx, Lenin, or Stalin had been firmly grounded in the Christian faith, either Catholic or Protestant, and if by reason of that fact this communistic experiment in Russia had been projected upon that basis, it would probably be declared to be one of the greatest efforts of Christian altruism in history to translate the ideals of brotherhood and charity as preached in the gospel of Christ into a government by men. The point is that the Christian religion could be imposed upon the communistic principles without doing violence to its economic and political purposes, the primary one of which is based upon "the brotherhood of men." Applying the same test to Nazism, the difference between the two is clear. The principles of the Christian religion cannot be imposed upon the Nazi philosophy, without destroying the political base of the state. Nazi philosophy makes the state superior to the Christian religion and is in fact a religion in itself. For that end it has tried to destroy Christianity in Germany through persecutions. Nazi philosophy creates a government which is in fact based upon the denial of the altruistic principles of the Christian religion. The Nazi state is deified. To it, war is a virtue. Brotherly love, charity, justice, and Christian virtues are indications of weakness and decadence if they conflict with the utilitarian needs of the state. The state is the church and the confessional. Force, power, might, as the expression of a Nordic and racial religion, are the base of the Nazi ideology.

To impose the Christian religion upon Nazism would be impossible. They are utterly antithetical.

That is the difference—the communistic Soviet state could function with the Christian religion in its basic purpose to serve the brotherhood of man. It would be impossible for the Nazi state to do so. The communistic ideal is that the state may evaporate and be no longer necessary as man advances into a perfect brotherhood. The Nazi ideal is the exact opposite— that the state is the supreme end of all.

DIARY   *Washington—July 7, 1941*

Had lunch with Sumner Welles today who is Acting Secretary in the absence of Secretary Hull. Wanted to discuss the Russian situation with him. Churchill has just announced that Britain will give "all-out" aid to Russia as allies, regardless of any conflicting ideologies and without thought of future postwar matters. I urged that the United States do likewise vigorously and promptly for two reasons: first, despite wealth and military strength, which I believe Russia had, my reports from Russia would indicate, it was nevertheless doubtful whether Russia's second line of defense—war mechanized industrial production—could in the long run stand up against German industrial war industry, and that Russia ultimately would have to have war supplies from here; second, that the Soviet leaders and the Russian people were proud and exceedingly sensitive. France and Britain had made the great mistake of flouting them in 1938 and 1939 with almost disastrous effect when they threw the Soviets into Hitler's camp. This Hitler attack, in my opinion, was a God-given break in the situation for nonaggressor nations and Soviet resistance should be stimulated in every way possible. In the event of partial success in the Ukraine, Hitler would undoubtedly make overtures of peace to them on the basis of the *status quo*. A situation where Soviet leaders might think that they had just been used to serve our purposes and to pull our chestnuts out of the fire should not be permitted to arise. Human nature was human nature. My own opinion was that the Soviet leaders were as realistic and hardheaded as any statesmen in Europe and would be disposed to reject any peace proposal of that kind because they know Hitler's promises are no good. They are not the kind who would sit on a red-hot stove the second time. Nevertheless, we should not be niggardly in our acceptance of their aid, for they were fighting Hitlerism.

Welles has a mind like a Swiss watch. He is a thoroughgoing individualist, a democrat, and naturally hostile to Communism, but he is heart and head in this fight to save this country from the menace of Nazi victory. He said that he felt that there was much force in my point of view and asked

January 22, 1940

My dear Joe:

    In order to make it possible for you to assume
the duties of your new post as Special Assistant to the
Secretary of State, I accept herewith your resignation
as Ambassador to Belgium and Minister to Luxembourg,
effective as of January sixteenth.

    I do this with less misgiving because through your
new work in the Department of State we shall continue to
have the benefit of your wide experience in Europe and
your critical estimate of developments there.

    Now that you are formally relinquishing the posts
in Brussels and in Luxembourg, I do want to assure you of
my deep appreciation of the excellent work you have done
there and I feel also that it is due you to say, particularly, that your reports from your recent posts, as well
as those sent previously from Moscow, were extremely
valuable.

    You exercised a happy faculty in evaluating events
at hand and determining with singular accuracy their probable
effect on future developments. Your judgments of men and
measures were sound and dependable. On this account I feel
it is particularly fortunate that we are to have the
continued benefit of your guidance and counsel in foreign
affairs.

                    Very sincerely yours,

                    Franklin D. Roosevelt

Honorable Joseph E. Davies,
Department of State,
Washington, D. C.

PRESIDENT ROOSEVELT'S LETTER ACCEPTING RESIGNATION AS
AMBASSADOR TO BELGIUM AND ANNOUNCING APPOINTMENT AS
SPECIAL ASSISTANT TO THE SECRETARY OF STATE.

whether I had seen the statement which he had already issued—somewhat along the purpose of my discussion. I had not seen it. In principle, he said, we are in agreement, for the Soviets were fighting Hitler, and therefore are fighting to protect our security here in the United States, both in the religious world as well as in the political sphere.

DIARY   *Washington—July 8, 1941*

My old friend, Jim Byrnes, asked me to come over to the White House to see him sworn in as a Justice of the Supreme Court. The Chief Justice of the Court of Claims, Dick Whaley, another crony of the Senator, and one of my oldest friends, was administering the oath. The ceremony was held in the President's office. Harry Hopkins was there, and immediately after the ceremony I went up with him to his room in the White House proper to talk about this Russian situation. I told him the story and urged that he look into the situation himself; that my old reports from Russia would give him a lot of facts which were based upon what I had seen myself and not on wishful thinking. On the wall there was a large military map of Europe. I pointed out on the map where the various industrial military manufacturing plants were located back of the Urals as long ago as 1937. I told him that I was suggesting to the President that he send word to Stalin direct that the United States was going to furnish all possible aid to Russia in the fight against Hitler.

THE SOVIETS "LEAP-FROG" THEIR INDUSTRIAL PLANTS

JOURNAL   *Washington—July 9, 1941*

Ambassador Oumansky had luncheon with me today at my home. I asked him whether in the event that Leningrad should fall, there would be danger that the industrial machinery there would fall into the hands of the Germans. He stated that he had definite information that arrangements were being made to dismantle and remove all the machinery of that character long before danger would be imminent.

The thing that impressed me greatly in Moscow was the sporadic bursts of energy with which work was frequently done. It was seen in the speed whipped up to complete the bridges near the Red Square for the Red Army Day celebration, and in many other situations. Taylor, who ran the Embassy residence and who went with us to Moscow, complained at times of the laziness of the Russian "house boys," but he has frequently said that when they went to it, they would each do the work of three men back home. That typical "reserve nervous and physical energy" is undoubtedly employed in this "leap-frogging" of industrial equipment, which is a part of the "scorched earth" policy laid down by Stalin.

Oumansky reluctantly agreed with me that Hitler's armies might possibly succeed in overrunning a part of the Ukraine, but he thought that it would be but a small part.

In reply to my question he said that undoubtedly the government and the Red Army High Command had laid their plans in contemplation of such a possibility. The plans of the Soviet government already made provided for a new seat of government in the interior if Moscow should fall, and included the insurance of an independent and self-sufficient army with adequate supplies which would be held in reserve for such new base. The plan of campaign which the war strategists of the Soviet Union had laid out did not contemplate or permit a decisive battle on the western front, as some of the strategists and commentators over here seemed to fear. The plan called for a definite strategy of withdrawal to draw the enemy into the interior; extend his line of communication and supply, and gradually to wear him down by making him pay dearly for each advance.

He said that the stories which came from the front describing the success of the Soviet defense against mechanized German attacks were extraordinary. A new chapter in the history of military strategy was being recorded by the strategy devised by Russian tacticians to meet the Panzer and air mechanized attack, projected by the Nazis.

He had been greatly heartened by the expressed desire of the President to give prompt and quick aid to the Soviet Union in their fight against Hitler. He was very uneasy over the time that was elapsing, necessarily perhaps, in getting the supply of war materials to the Red Army, for "every day men were dying."

RUSSIA'S NEW PLANES

DIARY   *Washington—July 12, 1941*

I had lunch with Ambassador Oumansky at the Soviet Embassy this day. General Golikov, the Assistant Chief of the General Staff of the Red Army, he said, is coming over via plane and should arrive in a few days.

He tells me that the Red Army has a new plane, MIG-3, a "fighter," which has just recently come into production. It is admittedly superior, he says, in both design and performance to either the British Hurricane or Spitfire, and much superior to the German Messerschmitt or the German fighters on the western front. He also described their new type of heavy armored bomber called the Stormovik. In ceiling capacity, speed, and defensive armor protection it is superior to anything which had yet appeared in this war. It was sufficiently fast, he said, and also sufficiently well protected to be able to make extended bombing flights without the need of accompanying fighter planes for its protection.

Oumansky is working night and day getting out the specifications, lists of materials, which the Soviet government wants immediately, and information desired by the War Department here. He is very much concerned over the delay in getting the material rolling.

DIARY   *Washington—July 15, 1941*

In the absence of Secretary Hull, I saw the acting Secretary, Sumner Welles. I prefaced what I had to say with the statement that I felt it was vital and possibly a turning point of the war, that Russia should receive every possible aid from this country and as speedily as possible. I was so deeply concerned over the matter that I wished to be of every possible help, freely, of course, to the Soviet Embassy here. I did not want to do so, however, unless it was with the complete understanding of the State Department that I was doing this, representing no one but myself, and that it was entirely agreeable to it that I should do so. Welles said that he understood and was certain that the Department would not misunderstand my action; that both he and the Department would have entire confidence that anything that I would do would be always conditioned upon the certain fact that my first loyalty would always be to the United States and to the policies of the President and the Department of State (which, of course, is the fact).

DIARY   *Washington—July 16, 1941*

Had a long conference with the President today at his office. Steinhardt in Moscow, he said, had been doing excellent work as his reports indicated. He wanted also to get my slant on the situation. He had noticed that the press had carried the story that in my opinion the extent of the resistance of the Russian army would "amaze the world," and that this opinion was at variance with that of most military experts and others who knew Russia. I outlined to him, at length, the reasons for my opinion and amplified certain facts which had not been contained in my reports to the Department.

July 18, 1941

HONORABLE HARRY HOPKINS

My dear Harry:

Here is a brief memorandum covering the matter we discussed. I do not have a copy of the brief which I compiled when I left Russia in June, 1938. It is on file with the State Department. You can readily obtain it upon request. It contained, I think, a reasonably accurate survey of the Soviet regime and the Soviet army at that time. I believe that in the course of a thirty-minute reading you could get the gist of it. You would, I think, find it of some help in evaluating the present situation.

MEMORANDUM REGARDING RUSSIAN SITUATION

The resistance of the Russian army has been more effective than was generally expected. In all probability the result will depend upon air power. If Hitler dominates the air, it is likely that the same thing will occur in White Russia and in the Ukraine that occurred in Flanders and in France, namely, the inability of land forces, without air protection, to resist the combined attack by air, mechanized forces, and infantry.

In such an event, Hitler will take White Russia, Moscow, and the Ukraine which will provide him with 60% of the agricultural resources and 60% of the industrial production of Russia.

When I was in Russia and for several years theretofore,

and I am sure now, a very substantial part of the Red Army was guarding the East against Japan. I was told by competent Russian authorities in 1938 that this army was completely self-sufficient and was provided with supplies and resources adequate for an independent campaign of two years, even though cut off from western Russia.

In addition thereto there was the so-called Volga Army also in the interior, which consisted of 400,000 to 500,000 regulars which might be held as reserves to fall back on.

At that time there had also been built enormous steel and aircraft plants in the interior of Siberia about 1000 miles east of Moscow. If Stalin is compelled to fall back to the east he will probably have these armed forces for such an emergency. The Ural and Caucasus mountains afford a very strong natural barrier to a mechanized attack.

If Hitler occupies White Russia and the Ukraine, as he may, and Stalin falls back into the interior, Hitler will be confronted with three major problems:

1. Guerrilla warfare and attack;
2. Sabotage by the population who resent that "Holy Mother Russia" has been attacked; and
3. The necessity of policing conquered territory and making it produce.

In 1918 under similar circumstances in the Ukraine, the Germans found that they did not get eighty per cent of the agricultural and other products which they had reasonably believed they could get.

Obviously, under such circumstances, it would be to Hitler's interest to put on a peace drive to induce Stalin to consent to an arrangement based on the then *status quo*, leaving Stalin to find his outlet to the south and east to China, possibly India.

Even though Hitler takes the Ukraine and White Russia,

in all probability Stalin can maintain himself back of the Urals for a considerable time.

From my observation and contacts, since 1936, I believe that outside of the President of the United States alone no government in the world saw more clearly the menace of Hitler to peace and the necessity for collective security and alliances among nonaggressive nations than did the Soviet government. They were ready to fight for Czechoslovakia. They canceled their nonaggression pact with Poland *in advance of Munich* because they wished to clear the road for the passage of their troops through Poland to go to the aid of Czechoslovakia if necessary to fulfill their treaty obligations. Even after Munich and as late as the spring of 1939 the Soviet government agreed to join with Britain and France if Germany should attack Poland or Rumania, but urged that an international conference of nonaggressor states should be held to determine objectively and realistically what each could do and then serve notice on Hitler of their combined resistance. They claimed that this was the only thing that would stop Hitler's aggression against European peace. The suggestion was declined by Chamberlain by reason of the objection of Poland and Rumania to the inclusion of Russia; and the disastrous unilateral agreements were then promoted and entered into by Britain.

During all the spring of 1939 the Soviets, fearful that they were being used as the "cat's-paw" to "pull the chestnuts out of the fire" and would be left to fight Hitler alone, tried to bring about a definite agreement that would assume unity of action and co-ordination of military plans to stop Hitler.

Even as late as August, 1939, the commissions of France and Germany were in Moscow for that purpose. Britain, however, refused to give the same guarantees of protection to Russia with reference to the Baltic states which Russia was giving to France and Britain in the event of aggression against Belgium or Holland. The Soviets became convinced, and with considerable reason, that no effective, direct and practical, general arrangement could be made with France and Britain. They were driven to a pact of nonaggression with Hitler.

The Soviet Union, from the beginning, never faltered in giving aid and assistance to China.

Throughout their participation in the League of Nations, the Soviet government led the fight for the protection of little nations vigorously and boldly. This was the fact in the case of Ethiopia and Spain.

No government saw more clearly or stated with greater accuracy what Hitler was doing and would do and what ought to be done to preserve peace and prevent the projection of a war by Hitler than did the Soviets. That is a fact regardless of whether their motive was ideological or whether it was for the safety of their own people.

I found among the leading Soviets a real friendliness to the United States possibly based on the fact that there was nothing that they had that we wanted, and that we had nothing that they could take; so there was a natural basis for a policy of "live and let live" between our two peoples. They bitterly resented the attitude of Britain and France to look down their noses at the Soviets, and this intensified their distrust and ultimately drove them into the Hitler camp.

Vis-à-vis with Japan, it is obviously to our advantage to have a friendly Russia at Japan's rear. It is my opinion that it is not their intent to seek to project Communism in the United States, nor would it be within the realm of possibility after this war or for many years thereafter for the Soviets to project Communism, if they wished, in the United States or even in Europe.

Specifically, I fear that if they get the impression that the United States is only using them, and if sentiment grows and finds expression that the United States is equally a capitalistic enemy, it would be playing directly into the hands of Hitler and he can be counted upon to use this in his efforts to project either an armistice or peace on the Russian front after he takes the Ukraine and White Russia. Word ought to be got to Stalin direct that our attitude is "all out" to beat Hitler and that our historic policy of friendliness to Russia still exists.

Faithfully yours,

SOVIET HIGH COMMAND STRATEGY

JOURNAL *Washington—July 31, 1941*

In the White House offices today I met General Philip I. Golikov, Assistant Chief of the General Staff of the Red Army, who had just arrived via London from the Russian front. He is a typical Russian. He is not a tall man, but gives the impression of great physical strength; as he talks, one gets the feel of a strong inner vitality in the man which is intensified by a quiet reserve. He does not talk English.

From what I gathered through Ambassador Oumansky, however, I find very much reassurance in the strength of the Russian defense. Hitler attacked without any notice whatsoever to the Soviet government; but the Red Army intelligence were aware of Hitler's mobilization and were prepared for any possibility. Hitler had a great initial strategic advantage in that he got "the jump" through surprise attack. It was estimated that Hitler had approximately thirty thousand tanks in this drive; "the Red Army also had a very large number of tanks."

The Soviet General Staff were completely familiar, through observation in France, with the Panzer mechanized attack and its technique, and had developed what they considered to be a defense. This they were trying out in the strategic retreat which the Red Army was conducting through the Baltic states. It involved considerable risk but they felt that they had the answer to it. Stated plainly, the technique was simply to allow these mechanized finger thrusts to get through the Russian lines and then have the Russian forces close in behind them, and finally use the same attack upon the attacker. It was recognized that some large section of the army might become surrounded, but they were expected to fight their way out, and the loss was allowed for and discounted.

He cited some of these segments as being fought to the last man. The plans of the High Command contemplate a strong reserve army and self-contained economy back of the Volga and in the Urals to support a government there in the event that Hitler takes a substantial part of the Ukraine. He confirmed Oumansky's statement that the Russians were already denuding their factories in the danger zones and transporting the machinery to the east.

For the regular German army he had great respect; they were good fighters, but in his opinion not so good as the Soviet regulars. The German reserve consists mostly of younger men who were not so good and could not stand up to the bayonet attack.

DIARY   *Washington—September 3, 1941*

Had a long talk with Ambassador Oumansky. His government has directed him to accompany the delegation to Moscow and serve as a member of the Russian committee there.

Oumansky does not think that he ought to return as Ambassador to the United States. He has an idea that some fresh man might be more effective. He feels that he has had a difficult time here during a period when his government was allied with Germany. This fact, he thinks, inevitably makes it more difficult for him to be as effective as some new man. He takes a very impersonal and fine personal attitude in the situation.

Oumansky has grown in my respect very much in these past several weeks. He has had a hard time of it with the American public, both as press censor in Moscow and here during the "late unpleasantness." I have found him very forthright, direct, and always on the level with me. I respect this attitude which he takes. It indicates size. I expressed the hope that Litvinov would come here as Ambassador in the event that Oumansky did not return.*

FINANCING SOVIET EMERGENCY PURCHASES

JOURNAL   *Washington—September 3, 1941*

Last night went to Will Clayton's house for dinner (stag). He is an exceptionally able businessman with a fine public outlook and is one of the outstanding men in the country, whom Jesse Jones has been able to bring into his organization here for public service during the emergency. He had been working on the exports which Russia could pledge to sustain a credit to cover immediate war purchases. He had asked Harry Hopkins, Averell Harriman, Jesse Jones, Jim Forestall, and myself in for the evening. Harriman was right "on top of the job" to work out ways and means for getting supplies to Russia and without delay. He is leaving with his delegation within a week.

The Soviet Agency Amtorg had almost exhausted its immediate cash balances, and had to meet its current obligations or break its long-established record of prompt payment for

---

* In view of the announcement that Ambassador Oumansky is not to return, I feel warranted in including this diary entry in this record.

American goods. Ambassador Oumansky had been able to get some advances on gold shipments which were en route to the United States. But that was not enough. Harriman had been working with Secretary Jones and with Clayton to solve the problems. Harry Hopkins was held up by another matter and couldn't get there. Harriman has the matter well in hand. He will do a good job in Moscow. Any misgivings that the Soviet leaders may have because of his "capitalistic antecedents" will fast disappear when they see him in action.

DIARY   *Washington—September 10, 1941*

This afternoon I had a cocktail party in honor of the three celebrated Russian fliers who had just arrived in Washington. Accompanied by forty other fliers, they came to Alaska in their own plane and thence to San Francisco. They were Brigadier General Michael Gromov, Colonel Andrey Jumachev, and Colonel George Baidukov. They all carry the highest decoration of "Heroes of the Soviet Union." They were fresh from actual combat. To meet these gentlemen fliers I had asked the leaders in the government, the press, and a good many members of the Diplomatic Corps. They did not speak English well, so I asked them whether they would object to having the group ask them questions in connection with their experiences. They graciously said, "No," and Ambassador Oumansky acted as interpreter. So out on the lawn we had seventy or eighty men circled about them, and from the questions there was developed considerable interesting information. To begin with, they are all fine-looking men. General Gromov is a scientist, as well as a distinguished soldier and flier. They spoke ably, temperately, and modestly. The questions were asked by Senator Barkley, Senator Guffey, Admiral Standley, Chairman Davis of the Red Cross, Colonel Monroe

Johnson, and a good many of the rest of us. Some of the most interesting information which was developed was as follows:

The new Soviet fighting plane which was just off the assembly line was, they said, the latest thing in aviation development. It was in fact superior to the British Spitfire and to the German Messerschmitt. Modestly, the General said that this was due to the fact that it just happened that these planes were coming off the assembly line at this particular time. The new Soviet bomber plane, he said, had a steel armament protection that was far superior to anything that the Germans had. So superior was it in point of speed, altitude, and armor plate that it could go on its mission without any necessity for fighting or pursuit planes to accompany it. This, he said, was unique. He also said that the Soviet planes would not give combat to these planes if they could avoid it.

He described the Stalin line and the "defense in depth" as a strategy developed by the Soviets from military experience in France, as a solution to the Hitler Panzer method of mechanized attack. In reply to the question of the number of Soviet prisoners taken by Germany, the reply was that it should be remembered that the Germans had evacuated whole villages of Russian peasants who were taken as prisoners, and that these were included in the figures. The old-line German fighters, they said, were first-class soldiers, but they gave indication of being worn out and tired. The younger reserves were not so good, and could not stand up to the bayonet. Their own soldiers did not surrender. If they were encircled, they fought themselves out or died in their tracks. This was said quietly, as a mere statement of what one was to expect. There is no question but what these fine, physical types of manhood, and apparently well balanced, made a strong impression upon the men present.

Telegram   **September 11, 1941**

AMBASSADOR CONSTANTIN OUMANSKY

AMBASSADOR OF THE U.S.S.R.

SIXTEENTH STREET

WASHINGTON D. C.

A PREVIOUS ENGAGEMENT, I DEEPLY REGRET, PREVENTS MY BEING WITH YOU TO DO HONOR TO THE PRESIDENT'S COMMISSION TO MOSCOW STOP IT IS A MATTER OF REAL GRATIFICATION TO ME, MR. AMBASSADOR, THAT YOU ARE ABLE TO PRESENT THESE GENTLEMEN TO YOUR GOVERNMENT AS THE UNQUESTIONED AND OUTSTANDING LEADERS OF OUR COUNTRY IN THEIR RESPECTIVE FIELDS STOP FOR MANY YEARS I HAVE PERSONALLY KNOWN CHAIRMAN HARRIMAN AS ONE OF THE GREAT LEADERS OF OUR AMERICAN BUSINESS LIFE, WHO HAS ALWAYS BEEN DISTINGUISHED AS A MAN OF PROGRESSIVE LIBERAL IDEAS AND GREAT EXECUTIVE ACTIVITIES STOP UNDER HIS LEADERSHIP I AM SURE THAT YOU WILL FIND THAT THE CONTRIBUTION OF THE VARIOUS MEMBERS OF THIS AMERICAN MISSION WILL BE HIGHLY EFFECTIVE IN THE CO-OPERATIVE WAR EFFORT WHICH WILL BE PROJECTED ALONG WITH THEIR DISTINGUISHED CONFRERES OF THE BRITISH AND SOVIET MISSIONS STOP THE COURAGE, VALOR, AND IDEALISM OF YOUR RUSSIAN MEN AND WOMEN NO LESS THAN THE FORESIGHT OF YOUR GREAT LEADER AND OF THE SOVIET GOVERNMENT COMMAND THE ADMIRATION OF THE WORLD BY YOUR VALIANT AND EFFECTIVE STAND TO REPEL THE ATTACK OF A TRAITOROUS NEIGHBOR TO WHOM THE HONOR OF THE PLEDGED WORD IS UNKNOWN STOP THE LIBERTY-LOVING MEN AND WOMEN OF THE WORLD REJOICE THAT YOUR GREAT PEOPLE AND GOVERNMENT ARE JOINED WITH THE DEMOCRATIC PEOPLE OF THE EARTH IN RESISTING THOSE FORCES OF AGGRESSION, DISHONOR, AND EVIL WHICH SEEK TO RULE OR RUIN THE PEACE-LOVING NATIONS OF A WORLD COMMUNITY STOP GOOD LUCK TO YOU IN YOUR FLIGHT TO MOSCOW WITH THIS MISSION.

JOSEPH E. DAVIES

IF HITLER TAKES THE UKRAINE

JOURNAL   *Washington—September 20, 1941*

And, if Moscow should be evacuated and substantial parts of the Ukraine occupied by the German forces, which is not impossible, what then?

If a line were drawn from Leningrad to Rostov and the territory west thereof were to be completely occupied by German troops, and if such occupation were to extend to the Volga River, it would involve a territory of approximately 700,000 square miles. Policing of this territory against the millions of Russians of the soil, and of hundreds—even thousands—of guerrillas and trained citizenry skilled in and taught all the devices of sabotage and barricade fighting, would be an enormous task. It would probably require an army of a million men. To make this fertile country fructify and produce without horses, and by means of mechanized equipment operated by a hostile civilian population, with all of the possibilities of sabotage which such a condition would supply to a Slav people who are bitterly resentful of an attack upon their homes, all assures a colossal task for their hereditary enemy, the German army. So far as the industrial plants are concerned, it can be assumed that the equipment of these great plants would have been removed far distant from the factories by the time the Germans arrived. It will be an enormous task for Hitler to police and administer this territory. It is much more apt to be a liability rather than an asset in the long run. For an army merely to invest such a territory imposes a great drain upon its man power and economy. It is a colossal task to support a line of communication and supply hundreds of miles from the home base. When the Germans occupied the Ukraine in World War Number I, they discovered from bitter experience that even upon the most conservative estimates of foodstuffs and materials which the authorities agreed to furnish, they were able to get only 20 per cent of such quotas.

RUSSIA'S "SCORCHED EARTH" POLICY

JOURNAL   *Washington—October 1, 1941*

The "scorched earth" idea to defeat the invader is not new in Russian history. It is significant that as early as 1937 and

1938 organizations for civilian defense were being promoted and developed by the military coincidently with their efforts to develop the military defenses against air and chemical attack. A campaign was even then being conducted to train farm workers and people in all walks of life, in various activities by which they could aid and support the army and provide mass public effort in the case of invasion. Undoubtedly the organization is today functioning and putting Stalin's "scorched earth" policy into effect.

On the twenty-third of June there were those supposed to be well informed who said that the Germans would be in Moscow in from three days to three weeks. The German *Blitzkrieg* marched through France to the coast to Abbeville —185 miles—in ten days. The Panzer Divisions supported by the most powerful air force then in the world drove the gallant Belgians, the magnificent British, and the French army back 65 miles in Flanders in 18 days. At the time of this writing—October 1—fourteen weeks have elapsed and the Russian Army is still holding the line. The Red Army has shown that it does not easily or long concede the initiative to the Germans but stands its ground, and attacks again and again.

HITLER'S MORALE CRACKS

DIARY   *New York—October 3, 1941*

Listened in to Hitler's Sportpalast speech on the short wave. There was much significance to me in the fact that he admitted that they had made one serious mistake and that was that they had underestimated the strength of the Russian military preparedness and the Red Army. Apparently he felt he had to explain to his people why the Red Armies were still fighting when they had been declared by him or his High

Command to have been destroyed each week for the last ten weeks.

It was a different Hitler than the one I have been listening to over the short wave for the last four years. To many Germans it must appear to be "kolossal" that the Führer, the self-proclaimed divinely inspired one, admits himself that he has made a mistake. It was the first crack that I have seen in the supreme self-confidence of the paranoic mentality of Hitler. Confidence is the essence of morale whether it be in the military or popular sections of the people. If the morale cracks at the top it is apt to spread very rapidly down below. This crack in Hitler's own morale reveals a more significant German weakness than any claimed by their Soviet enemies.

Hitler's invasion of Russia was his first serious military mistake. With cold weather coming on, the Red Army is still intact, and "General Winter" and "General Attrition" will be co-operating with the Soviet High Command.

SOVIET INDUSTRY BEHIND THE URALS

JOURNAL *Washington—October 15, 1941*

There is no question but what the occupation of the Don Basin and western Russia by the Germans will deprive the Soviet government of enormous manufacturing resources. But it should not be overlooked that east of the Volga there is a vast section of country and a highly industrialized region. It resembles the extended fertile spaces of the Mississippi Valley rather than Pennsylvania. This region east of the Volga is rich in iron ore, coal, and other raw materials. It might be said to be to the Donets Basin what St. Louis, Gary, and Detroit are to the industrial regions of Cleveland and Pittsburgh in this country. As a matter of fact, Magnitogorsk is spoken of by the Russians themselves as the Gary of the Soviet Union. This city derives its name from the mountain of high-grade magnetic iron ores which supplies the enormous steel plants there with iron ore. These plants were designed by American companies and American engineers and are equipped with the most modern blast furnaces, steel plants, and rolling mills. Farther to the west and connected by rail is the Kuznetsk Basin, where there is an abundant supply of coking coal. At both ends of this shuttle, there are these enormous steel plants with iron ore being transported in one direction and coking coal for the manufacture of steel in the opposite direction.

According to the report of the American-Russian Chamber of Commerce in 1938, the steel plants here consisted of a "series of shops comprising a complete steel-making cycle, from raw material to the finished steel, and auxiliary and service shops. The rolling of steel at Magnitogorsk follows the latest American technique, using the continuous conveyor process. In 1938 the Magnitogorsk works supplied 1,800,000 tons of pig iron, 1,600,000 tons of steel, and 1,260,000 tons of rolled-steel products."

In the heart of the Urals is the city of Chelyabinsk (population approximately 100,000). In 1939, according to the American-Russian Chamber of Commerce, the tractor plant was producing at the rate of approximately 15,000 tractors a year. It has undoubtedly been extended substantially since that time because of the feverish defense activity of the government during the last three years. The Ufa (population approximately 100,000) Motor Plant, according to the same authority, was producing at the rate of 10,000 motors a year. Also, in this district, at Perm, there are very large plants making Wright Cyclone Motors under license. Three years ago there was here alone a potential capacity of at least 10,000 tanks a year. There is no doubt but that this industrial region has been greatly developed by the defense preparedness of the last three years.

Sverdlovsk, the capital of this district, has enormous machine-building and armament factories. In 1938 it was the boast of the Soviet engineers that these plants could produce and duplicate anything that could be produced by the famous Krupp factories of Germany. At Berezniki and Solikonesk in this district, chemical industries have been highly developed.

Even in 1938, the production of machine tools, tractors, tanks, airplanes, etc., produced in this area approximated 30 per cent of the total produced in the Soviet Union. During the following years of enormous military and industrial preparation projected by the army, it is known that extraordinary efforts were directed to the development of these industrial regions in the interior in contemplation of possible military attack from the west. It was commonly understood, but information was withheld by the government, that the army also had developed extensive airplane factories in this region. The larger part of the nonferrous metal industries are located in the Urals.

AN AMERICAN INDUSTRIALIST ON RUSSIA

DIARY   *New York—October 27, 1941*

"Bill" Batt is just back from Russia. He was appointed a member of the President's Special Mission to the U.S.S.R., with the rank of Minister in Charge of Materials and Equipment. In the Office of Production Management (OPM), Batt is director in charge of assuring the supply of products and materials necessary for national defense. He is one of the industrial leaders of the country, drafted for defense work, who has made a very strong impression on Washington because of his drive, personality, and horse-sense. His work on the Mission had to do with all matters appertaining to the material and equipment required by the Soviets. I asked him whether he would give me a statement of what he thought of the Russian situation from what he saw, telling him I wanted to incorporate it in my book on Russia. I told him also that undoubtedly many of the readers of the book would like to get his "slant" in addition to the published statements of other members of the Mission. Here is what he had to say:

"We learned some things during our visit to Russia that are extremely important to the American public. They are important because the things we saw bear on a critical decision for this country: How far shall we go in helping Russia fight off the Nazis? During our brief visit I made up my mind clearly and positively on this point: We should go just as far as it is possible for us to go within the limits of our production, transportation facilities, and commitments to Britain and China.

"Why did I make this decision and why do I think it is the wisest and safest course for us to pursue at this time? Because I found the Russian officials, officers, and people capable, confident, and full of fight—determined to see it through, scornful of a separate peace with Germany. Because from all I could see and learn, Russian military equipment is generally excellent and, limited though it is, is being used to good advantage. Because we saw well-managed Russian factories of surprising size, operated by intelligent managers and skilled mechanics. Because I came away impressed with the feeling that if we worked as hard and as fast as we are capable of working, we can substantially bolster their defenses before the sheer weight of numerical superiority in equipment can win for the Nazis.

"With these facts and impressions of the physical strength and skill of Russia strongly in mind, other issues become secondary or irrelevant. The fact that their system of government and our system of government differ widely becomes a specious consideration. The fact that we *could* use some of the equipment we have undertaken to send them to produce more equipment in this country becomes a shortsighted argument against full aid now.

"One compelling set of circumstances emerges in my mind as the only thing worth considering: the Russians are fighting valiantly and well, they know how to use the materials and equipment we have promised them, and as long as they are fighting, the war will stay forever away from our shores. That is why I say deliver them the goods; deliver them now; deliver them by whatever means and at whatever sacrifices are necessary. To my mind, this is a common-sense, long-range, practical decision in the best interests of the United States of America."

WILL STALIN QUIT?

DIARY   *New York—October 28, 1941*

Upon the invitation of the Dutch Treat Club, I gave an off-the-record talk at lunch today, following up last night's talk for Russian relief at Madison Square Garden. Clarence Buddington Kelland was the Chairman and I gave them about twenty minutes of facts about Soviet Russia and Communism.

Afterwards there were questions:

"Can Russia hold out?"

"Is there freedom of religion in Russia?"

"Will Stalin make a separate peace with Hitler?"

The last question indicated to me how utterly people of this country misjudge the Russian situation. The real question which is vital now is, "Will WE force Stalin to make peace with Hitler again?" We, or rather the European democracies, forced Stalin into Hitler's arms in August of 1939. We—that is to say, England and America—could force Stalin into Hitler's arms again if Stalin were to believe that we were ready to let him down, use the Soviet army merely as a cat's-paw and double-cross him in the way that Chamberlain and Daladier did before and after Munich and up to the eve of Armageddon.

Stalin is a realist. Both he and the Russian people know that this is the ancient four-hundred-year-old struggle of Teuton vs. Slav and they know what fate has befallen their Slavic brethren in Czechoslovakia, Yugoslavia, and Poland at the hands of Hitler's Nazis. As I said at the rally last night, it is my opinion that "the Russian people would rather die as Slavs than live as slaves under Hitler." Neither Stalin nor the Russian people, now aflame with the sacrificial spirit of Russian nationalism and fighting a desperate war in defense of their homes and mother Russia against Nazi invasion, would tolerate any appeasement in the Kremlin.

Only one possible consideration would move Stalin or any other reasonable man under these conditions to make peace with Hitler. That would be the belief that further resistance was hopeless because the United States and Britain either could not or did not deliver the goods to enable them to do the fighting and that further resistance was hopeless. The instinct of self-preservation under such conditions might counsel the desperate expedient of making peace in the hope of living to fight another day.

If we would eliminate any possibility of another Russo-German treaty or a separate Russo-German peace, then—in my opinion—we must do these things. We must stand by our guns and deliver the goods. We must stop expecting other nations to have the courage of our conviction. We must satisfy the Soviet Union that we practice what we preach as to the right of nations to self-determination. This means that during and after the war we do and will accord to them the right to decide what kind of government they want for themselves. By so doing we can retain and deserve their confidence. By so doing we can make clear our belief that the American and Russian people can live as friends in a world devoted to peace.

LAST WORD

In the foregoing pages I have tried to set forth honestly and factually what I saw in Russia. I somehow have the feeling that in addition to the "Brief on the Facts" which I have presented, the reader would like to know what my own general "Conclusions" are. Briefly, they are these:

The Russia of Lenin and Trotsky—the Russia of the Bolshevik Revolution—no longer exists. Through gradual, stern, and often cruel evolution that government has developed into what is now a system of state socialism operating on capitalistic principles and steadily and irresistibly swinging to the right. Concessions had to be made to human nature, in order to make the experiment work. The present government professes to be a democracy. It is, I believe, sincerely devoted to peace both for practical and ideological reasons. The present government further proclaims and asserts constitutional protection for civil and religious liberty. Constitutional protections do not always work perfectly in certain regions because of political and personal purposes, as we know from our own experience here. In my opinion, the Russian people, the Soviet government, and the Soviet leaders are moved, basically, by altruistic concepts. It is their purpose to promote the brotherhood of man and to improve the lot of the common people. They wish to create a society in which men may live as equals, governed by ethical ideals. They are devoted to peace. They have made great sacrifices attempting to achieve those spiritual aspirations. They are fighting our fight now against Hitlerism and should receive every possible help as speedily and with as much friendly co-operation as we can extend.

The civilization we know has resulted from the constant concession of individual rights to centralized authority in the interest of the whole community. So-called progress has advanced at the same rate that this situation has constructively developed. This country and the democratic world have found that more and more private enterprises become vested with a public interest; therefore, the state either operates or controls them. The propulsion of war necessities now accelerates that movement, and more than ever the government takes over the operation of private industry. After this war the problem will arise of preserving or restoring for individualism as much private ownership and operation as is consistent with reasonable evolutionary progress. Then our test will come. This and the succeeding generation will face the problem of not losing the ship as well as the cargo.

The swing toward the left after this war will be acute. There will be real danger that it will be too rapid and violent. It would not surprise me if the experience derived as a result of the Russian revolutionary experiment will act as a brake upon this tendency. This laboratory in Russia must establish in the minds of all honest, intellectual radicals the fact that safe progress comes only through the gradual processes of evolution. Hereditary, nervous, and glandular reactions cannot be destroyed in a generation. Remedies too speedily applied frequently induce greater evils than those they are designed to cure.

The British Empire, the Americas, and Russia, along with China, are the great complementary powers of the earth. Their interests, their governmental ideas and purposes do not conflict. Moreover, their combined resources dominate the international situation in respect to man power, potential military and naval strength, strategic raw materials, industrial production, and reservoirs of accumulated wealth. These countries form a natural axis strong enough to defeat the Nazi-Fascist powers. They have the common purpose to thwart Hitler's effort to dominate the world and impose a program of pagan utilitarianism and Nordic mastery over Christian and other ethical peoples of the earth. They would have a common will and purpose not only to defeat the Nazi-Fascist forces, but also to aid the defeated people of the aggressor nations to re-form their own governments so that all men might live in a decent world, inhabited by civilized human beings and not by denizens of a jungle whose only rule is that of tooth and claw.

In this "Last Word," I wish to say that which I stated in the Foreword. From what I have seen in Russia and in Europe, I am more than ever grateful for our own form of government. It is the best on earth. It affords the greatest degree of protection to the life and property of the individual, even as against the state itself. It guarantees the maximum of civil and religious liberty. It provides equal economic opportunity to every man and woman and offers rewards according to the achievements and the abilities of each in all the fields of human thought and action. It is based upon the concepts of the Christian religion. Fundamentally, the government is not the master but the servant of the people. It rests upon principles of all those ethical systems from Confucius to Christ which have created what is known as civilization. No government on earth gives so many privileges and opportunities as does our representative democratic form of government. It is the last best hope for liberty and freedom in a threatened world.

I am confident that all of our citizens will hold everything else as naught in their purpose to defend and conserve it.

CHRONOLOGY

1936

3 President Roosevelt elected for second term, carrying all states except Maine and Vermont.

6 Britain and Italy sign a commercial treaty restoring economic relations to what they were before the attempt to impose sanctions on Italy in connection with the invasion of Ethiopia.

14 German government notifies signatories of Versailles Treaty that it no longer considers itself bound by provisions governing control of principal German waterways.

15 General Franco's advance troops penetrate University City in Madrid.

18 President Roosevelt sails for Buenos Aires to attend a peace congress.

23 A Russian court sentences E. I. Strickling, German engineer, to be shot on charges of sabotaging Siberian coal mines. Eight Soviet engineers also sentenced and Strickling's penalty commuted to ten years' imprisonment.

25 Stalin presents draft on new Soviet constitution to eighth All-Union Congress of Soviets.

DECEMBER

1 President Roosevelt tells Inter-American Peace Conference at Buenos Aires that New World nations should stand "shoulder to shoulder" in event of aggression from ·the Old World.

11 British Parliament ratifies abdication of King Edward VIII.

14 King George VI of England delivers first message to Parliament.

15 President Roosevelt returns from South American cruise.

16 The Inter-American Conference for the Maintenance of Peace unanimously adopts collective security, convention and nonintervention protocol.

1937

JANUARY

2 Britain and Italy sign Mediterranean agreement.

6 President Roosevelt tells Congress, "The judicial branch is also asked by the people to do its part in making democracy successful."

8 President Roosevelt signs Congressional resolution embargoing arms shipments to Spain.

23 Moscow trial of Karl Radek and others begins.

30 Hitler announces that Germany repudiates war-guilt clause in Versailles Treaty.

FEBRUARY

5 President Roosevelt submits his plan for enlarged Supreme Court to Congress.

8 City of Malaga in Mediterranean surrenders to General Franco.

MARCH

5 Central Executive Committee of Russian Communist Party announces introduction of secret ballot and expulsion of Rykov and Bukharin.

25 British government accedes to request of France and releases Belgium from obligations of material assistance under the Locarno Pact.

APRIL

19 British, French, German, and Italian warships begin patroling Spanish coast under Nonintervention Agreement.

MAY

1 President Roosevelt signs Neutrality Act.

12 George VI crowned King and Emperor.

17 Juan Negrin forms new Republican government in Loyalist Spain following failure of Largo Caballero to work with Communists.

28 Neville Chamberlain succeeds Stanley Baldwin as British Prime Minister.

29 Spanish Loyalists bomb German cruiser *Deutschland* off the Balearic Islands.

31 German war vessels bombard Spanish port of Almeria in retaliation for *Deutschland* shelling.

JUNE

11 Marshal Tukhatchevsky and seven other Russian generals sentenced to be shot for treason.

19 Franco's troops occupy Bilbao, Basque seaport in northern Spain.

20 Popular Front government of Premier Léon Blum resigns in France.

22 Camille Chautemps forms new French government with Blum as Vice-Premier.

23 Germany and Italy withdraw from Four-Power naval patrol of Spanish coast.

29 French government suspends gold and foreign-exchange payments.

JULY

2 Soviet government withdraws patrols and naval cutters from Amur River islands for which Japan disputes ownership.

17 England signs naval limitation treaties with Germany and Russia.

27 German government requisitions all wheat and rye crops.

29 Japanese bombing planes attack Tientsin in first major attack of Japanese undeclared war on China.

AUGUST

9 Japanese enter ancient Chinese capital of Peiping.

12 President Roosevelt nominates Senator Black to fill vacancy caused by resignation of Justice Van Devanter from the Supreme Court.

25 President Roosevelt signs modified Supreme Court Procedure Act.

26 Japanese machine gunners from low-flying airplane wound British Ambassador to China.

28 Secretary Hull notifies Japan and China that the United States reserves all rights on its own behalf and on that of its nationals in connection with wartime damages.

29 Chinese government begins nonaggression pact with the Soviet Union.

SEPTEMBER

6 Soviet government accuses Italian vessels of sinking two Russian vessels bound for Spain.

7 Hitler tells Nuremberg Nazi Congress that Germany, Italy, and Japan are linked to save Europe from "chaotic madness."

10 Britain, France, Russia, and six smaller Mediterranean nations announce that submarines will operate in the Mediterranean at their own risk. Germany, Italy, and Albania refuse to attend meeting at Nyon, France, from which the statement came.

14 President Roosevelt announces that merchant vessels owned by the United States will be permitted to carry arms and munitions to China and Japan.

25 Mussolini visits Hitler at Munich and reviews army maneuvers in Berlin the next day.

28 Mussolini proclaims solidarity of Rome-Berlin Axis in broadcast address at Berlin.

OCTOBER

5 President Roosevelt calls for a "quarantine" of "aggressor nations" in Chicago speech.

6 United States State Department condemns Japan for violating Nine-Power Treaty and Briand-Kellogg antiwar pact.

9 Italy refuses Anglo-French invitation to discuss withdrawal of troops from Spain.

13 Germany pledges to respect Belgian neutrality under all circumstances.

29 Germany declines Belgian invitation to Nine-Power Conference at Brussels to discuss the war in China.

NOVEMBER

6 Italy joins Germany and Japan in Anti-Comintern Pact.

28 Spanish Rebel government proclaims blockade of all Loyalist ports.

29 Italy recognizes independence of Manchukuo.

DECEMBER

12 Japanese bombing planes sink U. S. gunboat *Panay* on the Yangtze River.

14 Japan establishes new puppet Chinese government at Nanking.

24 Japan assures the United States in reply to *Panay* protest that American rights will be respected. The next day the State Department calls the reply satisfactory.

1938

JANUARY

12 First session of new Red Parliament opens in Moscow.

FEBRUARY

12 Chancellor Schuschnigg of Austria confers with Hitler at Berchtesgaden and consents to take five Nazi sympathizers into his cabinet.

21 Foreign Minister Anthony Eden resigns from the Chamberlain Cabinet because of the Prime Minister's insistence on concluding a pact with Mussolini, notwithstanding Italy's violation of the Nonintervention Agreement in Spain.

MARCH

9 Chancellor Schuschnigg of Austria announces that a plebiscite will be held on March 13 to determine whether the Austrian people prefer to maintain their independence or join Germany.

11 Chancellor Schuschnigg resigns as Austrian Premier to forestall immediate German armed intervention. The new Premier, Seyss-Inquart, calls for German troops and on March 13 proclaims the union of Germany and Austria.

APRIL

16 Britain and Italy sign a peace and harmony pact, contingent upon the withdrawal of Italian forces from Spain.

24 Konrad Henlein, leader of the Nazis in Sudetenland, reveals his eight-point "Karlsbad Program" of demands to be made upon the Czechoslovak government.

MAY

20 Czechoslovak forces mobilize in response to German mobilization on Czechoslovakian frontier.

JULY

2 The Czechoslovak government rejects several of the eight Karlsbad demands laid before it by the Sudeten Nazis.

AUGUST

3 Lord Runciman arrives in Prague as Britain's "conciliator and mediator" of the Czechoslovak crisis.

15 German army maneuvers of unprecedented size begin and continue for a full month.

22 The Soviet Union informs the German ambassador at Moscow that Russia will stand by its 1935 promise to support Czechoslovakia in the event of attack.

SEPTEMBER

12 Hitler tells Nuremberg Congress that Czech oppression of Sudeten Germans must end.

15 Chamberlain flies to Berchtesgaden to confer with Hitler.

18 Premier Daladier and Foreign Minister Bonnet of France confer with the British in London and agree upon dismemberment of Czechoslovakia.

22 The Czechoslovak government accepts Anglo-French terms calling for virtual surrender to Germany.

24 Chamberlain brings back from his Godesberg meeting with Hitler the day before a new list of German demands on Czechoslovakia, far exceeding those the British and French had urged the Czechs to make. Czechoslovakia mobilizes.

29 Mussolini, Hitler, Daladier, and Chamberlain meet at Munich and agree on terms calling for partitioning of Czechoslovakia.

30 The Czechoslovak government accepts the terms of the Munich Conference.

OCTOBER

10 German troops and Gestapo agents complete the occupation of the ceded areas of Czechoslovakia, sometimes going beyond the boundaries agreed upon at Munich.

NOVEMBER

7 Herschel Grynzspan, 17-year old Polish Jew, in a fit of manic depression, shoots Ernst von Rath of the German

embassy in Paris, following expulsion of all Polish Jews from the Reich.

13 Göring announces that German Jews must pay for damages done them by German mobs following the shooting of von Rath, plus a fine of one billion marks for the death of von Rath. This leads President Roosevelt to summon American Ambassador Hugh Wilson to return to Washington to report. The Germans also recall their envoy from Washington.

1939

JANUARY

25 General Franco's troops take Barcelona.

FEBRUARY

2 The Soviet Union severs diplomatic relations with Hungary because that country recently signed the Anti-Comintern Pact.

7 Over a million Spanish refugees enter France as Loyalist troops continue retreats.

28 Chamberlain announces that Great Britain will recognize the Franco regime as the legal Spanish government.

MARCH

10 Stalin delivers speech to 18th Party Congress of the Soviet Union criticizing appeasement and warning that Russia will not pull other nations' chestnuts out of the fire.

13 Hitler summons President Hacha, successor to Eduard Beneš as President of Czechoslovakia, to Berlin. Father Tiso declares Slovakia a separate state.

15 Hitler extends his protection to Czechoslovakia, extinguishing the republic, as German troops enter Prague.

20 Rumania signs a trade treaty with Germany.
21 Lithuania surrenders the city of Memel to Germany.
29 The remains of Republican Spain surrender to General Franco.
31 Great Britain guarantees Poland against aggression.

APRIL

7 Italian troops invade Albania and five days later King Victor Emmanuel II accepts the Albanian crown.
15 Roosevelt asks Hitler and Mussolini to pledge ten years of peace and lists 27 countries that they should promise not to attack.
28 Hitler rejects Roosevelt's peace proposal and denounces the Anglo-German naval treaty and his own nonaggression pact with Poland.

MAY

5 Foreign Commissar Maxim Litvinov, leading Soviet exponent of collective security, resigns his post and is replaced by Vyacheslav Molotov.
10 Prime Minister Chamberlain makes his first statement on his secret and unsuccessful efforts to secure Russian collaboration.

JUNE

7 William Strang of the British Foreign Office goes to Moscow to try to work out some Anglo-Russian agreement.
22 King George and Queen Elizabeth return from their visit to Canada and the United States.

AUGUST

13 Climaxing months of agitation and infiltration of Germans into the Free City of Danzig, Hitler invites Dr. Burckhardt,

League of Nations Commissioner, to a conference at Berchtesgaden.

22 German Foreign Minister von Ribbentrop flies to Moscow to sign a ten-year nonaggression pact with the Soviet Union.

25 The British and Poles sign a mutual-assistance pact in London.

27 Hitler refuses Daladier's appeal to make one more attempt to negotiate with Poland, insisting that Danzig and the Polish Corridor must return to the Reich.

28 France closes the German frontier.

30 Hitler rejects British appeal that he negotiate with Poland but does not show the Poles the terms that the British Ambassador in Berlin is told were offered to them.

SEPTEMBER

1 German troops invade Poland without formal declaration of war. The British and French ambassadors in Berlin announce that unless German troops are withdrawn immediately, their respective countries will fulfill their obligations to aid Poland.

3 After presenting a two-hour ultimatum to Germany, Britain declares war at 11 A.M. and France declares war at 5 P.M. Winston Churchill joins the Cabinet as First Lord of the Admiralty and Anthony Eden becomes Secretary of State for the Dominions.

8 President Roosevelt proclaims a national emergency "to the extent necessary for the proper observance, safeguarding and enforcing of the neutrality of the United States and the strengthening of our national defense within the limits of peacetime authorizations."

15 The Soviet Union and Japan agree to an armistice on the Far Eastern Front.

28 Molotov and Ribbentrop sign an agreement in Moscow partitioning Poland.

OCTOBER

 6 Following the victory over Poland, Hitler makes his "last peace offer" to the Allies.
19 Britain, France, and Turkey sign a mutual-assistance pact with proviso that Turkey shall not be compelled to fight Russia.

NOVEMBER

 4 President Roosevelt signs the amended Neutrality Act, lifting the arms embargo but adding the cash-and-carry clause. American shipping is forbidden to enter the war zones.
28 The Soviet Union denounces the nonaggression pact with Finland and two days later Soviet troops invade Finland while Soviet airplanes bomb Finnish cities.

DECEMBER

17 On orders from Berlin, the German pocket battleship, *Graf Spee*, is scuttled by its crew outside Montevideo.

1940

JANUARY

26 Russian troops begin to crack the Mannerheim Line.

FEBRUARY

12 The first Australian and New Zealand troops arrive at Suez.

MARCH

12 Russia and Finland sign an armistice which cedes western Finland to the Soviet Union.

19 Paul Reynaud forms a new French Cabinet to replace that of Daladier, receiving a majority of one vote.

APRIL

7 The Allies warn that they are mining the waters off Norway. Norway and Holland protest this as violation of international law.

9 German troops occupy Denmark without resistance and land in Norway at Narvik and Oslo.

MAY

3 Colonel O. B. Getz, Norwegian commander, asks for armistice and peace negotiations with Germany as British withdrawal continues.

8 Chamberlain's majority in House of Commons falls to 81 as 130 Conservatives abstain from giving government a vote of confidence.

10 German troops invade Holland, Belgium, and Luxembourg. The British Army moves into northern Belgium. Chamberlain resigns as British Prime Minister and King George VI asks Winston Churchill to form a new government.

11 Churchill forms a new Cabinet, retaining Halifax and Chamberlain, but adding three Labourites who had hitherto refused to hold office. Foreign Minister Arita of Japan announces that his country will not permit the Netherlands Indies to change hands.

14 Holland capitulates to Germany.

16 German troops pass Sedan, thereby in effect sealing the doom of France.

18 Premier Reynaud appoints Marshal Pétain Vice-Premier.

19 General Weygand succeeds General Gamelin as French chief of staff.

20 British troops begin evacuating Belgian ports.
22 British Parliament passes the Emergency Powers Defense Act giving the Churchill government unlimited wartime powers.
28 King Leopold of Belgium surrenders his army of 500,000 to the Germans.
29 Large-scale British evacuation of Dunkirk begins.

JUNE

4 The British evacuation of Dunkirk completed with 335,-000 men saved and more than 30,000 casualties.
10 Foreign Minister Ciano announces that Italy will consider itself at war with France and Britain. President Roosevelt says, "The hand that held the dagger has stuck it into the back of its neighbor."
14 German troops occupy Paris which the French had announced was an open city and would not be defended.
16 Premier Reynaud resigns and is succeeded by Marshal Pétain.
17 Marshal Pétain sues for peace.
22 French delegation signs armistice terms with Germany.
29 In response to Russian demands, Rumania cedes Bessarabia and northern Bukovina to the Soviet Union.

JULY

3 Great Britain takes over all French war vessels in British ports and disables part of the French fleet at Oran after the French commander refuses to accept a British ultimatum.
4 Rumania establishes a pro-German Cabinet.
5 The Pétain government breaks off diplomatic relations with Britain.

12 The British agree to close for three months the Burma Road to armament traffic destined for China.

AUGUST

16 After several weeks of increased air activity, the British repulse wave after wave of German war planes, inflicting 217 enemy losses in three days.

22 German planes launch first mass night attack on London.

31 Rumania cedes two thirds of Transylvania to Hungary.

SEPTEMBER

3 The United States transfers fifty overage destroyers to Great Britain in exchange for ninety-nine year leases to naval and aircraft bases in the Atlantic.

6 King Carol of Rumania abdicates.

8 Marshal Göring takes command of air attacks on Britain.

15 German air attacks on London reach their peak as RAF destroys 185 German fighting craft.

23 General de Gaulle and Free French forces, supported by British war vessels, withdraw from Dakar after failing to persuade local representatives of the Pétain regime to surrender.

27 Germany, Italy, and Japan sign a ten-year mutual-assistance pact.

OCTOBER

27 Italian war planes and troops attack Greece from Albania, following Greek rejection of a three-hour Italian ultimatum.

NOVEMBER

12 British aircraft seriously damage several large Italian war vessels in Taranto harbor.

13 Soviet Foreign Commissar Molotov visits Berlin.

16 German planes launch mass night attack on city of Coventry. Italians begin to evacuate their Albanian base at Koritza.

DECEMBER

6 Greeks capture Porto Edda and Marshal Badoglio resigns as Italian chief of staff.

10 British launch offensive against Italian troops in Libya and Egypt.

15 British drive all Italians from Egypt and pursue them into Libya.

23 Lord Halifax appointed British Ambassador to the United States to replace Lord Lothian who died on December 12.

1941

JANUARY

26 British troops capture Tobruk.

FEBRUARY

6 British troops capture Benghazi.

10 Britain severs diplomatic relations with Rumania.

MARCH

2 Bulgaria joins the Axis.

11 President Roosevelt signs the Lease-Lend Act.

APRIL

3 Axis land forces open drive on British troops in Libya.

6 German troops invade Yugoslavia.

13 The Soviet Union and Japan sign a neutrality and non-aggression pact.

14 Axis drive against British North African forces penetrates Egypt.

19 Pro-Axis Premier of Irak begins a series of uprisings which the British finally crush on May 31.

27 German troops enter Athens.

MAY

10 Rudolf Hess, Hitler's deputy and number three man in the Nazi hierarchy, flies to Great Britain and lands on the estate of the Duke of Hamilton.

20 Main Italian forces begin withdrawal from Ethiopia and surrender the country to Britain on June 1.

27 President Roosevelt proclaims an unlimited national emergency.

JUNE

1 British evacuation of Crete is completed.

8 British and Free French forces invade Syria.

18 Turkey and Germany sign a trade treaty and nonaggression pact.

22 German troops invade the Soviet Union.

JULY

7 United States troops announce the occupation of Iceland.

12 British and Free French troops complete the conquest of Syria.

16 Germans claim to have captured Smolensk and broken the Stalin Line.

25 President Roosevelt freezes Japanese assets; Britain follows suit the next day.

AUGUST

14 President Roosevelt and Prime Minister Churchill issue their eight-point peace aims.

28 Iran ends resistance to occupation by Anglo-Soviet forces.

SEPTEMBER

11 President Roosevelt orders American war vessels to shoot first at Axis warships in waters vital to the defense of the United States.

OCTOBER

3 Adolf Hitler announces that a huge new offensive against Russia is about to begin.

17 United States Navy announces the torpedoing of the destroyer *Kearny* on the Iceland patrol.

19 Joseph Stalin proclaims Moscow in a state of siege.

APPENDIX

Appendix Contents

Supplementary Report on the Stalin Conversation

Moscow, U.S.S.R.—June 10, 1938

MEMORANDUM IN RE CONFERENCE WITH STALIN
AND MOLOTOV FOR OFFICE PURPOSES

Strictly Confidential

Following the meeting with Stalin and Molotov and the discussions then had on June 5, I took counsel with Secretary Henderson and Counselor Kirk. We discussed the situation from all angles.

It was fortunate that Mr. Henderson had participated in the original debt negotiations and was personally familiar with all phases of the matter, and that some time ago he had also, at my request, prepared an able epitome of the history of the negotiations, together with a very clear analysis of the difficulties which arose, and upon which the negotiations foundered.

It was apparent that if this debt development were to be successfully worked out, it would be necessary to obviate those difficulties which prevented former success, and that therefore the proposal should be clarified and amplified to disclose exactly how it was proposed to work out the arrangement.

Accordingly, on June 8, I asked for another conference, which was arranged for one o'clock of that day. In order to prevent possible publicity which might arouse speculation on the part of the press and unwarranted assumptions, I asked Colonel Faymonville, driving his own car, to take me to the Kremlin, rather than use one of the chauffeurs here. I saw Mr. Molotov alone and explained the situation as above, and suggested that I desired to clarify in my own mind certain phases of their proposal and for that purpose had prepared two memoranda as a basis of discussion.

The conference lasted about an hour and fifteen minutes. Mr. Molotov stated that he would wish to give the matter some more thought and that he would let me hear from him later.

Before leaving, I suggested that in as much as my relations with his government had been entirely with the Foreign Office, I desired to have his consent to my taking the matter up with Foreign Minister Litvinov, to explain the situation to him, so that after my departure negotiations could be conducted through regular diplomatic channels on both sides. To this he said he had no objection and that he would ask Mr. Litvinov to get in touch with me.

On the following morning, June 9, I received a telephone call from Mr. Molotov's secretary asking whether I could come over to see the Premier, as he had an answer to the "proposals" which I had left the day before. I immediately (and quite sharply) said that I had made no proposals, that I had simply asked questions and left a statement of what I understood the terms of their proposal were and had asked them to verify that understanding, and that the memorandum which I had left with them would disclose that very clearly; that I was neither empowered to make a proposal nor would I make a proposal. He apologized profusely and stated that his English was faulty and understood thoroughly that it was not a proposal that we had made; that what he had meant to say was that Mr. Molotov wished to discuss further the questions raised in my memorandum.

Pursuant to this telephone call, I again called upon Premier Molotov at seven o'clock on the evening of June 9. Colonel Faymonville again drove me over to the Catherine Place, which is inside the Kremlin walls. Premier Molotov said that he had taken up the questions which I had submitted with all of his government associates and that they had agreed upon the terms of a definite proposal, which he had set forth in a reply to my questions. He handed to me a letter signed by himself, which was in the Russian language and addressed to me, setting forth seriatim the terms of the offer.

The Premier then stated that the memorandum was not in any sense a hard-and-fast proposition; that he agreed with me as to how the matter should be projected; that he would keep the situation from developing into a hardened state; that this would serve to make a start and to clarify the situation until he had heard further from me.

I then asked to have the Russian memorandum translated by them into English so that I could have their version of the meaning. They said they would have it for me and would deliver it promptly.

Premier Molotov then went on to say that the U.S.S.R. was in no serious need of credits; that they had been offered very large credits by Germany in the very recent weeks, which they were not going to accept under any conditions; that their balance of trade was favorable; that his govern-

ment and Stalin were, however, really desirous of getting
this debt matter cleared up because of their high regard for
the United States, etc., and that therefore they were initiat-
ing the matter in this manner; that they would like to know
from me as soon as possible what the reaction of the President and the Secretary of State would be to the possibilities of
some arrangement along the general lines of our discussion;
that, in any event, whether it was finally successful or not,
one thing at least would have been accomplished, to wit, the
manifestation of their good will and, finally, in any event
there would always be a kindly feeling in their minds with
reference to these discussions and these negotiations which
had been discussed by the heads of the government and by
Mr. Stalin with the American Ambassador.

Then to my surprise, he said that he thought it would be
better if the matter were kept out of the usual diplomatic
channels for the present. He stated that the matter had originated on the business side of the Soviet government's activities in the United States with Mr. Rosoff, head of Amtorg,
and that he thought it would be better to hold the matter
exclusively in that atmosphere until it had progressed into
stages where there was a possibility of having a definite agreement made. He therefore stated that the matter would not be
taken up by Ambassador Troyanovsky and he would prefer
not to have it discussed with him or with the Embassy in
Washington. He also said that they desired that I should not
take up the matter for the present with Foreign Minister
Litvinov. To this I demurred on the ground that it would be
difficult for me to communicate with him, except through our
diplomatic channels, or through their Foreign Office. He said
for the purposes of the immediate present he would find means
of communicating with me and that I could communicate
with him through Mr. Rosoff in New York.

Again I suggested that I felt that both the conventionalities and in fact my personal obligations required that the matter should be projected through our regular staff and through Mr. Litvinov. He stated that this would come in good time if the matter developed and that he would assume any responsibility for the situation so far as Mr. Litvinov was concerned; that he would take the matter up and explain it to Mr. Litvinov himself, if necessary.

In order that they should not obtain the idea that I had returned for details because of any possible lively interest on the part of the government of the United States on the assumption that I had communicated the matter to the President and to the Secretary of State, I stated to Mr. Molotov that I had not set forth the details of the debt proposal but had covered it and the discussions generally in my cable to the Department; that I had requested the Secretary of State and the President personally to be permitted to return to the United States to take my oath there and receive instructions before going to Brussels; that I had received such permission and was, therefore, going to the United States and would report the entire situation to my government, in the hope that it would start negotiations that might finally be successfully concluded.

He stated that his government and he were very glad that I was returning to the United States and would explain not only the proposal but interpret the spirit which actuated his government.

He also emphasized that at present he thought that the less publicity had and the fewer people who knew about this situation until the matter were agreed upon in principle, the better. With this I agreed heartily.

Brussels, January 17, 1939

TO THE HONORABLE THE SECRETARY OF STATE

SUPPLEMENTARY AND FINAL REPORT ON DISCUSSIONS
HAD WITH MESSRS. STALIN AND MOLOTOV PRIOR TO
MY DEPARTURE FROM THE SOVIET UNION

Strictly Confidential

Sir:

The purpose of this dispatch is to supplement and complete the reports heretofore filed and to provide in single compass a complete account of the conference held with Messrs. Stalin and Molotov, a history of subsequent developments relating thereto, and the status of the negotiations up to the end of my tenure as Ambassador of the United States to the Soviet Union.

On June 24, 1938, I returned to the United States upon the direction of the Department and conferred with the President, the Secretary of State, and the Undersecretary of State, after which I had several conferences with Mr. David Rosoff, the head of Amtorg, the Soviet business agency in the United States, who was authorized to discuss the matter with me. At that time I submitted to the Department the proposal of the Soviet government as authorized by Mr. Stalin and executed in written form by Mr. Molotov under date of June 9, 1938, at Moscow, together with an English translation furnished by the officials of the Soviet government at my request. The originals thereof are herewith enclosed.

After my discussions with the President, the Secretary of State, and the Undersecretary of State I was authorized to explore the possibility of securing a modification of the Soviet proposal, through discussions with Mr. Rosoff, with a view toward arriving at a project which could be recommended to the respective governments as affording a basis of discussion. In this connection, I was authorized to procure the advice and counsel of a prominent New York banker, Mr. Sidney Weinberg. Extended discussions were had with Messrs. Rosoff and Weinberg looking toward the possibility of obtaining a modification of the Soviet proposal along the line that a settlement would be confined to the payment of the Kerensky debt without prejudice to other claims, on a basis where compensating credits to be advanced to the Soviet Union through low rates of interest would make the settlement attractive to the Soviet government as well as to the government of the United States. During these discussions, it became quite apparent that it would be impossible for the government of the United States to consider a settlement on such a basis until the Senate of the United States had passed upon a somewhat similar proposal put forward by the Hungarian government. It was considered advisable, therefore, to await the outcome of the Senate's consideration of the Hungarian proposal. Pursuant to instructions, I advised the Soviet government through Mr. Rosoff in the manner as set forth in my letters of July 5, hereinabove referred to.

As a matter of good faith in my relations with the officials of the Soviet government it is incumbent upon me again to call to the attention of the Department the understanding that the entire matter is to be held in the strictest confidence, without publicity, until it is finally disposed of. I was also authorized to convey personally to the representatives of the Soviet government the information that the President and the Secretary of State were gratified at this gesture of friendship and the manifestation of good faith on their part to compose the differences and misunderstandings with reference to the debt settlement which had arisen subsequent to the Litvinov agreement.

My judgment on the situation is that the present Soviet government was, in June, 1938, sincerely desirous of clearing up the misunderstanding and bad feeling which were engendered by the failure of the debt payment negotiations under the Litvinov agreement. The principal difficulty lies in the fact that, practically, it would be impossible for the Soviet government to pay the prewar Russian debt without being obliged to give similar favorable treatment to 27 other different nations under its general treaty and contractual obligations. As a practical matter, this was financially impossible. The Kerensky debt situation is unique and is differentiated from other obligations, and therefore affords an avenue for partial composition. The difficulty arose primarily out of the fact that this situation was not frankly and unequivocally stated and recognized at the beginning, with the result that recriminations were indulged in and intense feeling was engendered on both sides.

A distinct advance was recorded in the fact that Messrs. Stalin and Molotov frankly made this statement to me and said that they desired to meet the government's obligations under the Litvinov agreement to the limit of their practicabilities.

During my stay in Russia, in interpreting the good-neighbor policy of the President and under express instructions from the President and the Secretary of State, I exerted every effort to cultivate mutual respect and good will between the two governments to the farthest degree consistent with the maintenance, firmly and aggressively, of the rights of the United States and the principles of democracy. The result was very satisfactory, for there was no doubt that when I left Russia there was a better understanding between the two governments than had existed for some time previously.

The responsible authorities of the Soviet government have

stated openly that in a world where they are surrounded by enemies, they have complete confidence in the objectivity, fairness, and honorable intentions of the government of the United States.

In my judgment, so long as the policy of the United States is to maintain relations with the Soviet government, it is desirable that these relations should be of a friendly character. The man power, resources, and strength of both the Soviet government and the Soviet people, their military and naval defenses, and their present economic and moral purpose of preserving peace constitute a factor which may be of great value in the maintenance of law and order and a moral concept as between nations, particularly in view of the aggressive disposition now apparent in the combined authoritarian states.

For reasons with which the Secretary of State is familiar, the appointment of my successor at Moscow has not yet been made. It was generally considered to be advisable, when I left, that such an appointment should be tendered to a man of the successful business or banking type who would be characterized not only by a familiarity with industrial and business problems but who was also known to be liberal in his political ideology, although not swayed by any communistic or extreme leftist attitude. I cannot recommend too strongly the advisability of pursuing such a policy in the interests of the United States. In view of subsequent international developments, it seems to me that a broad-minded, friendly type of independent personality, who would not needlessly offend the leaders of the Soviet government, would be most helpful in the maintenance of friendly co-operation to a degree that would appear necessary in view of the situation in the Pacific.* In that

---

* In connection with the appointment of Laurence Steinhardt, recently announced; his well-known business and professional success, coupled with his diplomatic success, made him ideally qualified for this post.

connection, I beg leave to direct the Department's attention
to the fact that, in the absence of some specific request on
the part of the President or the Secretary of State, Lieutenant
Colonel Faymonville's assignment as Military Attaché at Moscow expires this spring. If it is considered advisable to keep
him there in view of the discussions previously referred to,
it will be necessary to take prompt action.

Footnote on Sweden

NO. 454   *Moscow, July 28, 1937*

TO THE HONORABLE THE SECRETARY OF STATE

VISIT OF SWEDISH MINISTER FOR FOREIGN AFFAIRS,
R. J. SANDLER, TO MOSCOW

Sir:

During an informal conversation which I had with Litvinov, I brought up the question of Sandler's visit to Moscow.
Litvinov stated that Sandler was urging, as one of the reasons
for the elimination of smaller countries from the obligations
of Article 16, that such a course would enable the United States
to join the League, as it could then do so without committing
itself to joint action; and that, therefore, such course was advisable to strengthen the League, in bringing the United States
into its association. I replied that such reasoning seemed very
farfetched to me and that in my personal opinion no consideration, at the present time, could induce the United States to
become a member of the League even though Article 16 of
the Covenant were eliminated.

Litvinov's expressions were strongly impatient as to this
attitude of Sandler and were to the effect that it was "German
propaganda."

Litvinov's position is that some of the smaller neutrals wish to be relieved from a possible obligation to joint League action against Germany, under Article 16, as some of them had suffered severely from such action against Italy under sanctions imposed by Article 16. Sweden was taking the lead in this situation, according to Litvinov, and was thereby playing Germany's game. He believes that Hitler will destroy them all, one by one, unless they stand together, and that war anywhere in Europe will mean war everywhere for "peace is indivisible."

This looks like sense to me. A realistic military alliance of Britain, France, and Russia to oppose "Hit and Muss" is probably the only thing that will stop Hitler from doing what he has so boldly declared are his purposes.

I have had no indication of Sandler's attitude here, other than the above statement of Litvinov's. It is certain that neither the speech which Sandler made at Moscow, nor his statement to the press at Stockholm, indicates that Sweden is advocating a weakening of the Covenant or intends to change its policy of opposing, at least in theory, the conclusion of regional pacts of mutual assistance. It may also be possible that Litvinov is piqued at Sweden's apparent disbelief in the wisdom of regional pacts of mutual assistance and its preference for "mutual understanding between the Scandinavian countries" within the framework of the League as the most effective and universal instrument for preserving peace. Sweden's opposition to regional pacts of mutual assistance is undoubtedly as distasteful to Litvinov as the refusal of the United States to join the League. This appears to be borne out by Sandler's statement to the press in Stockholm that the aim of the close mutual understanding "between the Scandinavian countries is not for the purpose of creating unfriendly neighborly relations but should create mutual understanding

in the northern part of Europe and have a beneficent effect
within the League of Nations."

I shall find it of interest to explore this situation on the
occasion of my visit to Sweden next month.

I have the honor to be, Sir, respectfully yours,

Joseph E. Davies

The Baltic States Prepare for the Worst

THE TRAGEDY OF FINLAND: PRELUDE

NO. 456-A   *Helsingfors, August 2, 1937*

TO THE HONORABLE THE SECRETARY OF STATE

VISIT TO FINLAND—1937

Strictly Confidential

Sir:

Pursuant to schedule, I spent three days in Finland. While
there I had the opportunity of meeting personally the Premier,
Mr. Cajander, the Foreign Minister, Dr. Holsti, various members of the cabinet, and some of the prominent businessmen
of the community.

GENERAL CONDITIONS

Finland is enjoying a period of great prosperity. Industrial
production, agriculture, shipping, employment, and commercial activity bear the indices of a "boom." Exports have increased, as have also public revenues.

Finland's chief customer is England. This probably accounts, in part at least, for their disposition to follow the
political leadership of Great Britain in European affairs. It is
Germany, however, that now sells Finland the greater part

of its imports. German influence, I am advised, is very aggressive here.

Dr. Holsti, it will be recalled, visited the U.S.S.R. last spring. Upon that occasion the American Embassy tendered a reception in his honor, as previously reported.

FINLAND—THE U.S.S.R. AND THE SCANDINAVIAN BLOC

Finland was desirous of participating in the Scandinavian bloc (Norway and Sweden)—the dominant purpose of which, along with Denmark and recently Belgium, is to preserve peace and to maintain a position of security for themselves in the event of a catastrophe. Finland found that its participation in the "Oslo bloc" was not altogether viewed with favor by Sweden, because of the apprehension that the relationship between Finland and the Soviet Union was strained. It will be recalled that a source of irritation has existed between Finland and the Soviet Union during these many years, by reason of the problems arising out of the Finnish character of Karelia, which still remains a part of the U.S.S.R. and constitutes one of the constituent Soviet republics. The Soviet government has been engaged upon extensive fortifications and military preparations adjacent thereto on the Finnish border. In addition thereto, it appears that the U.S.S.R. was exceedingly suspicious that Germany had some sort of understanding with Finland, in the event of a German-Baltic attack on the Soviet Union.

These were the conditions, apparently, which prompted the visit of the Finnish Foreign Minister.

The position of Finland as between its two powerful neighbors is not an enviable one.

Since my departure, and a few days ago, the German fleet of nine or ten vessels have been on a friendly visit to Helsingfors. The official papers in Moscow have been violent in their attack upon this manifestation of friendliness on the part of Finland to Germany. The Finnish newspapers have, in turn, resented the suggestion that the Soviet Union should seek to determine for Finland what friendly courtesy it should extend to a friendly neighboring state. This is illustrative of the extreme sensitiveness of the situation here.

The Scandinavian bloc is, in my opinion, very close to the British Foreign Office.

CONCLUSIONS

There is a background of friendly feeling toward Germany in Finland. This has an historical basis and is due to the aid which Germany extended to the country in its struggle for independence against Russia.

On the other hand, the Finns are essentially a strong, democratic, liberty-loving, and independent people. The net impression which I get (and it is quite strong) from these various conversations is that the government of Finland is innately hostile to the Hitler concept and his governmental policies. Finland is instinctively not "*pro-German*."

Quite independently of both of these considerations, however, Finland's policy is based upon a realization of the exceedingly precarious geographical and military strategic position she occupies between two powerful enemy countries, and upon a determination realistically to avoid antagonizing either, if possible, and in any event to do her utmost to prevent her land from being converted into a battleground whereby both her political independence and economic freedom and independent well-being might be destroyed.

I have the honor to be, Sir, respectfully yours,

Joseph E. Davies

LATVIA AND HER NEBRASKA PRESIDENT

NO. 456-C   *Riga, Latvia, August 15, 1937*

TO THE HONORABLE THE SECRETARY OF STATE

REPORT OF VISIT AND TRIP TO LATVIA

Strictly Confidential

Sir:

I have the honor to report the following with reference to my visit to Latvia on August 13, 14, and 15, 1937.

DOMINANT PURPOSES OF FOREIGN POLICY

The government strongly adheres to the League of Nations for obvious reasons. Its entire foreign policy is based upon a desire to maintain its independence and the integrity of Latvian nationality. Peace is vital thereto. A balance and a strict neutrality as between Germany, Poland, and the U.S.S.R. are therefore imperative. It has a defensive and offensive alliance with Estonia. It is also a member of the so-called Baltic bloc. As near as I could sense, the officials are more favorably disposed toward Poland than to either the U.S.S.R. or Germany. England is their largest customer and has dominant influence.

DOMINANT PERSONALITIES

The President, Dr. Ulmanis, was for a time a lecturer at the University of Nebraska Agricultural College. The Secretary for Foreign Affairs, Munters, is a young man thirty-nine years of age (with a Scotch grandmother). He speaks Russian fluently, along with four other languages. He is an exceptionally brilliant, able, and personable man. The other three outstanding men appeared to be Minister for War, General Balodis; the Minister for Finance; and the Minister for Commerce; all of whom I had discussions with, with the exception of the President, who was away on a vacation.

RUSSIA AND THE WESTERN LOCARNO

If England and France were to make peace with Germany and Italy and establish a Western Locarno,* leaving Russia out from direct participation therein, it was the opinion of Secretary Munters that it would not be done without consideration being given and steps being taken to ensure the peace of eastern Europe. In that connection he stated that several months ago he had had a long political discussion with Neville Chamberlain, which developed the idea that the solution for the peace of eastern Europe might be found under an arrangement between Germany and the Baltic states, Poland, and Rumania, whereby Germany would enter into the same kind of treaties with these states, respectively, which the U.S.S.R. had with these states. With such pacts of non-aggression together with a clear definition of what constituted the aggressor, peace would be assured as far as treaties could effect that end and thereby there would be created a "roof" between Germany and Russia which would relieve the situation of the necessity for Russia and Germany to enter into a contract or treaty, as it was thought that Hitler would under no circumstances "sign any contract with the Soviet Union at this time." This arrangement, however, he said, would assure peace in eastern Europe at least for a time.

I have the honor to be, Sir, respectfully yours,

Joseph E. Davies

----

* It will be recalled that the Locarno Treaty (1925) was an effort to assure peace in western Europe. It provided that Great Britain and Italy would guarantee the frontiers of Belgium, France, and Germany from aggression by either side. These governments also mutually guaranteed that there would be no aggression each as against the other. It also provided for arbitration of differences between Germany and any of the countries—France, Belgium, Poland, or Czechoslovakia.

LITHUANIA LIVES ON FEAR

NO. 456-D   *Memel, Lithuania, August 16, 1937*

TO THE HONORABLE THE SECRETARY OF STATE

REPORT ON VISIT TO LITHUANIA—MEMEL

Strictly Confidential

Sir:

DOMINANT PURPOSE OF FOREIGN POLICIES

Primarily, of course, it is to preserve their national independence. It is in the heart of the danger zone as between the Soviet Union and Germany and, while desirous of maintaining strictly formal relationships with Germany, it is the most friendly to Russia of all the European states adjacent to the U.S.S.R. Innately it is anti-German. Its only real outlet to the sea is the port of Memel (Klaipeda) and it is in constant fear that the Nazi government has the intention of restoring Memel to German sovereignty. The government and the entire population are bitterly hostile to Poland. This situation has been accentuated from October, 1920, when, despite the agreement between the Polish government and Lithuania, Vilna (the then capital) was seized by the Poles and since continuously occupied by them. This bitter hostility is manifested by a tight military defense along and a complete shutting off of the border between the two countries. There is no intercourse between them, and as an illustration thereof, it was impossible for me to send a telegram to Ambassador Biddle at Warsaw from Memel. The Soviet Union is, therefore, more or less a natural ally in their hostile attitude to Poland and Germany.

The immediate objectives of their foreign policy are two:

(1) To recover its old capital of Vilna, now in possession of the Poles;

(2) To hold the port of Memel as against Germany. It is a member of the so-called Baltic bloc and collaborates with its two northern neighbors, Latvia and Estonia, but the hostility between Poland and Lithuania is a constant thorn in the projection of common purposes with the other members of the "bloc." Another fact which somewhat dulls this coalition is found in that both Latvia and Estonia fear being drawn into the Soviet orbit and would probably not desire to maintain too close a relationship if Lithuania were to become merely a puppet of the Soviet Union by becoming too closely and irrevocably tied up with the Soviet Union. In the last analysis it seems probable at least for the present that self-protection as against its two avowed enemies will be more controlling, as Lithuania will find its most effective protector, in case of war with either Poland or Germany, in the Soviet Union.

POLITICAL SITUATION AND GERMANY

So far as the Memel situation as an immediate issue between Lithuania and Germany is concerned, the situation seems to be better than it has been for the last two years. The last election in the Memel territory was held in 1934. At that time, for purposes of demonstration, Hitler appeared personally at Tilsit, just across the border, and it was reported that he had 25,000 men under arms stationed at that place. The election, it appears, was conducted by the Lithuanians with reasonable fairness. The result was that only five Lithuanians were elected to the governing body out of a total of 29. The population of the port particularly and of the territory generally is predominantly German and characterized by ardent pro-German sympathy.

The statement was made to me that the governor of Lithuania had been reliably informed within the past few months that Hitler "had no aggressive intention as to Memel for the moment."

I have the honor to be, Sir, respectfully yours,

Joseph E. Davies

DYNAMITE IN DANZIG

NO. 456-E   *Danzig, August 18, 1937*

TO THE HONORABLE THE SECRETARY OF STATE

REPORT ON VISIT TO THE FREE STATE OF DANZIG
AND THE POLISH PORT OF GDYNIA *

Strictly Confidential

Sir:

I had a most interesting discussion with Senator Frank and Dr. Blume. Dr. Blume is a man of about forty years of age, brilliant and epigrammatic. He is connected with the Foreign Office as an economist and apparently is a sort of secretary to the President. He was very frank in his attitude. He stated that he saw no solution for the intolerable conditions which existed in connection with the Danzig Free State, except one that possibly the future might bring and only "God knows when." He developed his idea of this possible eventuality by describing the perils which the Polish government confronted through the existence of serious unrest in the populace generally, due to the intolerable inequities between the different classes of Polish society and due to the existence of the very large bodies of Ukrainians and White Russians in that part of the Polish state adjacent to the Soviet Union. When, he said, the time arrived where these large Russian minorities in Poland became so infected with Soviet and communistic influence as to be able, together with the

---

* Report on Gdynia omitted as no direct relation to U.S.S.R.

other potential revolutionary elements in Poland, to project a revolution, then Poland would come to a realization that her real interest lay with, and that her real friend was, the German Empire. In such a situation he believed there would be a possibility of Danzig's being again restored to her proper German sovereignty, which would secure her economic and political rights. As to the attitude of the government of the Danzig Free State, he declared that if the average man on the street in Danzig were asked as to what he desired, he would state that not only was it necessary to be free from the domination of Poland, but that it was also necessary that the Polish Corridor be abolished. He recognized that this was impossible for some time because of the agreement of the German Empire with Poland, which did not expire until 1944.

VISIT OF KING CAROL—RUMANIA

In response to my inquiry as to the significance of the recent visit of Carol to Poland and the elevation of the Rumanian Legation to the status of an Embassy, he stated that Poland "would not get much even though they got Rumania." This feeling was illustrated by the common quip, to wit, "mania, dypsomania, kleptomania, and Rumania," he said.

DANZIG AND THE U.S.S.R.

The officials of the Danzig Free State manifested very little interest or curiosity in or as to the Soviet Union. The Polish authorities, on the contrary, were obviously very much interested and asked many questions. Their attitude was distinctly critical and hostile to the U.S.S.R., although they were very careful to qualify their comments as unofficial and indicated the necessity of Poland's preserving a strictly formal neutrality as between both Germany and the Soviet Union, in order to protect its own independence.

CONCLUSION

The net result of it all to my mind was that the situation here is artificial, unstable, and probably productive of ultimate trouble.

I have the honor to be, Sir, respectfully yours,

Joseph E. Davies

An Expert Report on Russia's War Industries

Moscow—October 16, 1937

MEMORANDUM FOR THE AMBASSADOR

SUBJECT: SOVIET INDUSTRY AS A SUPPORT FOR THE RED ARMY

1. Recent changes in the executive departments of the Soviet government have materially affected the organization of Soviet industry as a whole. The effect has been especially noteworthy in that portion of Soviet industry which is of direct usefulness to the Red Army. These changes include both the organization of new commissariats and the reassignment of bureaus and trusts among existing commissariats.

2. The most important of the changes was the creation last winter of a new executive department, the People's Commissariat of Munitions (defense industry), to handle the production of munitions for the Red Army. The change was the result of a suggestion made to the Drafting Committee of the new constitution and accepted and endorsed by Stalin upon the occasion of his report to the Extraordinary Congress of Soviets which approved the final draft of the constitution.

3. More recently, August 23, 1937, a new commissariat to be called the Commissariat of the Machine Building Industry was created from various bureaus which had been attached to the People's Commissariat of Heavy Industry.

4. Under the new arrangements, all industries and trusts

which are primarily responsible for the production of munitions for the Red Army are grouped in the People's Commissariat of Munitions. These activities include the aviation industry as a whole, the shipbuilding industry as a whole, all munitions plants, and certain sections of the steel industry and the light-metals industry together with their plants and research laboratories. The People's Commissariat of the Machine Building Industry will include production of tractors, machine-tool, locomotive, car, and agricultural machinery, works manufacturing machinery for light industry and for the food industry, and boiler, turbine and electrotechnical industries.

5. The reasons for these changes were both general and specific. In general, there appears to have been a recognition of the fact that highly centralized operations are not the most efficient type of industrial organization for enterprises so huge as the state industry of the Soviet Union. These highly centralized operations were inevitable during the early days of Soviet industry when technical knowledge and experience were confined to a small group of Soviet engineers assisted by foreign advisors and where the closest supervision over operations was essential. As the scope of Soviet industry widened, the centralized direction of operations became more and more difficult. Meanwhile, Soviet engineering schools were turning out more and more young engineers qualified to assume responsible positions in plants and factories. It thus became essential to decentralize operation at the same time that personnel became available for carrying out this decentralization.

6. The present situation in Soviet industry is in general one of highly centralized direction and control but decentralized operation. The increased number of industrial commissariats and the increased subdivision of industrial operations in trusts and in separate factories are evidences of this.

7. The specific reasons which led to the creation of the new manufacturing commissariats are understood to have been the complaints of army authorities at the lagging programs of munitions production and at the imperfections found in many of the factory products.

8. So far as concerns organization, the present arrangements made by the Soviet government for munitions production are almost ideal. The difficulties which arise are not those of organization. They concern rather the lack of technical skill among workers generally and the low productive capacity of Soviet labor, which in turn is due to various causes such as lack of training, low living standards, and possibly also political disaffection, sabotage, and the plots of wreckers.

9. The organization for munitions production, which is thought to be so nearly ideal, is based upon close co-ordination among the political, military, and economic aspects of Soviet life. The government, through its elaborate surveys which are constantly being enlarged, is in possession of necessary information regarding the natural resources of the country and the available supplies of raw material. Through its highly centralized direction of industry, the government is also in possession of information as to the present productive capacity of industry and the possibilities of further expansion in industry.

10. From the General Staff of the Red Army, the government receives information as to the extent of industrial preparedness essential to support any proposed plan of military action. Knowing these basic facts, the government is thus able to frame its political policies with a sure knowledge of whether or not the policies can be carried through by force in case diplomacy fails.

11. The General Staff of the Red Army, having received from the government an indication of the several possible

strategic situations in which it may be called upon to act, is in a position to compute its requirements, which must be met before successful military action can be expected. These requirements would naturally include man power, the necessary clothing and munitions with which to equip man power, and the financial and industrial support essential to keep the flow of munitions uninterrupted throughout the estimated duration of an emergency.

12. The requirements of the General Staff for each of the several strategic situations considered are no doubt carefully examined by the government. The assumed strategic situations would naturally include the case of defense against a single invader, defense against a combination of enemies, and offensive operations on one front combined with defensive operations on another front. Upon approval by the government, the General Staff's requirements would naturally be transmitted to the national planning agencies which would be required to meet the industrial needs of the Red Army. Satisfaction of these needs has heretofore had first place in the projects of the State Planning Commission.

13. The planning commissions, through their centralized control of all industry, are in a position to assign to munitions production an adequate share of the natural resources, sufficient fuel and power for the operation of defense industries, and sufficient man power and money to guarantee successful operation of these industries. The principal commissariats affected under such plans are the Commissariat of Munitions, the Commissariat of Heavy Industry, the Commissariat of Light Industry, the Commissariat of the Machine Building Industry, the Commissariat of the Food Industry, and the Commissariat of Transportation. It is on these executive departments that the chief burden of industrial preparedness will lie.

14. It may be concluded that the socialist economy which prevails in the Soviet Union, through its complete control of all the industry of the nation, provides the essential industrial support for the military plans which have been decided upon by the government. Industry has been so organized as to make available for military use any required share of the raw materials, productive capacity, and man power of the nation. As a result of the highly centralized control methods which obtain in the Soviet Union, production programs can be adopted instantly by executive decision alone without legislative or other checks. Difficulties in carrying out production schedules would be sure to arise, but these difficulties would be technical and political, and the framework of the organization for industrial production in the Soviet Union may be considered sound.

Inventory on Russia's Richest Region

MEMORANDUM ON SOVIET INDUSTRIAL REGIONS

Before leaving the Embassy in Moscow, I had prepared from published material a dossier upon the various plants that we were going to visit, and after dinner in the dining car the Soviet Economic Expert of our Embassy staff, Mr. Shiffer, gave us a regular lecture of thirty or forty minutes on what we would see the next day.

Our first stop was in Kharkov, a city of approximately 700,000 people.

After World War No. 1, the capital of the Ukraine was shifted from Kiev to Kharkov, but it was subsequently shifted back to Kiev. Kharkov was considered to be the most Russian of all cities. What we would call a municipal center had just

been completed away from the old section of the city and
centered about a handsome park. The buildings were imposing, neat, efficiently arranged, and formed practically a separate community. That sort of thing was typical of every
place I visited in Russia. The building tempo was very rapid.
Here at Kharkov we were interested in seeing one of the new
tractor plants which had been built as a part of the Five-Year
Plan. It was located some eight or ten miles from the city on
a wide, modern asphalt road stretching out into the broad
steppes of the Ukraine. This plant had an annual capacity of
37,000 tractors of the wheeled type and employed 12,000
men when in full operation. When we were there a large
part of the plant was being shifted over for the production
of caterpillar tractors under a plan which called for the production of 15,000 annually. We all agreed that the shift to the
caterpillar type of tractor was really for the purpose of making
caterpillar tanks for the army.

The plant had been designed in consultation with the best
engineers of the United States, Britain, France, and Germany.
Under the Five-Year Plan the Soviet government had been
almost profligate in paying any amount of money to get the
best engineering, technical, and planning skill that any of
the western countries could offer. This plant had been built
in 1931. Approximately 60% of its machinery had been built
in the United States. We were advised that there were then
working at the plant some 9000 men and women, including
121 technicians of various nationalities. Adjacent to the tractor factory we saw an enormous housing project of modern,
clean-looking apartment buildings. They were to provide living quarters for the workers and their families. They were
typical of the new type of workers' apartments which I found
quite generally in other Russian communities. We visited
these apartments and inspected a crèche later—a baby nursery

where the babies of the women workers were left in the care of trained nurses while the mothers were working in the plants, taking time off to return to the hospital to nurse the babies as necessity—and the babies—required.

This tractor plant itself, as well as its equipment and the arrangement of the equipment, was the last word in factory plan and design. It was impressive. Just as in the Ford plant at River Rouge, machines were arranged in series so that the material processed itself through into the final product without crisscrossing or backtracking. The different processes were so arranged consecutively that there was a constant flow from raw material to the finished product, and the conveyor and belt system was used wherever possible. It was a line-assembly plan for production. In fact, they were running tractors through on this assembly line when we were there.

The plant seemed to be working efficiently. There didn't seem to be quite the same speed or high degree of activity that one would find in the usual automobile factory in this country. As a matter of fact, the Russian technicians publicly reported at that time that the productivity of Russian labor, while constantly getting better, had only reached 40 per cent of that of the American mechanic. I should say on the whole that it looked to me as though they were working upon that basis of efficiency. In performance the plant did not compare with its construction, planning, and facilities.

An economic institution connected with the factory was the so-called "scientific technical section" which was housed in one of the large handsome buildings of the plant. It provided lecture rooms, a special hall for motion pictures, individual study rooms, a technical library, and a room of technical exhibits. Its avowed purpose was to improve the technical knowledge and qualifications of the personnel of the plant and the building was designed for this specific purpose. The walls were covered with graphs and charts, currently kept up, indicating the manner in which factory management was keeping track of the various factors which made for efficiency and non-efficiency in production. The records were apparently up to date and covered a wide variety of data, including the productivity of man power for various departments and the number of Stakhanovites, or pieceworkers.

The library was particularly interesting as disclosing the earnestness and interest of these young Russian engineers and technicians. It was in charge of a pretty young woman who took great pride in showing, not only her collection of the best engineering technical textbooks and authorities upon tractors, but also her cataloguing system and card index. On the table of the library it was interesting to see technical trade journals and magazines published in different languages from practically all of the industrial countries of Europe and the United States. Classes were held nightly in the building.

The tractors themselves as they came off the line looked sturdy. They were not equipped with many gadgets, but looked as though they were designed for use and would stand up. In fact, I subsequently saw a great many of them on the collective farms in Russia where they seemed to have withstood hard usage.

The wage scale of this plant and, in fact, of all of these industrial plants, was interesting in view of the enormous amount of gold value that had been expended and was being expended by the Soviet government in industry. Its productivity for war purposes or other purposes is greatly enhanced by the low labor costs, for unlimited man power is one of Russia's greatest industrial resources. At this plant, for instance, the average monthly wage was 230 rubles a month, which, at the then current rate of official exchange, would be about $45, but which at the then existing bootleg rate in rubles was about $23 per month. The average wage for skilled workers was about twice as much. The highest wage for the Stakhanovite pieceworkers was about $80 per month, whereas the managers, up to and including the director, did not receive more than $2500 a year.

Near Kharkov is also located a turbine generator and an electric mechanical plant. It makes machinery for the Soviet's metallurgical, coal, iron-ore, and electrical-power industries. We spent hours going through it. It employs 38,000 men. Of the 2500 machine tools in the plant, we were told that about one half were of foreign make. It had an annual capacity of 30 turbines of 50,000 kilowatts each. Here, too, in connection with the small machine production, the conveyor-system belt line was employed according to the best technical practice of factory management. The largest traveling overhead crane in the factory had a capacity of 200 tons. We saw an enormous turbine in process of construction. It was designed for a capacity of 100,000 kilowatts. Of the 38,000 workers, 1200 were technical engineers. Their maximum pay was about $1200 a year. Among them, there were 1500 foreign specialists. Here, again, characteristic of the kind of men in charge of these enterprises, the management took great pride in showing us the details of their technical, engineering, and chemical laboratories, their cost-accounting systems in factory management, and the educational departments, classrooms, etc.

Here, again, however, there was the same indication of lack of real businesslike running of the plant, so far as the workers were concerned, which we found in the other plant when compared with the tempo of production in plants which I have seen in the United States. Nevertheless, the output and performance were impressive for a nation which had only recently adapted itself to a modern industrial system.

We boarded our train and went from Kharkov to Zaporozhe, which was quite a long trip. After dinner we again had our lecture upon what we would see the following day.

Zaporozhe is a city of 125,000 people in the heart of the great industrial region of the Don Basin and is a typical part of the gigantic plan covered by the Soviet government in industry. This region centers around the Dnieper Dam, midway between the great iron-ore and coal deposits of the Ukraine. Ever since the time of Catherine the Great, attempts have been made to make the Dnieper River navigable and to erect dams at this point. After many failures, finally our American Colonel Cooper was retained by the Soviet government to do this job. He did it successfully. This so-called Dnieper Dam or Cooper Dam was then the largest dam in the world, with the single exception of Boulder Dam. About this great central reservoir of electric power there was built, in the course of four or five years, enormous manufacturing plants of different kinds. Practically overnight the new city of Zaporozhe was constructed. It looked like what you would expect to find in a pioneer community created for the purpose of efficiency, housing, and service for an industrial community. The buildings were of the utilitarian dormitory type, of three or four stories, neat and well built. The streets were laid out in rectangular fashion like the average American prairie town. There were some attempts at beautification of the local park— the so-called Park of Culture and Rest. There were streetcar facilities and a rather handsome modernistic moving-picture house. The streets were clean.

We came here to study the relation between the dam and the industries which it served. What we wanted to see was the city itself, the Cooper Dam, the enormous steel plant which was in process of completion—partly in operation and about half completed—and the aluminum plant which was unique in Russia and one of the largest in the world. We motored across the enormous dam and spent several hours in the turbine rooms which were operated by Soviet engineers. They spoke in terms of great admiration and affection for Colonel Cooper. The building of the dam, said they, was started in 1927 and completed in 1932. It supplied a region of 80,000 square miles. The maximum distance for the transmission of power was 500 miles. They have auxiliary steam plants for winter use. Despite these auxiliary plants, the Cooper Dam does not begin to provide the power demanded for this region. Plans were then being made for the building of four more of these electric-generating power plants, two of which were then in process of construction. It is an interesting fact, in this connection, that the Soviet Union produces more electric power than all of the rest of Europe put together and is second only to the United States in volume of production. This plant has some 2000 substations in the agricultural districts from which it distributes power in a rural electrification program somewhat similar to our own TVA and REA programs.

The engineers in charge were fairly typical of their profession. They were strong, modest, well-balanced men, if I am any judge of character. Their whole outfit looked as clean and as well ordered as a battleship. I have not seen power plants in the United States, but I could conceive of nothing that gave the appearance of being more well kept or efficiently ordered and directed than this one.

Adjacent to the dam and across the river from the turbine plant is a huge aluminum plant built in 1931 and 1932. It was located here because of the availability of the large quantities of electric power which are required in the production of aluminum. It was originally designed for an annual capacity of 20,000 tons of pure aluminum, but its capacity has since been doubled. The total production of aluminum in the United States at that time was 45,000 tons, according to the director. The plant was designed by French engineers connected with the French Aluminum Company, and consumes about one half of all the electric power generated by the Cooper Dam. Bauxite, the principal raw material, is brought down from the Leningrad district and also from large deposits in the Ural Mountains. The aluminum produced was sold to various state industries for cables, aircraft, automobiles, etc. The demands of Soviet heavy industry could absorb all of the aluminum produced by the plant and more, according to the Director.

This Director impressed us all very much. He was a great big fellow. He looked like my old friend, Alec Legge, of the International Harvester Company, but was slightly broader and was a sort of combination of Alec Legge and my friend, William Knudsen. This man would be a big man in any community and in any situation. His plant gave every indication of being run by that type of executive. In reply to our inquiries, he told us that this plant was operated on a profit basis. The norm or quota was determined by the Central Commissariat. Any profit over and above that norm was a bonus to the plant and to the management. It was used for bonuses for individual records of efficiency and also for improving social facilities for the workers. Living quarters, he said, were provided at a rental of from 12 per cent to 15 per cent of the family wage and from three per cent to five per cent for bachelors living in dormitories. It was noticeable that the machines in the electric department were largely of German make.

The largest enterprise in this region is the steel plant designed to produce pig iron, steel wire, high-quality rolled products, ferroalloys, etc. When we were there, it was about one half completed but this half was in operation. We were told by the Director that the cost was estimated to be about a billion rubles ($200,000,000 at the official rate of exchange). When finally completed it was to have four blast furnaces, three steel shops, and three rolling mills.

The original plant contemplated the production of 1,970,000 tons of pig iron; 1,800,000 tons of open-hearth steel; and 1,800,000 tons of rolled sheet iron. In this locality an American company was at that time engaged in installing a continuous hot and cold strip-sheet rolling mill and finishing department. The American machinery furnished for this plant alone, so the Director said, cost $4,000,000. There were only two other comparable thin-sheet rolling mills in the world. These two were in the United States. When completed, the steel plant would employ 35,000 men.

From Zaporozhe we went on to Dnepropetrovsk which was some 250 miles to the east. Dnepropetrovsk was a lovely old-fashioned type of Ukrainian city. It had broad avenues, beautiful trees, and handsome old buildings and homes. The new buildings were typically modernistic and for the most part apartments and workers' dwellings. The principal factory which we were interested in seeing was a steel-tube manufacturing plant which employed 9000 men and was engaged in turning out pipes and tubing and other forms of finished steel products. A new special section had just been built for the manufacture of seamless pipes. This section had been in operation for only two years. It had a nut-and-bolt department, pipe-rolling department, and three open-hearth furnaces. Its open-hearth steel capacity was 440,000 tons. We went through the plant and in a general way found much the same conditions to exist as we had found in Kharkov.

Here again, the most interesting fact in connection with this plant was the Director himself. When we went to the main office to call upon him, we found a typically well-furnished and well-equipped head office, similar to that of any organization in the United States. When ushered into the room of the Director, a young man of about thirty-five years of age met me at the door and in perfect English said, "How do you do, Mr. Ambassador. I am very glad to welcome you here." He was a clean-cut, well-groomed man in a well-tailored suit who might be mistaken in New York for a lawyer or businessman. We followed our usual course of asking various questions of a technical character and upon matters affecting the plant, such as management, etc. He sat back of a glass-top desk and in a very quiet but keen way answered all the questions confidently. Most of the answers were at the tip of his tongue. Sometimes he referred to charts and tables of figures which he had under the glass top of his desk. What he didn't have there he had in a little notebook which he took out of his vest pocket. This was filled with finely written data apparently referring to facts connected with the plant and its management.

When he told us of the installation of the new department for the making of seamless pipes, I asked him whether he knew of the installation of the Smith Brothers plant in Milwaukee where labor costs have been enormously reduced by the use of electric machinery. He said that he had studied the plant in Milwaukee, as well as another plant of similar character in Ohio, and that this installation, with the advice of American engineers, embodied the best features of both. He added that he thought it was better than either. Before I left, I asked him whether he would excuse me if I asked him a few personal questions about himself. He said, "Of course!" It developed that he was born the son of a peasant some 25 miles from Dnepropetrovsk. He was one of a family of eleven children who had lived in a typical, primitive, floor-less hut of the sort commonly found in the agricultural districts of Russia. He had never worn shoes until he came to Dnepropetrovsk to go to school.

At the expense of the state, he finished his common-school education at Dnepropetrovsk and then attended the local university which had a mining, metallurgical, and technical faculty. He stated that it was a type of higher university or technical institution something like Carnegie Tech. His course was four and a half years. He graduated in the metallurgical section and obtained his diploma at the age of 23 years. I asked him how large the university was. He said it had 25,000 students at the present time. All students were given stipends by the state for clothing, living expenses, theater, etc. After finishing his course at the local university he spent some time in technical schools in Moscow and Leningrad and then he went to Germany, France, and the United States to finish off his technical education by familiarizing himself with methods of other countries. He spent seven months in the United States visiting Pittsburgh, Youngstown, Cleveland, Chicago, and Detroit in order to study American methods. He had returned to become one of the assistants in the management of the plant and at the age of thirty-five was now in charge of the entire organization.

AGRICULTURAL MACHINERY

From Dnepropetrovsk, we went on to Rostov-on-the-Don, on the northern shore of the Black Sea, where there was a very large plant for the manufacture of agriculture combines and farm machinery. It is not generally known, but it is the fact that the Soviet Union produces more agriculture machinery than any country in the world, even including the United States. They are our competitors—and serious competitors— all through the Near East and even in Asia. The agriculture-machinery plant is the largest of its kind in the U.S.S.R. It was located on the outskirts of the city, which, incidentally, has a population of 500,000. Before the Revolution, Rostov-on-the-Don was the headquarters of the Don Cossack military organization. Today it is one of the largest cities in the Don Basin area and not far from the region which contains the largest coal-mining industry in the country, as well as some of the largest steel and chemical industries. The district is also rich in anthracite and soft coal, some of which is of very high coking quality. At that time 30 per cent of the steel furnaces in the Soviet Union were located in this region, as well as twenty-one coke and chemical plants and five basic chemical plants. The farm-machinery plant covers 180 square hectares (about 446 acres). It manufactured caterpillar tractors, harvesters, harrows, plows, etc. Here, again, we found definite indications that pointed to the fact that the plant was being converted into war use. The foundry, the Director said, was "closed for repairs." When he said this, Demaree Bess winked at me. All Russia, including ourselves, was thinking and talking in terms of the war preparations in which the Soviets were so intensively engaged. The assembly-line, conveyor, and belt systems were used and seemed to be working very well. From the point of facilities, arrangement of machinery, and plant planning it was as good as anything I have seen. Here, again, it did not seem to be geared up to the rate of production that would be found in our own plants with which I am familiar. Nevertheless, it was going along. I got on the chassis at one end of the assembly line and in a very few minutes we were leaving the plant on our own gas, a complete unit.

In the mechanical section of the plant it was noticed that most of the machinery was of either American or German make. In the course of our tour, another interesting thing occurred. We were going through the woodworking shop where we found most of the machinery of American make.

We were introduced to the manager of this section which employed 1000 men. He was about 30 years of age. He said to me, "Mr. Ambassador, you come from Wisconsin, do you not?" This in perfect English. I said, "Yes, why?" His reply was, "I studied two years at the University of Wisconsin in Madison. What a great university it is and what a lovely city." He added that he had visited most of the large machinery-manufacturing plants of the United States after his technical education had been completed. Here, again, was an indication of the youth and quality of the junior executives of these organizations. When we left this plant, it was the consensus of my unofficial advisers, the newspaper contingent, that this plant was being converted into caterpillar construction for large tanks.

NO. 1318 *Moscow, June 1, 1938*

Dictated at Batum, May 22, 1938

TO THE HONORABLE THE SECRETARY OF STATE

THE PORT OF ODESSA AND INDICATIONS
OF SHIPMENTS TO SPAIN

Confidential

Sir:

Odessa, on the northwest coast of the Black Sea, is one of the largest of the Russian Black Sea ports.

Alongside the wharves there were six Spanish ships which were apparently interned, and another dozen in other Russian Black Sea ports. I was informed during my recent visit to Odessa that the members of the Spanish crews were allowed or paid 50 rubles a month each by the Soviet government, in addition to their food; but were required to employ their time in painting and otherwise keeping the vessels in condition. This was generally presumed to be done for the reason that it was expected that the Soviet government would ultimately retain the vessels in compensation for goods delivered. It was also stated that British and Greek bottoms were chartered by the Soviet government to transport merchandise to Spain from this port. I counted approximately 200 trucks of Soviet manufacture on the docks apparently destined for the Spanish government.

We arrived at Odessa on the morning of May 17. During the day we visited two rest homes and a large recreation project, which consisted of a type of park and bathing beach.

The old residences of the *bourgeoisie* and noblesse situated on the outskirts and overlooking the sea in the residential districts have been converted into sanatoriums and rest homes, which are characterized by a great deal of fresh paint both on the buildings and on the surrounding walls. The larger of these was a beautiful place of approximately 60 acres on the outskirts of the city of Odessa overlooking the Black Sea. It was formerly the home of the wealthiest banker in the community. It is now being used as a sanatorium for heart and nervous cases. It is presently occupied by the management and 220 patients. It was kept in a very spic-and-span condition, and gave indications of being well run.

I have the honor to be, Sir, respectfully yours,

Joseph E. Davies

NO. 1325   *Moscow, June 1, 1938*

Dictated at Batum, May 22, 1938

TO THE HONORABLE THE SECRETARY OF STATE

BREAD-BAKING FACTORY IN ODESSA

Sir:

On the occasion of my visit to the city of Odessa on May 17, I had the opportunity of inspecting one of the largest bread factories of the Soviet Union—the so-called Stalin bread factory.

The factory was exclusively devoted to baking a rather coarse type of brown bread. The factory building was quite large and rather impressive. It was painted white and yellow and both inside and out gave indications of orderliness and cleanliness. In the arrangement of the plant there was evidently quite a pretension of hygienic and sanitary precautions on the part of the management. Visitors are required to don white coats, and employees, it was said, must take shower baths before entering and upon coming out of the factory. The management also took considerable pride in its chemical laboratory, in which chemical tests of each batch of dough and bread were currently made. The machinery was part English and part Soviet. As is usually the case, there were several Soviet duplications of foreign machines. Here again the management was quite distinctive and marked by the youth of the engineering director and the earnestness and self-assurance which seems to be characteristic of the Soviet engineer.

The plant management procures its own raw materials by purchase. It reports to the central administration. It is operated on a basis of norms—the "plan" of the central administrations. It became entitled to a Director's fund as a premium and additional compensation for the workers, the management, and the plant, if the norms "of profit" were exceeded through the efforts of the plant management and workers. The profit incentive, here also, is resorted to as a stimulus for efficiency and effort.

I have the honor to be, Sir, respectfully yours,

Joseph E. Davies

NO. 1311   *Moscow, June 1, 1938*
                                  Dictated at Batum, May 22, 1938

TO THE HONORABLE THE SECRETARY OF STATE

PORT OF BATUM AND THE SOVIET BOTANICAL
GARDEN AND EXPERIMENTAL STATION; CITRUS
FRUITS, TUNG TREE

Sir:

Batum, the chief port of export of the U.S.S.R. for petroleum products, is located in the southeastern corner of the
Black Sea in the smallest republic of the Soviet Union—the
Adzhar Republic. It is in the subtropical region and has a
population of approximately 75,000 people. There is enclosed
herewith a memorandum setting forth certain basic facts regarding the port of Batum.

The two principal pipe lines of the Soviet Union extend
from Baku on the Caspian Sea to this port—a distance of 800
or 900 kilometers. Oil or oil products constitute from 53 per
cent to 90 per cent of the total exports of the port. Other
shipping is relatively negligible. Among other exports are
green tea, some timber, and miscellaneous products. The
cargo turnover of the port has increased threefold since 1913.

The city itself is clean and orderly. In this respect it compares most favorably with similar subtropical cities of the
Spanish-American continent. The principal streets are as-
phalted and practically all of the streets are paved. There are
many indications of an attempt at ornamentation with greens
and subtropical plants. The parks are quite pretentious and
give indications of a great deal of care. Within the past few
years, the city has become more or less of a health resort. I
am advised that there are now 15 sanatoriums or rest homes

scattered among the foothills of the mountains immediately adjacent to the city. The people appear to be better clothed and more prosperous generally than the population of Moscow, and their faces also seem happier.

In a valley, approximately 12 miles outside of the city, reached by a mountain road over a range of foothills, there lies the largest botanical garden of the Soviet Union. It was founded in 1912 and includes an area of approximately 100 hectares, or 247 acres. It stretches from the sea up the mountainsides. Along the crest of the foothills a drive through the garden affords a beautiful view of the mountains, the sea, and the city.

The Botanical Garden is also an agricultural experimental station. The staff of 120 employees includes, besides gardeners, laborers, and so forth, 21 so-called scientists. When we made a visit to this enterprise, we were met by the Director and a young woman who was introduced as the Chief Agronomist. She was a sturdy type and highly intelligent. She speaks several languages; and spoke English quite well.

The experimental station is conducting experiments in tea planting, citrus-fruit growing, cultivation of the quinine, ether, and rubber-bearing plants, the development of the tung tree, and in the various fields of plant physiology which this region would permit. It extends practical aid, advice, and assistance to the collective and state farms. The garden prides itself on the Japanese and Chinese plants which it has assembled in the Japanese garden, which is unusual and attractive. The agronomist stated that there were approximately 1300 different varieties of trees and plants in the entire Botanical Garden.

The enterprise gave indications of being very well administered. Again, the character of the directing personnel and the earnestness and the intelligence of the "scientists" in charge of the work were impressive.

I have the honor to be, Sir, respectfully yours,

Joseph E. Davies

NO. 1327   *Moscow, U.S.S.R., June 1, 1938*

Batum, May 22, 1938

TO THE HONORABLE THE SECRETARY OF STATE

INSPECTION OF OIL REFINERY AND GASOLINE-
CRACKING PLANT AT BATUM ON MAY 22, 1938,
AND GENERALIZATIONS WITH REFERENCE
TO THE SOVIET OIL INDUSTRY

Sir:

Batum, a city with population of 75,000, is the largest port of export for Soviet oil and oil products. The annual export of oil ranges from 53 per cent to 90 per cent of the total exports of this port. Within one mile of the harbor is located one of the largest oil-refining and gasoline-cracking plants in the Soviet Union. Of the four oil pipe lines in the Soviet Union, two lead into this plant and this harbor, carrying oil from Baku, the center of Soviet oil production. This Batum plant handles 2,000,000 tons a year which constitutes about 7 per cent of the total Soviet production of about 30,000,000 metric tons in 1937.

It was installed by an American firm in 1929. The machinery is of American make. The machines bear the name plates of Winkler-Koch, Jenkins, and Foster-Wheeler.

There is attached hereto a memorandum covering the stenographic report of the dictation given and discussions had on the occasion of our visit to this plant on May 22, 1938.

The net general impressions which I received were:

1. That extensive general geological explorations are being conducted for oil; that the prospecting has not been as

successful as was anticipated; and that there are, however, some new fields coming into production. It was stated that within past months a new oil well, with a production of 150 tons a day, has opened up an additional 20 hectares (approximately 60 acres) in the Baku oil field;

2. That while in certain quarters a great deal has been made of the fact that during the year 1937 there has been a substantial slipping in the production of Soviet industry on account of the dislocations caused by the "purge" and political conditions, the fact remains that the total oil output for the year 1937, while substantially less than the planned production, was nevertheless in excess of the 1936 production;

3. That the oil-refining plants are generally pretty good but relatively antiquated. It was in 1923 that Serebryakov, who was condemned to death in the Pyatakov trial, instituted a five-year plan to modernize and equip the Soviet oil industry. The plants are generally of that vintage, as I am informed. The Soviet technicians and experts themselves now complain that in technological equipment the oil industry is antiquated and that they are handicapped by the inadequate machinery. This fact accounts probably for the heavy imports from the Pacific Coast of the United States. They are not yet producing the high-quality gasoline required for airplanes; and

4. That the operation of this refinery and gasoline-cracking plant in Batum indicates a fair standard of efficiency. The premises were orderly and apparently well administered. The plant seemed to be well run. The administration was in the hands of young men—technical and scientific experts, educated in the Soviet universities—who had also practical experience and who appeared to be very earnest and hard working. From superficial appearances, I would judge that the tempo of this plant was about 50 per cent of what would appear in a similar plant in the United States.

Labor, living, and employee-profit conditions were much the same as reported in previous reports. They have their director's fund here also but in a somewhat modified form. The profit motive is of course again relied upon to stimulate individual effort. The standard of living of the workers appears higher than in any Soviet industry that I have inspected. The living quarters and apartment buildings were the best that I have seen in Russia.

This plant employs approximately 1000 workers. It produces gasoline for automobile consumption; also kerosene, ligroine, and coal oil products. Its entire product is shipped out by boat.

The harbor facilities, so far as the shipment of oil was concerned, were nothing extraordinary. Of the 13 berths provided in the docks for ships, five were designed for oil tankers. A visit to this section of the harbor, where a tanker was in process of being loaded, disclosed a network of pipe lines, valves, and so forth, which are adapted to the discharge of various oil products direct from the factory or from the pipe lines to the ship's hole. Neither in extent nor in character did the equipment seem to be particularly modern or unusual.

There were absolutely no indications of any plan for the extension of facilities for the export of oil. The reservoirs for supplies were also noticeably meager.

As a matter of fact one could predict with reasonable assurance that the Soviet Union will not export oil in substantial quantity for some time to come. This country can consume all of the oil it can produce for some time, unless its quantities are greatly extended. The production of automobiles and trucks is now only approximately 250,000 a year. With even that relatively small demand for gasoline, there is scarcity of supply. An extensive effort is being put forth to build new roads. The population is keenly interested in automobile transportation.

There is every prospect that the increase in demand will out-strip production for some time. In addition thereto are require-ments of heavy industry and mechanized agriculture which are already putting a strain on the oil industry. The govern-ment, moreover, is bending every effort to provide oil reserves for what they consider to be an inevitable war.

These factors indicate an enormous and growing demand within the Soviet Union itself, which for a long time will tax Soviet oil production.

Attached hereto also is an abstract, as made by Mr. Gordon at my request in anticipation of this trip, of the oil reports on file in this mission, including the Riga reports and the recent excellent dispatches on oil prepared by Mr. Chipman.

I have the honor to be, Sir, respectfully yours,

Joseph E. Davies

Batum, U.S.S.R., May 22, 1938

VISIT TO THE OIL REFINERY AND CRACKING PLANT

On the afternoon of May 22, 1938, the oil refinery and cracking plant which is not far from the port of Batum were inspected by the Ambassador and party, which included Mr. Spencer Williams of the American-Russian Chamber of Commerce and the writer. We were conducted to the office of the Director with whom the Ambassador had an interview and who supplied certain information in reply to the Ambas-sador's questions. A record of the interview follows:

AMBASSADOR: For your information, I wish to say that your government has extended to me as the American Ambassador the opportunity of visiting and inspecting a great many of your individual enterprises and I was desirous of seeing your refining and cracking plant here and the port facilities which you have here for the shipment of oil and oil products. With

your permission I would like to ask some questions. If they
are in any way embarrassing please do not answer them.

QUESTION: As I understand it, your supply of crude oil
comes into your plant through two pipe lines. Is this correct?

ANSWER: Yes, piped from Baku.

QUESTION: How much crude oil goes through the plant
here each year, in metric tons?

ANSWER: About 2,000,000 tons a year production.

QUESTION: You produce kerosene, gasoline, ligroine, or
all three here?

ANSWER: Yes, all three.

QUESTION: In what proportion?

ANSWER: More kerosene.

QUESTION: What is your percentage of recovery in making
gasoline?

ANSWER: 3.2 per cent from the crude oil; depends upon
quality of the oil; and an additional 9 per cent through
cracking.

QUESTION: What percentage is ligroine and what percentage kerosene and gasoline?

ANSWER: Gasoline 3, ligroine 4, and kerosene 28 per cent.
The residue after refining and cracking (about 65 per cent) is
mazut fuel oil.

QUESTION: What is the length and the diameter of these
pipe lines from Baku?

ANSWER: Can't say as to the length. The diameters are
8 and 10 inches.

QUESTION: How many employees have you in this plant?

ANSWER: 1000 persons including technical personnel.

QUESTION: Do you employ any women?

ANSWER: Yes, 150.

QUESTION: What percentage of the workers are Stakhanovites?

ANSWER: 85 per cent, including Udarniks.

QUESTION: What is the average monthly wage?

ANSWER: 530 rubles.

QUESTION: And the Stakhanovites' wage?

ANSWER: Depends upon qualifications, 700 to 800 rubles, although a few make 2000 rubles a month.

QUESTION: Do you happen to know how many refineries and cracking plants there are in the Soviet Union?

ANSWER: No.

QUESTION: How long ago was this plant built?

ANSWER: 1929.

QUESTION: By whom?

ANSWER: By an American firm.

QUESTION: Was this plant originally built by the Standard Oil technical experts employed by the Soviet Union?

ANSWER: Foster-Wheeler, and Winkler-Koch.

QUESTION: Were these apartment houses for the workers built at the same time?

ANSWER: Yes.

QUESTION: Do the workers receive anything in addition to their wage in money?

ANSWER: Yes, in the Soviet Union we have government insurance for the workers.

QUESTION: Do the workers here pay rent for living quarters?

ANSWER: Yes.

QUESTION: On what basis?

ANSWER: They pay not on the basis of wages but on the amount of space they occupy. The plant, however, pays 80 per cent of a worker's rent and the worker himself pays 20 per cent. They also receive such conveniences as heat, water, light, services, and repairs, as these are provided by the plant free of charge.

QUESTION: Does the factory provide a restaurant and food?

ANSWER: Yes.

QUESTION: What do the meals cost?

ANSWER: Breakfast and lunch, 75 kopecks each; dinner consisting of 2 courses (soup or borscht and various kinds of meat), 1.20 rubles.

QUESTION: Do you have a Director's fund?

ANSWER: Yes.

QUESTION: How do you get that fund?

ANSWER: The Director's fund usually comes out of the plant's profits over the planned norm.

QUESTION: How do you compute the profits and who decides what the planned allowance for costs should be?

ANSWER: We know how much the crude oil costs and we make our own calculations and set the norms and prices.

QUESTION: You get the crude oil at a certain price. Who determines that price? Is it a trust or some subdivision?

ANSWER: Azneft (the Soviet oil trust in Azerbaidzhan which controls oil production in the Transcaucasus), who supplies us with oil.

QUESTION: The trust decides the plan and norm for you?

ANSWER: The trust at Baku sets the norms for the plant and production, but we calculate the costs of production. They provide us with crude oil and set its cost to us.

QUESTION: How do you arrive at the profit for the Director's fund? Give us an example.

ANSWER: If the plant is producing well, that is the first thing. Then there is the cost of raw material and the cost of obsolescence to be taken into consideration. Any savings which we make through efficiency in use of materials or extra-efficiency in labor create the profit.

QUESTION: Do I understand, then, that whenever you do better than what the plan calls for, you have an additional profit out of which you receive a premium, which is the Director's fund?

ANSWER: Yes, the more we receive then for the Director's fund.

QUESTION: What is the Director's fund used for?

ANSWER: The main purpose is to improve the cultural and living conditions of the workers.

QUESTION: Does it also provide premiums to the heads of departments and workers according to their merits?

ANSWER: No; under our system here, that doesn't come from the Director's fund; that is a direct payment.

QUESTION: Do the directors, managers, and brigadiers receive premiums for doing better than the plan calls for as they do in other industries?

ANSWER: No; not from the Director's fund, but we have a special system for the payment of progressive-scale wages. Everyone works under this system except three persons—the Director, the Chief Engineer, and the Assistant Director.

QUESTION: Is what you have just described the so-called Stakhanovite system?

ANSWER: No, the Stakhanovite system is a separate movement based on overfulfillment of certain norms. There is both a Stakhanovite system and a premium system for production over the norms.

QUESTION: Do you have losses in transportation?

ANSWER: Yes.

QUESTION: Where do the greatest losses occur?

ANSWER: Chiefly in transportation by rail.

QUESTION: What proportion of your crude oil comes by rail and what proportion by pipe lines?

ANSWER: We receive only through pipe lines.

QUESTION: Where does the crude oil shipped by rail to Batum go to?

ANSWER: To the organization that does the selling. The oil you saw yesterday being transported by rail goes to another organization, Glavreft, of the People's Commissariat for Heavy Industry, which handles the export of oil through the port.

QUESTION: Do you export any petroleum products from this plant or is it used in the Soviet Union?

ANSWER: We deliver our product to Glavheftessyt (Soviet trust for the distribution of oil and petroleum products), which has an office here in Batum.

QUESTION: Where did you obtain your technical training?

ANSWER: I received my higher technical training at the Donskoi Polytechnical Institute at Novocherkassk.

QUESTION: How many students attended that institution then?

ANSWER: In 1929 there were about 7000 students.

QUESTION: How large a city is it?

ANSWER: It is not small; it was formerly capital of the Don Cossacks.

QUESTION: How many years did you spend in obtaining your technical training?

ANSWER: Five.

QUESTION: And before that?

ANSWER: Eleven years.

QUESTION: How old are you?

ANSWER: 37.

QUESTION: How long have you been Director here?

ANSWER: Two years.

QUESTION: Have you worked only in this plant?

ANSWER: Only here.

QUESTION: Have you brothers and sisters?

ANSWER: One brother.

QUESTION: Is he also a scientist?

ANSWER: He is a mining engineer.

QUESTION: What did your parents do?

ANSWER: My father was a railway conductor.

DIRECTOR: What can I show you about the plant?

AMBASSADOR: We would like to go through the plant and have you point out what you think is of interest.

QUESTION: What grade of gasoline is produced here?

ANSWER: For automobiles; no high-grade gas.

QUESTION: Do you also store gasoline here?

ANSWER: Yes.

QUESTION: Who built this gasoline-cracking plant?

ANSWER: An American firm, Foster & Wheeler. The machines are Winkler-Koch and Jenkins.

QUESTION: Was it satisfactory?

ANSWER: Yes.

We went through the pump house; saw 4 Jenkins pipe stills and the cracking department; also a large electric-power building with five chimneys. The plant produces its own power.

QUESTION: How many stills have you here all together?

ANSWER: 4 Winkler-Koch; 4 Jenkins; and 4 Foster-Wheeler.

QUESTION: Are there any American technical experts here?

ANSWER: No, they left in 1931 after six months here.

QUESTION: How do you ship your products?

ANSWER: The oil is pumped into storage tanks and from there direct by pipes onto the ships.

QUESTION: Do you produce high-test airplane gas here?

ANSWER: No.

QUESTION: Is it produced in the Soviet Union?

ANSWER: Yes.

QUESTION: Do you need a special kind of crude oil to produce aviation gasoline?

ANSWER: No; it depends on the type of equipment used; the production of high-test aviation gas requires a second cracking process.

DICTATED BY THE AMBASSADOR AT THE HARBOR: The harbor entrance is guarded by an armed sentry who required directions from the main office before we could get through the gate. A ship alongside is being loaded with oil. There is a network of pipe lines laid up to the side of the dock at the different berths for oil tankers, along the harbor sides. The oil is being pumped through an extension of the pipe direct into the tanker.

THE SOVIET ATLANTIC CITY

NO. 1328   *Moscow, June 1, 1938*

Sochi, May 24, 1938

TO THE HONORABLE THE SECRETARY OF STATE

REPORT ON SOCHI—"THE CAUCASIAN
RIVIERA"; SOVIET SANATORIUMS AND REST
HOMES; THE RED ARMY SANATORIUM

Sir:

One of the phases of Soviet government activity much stressed by the proponents of the system is the attention that is devoted by the government to the well-being and health of the workers, and the sanatoriums and rest homes that are also provided by it for the proletariat.

Sochi, on the eastern shore of the Black Sea, is much heralded and extensively publicized as the "Caucasian Riviera," that is devoted to the health and holiday happiness of the workers. During the tsarist regime, in 1901, the village of Gagri, about 70 kilometers distant from Sochi, was established as a bathing resort. The Soviet government, beginning in 1925, proceeded to develop Sochi as the center of their sanatorium-palaces and rest homes. It is here that Stalin has his summer rest home or *dacha*. I visited Sochi on May 24, 1938.

The character of this community is quite in keeping with, and indicative of, the rapidity with which the industrial and building program here has been projected in the last years. The city is practically new. It is located in the foothills of the snow-peaked Caucasian mountains which reach to the edge of the Black Sea. There is no natural harbor here. The city extends sheerly from the shore line of the Black Sea, and scatters itself up the hills.

The entire landscape is dotted with large, newly constructed white buildings of a pretentious character. All these are the rest homes and sanatoriums of either the government itself or of organizations of the trade unions connected with the various commissariats. The community abounds in new structures of modernistic character, all painted white or yellow and white. There is a very creditable hotel, a new, large, and handsome opera house, and a community of brand-new "stores" just being finished. The main street, extending from a park at one end to the "new" sulphur baths, is in fact a very handsome and impressive four-lane cement boulevard running along the sea for a distance of eight miles. There are boulevard lampposts with white "soap-bubble" lamps, and exceptionally good-looking covered waiting stands which serve bus patrons and give character to the highway. Wherever the surface of the mountain had to be cut to preserve the grade, the sides were handsomely faced with rock walls. One obtains, somehow, the very definite impression that there is a very obvious attempt here to create a show place that would be illustrative of the great achievement of the Soviet Union, in making the populace "happy and bright." The shopwindows along the boulevard are attractive and the interiors, as well, are quite pretentiously laid out. On the shelves there are a substantial amount of consumers' goods of all kinds that would attract the holiday tourist. They are the best shops I have seen in the Soviet Union. They are by no means typical, but they are very significant of what they are aiming at, of measurably what they can do, and potentially of what the future may develop if the present regime manages to sustain itself in power.

Practically every residential dwelling in the community is either a rest home or sanatorium. It is claimed that there are 70,000 patients and holiday-makers in this community during the "season," which extends from May 25 until October 15. All of these new sanatoriums are handsome. They are built usually by the trade unions of the various government agencies which seem to vie with one another in creating these institutions. Two of them are particularly impressive: the Central Sanatorium of the Red Army and the Sanatorium of the People's Commissariat for Heavy Industry.

Attached hereto is a memorandum containing stenographic notes taken and dictated on the occasion of a visit to the Red Army Sanatorium on May 24, 1938.*

The domain upon which this sanatorium is built extends from the edge of the Black Sea up the hillside a distance of approximately 2100 feet to a height of approximately 250 feet. A funicular or inclined railway leads from the bathing-beach pavilion to the principal buildings which are located on the topmost terrace. Midway up the hillside the boulevard heretofore mentioned traverses the terraced part of this beautiful estate, with the inclined railway running beneath it. On the top terrace of this series of terraces, all of which are laid out in rose gardens and formally landscaped, is the main

---

* Not included for reasons of space.

building. It is in the shape of a horseshoe. In the center of the horseshoe is the top terraced patio. The main building and wings are approximately four stories in height. The whole building is characterized by an appearance of sanitary whiteness, and a profusion of windows with verandas and porticos for each room on each floor.

Both from the outside and the inside one obtains the impression of an efficient, comfortable, sanitary, well-organized, and remarkable institution. The details of my impressions are to be found in the attached memorandum mentioned above.

The cost of this institution was stated to be 20,000,000 rubles ($4,000,000 at the official rate of the ruble). On an actual gold-value basis for the ruble this would probably range from $600,000 to $2,000,000 depending upon whether the value of the ruble is computed at the prevailing rate of the "black ruble" of the past year or at the most conservative estimate of the real gold value of the ruble. In my opinion it would be difficult to produce this plant in the United States short of $800,000 to $1,000,000, exclusive of the cost of the land.

The entire cost of erection, maintenance, and operation is borne by the Red Army. It is both a sanatorium and rest home and place of recuperation for the army officers and their families. It has a capacity for the taking care of 6000 persons each season; 500 patients at one time. Admission is determined by a medical commission in each subdivision of the army. A medical clinic is provided. Sulphur baths are also available. Facilities for bathing and all kinds of sports, including tennis, volley ball, and so forth, are provided.

The number of employees connected with the institution is 500, including domestic staff and so forth.

The management and administration appear to be first-class and typical of the relative cleanliness and efficiency of the Red Army.

This situation illustrates the departure of the Soviet government from the communistic principle. This sanatorium can accommodate but a very small percentage of the Red Army officers and their families. To be permitted to enjoy this beautiful place is a very special "privilege." It can attach only to a very small "class." It provides for a "class" exclusively. The members of even that class who can come and enjoy this beautiful institution are determined by a small group of medical officers all of whom must be amenable to those elements of power and influence which always have been projected by those who are the most powerful in that particular class. Of course, it must be said, however, that the ideal that is behind even a profession of caring for the health and well-being of the proletariat must command respect.

I have the honor to be, Sir, respectfully yours,

Joseph E. Davies

MOUNTAINS OF CEMENT ROCK

NO. 1330   *Moscow, June 1, 1938*
                          Dictated at Novorossiisk, May 26, 1938

TO THE HONORABLE THE SECRETARY OF STATE

CEMENT INDUSTRY OF NOVOROSSIISK;
SHIPPING FACILITIES FOR EXPORT OF
CEMENT IN LARGEST PORT OF SHIPMENT
OF CEMENT

Confidential

Sir:

The cement industry is of vital importance to the Soviet Union. While, during the first and second Five-Year Plans, the production of cement increased in striking manner (25% greater in 1937 than 1935), the needs of the Soviet Union for cement have been even greater. For this reason, in part at least, the exports of cement from the country have decreased and the imports have increased. Everywhere, during my stay here, however, the evidence of construction and building impressed me as being extraordinary. In connection with the present regime, the extent of government building and construction is one of the chief outstanding economic facts in this situation. Enormous amounts of cement are required for the construction of hydroelectric-power and industrial plants, for buildings, for highways and also recently, it has been stated, for the construction of reinforced concrete fortifications along the frontiers. Of the 41 districts into which the country is divided, cement is produced in only 12 of them. The productive area is confined practically to the southern part of the Union of Soviet Socialist Republics in the territory adjacent to this port. According to the Moscow authorities 30 per cent of the total cement output of the Union of Soviet Socialist Republics is actually manufactured in Novorossiisk.

Novorossiisk, with a population of 110,000, is located on the eastern coast of the Black Sea. It has an excellent natural harbor which is supplemented by a breakwater.* There are four large cement plants located immediately upon the harbor front. A mountain of raw-material supply lies immediately back of these plants. The rock is being quarried and hauled down to the water's edge for a distance of not exceeding 2¾ kilometers at any point.

On May 26, 1938, I visited the largest of these plants. Attached hereto is a stenographic transcript of the dictation

---

* This is the harbor to which the Soviet Black Sea Fleet will probably make its base, if Sevastopol should fall.

given and discussions with the Director and engineer upon
the occasion of that visit.*

This particular plant was built about 50 years ago by French
concessionaires. Since the Revolution, it has been supplemented by modern foreign machinery and some of Soviet
make. The raw material is quarried by mechanical excavators
and transported to the plant in narrow-gauge railway truck
buckets which are hauled in by cables which lead from the
quarry to loading; generally speaking it is handled mechani-
cally. The finished product is discharged into the holds of the
ships on the docks adjacent to the plant by means of overhead
mechanical conveyor systems and mechanized barrel loaders
on the dock itself. The plant appears to be well planned and
well equipped and organized; and to be an efficient unit.

The average wage of the workers was from 300 to 320 rubles
a month; Stakhanovite wages were as high as 900 rubles per
month. The plant also operates under the prevailing profit
system which obtains in other plants visited and as reported
in previous dispatches.

Provision for the housing and feeding of the workers are
similar to those described in previous dispatches.

My general conclusions were: that the plant was a good
one; that, by and large, it was producing a substantial amount
of cement; that in efficiency of operation, however, it would
not compare favorably with operations of plants in the United
States. Due to the extent of mechanization, however, the volume of output would not be so seriously affected by labor
inefficiency as it would be in some industries; that there is
an enormous supply of raw material available in the Union of
Soviet Socialist Republics and that there is distinct oppor-

* Omitted because of space limitation.

tunity for the introduction of American machinery to the advantage of both parties.

Attached hereto is a memorandum prepared at my request by the Economic Division of the Embassy staff with reference to the port of Novorossiisk and available published data upon the cement industry and port facilities of the harbor.*

Confidential

There were some indications from things that were dropped in the course of discussions with the Director and chief engineer that led to the opinion that the plant, along with Soviet industry, had been suffering from the purges and political shakeups of the last year.

The character of the management of this plant struck my mind as being significant of the conditions which have recently obtained in industry because of the purge and the general political activities of the N.K.V.D. (People's Commissariat for Internal Affairs), or the secret police. The Director, for instance, had only been connected with this plant for two months; the engineer for only seven months. The Assistant Director, however, had been with the plant since 1921. The engineer was of the type of scientific man, pure and simple. He apparently knew his job and looked like the kind that would not be interested in politics. The Director, on the other hand, was quite a different type. He impressed me distinctly as having a political psychology. He was shrewd, keen, well balanced, and always more concerned with anticipating the effect of the answer of my question upon the good repute of Soviet industry than with anything else. He was the first Director on this trip who directly refused to answer a question. He did it, however, adroitly. In all probability he was the

---

* Omitted because of space limitation.

representative of the party recently installed in the plant to oversee the work of the technical and practical workers.

I have the honor to be, Sir, respectfully yours,

Joseph E. Davies

THE TSARS' WINERY

NO. 1332   *Moscow, June 1, 1938*

Yalta, May 29, 1938

TO THE HONORABLE THE SECRETARY OF STATE

REPORT ON THE WINE INDUSTRY AT
YALTA; COLLECTIVIZATION METHODS
APPLIED TO VINEYARDS

Sir:

On the very beautiful southern coast of the Crimea at Yalta, the former tsars and noblesse of the old regime built up a very beautiful community. All of these beautiful old palaces and villas built by them have now been converted into institutions by the trade unions of the various commissariats of the Soviet government. The region is now one of the chief centers for Soviet rest homes and sanatoriums.

The palaces of Alexander III and Nicholas II were built on a beautiful estate called "Livadia." It is located on the coast about five or six miles from the harbor of Yalta. Included in this domain were the tsars' vineyards, approximately 7000 hectares, or 16,000 or 17,000 acres, in extent, and located in one of the most famous wine-growing districts of Russia.

These old vineyards are now being operated as state farms. The handsome old Massandra winery, finished in 1897 and commemorating the "happy reign of Nicholas II" (as appears on the bronze plaque imbedded in the wall of the building), is now under the administration of and operated by the Soviet government under the direction of a Soviet "scientist," a graduate of the Agronomic and Grape Institute of Crimea, 34 years of age, who had ten years' experience in administering these grape-growing state farms before he assumed his present duties. Attached hereto is a stenographic report of the dictation given and discussions which took place on the occasion of a visit to this plant on May 29, 1938.

The winery, situated in the foothills of the region, is located about 12 miles from the harbor of Yalta. It is a very handsome and substantial building. Fifty people, of whom 15 are women and 80 per cent of whom are Stakhanovites or brigadiers, are employed in the winery. The average wage is from 300 to 350 rubles a month and the Stakhanovite's wage ranges from 400 to 600 rubles a month. Practically all kinds of wines in fifteen varieties are being produced at this winery. The Director stated that the muscat grape in this particular region is famous the world over and that the muscat wine produced at this vineyard is still very widely known.

In one of the caves there was stored a wide assortment of old wines, some dating back to 1775. These old wines, together with an assorted collection of modern European wines, were kept intact for purposes of scientific experimentation and study in connection with their present processes. There was considerable pretension of scientific chemical testing of the various wines produced in order to procure the best possible product. In answer to a direct question as to whether they were now trying to make a synthetic wine the answer was very vigorously in the negative.

The Director stated that both state and collective vineyards there were provided with tractor stations for mechanized agriculture. He stated that these tractor stations eliminated a great deal of hand labor and made for efficiency over the old methods but that mechanization could be applied only in tilling the ground and cultivating the soil and eliminating weeds; that the grapes were still picked and harvested by hand.

Here again I was much impressed by the type which the Director represented. He had spent ten years up on a collective farm and four years in an agricultural institute. He is now Director of the entire Crimean Grape Trust. (The trust is the business organization that handles the government operation of various industries.) He was a strong-looking, fine type of physical manhood with a fine face and well-balanced head. He gave the impression of a great deal of reserve strength, modesty, earnestness, and balance. He was typical of the kind and type of young men that I have found generally in charge of the industries which I have inspected.*

I have the honor to be, Sir, respectfully yours,

Joseph E. Davies

Yalta, U.S.S.R., May 29, 1938

INSPECTION OF THE MASSANDRA WINERY AT YALTA

This afternoon the Ambassador and party proceeded to Massandra, a winery of the People's Commissariat of Food Industry of the U.S.S.R. in Yalta.

The Director, Mr. Sobolev, conducted us on a tour of the establishment.

---

* After inspecting the plant and the wine "caves," the Director invited us all into the "winetasters'" room, where an excellent luncheon was served with many different varieties of wine. Actuated by both pride in Soviet achievement and by Soviet hospitality, our hosts insisted that we should taste and enjoy each of these wines. We did enjoy them and did taste them too, at least partially; and at least to a degree which caused some of the party to insist upon performing acrobatic tight-rope-walking stunts on the wine casks of the courtyard. Some of the rest of us became like Sandy McNab's Scotsman:

"After we dined we wined.
After we wined every mon wanted
to make a speech."

AMBASSADOR DICTATES: Upon arrival we were met by the Director, Mr. Sobolev, and the Assistant Director, who conducted us on a tour of the establishment. We entered a very handsome old building, construction of which was begun in 1894 and finished in 1897. Imbedded in a wall of the entry was a bronze plaque giving the date of the erection of this plant during the "happy reign of Nicholas II."

QUESTION: How many of these corridors such as we are now in do you have in this winery?

ANSWER: Seven tunnels each 150 meters long.

AMBASSADOR DICTATES: In each tunnel there is room on either side for rows of hogsheads which are piled three high. The corridors appear to be about 12 feet high. The hogsheads are about 32 inches in diameter.

DIRECTOR: The wine in these barrels is 1937 wine.

QUESTION: Of what year is the oldest bottle of wine which you have here?

ANSWER: 1775.

AMBASSADOR DICTATES: There is a small narrow-gauge track in the various caves or corridors apparently used for hauling of these large barrels.

QUESTION: How many barrels are there in each of these corridors?

ANSWER: 800 barrels in each tunnel.

QUESTION: How much wine does each barrel contain?

ANSWER: 50 decaliters.

QUESTION: What is this bulletin board I see posted here?

ANSWER: Each tunnel has a different board.

AMBASSADOR DICTATES: In one column the wines are numbered from 35 to 89. In the next column is the number of barrels, and in the next is the total literage in the barrels.

QUESTION: Where do you get your grapes?

ANSWER: From seven state farms.

QUESTION: Are they the old farms of the Tsar?

ANSWER: Yes.

AMBASSADOR DICTATES: In one of the corridors or tunnels through which we were passing there were four immense hogsheads about ten feet in diameter.

QUESTION: What are these used for?

ANSWER: To mix the wine.

QUESTION: Do you empty the wine after it is mixed from these big hogsheads into the small barrels?

ANSWER: Yes.

QUESTION: How many different kinds of wine do you blend here?

ANSWER: Very many; as many as 35.

QUESTION: How many hectares of vineyards do you have in the seven state farms?

ANSWER: Up to 7000 hectares.

QUESTION: The grapes are cultivated by hand?

ANSWER: Everything is mechanized and the work is done by the tractors.

QUESTION: Do you have tractor stations, as do certain collective farms?

ANSWER: In the state farms they have their own tractor stations.

QUESTION: Does that result in the elimination of a great deal of hand labor?

ANSWER: Yes, very much.

QUESTION: How does it compare with the mechanization of wheat growing? Can you use mechanized tractor stations to the same advantage in growing grapes as in growing wheat, for example?

ANSWER: No; harvesting the grapes is done by hand as the grapes are picked, but in the cultivation of the ground and elimination of weeds we have mechanized agriculture and that saves labor.

QUESTION: What are the various processes which you have in this factory? Can you show us where the grapes come in and how they go through the plant?

ANSWER: In this particular wine cellar we don't crush the wine; it comes here in barrels. We blend and bottle it.

QUESTION: I notice here an inclined traveling crane. What is this used for?

ANSWER: We have a machine that washes the bottles. This is a conveyor of Soviet make, but the bottle washer is of foreign manufacture.

QUESTION: What is this small machine here?

ANSWER: This is the machine which corks the bottles after they have been washed and brought down here.

QUESTION: Where do you bottle it?

ANSWER: Bottling is not mechanized. It is done by hand.

QUESTION: We see here two small machines. What are these machines for?

ANSWER: We have five such machines to cork the bottles.

QUESTION: Each machine requires one person to operate it?

ANSWER: Yes.

QUESTION: And this machine is supplied by hand by the person who operates it?

ANSWER: Yes.

QUESTION: The operator takes the bottles out of the cases?

ANSWER: Each woman operator has a case near the machine. As soon as the bottles are full they are corked.

QUESTION: How many persons are employed in this plant?

ANSWER: Fifty.

QUESTION: How many women and how many men?

ANSWER: 15 women and 35 men.

QUESTION: How many Stakhanovites and brigadiers?

ANSWER: Forty Stakhanovites.

QUESTION: What is the monthly wage of the Stakhanovite?

ANSWER: From 400 to 600 rubles.

QUESTION: What is the average wage of those not Stakhanovites?

ANSWER: About 300 to 350 rubles.

QUESTION: Is this under the administration of the Food Commissariat—Mikoyan?

ANSWER: Yes; Ilinsky, not Mikoyan.

DIRECTOR: We have overfulfilled the plan.

QUESTION: How long do you age the wine; how long is it fermented in the wood? [See explanation below.]

QUESTION: What kinds of wine do you make here?

ANSWER: 15 or 20.

QUESTION: What is this machine?

ANSWER: It is a French filter to filter the wine.

AMBASSADOR DICTATES: The Director then took us down into the subterranean cave. It was a corridor about 40 or 50 feet high and 20 feet wide, and on either side it is noted that there are cement receptacles about 4 feet deep, 4 feet high, and about 6 feet wide. The receptacles are supported by cement or stone 6 or 12 inches thick. On the bottom, midway between the floor and the ceiling, is a walkway about 2 feet wide that goes the full length of the cave and is guarded by a railing. The center of the corridor is apparently used for large hogsheads of wine piled one upon another 4 casks high.

QUESTION: Is this old or new wine in this tunnel which we are now in?

ANSWER: This wine has been kept here for from three to seven years.

QUESTION: Do you have similar tunnels under each of the corridors? How many are there?

ANSWER: Yes; also seven.

AMBASSADOR DICTATES: We are now in another cave which has two instead of four receptacles on either side and in the center. Each of these different sections has various wines of different ages that range from 1775 to the present time.

QUESTION: What are the best wines of the sauterne type that you have here?

ANSWER: White muscatel; Livadia.

QUESTION: How old?

ANSWER: 1897, 1910.

QUESTION: Which is the best year?

ANSWER: I think 1910.

QUESTION: Do you sell this now?

ANSWER: No; this is a special collection of wines.

QUESTION: What do you keep it for?

ANSWER: For purposes of scientific research work. We open up a bottle to see what has happened to the wine and apply the principles.

QUESTION: How many different types here?

ANSWER: More than 100.

QUESTION: What is the oldest?

ANSWER: 1775.

AMBASSADOR DICTATES: The Director showed us an old bottle; it had a label in red with the inscription "Vino de Jerez Imperial," date 1775. It is a Spanish wine with the Spanish coat of arms.

QUESTION: Is this wine still good or is it corked? In other words, will it keep that long?

ANSWER: We have not tried it or tested it yet.

AMBASSADOR: Let's see the oldest Russian wine.

AMBASSADOR DICTATES: The Director showed us also a square bottle containing wine put up in 1888. The bottle is ornamented with the crown and the coat of arms cut in on each side; a large rose cut in or blown in the glass on one side, commemorating the coronation of Nicholas II.

QUESTION: What kind of wine is it?

ANSWER: Pinogri wine.

QUESTION: What kind of wine is in this strangely shaped 1895 bottle?

ANSWER: Port wine.

AMBASSADOR DICTATES: It is noted that in one of these receptacles there are many different types of Spanish wine of recent manufacture. It was explained to us that they were obtained for analysis and scientific study in connection with the production of their own wines. Here also is a Massandra wine of 1841.

QUESTION: What are these different quaint bottles that look like Benedictine bottles?

ANSWER: "Seventh Sky." Gallitzin coat of arms on the bottles.

AMBASSADOR DICTATES: In this tunnel all the wines are new; Soviet-made.

QUESTION: How many varieties?

ANSWER: Fifteen sorts.

QUESTION: And from what year to what year?

ANSWER: From 1931 on.

AMBASSADOR CONTINUES DICTATING: The bottles for new wine were in some instances quite ornate; designs either cut in or blown into the bottle, I see here some test tubes on a rack bearing numbers at the bottom.

QUESTION: What is this for and what is in these tubes?

ANSWER: Before the bottles are corked a sample of wine is put into the tubes. This is part of the process before corking and labeling the bottles.

QUESTION: Do you have a wine-crushing plant here?
ANSWER: No. It is on the state farms.
QUESTION: How far are the state farms?
ANSWER: They are from 6 to 150 kilometers away.
The party then returned upstairs to the ground floor.
QUESTION: What room is this that we are now in?
ANSWER: The winetasters in charge of the various vineyards come here and taste the wine. This is their meeting room.
QUESTION: Are any of the Directors of the state farms here that I might talk to?
ANSWER: No; they are in their various districts.
QUESTION: About how many people are employed on these seven state farms?
ANSWER: 7000.
QUESTION: And about what percentage would be Stakhanovites?
ANSWER: About 32 per cent.
QUESTION: Do you know the average wage of those Stakhanovites?
ANSWER: 500 rubles a month up, on the state farms; a tractor Stakhanovite makes 1000 rubles.
QUESTION: And those who are not Stakhanovites?
ANSWER: 250 to 350; it is piecework.
QUESTION: About how many months a year are they employed?
ANSWER: The year round.
QUESTION: Do the state farms provide them with houses in which to live?
ANSWER: We receive credits from the government every year to build.
QUESTION: Is that out of the Director's fund?

ANSWER: 50 per cent comes from the Director's fund and 50 from the People's Commissariat for Food Industry.

QUESTION: And the workers pay rent for their apartments according to the space occupied?

ANSWER: They pay 35 kopecks a square meter from their own wages.

QUESTION: Do they have a central restaurant for this place here?

ANSWER: Yes. In every state farm they also have a kitchen, nursery, clubs, and so forth.

QUESTION: About what is the price of the principal meal of the day on the state farm?

ANSWER: Dinner varies from 1.20 to 4 or 5 rubles. Special orders cost more than the standard meals.

QUESTION: What is the price of the standard meal; the principal meal of the day?

ANSWER: 1.5 rubles.

QUESTION: How many courses?

ANSWER: Two.

QUESTION: And for breakfast and supper?

ANSWER: 45 kopecks for breakfast; 65 for supper.

DIRECTOR: In tasting these wines, we shall start with white and red; and then taste the sweet wines; followed by dessert wines.

QUESTION (Laughingly): After we taste all of these wines here, where do we go?

ANSWER: Rest.

QUESTION: Is the Director a scientist?

ANSWER: I finished at a special Agronomic Institute. I managed a state farm for ten years and after that went to the State Institute in the Crimea for the study of agriculture and grape culture—Nikitsky gardens—for four years.

QUESTION: Just studying the production of wines?

ANSWER: Studying tobacco, wine, and so forth.

QUESTION: And after that?

ANSWER: I am now the Director of the entire Crimean trust.

QUESTION: How old are you?

ANSWER: 34.

DIRECTOR: What kinds of wines would you like to taste? This wine (cabernet) is light and dry; something like a Burgundy. It is a red wine and very good for the stomach. There is a city in France called Cabernet.

QUESTION: After pressing it is put into casks and brought here?

ANSWER: The wine is filtered at the crushing plant and then sent here.

QUESTION: They don't hold the wine there?

ANSWER: Not for more than six months; one fermentation takes place there.

QUESTION: When it comes here do they change it into other casks?

ANSWER: It is tested right here; if necessary it is filtered and then bottled.

QUESTION: In the same casks?

ANSWER: It is refilled here.

QUESTION: And then how long does it set?

ANSWER: 3 to 7 years.

QUESTION: Do you do anything with it in that time?

ANSWER: We do refilling; put the wine through technological processes; a kind of gelatine and glucose treatment.

QUESTION: What does that do to it?

ANSWER: A chemical action occurs causing cloudy reaction, it settles and is poured off; this is the clearing process.

QUESTION: During that 3 to 7 years how many times do they pour it off?

ANSWER: 15 or 16 times in the 7 years.

QUESTION: Each time it gets less, evaporates, and you put in more wine?

ANSWER: No; we only refill once. If necessary, depending on the quality of the wine, we do it twice.

QUESTION: What occurs that makes you know it is time to fill it? The port and muscatel sets 4 or 5 years; it is tested, put into the bottles, and not touched until it is used?

ANSWER: When it is corked it sets for six months; then we pull the cork and refill after removing the sediment. After decantation it is put into the bottles and then sets.

QUESTION: After it has been put through the final process how long does it set before being put on the market; do you age it further or is it ready immediately?

ANSWER: Aged about one month then and we send it out. We have plants in Moscow, Leningrad, Kiev, and elsewhere where the wine is bottled.

(We all tasted Soviet Madeira No. 83, 1932.)

QUESTION: Is the quality of the wine the result of the quality in the grape or the region?

ANSWER: Muscat wine made from muscat grapes in a particular section near here is the best muscat wine in the world, and it is due to the character of the soil, climate, and climatic conditions.

AMBASSADOR: Please tell the Director and his associates here that we are very much obliged to them for their courtesy and that we appreciate all the trouble which they have taken to make our visit interesting.

DIRECTOR: Do you still have the dry law in America?

AMBASSADOR: No, the Federal dry law has been repealed.

DIRECTOR: The Communist Party and our government are fighting in order to achieve the highest quality of wine.

AMBASSADOR: Commissar Mikoyan, the head of your Food Commissariat, told me at some length what you were doing a year ago and I was very glad to have the opportunity of seeing your plant here.

(We also had port wine No. 80.)

QUESTION: We were told by Mikoyan that you did not age your wines; that you did it synthetically. Do you do that here as well?

ANSWER: No (emphatically), only natural; no synthetic processes here.

AMBASSADOR: Do you export these wines?

ANSWER: Two years ago we exported much wine but now we don't.

DIRECTOR: Nicholas, the former Tsar, tasted wine here and pretty soon we couldn't find him; he was lying behind a barrel!

QUESTION: Where are these queer-shaped glasses made?

ANSWER: Constantinovsky Factory.

DIRECTOR: In the whole world there are 15,000 different kinds of wine.

(The Ambassador purchased a few bottles of four kinds of wine, as follows:

1. Cabernet
2. Port No. 80
3. Madeira, No. 83
4. No. 85 white muscatel [Livadia].)

QUESTION: Where does the muscat grape grow in this country?

ANSWER: Only in the Crimea; Alushta, in the Yalta District. The Director offered a toast to the friendship between the people of the United States of America and the people of the Soviet Union, and also to Ambassador and Mrs. Davies.

The Ambassador returned a toast about as follows:

To the great people of Russia. The people of the United States and the people of Russia have been friends for 200 years. Russia refused to aid England against the United States in 1776; during the American Civil War, Russia refused to aid the rebellion; President Wilson insisted upon Russia's right to self-determination after the Great War; the Red Cross of the United States came to the relief of Russia during the famine. Our peoples have had a traditional friendship for more than 150 years. Here's a toast to the great things which the Russian people have been doing, and to all those good things that Stalin has done, and to a continuance of such good work in the future.

RECREATION CAMPS FOR SOVIET YOUTH

NO. 1333 *Moscow, June 1, 1938*
Yalta, May 29, 1938

TO THE HONORABLE THE SECRETARY OF STATE

VISIT TO THE PIONEER CAMP ARTEK AT GURZUF, NEAR YALTA

Sir:

An institution which will have an important bearing on future life in Russia are the organizations of youth which the Soviet government projects and fosters. It is analagous to the Boy or Girl Scout movement in the United States. The organizations are practically, I am advised, training camps for the Communist Party. The "Octobrist" organization is the first step in the training of Soviet youth, covering children from the ages of 6 to 10. The "Pioneer" organization, covering the ages from 10 to 15 or 16, prepares the children for membership in the Komsomol (Communist Youth), from which the young men and young women are recruited to fill the ranks of the Communist Party.*

In all of the larger cities there are so-called Pioneer Houses. On the occasion of an inspection trip to Kharkov last year I visited the Pioneer House there (one of the most widely publicized in the country) and my dispatch No. 116 of March 12, 1937, covers a description of the activities I found there.

Throughout the Soviet Union, I am advised, there are sustained Pioneer camps, similar to the summer camps for the youth in the United States. The most important and pretentious of these camps is located at Gurzuf, near Yalta under the shadow of Bear Mountain on the Crimean coast which thrusts itself into the Black Sea.

On May 29 I took occasion to visit this camp. It is located on an extensive domain, approximately 800 hectares in extent (1900 acres), on a very beautiful portion of this rocky coast. The camp has four divisions; two are situated in the hills and two on the beach. All have their own head "doctor," but nevertheless under the administration of a central Director. The camps immediately adjacent to the shore have been recently constructed. They are clean, attractive, well laid out, and prepossessing. The two hillside camps center about two beautiful villas of the *bourgeoisie* of the old regime, located in what is really a large park, beautifully landscaped. All of the camps have facilities for sports, outdoor games, and beach bathing. One of them has a stadium which would seat approximately 2500 people.

The four camps accommodate approximately 900 children

---

* One of the most significant facts connected with totalitarians which I noted in Europe is the manner in which, and the degree to which, they give attention to the youth. "As the twig is bent, so grows the tree."

between the ages of 10 and 15 of both sexes. They come from all sections of the Soviet Union and stay for a period of 40 days. The camp is open the year round; but the principal season is between May 15 and October 15. The privileges of the camp are accorded to children who established themselves, in scholarship competition, as leaders in their respective communities. The children have a uniform similar to our Boy and Girl Scout costumes, with sailor collars and red scarves about the neck, which are drawn through a metal ring bearing the Pioneer motto "Be prepared."

At each of the camps the children, with much spirit and for our entertainment, put on an exhibition either of volley ball, or of singing, dancing, or recitations.

This group of children was the final result of a selective process that culled out the keenest, brightest, and most intelligent and sensitive of the school children in the Soviet Union. Both in appearance and conduct the children, as a whole and individually, reflected that fact. They were exceptionally fine-looking, well co-ordinated physically, with generally handsome features, of a sensitive character, and with well-balanced heads. They looked well and healthy. While predominantly Russian, they were of all types—White Russians, Mongolians, Armenians, Jews, and so forth. They were eager, enthusiastic, most friendly and kindly to the "Amerikanskis." As illustrative of the quality of their mentality, one of the children, aged 10, asked where we came from and, when being told "From the United States," immediately rejoined with the question, "Why doesn't the United States permit arms to be shipped to the Republican government in Spain in their noble battle against the Fascists?"

As indicative of the talent of these youngsters, there is attached hereto, together with an English translation, a copy of a revolutionary poem,* the author of which is alleged to be a little girl about 12 years of age. Before the stadium in which we were seated together with 200 or 300 children and the directors, this little child recited this poem. She did it exceedingly well; with much poise and naturalness and also with great intensity and dramatic fervor. She was what we, at home, would call "a natural."

Among the children was a group of fifty-one Spanish refugee children, both girls and boys, all of whom looked well and were fraternizing with the Soviet children and apparently happy.

It is claimed by the Soviet government that approximately 2,000,000 Soviet school children will be accommodated in Pioneer camps scattered about the country this summer. In addition to what the Soviet of People's Commissars is doing a great many school children will be accommodated and provided for by various trade-union organizations. The Soviet

---

* "Wreck of Soviet Steamer *Komsomol*"
    All Soviet land heard
    How our own steamer perished.
    It slowly sailed loaded with ore
    And had no weapons aboard.
        But the ships of pirate-brutes
        Noticed it from afar.
        The *Komsomol* slowly moved on,
        And they surrounded it from all sides.
    Without sparing anything at all
    They began to destroy it by fire.
    It perished—all alone among foes
    With an immense desire of revenge to the Fascists.
        But the Fascist force should remember
        That with our hundreds of shock brigades
        We shall give to our great country
        Hundreds of other ships!
    Times will come
    When the Fascists will be given a punch in the jaw
    And in the whole universe
    Death will be the fate of Fascists and lords! ! !
                        F. GORER

of People's Commissars for the current year has allocated
203,300,000 rubles to Pioneer camps and children's sanatoriums. At the official rate of exchange this would be $40,000,000.
Upon the "Citrine basis" of gold value it would amount to
$10,000,000. Of this total approximately 140,000,000 rubles is
for the upkeep of the camps, 20,000,000 rubles for the organization and equipment of camps, and 40,000,000 rubles for
the care of children who need special medical treatment in
the sanatoriums. In addition to this sum it is stated that
approximately 30,000,000 rubles more have been appropriated by the trade unions to defray the children's expenses in
the Pioneer camps. It is interesting to note that in a current
news item in the Moscow press it is stated that:

> If the city child's parents wish to send him to camp they find the
> number of such institutions constantly on the increase while the
> cost to them is scaled according to their income.

From this it will be observed that the Soviet system of
taking care of city children at children's camps runs to the
class distinctions of the families of "haves" and the "have-
nots," communistic theory to the contrary notwithstanding.

If, however, the present regime manages to maintain itself
and will be able to direct these huge capital investments of
the last ten years into the production of additional wealth,
and will also continue to project this character of education
and solicitude for the young, a very extraordinary situation
will develop. There will also be produced here an extraordinary amount of talent and genius out of the hitherto unmined
millions of the human wealth in the country. It is a factor
that is pregnant with many possibilities.

I have the honor to be, Sir, respectfully yours,

Joseph E. Davies

COLLECTIVE FARMS IN THE UKRAINE

NO. 1335 *Moscow, June 4, 1938*

Kiev, June 2, 1938

TO THE HONORABLE THE SECRETARY OF STATE

VISIT TO A COLLECTIVE FARM IN
THE UKRAINE

Sir:

On June 2, 1938, I had the opportunity to inspect a *kolkhoz* (collective farm) approximately 60 kilometers distant from Kiev, the capital of the Ukraine. Arrangements had been made by the Soviet officials for me to see this particular farm. It was apparently a model farm of the region.

The countryside through which we motored to reach the farm was in the heart of one of the richest and most fertile districts of the Ukraine in the valley of the Dnieper River. It was a gently rolling rich country, with scattered groves of pines and plains of waving grain fields as far as the eye could reach.

The Ukraine, of course, is one of the richest and most fertile agricultural districts in the world. The entire territory of the Ukraine covers 443,000 square kilometers and has a population of about 32,000,000 people. In the Kiev district are concentrated about 14 per cent of the tractors and combines used in mechanized farming. This small percentage is due to the large proportion of diversified farming and sugar-beet raising which obtains in this area in contrast to the grain-growing plains. The Kiev district produces approximately 3 per cent of the total crop of cereals of the U.S.S.R. and is considered the largest and most important agricultural region of the Ukrainian Republic. Of the total agricultural farming units in the Kiev district, approximately 92 per cent are collectivized which are practically all serviced by machine tractor stations.

This particular *kolkhoz* was a community covering approximately 1800 hectares (about 4500 acres) upon which there lived 1328 people, 675 of whom were workers. Of this number 375 were women and 300 men. There were 317 families on the estate.

The farm was devoted to diversified agriculture. Approximately 300 acres were in wheat, barley, and rye; 1900 acres in hay; 130 in orchards; and 125 in truck farming. In the truck-farming area there were hothouse beds and special sod-covered cellars for the storage and protection of seed.

A very creditable stable, built in 1933, about 235 feet long by 60 feet wide, was provided for 221 horses. One hundred and twenty of these were used for farm work and the remainder for breeding purposes. They had some blooded stock including a Percheron stallion which was housed in a box stall. We saw some twenty or thirty very good-looking colts which were in part being bred for the army.

A similar new barn was provided for eighty-five cows, which were hand milked.

The dairy end of the stable, while reasonably clean, was nevertheless quite simple. The milk is not sterilized or pasteurized on the farm.

Mechanized farming is employed here only for the plowing and cultivating of the ground. The *kolkhoz* is served by a tractor station in the neighborhood which serves twenty-four other *kolkhozes*.

In spite of the fact that this visit had been arranged by the Soviet officials, and I had been told that the president of the *kolkhoz* would be there to greet us, we found, upon our arrival, that he was not present, but had "just left." It was with some difficulty that we were able to elicit any information from one or two men who, we were told, were subheads in the organization. Finally the Assistant Director appeared and advised that he had been delegated to talk to us. It was quite evident that he and they were embarrassed and would have much preferred not to have to speak to us. They seemed suspicious or afraid. In spite of the protestations of the Soviet officials who had accompanied us, the Assistant Director would not consent to our taking any photographs of the premises. Such information as we were able to elicit was procured only after considerable time and with the greatest difficulty. From that point of view the visit was unsatisfactory. From another point of view, it was highly illuminating. It indicated the degree to which the influence of the Kremlin reaches out into the rural districts, hundreds of miles away. This may be explained by the fact that there has been projected recently a campaign by the government against the managers and directors of collective farms, who are alleged, in the Soviet press, to have diverted too much of the earnings of the collective farms to administration expenses and investments in improvements with the result that the workers did not receive adequate compensation as their yearly wage. When the Assistant Director asked what government we represented and was advised that it was the United States of America, he seemed to thaw out somewhat.*

One of the most interesting facts elicited was the opinion, which we were finally able to get, of what the earnings of a member of this *kolkhoz* were per month in contrast to the industrial worker of the city. The farmer on this collective pays no rent; the government has given to him in perpetuity two thirds of a hectare of ground and his habitation. He also has

---

* This was an indication of the violent campaign which the Kremlin was at that time conducting against "foreigners."

from one to three cows and some fruit-bearing trees. He is paid on a basis of piecework and the amount varies according to his efficiency. The average is 1.43 rubles in money for each workday. In addition thereto he receives certain amounts of grain, produce, hay, and straw from the collective and grows his own green vegetables and fruits. It was the opinion of this man and his associates that the average farmer on this collective earned approximately 150 to 200 rubles a month and the Stakhanovites and brigadiers from 200 to 300 rubles a month which was somewhat less than the city worker.

Attached hereto is a stenographic report of dictation given and notes taken by Mr. Gordon upon the occasion of this visit, to which reference may be had as to further details.

I have the honor to be, Sir, respectfully yours,

Joseph E. Davies

Kiev, June 2, 1938

INSPECTION OF COLLECTIVE FARM (KOLKHOZ)
IN THE UKRAINE NEAR KIEV

Upon arrival at the farm the Ambassador and party were introduced to Mr. Primar, the field superintendent, who conducted us on a tour of the farm and supplied the following information in reply to the Ambassador's questions:

QUESTION: When was this farm organized?

ANSWER: In 1930.

QUESTION: How many hectares?

ANSWER: 1823 hectares under cultivation.

QUESTION: What do you grow?

ANSWER: Various crops; hay, grain, truck farming, and orchards.

QUESTION: Apples?

ANSWER: Yes; also pears. We also grow flax.

QUESTION: Wheat and rye?

ANSWER: Mostly technical cultures: flax, high-grade cauliflower, seeds, and so forth, and we have many hothouse cultures.

QUESTION: How many families live on this *kolkhoz*?

ANSWER: 317.

QUESTION: How many workers?

ANSWER: 675. 1328 is the entire population.

QUESTION: How many men and how many women?

ANSWER: 375 women and about 300 men.

QUESTION: How many Stakhanovites?

ANSWER: 95 persons.

QUESTION: Are they all paid by piecework?

ANSWER: Yes. All the work is piecework.

QUESTION: Do you do mechanized farming?

ANSWER: No. It is all hand work.

QUESTION: Do the machine tractor stations help you?

ANSWER: Yes.

QUESTION: What do they do?

ANSWER: They do all the work they can; plow, thresh, and so forth, in season. The station is 8 kilometers from here.

QUESTION: What percentage of the crop does the machine tractor station get?

ANSWER: 5 to 10 per cent, depending upon what they do.

QUESTION: What per cent of the product goes to the state?

ANSWER: 7 or 8 per cent, depending on the crop.

QUESTION: This horse stable that we are walking through was built in 1933?

ANSWER: 1933, yes.

AMBASSADOR DICTATES: About 200 to 235 feet long and 60 feet wide, with 4 rows of stalls, some box stalls and some ordinary stalls, all whitewashed inside. In the box stalls they have some blooded stock (horses), including a Percheron stallion and a thoroughbred.

QUESTION: How many blooded stock do you have?

ANSWER: About 42 thoroughbreds.

QUESTION: Do you make a specialty of raising blooded stock?

ANSWER: Yes, for sale.

QUESTION: What is the total number of cows?

ANSWER: 85 milking cows belonging to the collective farm. Each individual farmer has his own cow. Some have one and some two or three.

QUESTION: How many horses on the place?

ANSWER: 221.

QUESTION: Do you work all the horses in cultivating the land?

ANSWER: 120 are work horses and the others are for breed- ing purposes.

QUESTION: Do you breed for the army?

ANSWER: Yes. We have 20 to 30 colts.

QUESTION: Do you have any scientists here who are experts on breeding?

ANSWER: Yes, we have a veterinary, a zoological technician, and so forth.

QUESTION: Do you do any breeding by artificial insemina- tion?

ANSWER: No.

QUESTION: Now as to the distribution of the income; 5 to 10 per cent goes to the machine tractor station, and 10 per cent to the state. That's 20 per cent. Where does the re- maining 80 per cent go?

(Not answered here; see below.)

QUESTION: Where do you keep the cows?

ANSWER: We have another barn for the cattle.

QUESTION: What are these other buildings I see?

ANSWER: Some repair shops, storage space, and so forth.

QUESTION: Do you do all your own horesshoeing on the *kolkhoz*?

ANSWER: Yes.

QUESTION: How many blacksmiths do you have?

ANSWER: Six.

QUESTION: How many machine repairers?

ANSWER: Only one mechanic; mediocre.

QUESTION: Do you use tractor cultivators or horse cultivators?

ANSWER: Horse cultivators.

QUESTION: What do you use the tractors for, mostly for plowing?

ANSWER: Yes.

QUESTION: How many hectares do you have in grain?

ANSWER: 100 hectares in grain; 200 in barley and rye, 45 in oats, 783 in hay; 1821 hectares in the whole farm.

QUESTION: How many hectares in orchards?

ANSWER: 55.

QUESTION: How much in truck farming?

ANSWER: 45.

QUESTION: The remainder in potatoes and vegetables?

ANSWER: Yes.

QUESTION: Have you any new houses for the workers?

ANSWER: No new ones; only old ones. The club and school are new.

AMBASSADOR: I see this good-looking house over here, surrounded by a fence. Who lives there?

ANSWER: A kulak lived there, it is now being prepared as a laboratory.

QUESTION: How many hectares does each family have for its private use?

ANSWER: One third of a hectare.

QUESTION: Where is the *kolkhoz* bazaar?

ANSWER: 5 kilometers from here; we also dispose of our produce at Kiev.

QUESTION: Do you furnish Kiev with your vegetables?

ANSWER: Yes.

QUESTION: Does the collective farm have a collective eating place or does each family supply its own?

ANSWER: We have no community dining room.

QUESTION: How many teachers in the school?

ANSWER: 15, teaching 350 children a 10-year course.

QUESTION (by the Ambassador): Is there anything you would like to show us as of interest?

(The Director took us over to see the cow stables.)

QUESTION: Are all the cows milked by hand?

ANSWER: Yes.

QUESTION: How many collective farms are served by the same machine tractor station that serves you?

ANSWER: 24. It has 43 tractors and 4 combines.

QUESTION: How many people work at the machine tractor station?

ANSWER: I don't know.

QUESTION: What do you do with the milk when you get it from the cows?

ANSWER: We have to send some to the government and the remainder is sent to the collective bazaar.

QUESTION: Is the milk sterilized?

ANSWER: No. It is sent out fresh.

QUESTION: Do you wash the cans in cold water or hot water?

ANSWER: Hot, boiled water.

QUESTION: Do you heat the water right here?

ANSWER: Yes. We have three water boilers.

QUESTION: Were these hothouses that we are now passing built before the Revolution?

ANSWER: No; during collectivization in 1930.

QUESTION: What was the wage of the average worker here last year?

ANSWER: For a workday, 1.43 rubles in money. Also 2.6 kilos of grain; 8 kilos of potatoes; 1.5 kilos of hay; 1.5 kilos of straw. In addition, each one has his own green vegetables and fruits. Those who haven't got it can always get it on the farm.

QUESTION: What does it all really amount to each month, in your opinion, compared to industrial workers?

ANSWER: Industrial workers receive more than collective farmers.

QUESTION: What does the average collective farmer here get a month, approximately?

ANSWER: 150 to 200 rubles a month, figured at our prices.

QUESTION: And Stakhanovites and brigadiers?

ANSWER: 200 to 300.

QUESTION: Thus the collective-farm worker makes 100 to 300 rubles a month as compared to the industrial worker?

ANSWER: Yes.

QUESTION: Does the collective farmer pay rent for his house and land?

ANSWER: No. They were given to them by the government in perpetuity.

QUESTION: Do you include, in figuring pay, the value of the cows' milk or is that left out?

ANSWER: What he makes on his own place is extra.

QUESTION: What are these beds we see here?

ANSWER: They are for hothouse purposes.

QUESTION: We saw some cucumbers planted under glass

in quite a number of rows about 5 feet wide and 35 to 40 feet long. How many of these frames do you have?

ANSWER: 1030.

AMBASSADOR DICTATES: 12 in a row, about 100 rows in all. They also have cellars 60 feet long and 12 feet wide covered with earth 8 feet high which are used to store seeds. There is also quite a pile of brick on the premises with which they are going to build hothouses.

QUESTION: How large are the hothouses which are being planned?

ANSWER: 23.6 meters long by 6.9 meters wide. This year we will build two.

QUESTION: What fruits do you have in this orchard?

ANSWER: Apples, pears, cherries, and so forth.

QUESTION: Do you plow up and cultivate the ground between these trees each year?

ANSWER: Yes; but it has not been done this year as yet.

QUESTION: Do you spray the trees to kill off worms?

ANSWER: Yes, twice a year.

AMBASSADOR: I see some beehives here; how much honey do you get a year?

ANSWER: 32 kilograms from each hive. We have 180 beehives.

QUESTION: The *kolkhoz* is managed by the Director and whom else?

ANSWER: There are three of us: the Chairman, his Assistant, and the Field Superintendent.

QUESTION: And after you pay all the expenses and make the necessary improvements on the farm, you divide the balance among the workers?

ANSWER: When we have finished paying the machine tractor station and the government we divide according to the work done.

QUESTION: Who decides what will be done with the rest of this money?

ANSWER: We have a general meeting of the members of the collective farm which decides that.

· QUESTION: Do they also decide upon the rates paid for piecework; or who decides that?

ANSWER: The management and the brigadiers.

QUESTION: And each shares in the surplus according to the amount of work performed by each?

ANSWER: Yes.

QUESTION: So that the best workers get larger percentages than the others?

ANSWER: Yes; according to what they manage to produce.

Documentation on the Démarche That Failed

NO. 1105 *Moscow, April 1, 1938*

TO THE HONORABLE THE SECRETARY OF STATE

INCIDENT OF PROPOSED PROTEST OR *démarche* TO THE SOVIET FOREIGN OFFICE BY THE DIPLOMATIC CORPS WITH REFERENCE TO CUSTOMS AND CERTAIN OTHER MATTERS AFFECTING THE DIPLOMATIC CORPS

Strictly Confidential

Sir:

I beg leave to advise that I submit herewith a résumé of the above-entitled incident.

While the details of the subject matter are relatively unimportant, the circumstances, which developed incident thereto and are illustrative of conditions here, may be of significance

and value to the Department. It is for this reason that I am
transmitting herewith this report in some detail.

BACKGROUND

The situation arose out of the fact that for some time, and
particularly in the recent past, a great deal of indignation in
the Diplomatic Corps has been aroused by the attitude of
Soviet customs officials toward departing diplomats. Upon
the departure of chiefs of mission or diplomatic officials other
than heads of missions, the Soviet Union has insisted upon
rigorously administering Soviet customs laws without regard
to the diplomatic usages and customs generally obtaining
among nations. The government here has insisted upon the
right to inspect (in the residence of the departing chief of
mission) all the personal effects of a chief of mission which he
is taking out of the country, and, while relieving him from
the payment of customs duties, nevertheless exacts the payment of an appraisal or administrative fee of three per cent
on objects procured in the Soviet Union, even though such
effects be for personal use. In connection with diplomatic
officers other than chiefs of mission, the Soviet Union has required that the personal effects be examined not at the residence but at the government customhouse, which involves a
real hardship. There have been other restrictions upon the
Diplomatic Corps in connection with sales of automobiles as
between each other; and again the importation of printed
matter through the mails to missions has been denied diplomatic immunity.

Recently this customs problem was intensified by reason
of the departure of the Danish and Swedish Ministers. While
protesting most vigorously, they were nevertheless compelled
to pay the administrative appraisal fee of three per cent, as
a condition of getting their goods out of the country. Some

time ago, the Dean of the Diplomatic Corps protested to the Foreign Office on behalf of the Diplomatic Corps, without result, except that there followed shortly thereafter a very extraordinary attack upon the Afghan Ambassador in the official Soviet press.

Generally speaking, there has also developed an increase of asperity as between the Soviet government and the diplomatic representatives of certain other governments during the past several months. The hostility of the Fascist states became more vocal and more aggressive. It has been quite noticeable that recent Hitler successes have had an influence upon the attitudes of some of the diplomatic representatives of the smaller European nations who have representation here. On the other hand the Soviet government has been severe, almost to the point of ruthlessness, in requiring the closing of consulates of foreign powers in the Soviet Union, and in other matters. Whether justified by the facts or not, the Soviet officials and press do not hesitate to charge openly that certain capitalist countries are secretly conspiring within the Soviet Union to overthrow the present regime and are employing their consulates and diplomatic agencies for purposes of spying, espionage, and interior hostile actions in conjunction with alleged counterrevolutionary forces. Every propaganda agency has been diligently employed to impress upon the masses this alleged danger to the country. Soviet officials have not hesitated to state to me that they are convinced that the Soviet government is isolated and surrounded by enemy states, and that they must and do rely only upon themselves and must make and are making preparations to be completely self-contained economically and from a military point of view; that they can only rely on their own strength and must be "safe." Characteristic of the Stalin regime, the government has not hesitated to attack first and vigorously. The treatment of many of the diplomatic representatives here has been characterized by what would appear to be an astonishing indifference as to the consequences that might flow therefrom even to the point of withdrawal of diplomatic representation.

This was the general condition that obtained and in which the projected joint *démarche* was proposed.

It should also be noted that joint *démarches* by the Diplomatic Corps here in the past, in several instances, have been rejected quite without exception and have been resented by the Soviet Foreign Office as an indication of the hostility of the capitalist states.

THE LETTER OF THE BRITISH AMBASSADOR, THE ACTING DEAN OF THE CORPS

Under date of March 17, the British Ambassador, in his capacity as the Dean of the Diplomatic Corps, sent to the chiefs of mission here a proposal for joint action and protest with reference to the above-described practices, affecting the Diplomatic Corps, for the purpose of calling to the attention of the Soviet government the importance which was attached to the re-establishment of practices more in accord with international usage with respect to these matters, and the opinions of the various chiefs of mission were requested as to the timeliness of such a *démarche*.

CONFERENCE WITH THE BRITISH AMBASSADOR

In view of the Department's instructions, I called upon the British Ambassador so that I might be able to inform the Department more fully as to the method and manner that were to be employed in bringing this to the attention of the Foreign Office, and particularly whether it was to be by formal note formally signed, or orally. Briefly, the summary of the discussion was as follows:

I suggested that in my opinion my government would be desirous of co-operating with the British government and other governments here represented, in an effort to protect here the proper and established diplomatic usages and conveniences which have existed for so many years in the intercourse of other nations; but that I desired to confer with him as to the procedure to be followed, to be able to advise my government fully in the premises. Further, I felt confident that he recognized fully with me the delicacy of the situation here, arising out of the hostility which existed at the present time (whether justified or not) toward capitalist nations. The method and manner in which it was proposed that joint action should be projected was, therefore, of importance. In view of previous rebuffs to similar joint *démarches* on other occasions, there was danger of a rebuff by the Soviet Foreign Office, unless the matter were broached in an atmosphere of friendly remonstrance rather than as a formal joint action. The question had occurred to me as to whether there might not be more probability of success through a common concerted plan, simultaneously projected but by individual approaches of the various heads of mission to the Foreign Office, as this might forestall the possibility that this action might be construed as a joint hostile action and a "ganging up" of the representatives of capitalist nations against the Soviet Union. If the *démarche* were to be projected by a joint note signed by all heads of mission or by an *aide-mémoire* in a formal manner, it might induce a possible public rebuff by a note from the Foreign Office, which would afford no relief as to the matters desired and might affect the general situation adversely. I also suggested that while the matter of these customs regulations was important, if the incident assumed a political aspect it might adversely affect more important objectives of policy, which either existed or might possibly exist in the future. Specifically, I referred to the world's hope that the Chamberlain government would bring peace in Europe and the establishment of international order; but that in the possible event of failure the attitude of the Soviet Union and its enormous power, both in resources and men, might be of serious importance to peace and the principles of international justice; and while this incident would not be conclusive upon the attitude of the Soviet Union, that it would be unfortunate to intensify the hostility to *all* nations, particularly if the results we sought were also not obtained.

The British Ambassador assured me that he was entirely in accord with this analysis and outlook; that the French Ambassador prior to his departure had also suggested that the matter be not taken up formally by note or *aide-mémoire,* but purely on a personal, friendly and administrative basis; that he felt also that it was important to make these representations as otherwise conditions and restrictions would grow constantly worse. He assured me that he would only conduct these discussions provided it could be done in a friendly atmosphere and in such a way as could not give offense. He stated further that in view of the fact that the Danish Minister had departed and that the situation as to the departing Swedish Minister was closed, there was no need for immediate action for several weeks. Thereupon, I stated to Lord Chilston that the doubts in my mind had been clarified and that I was much reassured and would communicate with my government and advise him upon receipt of instructions. At the close of the conference Lord Chilston stated that he appreciated my coming and discussing the matter with him. I left with the impression that the matter could be disposed of by mail rather than by cable to the Department.

TELEGRAPHIC REPORT TO THE DEPARTMENT

On the following Saturday evening, March 26, on the occasion of a reception at the Embassy here, Lord Chilston approached me and asked whether I had reported to my government; to which I replied that a report was in process of preparation and that I assumed there was no hurry about the matter. He then asked that I communicate by telegram. I told him that I would do so. I also stated to him at that time that I would recommend to the Secretary of State that I be authorized to join in the proposed action. He then stated to me again that unless there was unanimity among the chiefs of mission here he would not proceed further.

DEVELOPMENT OF ONE COUNTRY'S ATTITUDE

Later we learned that the Spanish Charge d'Affairés had declined to join the proposed *démarche*.

On March 29, the ———— Minister called on Mr. Henderson and discussed the proposed joint action. Mr. Henderson's memorandum of this conference is enclosed. The gist of it is: that he [the ———— Minister] had heard that the American Ambassador had thus far failed to join in the proposed *démarche*; that he sincerely hoped he would not join in this procedure; that, while he had previously advised the British Ambassador that he would participate, he now proposed later in the day to inform Lord Chilston that under instructions from his government he felt it was his duty to refrain from doing so; that he had learned that a copy of the circular note had reached Litvinov; that it had aroused resentment and that the disinterestedness of Lord Chilston was challenged; that the *démarche* would be rejected; that if no *démarche* were made the Foreign Office hoped to bring about an improvement in conditions and that the *démarche* could have only negative results and lead to increased friction and that it might result in attacks in the Soviet press similar to that which appeared against the Afghan Ambassador.

SECOND CONFERENCE WITH LORD CHILSTON

Immediately upon receipt of this information I called upon the British Ambassador. I confirmed the letter which he had received from me advising that I had reported to my government and had recommended that I be authorized to co-operate with him in this matter and that I based this recommendation upon my confidence that the matter was entirely safe in his hands and would be handled certainly in a manner which would not give a political character to the incident and produce no harmful results. I then called to his attention that information had reached us that the Soviet Foreign Office had already received a copy of his letter; that it had been offended by it; that the proposal would be rejected; and that he would also doubtless receive similar information.

Lord Chilston regretted that the situation should have developed in this manner. He expressed great appreciation for the manner in which I had frankly discussed the matter with him and for my friendly and frank co-operation. He thought it would be exceedingly unfortunate if anything should transpire that would increase the growing hostility of this government toward outside nations and particularly the democracies, and that he recognized fully the potentialities in the European and world situations where it might be important that the Soviet government should not obtain the erroneous impression that all governments were hostile and were carrying such hostility even into small matters. He advised me then that he had decided that he would not present the *démarche*.

I immediately cabled advice to this effect. Personally, I think this is a fortunate disposition of the matter. While disagreeable, irritating, and measurably important, the whole matter was relatively *de minimis* in contradistinction to the broader objectives of policy in connection with what is potentially a serious situation here in connection with this growing hostility against foreigners and foreign nations, and the implications that arise therefrom.

And it is fortunate that the incident is disposed of without the possibility of misconstruction or misunderstanding.

I have the honor to be, Sir, respectfully yours,

Joseph E. Davies

NO. 1152 *Moscow—April 12, 1938*

TO THE HONORABLE THE SECRETARY OF STATE

PROPOSED DIPLOMATIC DÉMARCHE RELATIVE CUSTOMS
DUTIES AFFECTING DIPLOMATIC CORPS, ET CETERA

Sir:

The conditions which caused the British Ambassador to drop the proposed *démarche*, as heretofore reported, were: that Lithuania and Spain refused to join; that information had come that the Soviet Foreign Office already had obtained a copy of Lord Chilston's letter, was bitterly incensed thereby, and would reject the *démarche;* that the British Ambassador's disinterestedness was challenged; and that if the matter did not assume an aggressive political character the Soviet Foreign Office had hoped in its own way to work out relief as to the customs situation.

On April 2, to my surprise, the British Ambassador told me that he had changed his mind; that he proposed to go ahead regardless of lack of unanimity and of the above conditions, lest it might be construed as "a backing down" to do otherwise; and he expressed the hope that he would have my co-operation.

Frankly, but in a most friendly manner, I stated to the British Ambassador that my personal advice would be that he go slowly; that the proposed action would probably get nowhere; that it might make an already bad situation worse; whereas if he waited for the situation to cool off and take the matter up later it is quite possible that he would obtain the relief desired. I told him also that the Lithuanian and Czechoslovakian Ministers had approached me on their own initiative and urged that I express this opinion to him, as it was also their belief.

To this the British Ambassador replied that he would await my instructions from the Department, but that he was anxious to take action before the Diplomatic Dean, the Afghan Ambassador, returned to the city.

It is my judgment that if the Department should instruct me generally to participate only in case of unanimity of all missions as first proposed and not otherwise it would dispose of the question for the present, and that the situation could be worked out satisfactorily later after the present heat has subsided.

On the other hand, I can assume the responsibility, if in accord with the views of the Department, and state that under the circumstances my recommendation to the Department is that our participation therein would be inadvisable, except as the action is unanimous.*

I have the honor to be, Sir, respectfully yours,

                                                              Joseph E. Davies

---

* The Department instructed me to follow my own judgment; and I promptly advised the British Ambassador that I had decided not to join in the proposed *démarche,* and that I felt entirely free to take this course in view of our understanding that my acquiesence depended upon unanimity in the Diplomatic Corps on this question.

NO. 1233   *Moscow—April 30, 1938*

TO THE HONORABLE THE SECRETARY OF STATE

THE PROPOSED PROTEST OF THE DIPLOMATIC CORPS AT
MOSCOW TO THE PEOPLE'S COMMISSARIAT FOR FOREIGN
AFFAIRS, REGARDING CUSTOMS MATTERS

Sir:

With reference to my previous communications to the Department relating to the proposal of the British Ambassador, Acting Dean of the Diplomatic Corps, to register a protest against the manner in which Soviet customs authorities have been treating members of the Corps, I have the honor to report that the British Ambassador has decided to drop the matter for the present at least.

The British Ambassador left the Soviet Union last evening on an extended leave and will not return until after the Afghan Ambassador has already assumed his duties as Dean of the Diplomatic Corps. In my opinion it is doubtful that the Afghan Ambassador will take any steps in the matter.

It is well closed in my opinion and "much ado about nothing."

I have the honor to be, Sir, respectfully yours,

Joseph E. Davies

Documents on Debt and Trade Talks

MEMORANDUM OF DISCUSSIONS BETWEEN MR. NEYMANN OF THE
FOREIGN OFFICE AND AMBASSADOR JOSEPH E. DAVIES, ON
JULY 8 AND 9, 1937, IN CONNECTION WITH THE COMMERCIAL
AGREEMENT

Shortly after my conference with Mr. Litvinov on July 2, I had an opportunity to discuss the situation, informally, with

Mr. Neymann. He stated that Mr. Litvinov had discussed the matter with him and that he hoped that I would bear patiently with them and not think them "meticulous" in the discussions which were in process with Messrs. Henderson, Kennan, and Durbrow; that as a matter of fact they were under obligation to bring certain matters up which they felt had to be discussed; but that they were sincerely desirous of projecting the matter on a broad, equitable, and fair basis.

I then stated to Mr. Neymann, in effect, what I had said to Mr. Litvinov, and impressed upon him the full measure of the advantages which they were receiving under the new commercial treaty, over and above last year.

He stated that they were having difficulty, in connection with guaranteeing $40,000,000 of purchases in the United States; that they also felt obliged to insist that the most-favored-nation obligation should be upon a bilateral and reciprocal basis, and finally that they would have to insist that the arrangement should apply to exports as well as imports.

To this I replied that I could sympathize with them in their attitude of desiring to have the obligation a bilateral one (this for reasons of possible *amour-propre*), and this even though it was perfectly clear to me that what they were seeking was to appear to give us something that we did not want because, realistically, it had no value; that as a practical matter whether the Soviet government, which made these purchases, should exact an import duty or not, or should impose on what it sold an export tax or not, did not affect American interests in any way; and for these reasons, I could (personally) see no reason, if they wanted it, why they should not have it so provided in the agreement. In connection with the proposed "exportation clause" and exports, however, I stated that I thought there would be difficulty because of the passage of the neutrality laws subsequent to the passage of the law which vested the power in the Executive to negotiate these agreements.

I stated quite frankly, however, that while, personally, I made these admissions to him "and against interest," that quite as frankly I had absolutely no tolerance for a position that would haggle over an increase of $10,000,000 in purchases (from $30,000,000 to $40,000,000) in view of both the equities and the practicalities of this situation; that in my opinion it was not an evidence of approaching the matter in a broad-minded and appreciative attitude of the position which Secretary Hull had taken so fairly and in such a large-minded way on this particular problem. I elaborated at some length on the difficulties which had confronted Secretary Hull.

Mr. Neymann manifested a very fair-minded attitude in reply and stated in conclusion that he would not be disposed to quarrel with that point of view; that he felt that we could arrive at some agreement on the question of purchases in the United States, but that on the other matters he felt that he might have to insist upon their point of view; but that he would try to approach it in a manner that would be fair and designed to bring results.

MEMORANDUM OF CONFERENCE BETWEEN MR. NEYMANN, MR. ROSENBLUM, MR. KAMINSKY, MR. VINOGRADOV, AND AMBASSADOR JOSEPH E. DAVIES, AT THE FOREIGN OFFICE, MOSCOW, JULY 15, 1937, WITH REFERENCE TO THE COMMERCIAL AGREEMENT. MR. GEORGE T. KENNAN, SECOND SECRETARY OF THE EMBASSY, WAS ALSO PRESENT

I opened the discussion by again outlining the situation from our point of view, in the manner as heretofore described in memoranda of conferences with Mr. Litvinov and Mr. Neymann.

I then stated that the matters in disagreement had now resolved themselves into three:

1. The matter of the proposed bilateral character of the
agreement.

2. The matter of the proposed exportation clause.

3. The matter of the amount of Soviet commitment for
purchases in the United States.

Taking up the first matter in difference, I recalled to Mr.
Neymann that personally I had been disposed to recognize
the validity of their position and even to recommend that the
Department yield upon that point, and in that attitude I had
felt I was on logical ground. Subsequent thereto, however, it
had developed that the Soviet Foreign Office would find no
value in such a bilateral agreement, unless it provided for
exceptions with reference to Baltic countries and countries
in southern and eastern Asia.

In view of this development, I was now obliged to withdraw
from my previous position, for such a condition, in my opinion, completely changed the situation and would be inequi-
table clearly to my mind. I then stated, in view of their attitude, that the exception of these countries was a *sine qua non*
to the bilateral character of these agreements; that I had been
instructed by my government that the bilateral agreement,
as proposed, could not be accepted and that, therefore, further discussions thereof would be useless.

Second: With reference to the exportation clause, the
Department had taken the position that to work this out
(even if it were now agreed upon in principle) would require
a great deal of careful consideration which would necessarily
take some time and which would involve serious delay in
the completion of the agreement.

Third: With reference to the amount of purchases, it was
our confident position that we could expect, in view of the

very substantial concessions which we were making to them (amounting approximately to $1,000,000 a year), that they would not belittle themselves or us by proposing anything less than $40,000,000.

In conclusion, I stated to them that, quite frankly, the situation had now narrowed itself down to this: that the agreement could be promptly closed, provided it was unilateral in character and provided $40,000,000 could be the amount agreed upon for purchases by the Soviet government in the United States.

After considerable discussion they seemed to concur that the bilateral character of the treaty was out of consideration. They insisted, however, that as a matter of principle they were entitled to an agreement that covered a most-favored-nation treatment of exports as well as imports; that there was no real justification for a discrimination against them in the matter of exports; that under the circumstances it was rather an invidious suggestion that exports should be omitted as it contained some implied aspersion, which they could not see as justified, and that they particularly felt that they should not be discriminated against, provided they undertook to purchase a definite amount of goods in the United States, in contrast with other nations similarly situated, who have made no definite commitment whatever for purchases in the United States.

They also stated that they appreciated the difficulties which we had outlined, in connection with the neutrality legislation and the possibility of the necessity for change of provisions, in view of such legislation, but they stated that they would be entirely willing to accept the language contained in the Netherlands Treaty adapted to a unilateral agreement, together with the second paragraph of Article 11 of the Netherlands Treaty, and in connection therewith would be

willing to commit themselves by supplementary letter that
they would accept any modification of the language which
the United States required and obtained from other nations
similarly situated, provided only that there should be no
discrimination as between the treatment accorded the Soviet
Union in contrast with the treatment accorded to others
having similar rights with reference to exports from the
United States.

I then asked them whether, in their opinion, I would be
reasonably justified in stating to the Department that in the
event their proposal with reference to the exportation clause
would be acceptable that there would be no trouble in connection with the $40,000,000 commitment for the purchase
of goods in the United States. They stated that I would be
reasonably justified in making that statement, but that there
was a reservation that they were not prepared to be committed definitely to a $40,000,000 amount. The implication,
however, was quite clear that they would recommend it and
that it would go through, but that they did not wish to be
definitely committed.

I then stated that it might be that it would take considerable time to work out suitable language, in connection
with the exportation clause, if the Department were willing
to accede to it; that the Department might prefer to have
time to work it out rather than to accept the language contained in the Netherlands Treaty, and I asked them whether
it would be agreeable to them to enter into the agreement,
unilateral in character, with a commitment of $40,000,000
now and dispose of that with an ancillary exchange of letters,
setting forth that a supplementary agreement will be entered
into within a period of sixty or ninety days covering exports,
in such language as could be mutually agreed upon and as
would ensure that the Soviet Union would not be discrimi-

nated against in contrast with other nations enjoying the same treaty privileges, which letters should provide that unless such supplementary agreement was concluded within such period of sixty or ninety days that within ten days thereafter the Soviet government might abrogate the principal agreement hereinbefore described. Their reply to this was also in the affirmative; that they thought it could be worked out that way if it were desirable.

The distinct impression which I received was that they are working in a very tense atmosphere, where officials are disinclined to assume responsibility because of the extent of current criticism which obtains everywhere in government circles, and also because of the general "hate" that is "on" in connection with relations with all capitalistic enemy states (particularly since the Stalin speech of March 5, last), but that nevertheless they were seriously and honestly concerned with what they regarded as a necessity from their viewpoint; i.e., the prevention of an appearance on the face of the treaty that there was a discrimination between the treatment accorded to the Soviet Union and other nations, who had similar treaties with the United States. It appeared to me to be a question of *amour-propre*, and, as a matter of fact, it was difficult for me to make an effort to maintain that there was serious justification for such discrimination, particularly in view of the fact that the treaty was to obtain for only one year.

We then discussed within what time we might be able to conclude this treaty, if we could agree, in principle, along the line discussed, and Mr. Neymann said that he thought it would take at least a week or more to arrange all of the details before the signature and formal closing could be had and that so far as they were concerned that delay would not seriously affect them.

The Ambassador's Farewell

Moscow, June 9, 1938

SPEECH OF FAREWELL TO THE EMBASSY STAFF AT MOSCOW DE-
LIVERED BY AMBASSADOR DAVIES ON JUNE 9, 1938

Ladies and Gentlemen of the Staff:

I asked Mr. Ward to ask
you to assemble here this noon, because I wanted to see
you all, to bid you all au revoir—not "good-by"—because I
hope to see you many times again—at least many of you—not
here but back home or wherever our paths may cross.

In the name of our government, I wish to thank you all for
the splendid service you have rendered during my administration as Ambassador. To our Soviet employees who are here,
I wish also to express my appreciation for their diligence, their
faithfulness, and their loyalty. Of course, their primary loyalty
is to their own government which to them is first and should
be first. That, fortunately, in this Embassy, can never require
any lack of loyalty to their employer, the United States. Each
loyalty obtains in its respective sphere. You have been loyal
and, I am sure, high-minded and honorable in keeping that
which is of the United States to the United States, and that
which is of your government to your government.

To the members of our own service, I have a few special
things to say, as I am departing for my new post. I haven't
seen as much of you all as I should have liked. I found that I
could do better and more intensive work up at my office in
the Spazzo House, so I have not been here among you so much.
I wish to express here my particular appreciation to my immediate colleagues—Secretary Henderson, Counselor Kirk, Colonel Faymonville, and Secretaries Kennan, Durbrow, Chip-

man, Page, Grummon, and Bohlen and Dr. Rumreich. To each I am indebted for the splendid help which he has given to me; and I wish to express my appreciation in this manner. I should not have been free to devote a great deal of my time to the serious work I have tried to do, but for the splendid ability of Mr. Henderson and fine efficiency of Mr. Ward in relieving me of much of the administrative work in the conduct of this mission. For this situation and for these services, I am very grateful.

That situation, however, did not mean that I was unfamiliar or out of touch with the work which the staff was carrying on. I was familiar with it, and I want to say to you that you have a fine batting average; you have not known what it was to look at the clock in emergencies; you have never hesitated to volunteer to continue the work long into the night when dispatches had to be got out; you have been what I would expect of a fine group of men in the service of our great government. I want to say that to you as I am leaving. To you, my associates, I want to express my thanks particularly for your generosity toward your chief. At times it has not been altogether easy, for I have been accustomed to rather forceful and direct action as the head of my own outfit; and I fear that at times I may have appeared to be exacting and inconsiderate in my desire to get things done. I fear I may not be an easy man to work with for that reason. If so, I am sorry. In any event, I have found very generous and loyal response always from Mr. Henderson and each of my colleagues. I feel sure that you all knew that my heart was right. It's hard to teach an old dog new tricks.

There is one thing in particular, in which I take pride in connection with this staff, during my administration, and that is this: as I have mingled with the Diplomatic Corps representatives of other nationalities, I have frequently marveled at the indiscretion and poor taste—and of course I am saying this in the bosom of the family—of some members of the Diplomatic Corps. It was not infrequent that I found those who were accepting many courtesies and hospitalities at the hands of the government to which they were accredited had the bad taste and bad judgment to go out of their way to find fault and criticize, quite uselessly, many things which reflected upon or would needlessly offend the sensibilities of officials here with whom they were doing business and from whom they were accepting courtesies. As a practical man of business affairs, I could not understand it. If diplomacy means anything in government or if it means anything in business, it means the art of getting along and getting matters in difference settled with the least amount of irritation and with the least amount of difficulty—all, however, consistent with the fundamental principle that one never yields self-respect or stanch standing up for the ideals of our government whenever or wherever necessary. As a matter of plain common sense, it is elementary that one should not needlessly and uselessly offend people with whom one has to do business. I am not a professional diplomat of state; but I have consorted with high professional and business diplomats for many years. It is my observation that diplomats, whether political or business, if they are big men, do not everlastingly have to proclaim their own virtue to maintain their self-respect. That is sufficiently strong to be taken for granted. Nor do they ever try to add to their own stature by needless detractions of others. Such men never fail to do battle with a broadsword when the occasion honorably requires that they take a stand for principle. The great diplomats of our own service never needlessly give offense. From Benjamin Franklin to the present day, our diplomats have not required the tutelage of Chesterfield to give them consideration for the feelings of others.

And I am happy to say that I have found very little, if any, of that in my own staff. It has gratified me immensely. It is a reflection of good judgment and fine impulses. It is creditable to the principles of our own great country. In such conduct you are reflecting and representing the strength, tolerance, and Christian character of our great people. And what a country it is, and what an honor to be its representative!

I never go back home from Europe but what I reverently thank my mother's God that my forebears had the courage and self-reliance and the hardihood to brave the wilderness, 150 years ago, and migrate to the United States of America, and through their sacrifices make it possible for my children and my grandchildren to enjoy the beneficences of a democratic form of government and the privilege of living in the United States. I never go back home from Europe but what I feel how blest the American people are. Think of what we enjoy in contrast to many European countries!

We have liberty—personal freedom.

We have the right of free speech.

We have the right of peaceful assembly.

We have the right to think freely.

We have the right to worship God as our conscience may dictate.

Our liberty, our lives, our property, our rights are protected even as against the government itself.

Every man is a king in his own castle.

Our liberties and our lives are protected by laws by which even an all-powerful government is required to prove guilt beyond a reasonable doubt, before a man may be punished.

What would millions of men and women in Europe today give to be assured of and enjoy these blessings!

The dignity of manhood and womanhood, the sanctity of human life and liberty, the self-respect of the human spirit, are the best product which civilization has brought into this world. These are found in the United States of America to a degree that is found no place else in the world.

I don't care how much totalitarian states or dictatorships may provide in material benefits or social benefits to childhood or old age. If liberty and freedom have to be sacrificed, then the price is too high to pay.

So while we have something that we should very jealously protect and guard in our own country, we also have institutions and ideals that are so noble and so high that it imparts a great obligation upon us to hold them high and guard them loyally in our conduct abroad when we have the honor to represent them and to carry the standard of the United States.

And as I say, I am very glad to be able to feel that in my staff, while I have been here, there has been that fine self-control that has enabled you to keep your principles to yourselves; not to be needlessly irritable toward the government to which we are accredited; being tolerant and generous as the religion of your mother and my mother and your father and my father taught us to be.

So I am going away, and I shall carry with me pleasant memories, and I shall be glad to recall these many friendships, and wherever you may be, if you ever come across our paths, don't hesitate; come and see Mrs. Davies and me and we will be delighted to see you, because you are one of our boys in Moscow.

INDEX

Albert, King of the Belgians, 256
Alexander III, Emperor of Russia, 596
Alfred the Great, King of the West Saxons, 380
Allen, Robert, Congressman, 452
American-Russian Chamber of Commerce, 6, 286, 287-288, 352, 506, 581
Amtorg, 61, 62, 127, 346, 372, 499, 540, 542
Anderson, member of U.S. Embassy staff in Moscow, 321
Andrea del Sarto; see Sarto, Andrea del
Antireligionznik, 118
Arita, Japanese Foreign Minister, 529
Arnold, Laurence, Congressman, 452
Associated Press, 98, 165, 275
Atherton, Ray, U.S. diplomat, 149

Badoglio, Pietro, former Italian chief of staff, 532
Baldwin, Stanley, British statesman, 519
Balodis, J., Latvian Minister of War, 551
Baltrusaitis, Jurgis K., Lithuanian Ambassador to U.S.S.R., 161, 336
Bardikov, George, Soviet colonel, 500
Barkley, Alben, Senator, 5, 220, 221, 450, 500
Barkov, Vladimir N., Chief of Protocol Division of Soviet Foreign Office, 16, 17, 20, 229, 341, 343, 369

Barnes, Joseph, *New York Herald Tribune* correspondent in Moscow, 17, 223, 275, 321-322, 352
Barnes, Mrs. Joseph, 17
Barton, Bruce, Congressman, 452
Baruch, Bernard M., American financier, 226
Batt, William, director of Office of Production Management, 507-509
Beaverbrook, William Maxwell Aitken, Baron, British publisher and member of Churchill cabinet, 485
Beck, J., former Polish Foreign Minister, 458
Belasco, David, 43
Bender, Philip, employee of U.S. Embassy in Moscow, 228, 313, 331, 369
Beneš, Eduard, former President of Czechoslovakia, 226, 525
Bess, Demaree, *Christian Science Monitor* correspondent in Moscow, 17, 49, 98, 220, 225, 352, 572
Bess, Mrs. Demaree, 220, 225
Biddle, Anthony J. Drexel, U.S. Ambassador to Poland, 369, 553
Biddle, Mrs. Anthony, 369
Bingham, Robert Worth, former U.S. Ambassador to London, 149, 151, 214.
Bingham, Mrs. Robert, 149
Black, Hugo, Associate Justice of Supreme Court, 520

Houdon, Jean Antoine, French
sculptor, 222
House, Edward M., American
diplomat, 139-140, 143-144
Howard, Roy, president of Scripps-
Howard newspapers, 72-73
Hrinkevich, 413, 420, 421, 424
Huddle, Jerome, inspector of American foreign service, 12
Hudson, George, President of British Board of Trade, 435, 436, 455
Hull, Cordell, Secretary of State,
26, 57, 58, 59, 64, 140-141, 147,
178, 215, 226, 263, 291, 307, 342,
370-371, 372, 373, 430, 432, 450,
463, 487, 492, 520, 637

I Found No Peace (Miller), 149
International Bible Students' As-
sociation, 151
International Business Machines
Company, 212-213
International Chamber of Com-
merce, 213
International Harvester Company,
568
International News Service, 68, 275,
286
Ivanov, Vladimir I., Commissar for
Timber Industries, 262
Izvestiya, 47
Izac, Ed V., Congressman, 452

Jarman, Pete, Congressman, 452
Jenkins, American engineer, 56
Johnson, Hiram, Senator, 348
Johnson, Luther, Congressman, 452
Johnson, Monroe, member of I.C.C.,
500-501
Johnson, Nelson, U.S. Ambassador
to China, 29
Johnson Act, 63

Jones, Jesse, Secretary of Commerce, 3, 5, 141, 499, 500
Jones, Mrs. Jesse, 141
Jumachev, Andrey, Soviet colonel,
500

Kaganovich, L. M., Secretary of the
Communist Party, 403
Kalinin, Mikhail, President of the
Praesidium of the Supreme Soviet
of the U.S.S.R., 16, 21, 24-28, 46,
50, 56, 188, 230, 231, 232, 233,
240, 306, 338, 340, 341-343, 344,
355, 356, 403, 412, 442
Kamenev, S. S., old Bolshevik, 32,
403
Kaminsky, G. N., chief of Foreign
Trade Policy Section of Commis-
sariat of Foreign Trade, 169, 176,
177
Karakhan, former Soviet Ambassa-
dor to China, 169, 257
Karp, S. B., head of State Planning
Commission of Central Soviet,
252
Kee, John, Congressman, 452
Kelland, Clarence Buddington,
American writer, 509
Kennan, George P., secretary of
U.S. Embassy in Moscow, 80,
177, 636, 642
Kennedy, Joseph, former U.S. Am-
bassador to Great Britain, 370,
440
Kerensky, Alexander, Russian pre-
mier, 61, 232, 339, 347, 349, 350,
543, 544
Khalotsky, Soviet official, 343
Khatskevich, Secretary of the
Soviet of Nationalities of the Cen-
tral Executive Committee, 26
Kirk, Alexander, U.S. Ambassador
to Egypt, 350, 353, 537, 642

ABOUT THE AUTHOR

Joseph Edward Davies served as Ambassador of the United States to the Soviet Union from the end of 1936 to the middle of 1938, shortly before the Munich Conference. Before assuming this post, Mr. Davies had long experience in law, politics, and international affairs. On leaving Moscow, he was appointed by the President as Ambassador to Belgium and was then called back to serve in the State Department as special assistant to the Secretary of State in charge of Emergency Problems and Policies. Mr. Davies is Wisconsin-born. He received his A.B. degree from the University of Wisconsin in 1898 and was graduated from the Law School of the same University in 1901. He then practiced law in Wisconsin until 1912 when he became Western Campaign Manager for Woodrow Wilson. The next year he moved to Washington to become Commissioner of Corporations.

In 1915 President Wilson appointed Mr. Davies chairman of the Federal Trade Commission which made him, ex officio, a member of Bernard Baruch's War Industries Board. In 1918, Mr. Davies ran for the United States Senate from Wisconsin and, failing election, turned to the practice of law in Washington. As a specialist in corporation tax and antitrust law, he was associated as counsel for many years with many nationally important corporations and banking firms. At different times he represented the governments of Holland, Mexico, Greece, the Dominican Republic and the United States in cases involving international legal matters and international arbitrations. He also served as counsel for the taxpayers in the celebrated Ford tax case. He is the author of Trust Laws and Unfair Competition *and other legal publications. Mr. Davies was chairman of the Roosevelt Inaugural Committee in 1941 and chairman of the President's Committee for Coordination of War Relief Activities and Agencies. His chief hobbies at the present time are golf, poker and the collection of Russian paintings and he has recently given the University of Wisconsin his own superb collection of Russian pictures and icons.*